THE RHINO RECORDS STORY

THE RHINO RECORDS STORY

Revenge of the Music Nerds

Harold Bronson

SelectBooks, Inc.
New York

This edition published by SelectBooks, Inc.
For information address SelectBooks, Inc., New York, New York.

First Edition

ISBN 978-1-59079-128-8

Library of Congress Cataloging-in-Publication Data

Bronson, Harold.
    The Rhino Records story: revenge of the music nerds / Harold Bronson. –
First edition.
        pages cm
    Includes index.
    Summary: "Co-founder of Rhino Records label, which he ran with his
    partner for twenty-four years, charts the course of the company started by
    two music fans in the back of their record store and has frequently won the
    award for label of the year. Author profiles many of the label's artists,
    including the Monkees, Turtles, and Tommy James"–Provided by publisher.
    ISBN 978-1-59079-128-8 (hardbound book: alk. paper)
    1. Rhino Records–History. 2. Bronson, Harold. 3. Foos, Richard. 4. Sound
    recording executives and producers–United States. 5. Sound recording
    industry–United States–History. I. Title.
    ML3792.R55B76 2013
    384–dc23
                        2013016154

Manufactured in the United States of America

10 9 8 7 6 5 4 3 2 1

Contents

The Intro

When Richard Foos and I kick-started the Rhino Records label from the back room of our record store, our ambition was limited to making enough money so that we wouldn't have to get real jobs. Ignoring the constraints of commercial radio, we dreamed of having hits by producing novelty records like the ones we grew up listening to in the 1950s and 1960s. A bit later, when we started to make available the great records of the past, we went against the standard business practice of allocating as little as possible on these reissues by spending more money on the product as a reflection of how important the music was to us. We didn't set out to create America's best record company,* or one that made tens of millions of dollars. Our success was the result of our passion, inherent business sense, and the commitment of our employees.

In my own mind, I envisioned myself as a Rod Stewart or Marc Bolan type of mod, but without the drive or clothing budget. One morning in the early days of the label Richard announced, "It's clothes buying time!" solely so he could persuade me to part with the out of fashion cardigan I had worn to work that day. Of course, he was right. I had worn it in high school. He gave me twenty-five dollars for it, and then deposited it in the wastebasket.

Richard was content to look like a hippie follower of the Grateful Dead, except that he wasn't a fan of their music. Blow away the fantasy dust and

---

*I would have preferred Record Label of the Year, but the National Association of Record Merchandisers (NARM) awarded Rhino the Entertainment Software Supplier of the Year award for 2001. It's wordy but it meant that we were chosen over all the major record companies and the software manufacturers whose products also made their way into record stores.

Richard's take isn't that far off the mark: "We were a couple of record nerds who had a little more business savvy and slightly more social skills than the average record nerd who lived with their parents until they were forty. And if they ever got married, it could have easily been with a mail-order bride."

Because we didn't have hits, we weren't respected by the music industry or happening new artists, and no models or starlets flocked to our sides. For a number of years our main social activity was crashing other people's parties. We did, however, get to know many of the performers whose music we loved. We showed them interest and respect—compared to their era in which artists were routinely ripped-off by their original labels—and in a number of instances, helped to revive their careers.

For someone like me, engaged in the entertainment business, it might come as a surprise that I was initially inspired to write my memoirs after reading *Iacocca: An Autobiography* in 1985. Lee Iacocca, the veteran automotive executive, broke new ground in the way he revealed his personal life and professional career. Most autobiographies by celebrities and businessmen are not "written" by them. Mostly they talk into an audio recorder or to a ghostwriter. A transcript is written to which the "author" adds and edits the copy. I thought that, having been a writer in my twenties, I could manage to be more literate in telling my story by writing it directly.

I had intended to pounce on a history of Rhino not long after I left the company at the end of 2001, except it took me much longer to finish the film I was producing than I had anticipated. The subsequent head of Rhino changed the name of the company to Warner Strategic Marketing and stopped promoting the brand—although it was still used on the product. Primarily because of Rhino's decreased visibility, combined with the music industry's decline, I decided to put off the project.

But the more I thought about our story—how much music fans loved our product, how we inspired other companies to care for their archives, of all the good we brought to our employees and the community, of all the wacky things we did—the more I thought it was one that needed to be told.

It was a dream job, except nobody had given it to us. We had to develop and define it. We did it on our own, with no funding from a deep-pocketed relative, and with no mentor to show us the way. Because we had no boss telling us what we couldn't do, the company was largely a reflection of who we were as people, the imagination as well as the humanity. We had a good relationship with each other, and realized the need to express ourselves. Neither of us had been to business school or had formal training in the record business but this lack of experience, more often than not, had us doing the right thing rather than what would have been expected of us in an ongoing business. The end result was a good product with a positive effect. Listening to music makes people feel good. It doesn't add calories like a sweet dessert, and it can help to take them off, when providing a sound-track for exercise.

At the end of our tenure, our profits and sales were good. Viewed from within the decline the industry experienced they were exceptional. To some degree, we were still propelled by our mission: to make the great music of the past available. Our successors, presumably, were ruled by more domi-nant and conventional motivators: keeping their jobs, pleasing their boss, hitting their financial targets, bolstering the company's stock price. Those were not our concerns and we, as well as our customers and employees, were all the better for it.

*   *   *

The chapters are sequenced somewhat chronologically. Later entries will illuminate earlier ones, adding pieces to a puzzle with more revealed at the book's end. Although what follows are my impressions, opinions, and recollections, there is a desire on my part to present an accurate account of what transpired in the world of Rhino.

Take the Quiz

How was Rhino Records named?

A. The alliteration—it just sounded good.

B. Inspired by Eugene Ionesco's play *Rhinoceros*, which dealt with the issue of nonconformity. Because we considered ourselves nonconformists, we called the company Rhino.

C. One of Harold's favorite rock groups was England's Bonzo Dog Band. The label name was inspired by the number of references to rhinos in their songs.

D. The R stands for Richard. The H stands for Harold. When Harold wrote out the abbreviation for incorporated, INC, the "c" was nearly closed, and looked like an "O," spelling the word "RHINO."

Rhino in High Fidelity

Best Damned Record Store in California
R. Meltzer, *Coast Magazine*, July 1976

When I arrived back at the store, Jeff and Lee were battling again—not with their fists, not with their voices, but with records as weapons. They alternated their selections on the turntable, trying to drive each other crazy. Lee played cacophonous avant-garde jazz artist Anthony Braxton; Jeff followed with the ragged punk of the Clash's second album. The taunting climaxed with Lee telling Jeff not to say another word, at which point Jeff responded with "Word, word, word, word!" The two customers seemed blasé about the exchange. At times I reprimanded them, but why listen to me? I was only the manager.

*   *   *

When Richard Foos moved his record concession from Apollo Electronics in Santa Monica into his own space, his intention was not to create the world's best record store. His primary goal was a modest one: to make more money than he earned from his community social work. He was looking for a business to run, one in which a hippie like himself would feel comfortable. He thought of a revival-run movie house, a small repertory theater, even a local newspaper like *The Venice Beachhead*, in which he had a column. Because there were a number of chain record stores in the immediate UCLA area, he reasoned that what the students needed was a used record outlet where they could stretch their meager budgets. His inspiration was Aron's on Melrose Avenue in Hollywood, which was a favorite of savvy buyers for the promotional copies of new releases—usually referred to as "promos"—in their used bins.

Although Richard had secured a small loan from his friend Richard Weinstein, Westwood Village rents were out of the question. He went a few blocks south to 1716 Westwood Boulevard where he split the space and the $200 a month rent with the electronics repairman already occupying the store, Dave Nyan. The building was slightly dilapidated, the neighbors a Chinese laundry and a flower shop.

Before I left for London in September 1973, Richard didn't know what to name the store. I had suggested Waterloo Sunset Records after my favorite Kinks' song. While I was away, Richard and a group of his friends were tossing around names when Jerry Kaye—a budding DJ—suggested "Rhino Records." At the time, it was primarily the alliteration that Richard found appealing. He hung a parachute from the ceiling and emptied his entire collection of records into orange crates placed on large telephone cable spools. He had his friend John Farkash (aka "Fark") paint a large sign depicting a rhinoceros, identifying the new establishment as Rhino Records.

As a shy individual, when Richard opened the store on October 23, he was looking forward to the excitement of new encounters, and of making deals to buy records. Contrary to his expectations, UCLA kids continued to favor Westwood Village's chain stores, and as foot traffic was slow, so was business. Richard soon realized that the counterculture consciousness of the late 1960s had passed by the time he opened. Most students who came by, Richard felt, were disgusted by what they saw. They wanted the polish and shine of a large, modern record store, and they wanted the hits. They weren't interested in the classic jazz and blues albums he stocked. Richard remembered one day when there wasn't a single customer at all. Still, there were the collectors, and there was some business. Sometimes he was kept on his toes by the small explosions and flying sparks emanating from Nyan's electronic handy work in the back room.

In the earliest days, Richard employed his roommate, Pete Parks; Steve Cooper ("Coops"), a Cat Stevens lookalike folk singer; and Jeff Gold, a high school senior. Jeff cringes when he remembers Richard salting the bins with thirty dollar collector's items like John's Children's *Orgasm, Yardbirds Live,* and *Longbranch Pennywhistle*—all marked at regular price to encourage collectors to make Rhino a necessary stop on their rounds.

Richard liked the wheeler-dealer aspect of the record business, as he knew it. He also delighted in picking up records at U.S. Postal Service auctions of parcels that were undeliverable. At one postal auction he bought two record-pressing machines. Unaware of the vast setup needed to activate the presses, the two machines sat in Fark's driveway for so long that they sank partially into the ground before he had them hauled off by a junk dealer.

In those early days, Rhino's stock of hits was minimal because the albums cost too much for such a small markup. Mostly it was used albums, bootlegs (unauthorized, mostly live recordings), and cutouts (perfectly good, sealed albums no longer manufactured or listed in the catalogue and dumped at a low price).

Because he was bored from having so few customers, Richard amused himself by making crudely-lettered signs that he posted in the store. One listed credit cards that the store accepted, like the Rocky & Bullwinkle card. In fact, Rhino didn't accept any credit cards, only cash and checks. A favorite was "The Ten Most Asked Questions," which included the following: *Q. How come I'm only getting ten cents in trade for this Black Sabbath album, I only played it once? A. Next time don't use a Bic Pen as your needle.* In a reference to the freeway car pool lane: *Please Observe Diamond Lane. All persons in lane between 3-5 p.m. Monday thru Saturday must be holding at least 3 records. — Notice — All violations will be ignored.* Tape strips fashioned into diamonds similar to ones on on-ramps marked the store's left aisle.

Richard introduced me to the concept that you could have humor in retail. It wasn't a tactic to get more customers, nor was it a conscious effort to brand the store and give it a unique identity. By the same token, while it might have appeared to be, it wasn't an attempt to sabotage the business. Even today, from chain store to boutique, one rarely sees any intended humor expressed.

Richard expanded the exercise of his humor in coming up with contests. One idea was prompted by an effort to get rid of a stack of albums by the Partridge Family's Danny Bonaduce. Richard couldn't sell them, so he initiated Rhino's first promotional effort by paying customers five cents to take the album home, and an additional fifteen cents if they promised to listen to it. Richard got the idea of the first big Rhino customer-participation promotion because he had a quantity of impossible-to-sell Glen Campbell posters that he acquired as part of a lot that included those of the Beach Boys and Vanilla Fudge. "The Glen Campbell Poster Deface Contest" inspired customers to break out all manner of crayons, paints, and Marks-a-Lots to decorate the singer's image. The winner was the ten-year-old son of the family that owned the Chinese laundry two doors down. Following that was the "Guess How Many Records Are in the Trash Can Contest," which permitted Richard to rid himself of many unsalable bargain bin LPs with a few desirable records on top to interest the participant. The thought of winning a trash can full of albums (invariably the winning number was around 238) excited many customers, and it proved a perennial favorite.

Rhino developed a bohemian, Beat coffeehouse image—a place where hipsters could hang out, similar to San Francisco's City Lights bookstore. Informal Friday night jam sessions were held, with Richard playing his bass alongside John Weider, who had been a member of successful English bands like the Animals and Family and who lived in the area.

After my unemployment ran out, I asked Richard for a job. It took a while, but when Coops left in April 1974, I was hired. By that time, Nyan was out of the picture. I opened the store each morning, allowing Richard to look for deals downtown and to pick up product at West Coast one-stop. (A one-stop was a wholesaler that carried product from a majority of the labels.) When I swept the floor, I always paused to note that our stack of Otis Redding and Carla Thomas's *King and Queen* album hadn't diminished, even though it was priced at two dollars.

Is this what my twenty-three-year-old, UCLA-educated life had come down to? Sitting on a ledge behind the counter in a dilapidated record store, munching on a spinach and almond butter sandwich and waiting for a few customers to buy used albums? It was a far cry from working at a prestige store like Tower Records, yet I felt lucky.

With so few customers, there was only so much time I could spend organizing the records in the bins. I read *Newsweek* and on occasion called Howard Kaylan, who always seemed up for a long chat. The afternoon sun penetrated the large glass window. A shelf behind the counter blocked most of it, but the area still got hot.

When Kareem Abdul-Jabbar first came in, it was a surprise, as we didn't get celebrities. Head down, he headed straight for the jazz bins. Nobody bothered him. After a while, I looked over and noticed that he had a pile of thirty albums. Sure, they were all two dollars each, but I was anticipating a big sales day for the store. After about an hour, he placed two albums on the counter, totaling four dollars. I couldn't understand it. With the big salary he got as an NBA star, that's all he bought? He didn't come in often, but the routine was repeated; I only saw him purchase one or two albums per visit.

I learned the retail record business, or at least Richard's version of it. Being a record fan, I thought it would suit me to work at Rhino, but the prospects were too limited for me to think of it in the long term. I was biding my time, still hoping to get a job at a record company. An opening came up for a writer at *Cash Box* magazine, and Toby Mamis recommended me for the position. *Cash Box* was a trade magazine, a second-rate *Billboard*. It wasn't a record company, but it was working within the industry, and I started the last week in July. Idealistically, I was looking forward to improving the publication's editorial content. Two weeks later I was fired, on August 8, 1974, the same day President Nixon resigned. I took writing seriously and didn't realize, as it was explained to me, that the articles were merely to fill in the space between ads, and that being solicitous to the advertisers was paramount. I attributed my dismissal to turning down an interview with Jim Capaldi for a column that was backed up by six weeks. I had interviewed Pink Floyd's Rick Wright only a few days before and by comparison didn't think the ex-drummer of Traffic was important enough. The record company complained to the publisher, and I was out.

When I interviewed producer/manager Peter Asher, he told me how insecure the record business was, how you could be fired for no reason, because it happened to him. And then it happened to me. I needed more stability, and Richard gave me my job back. I noticed stacks of old, unpaid bills atop Rhino's barely-functioning cash register. Richard was laissez-faire about finances. He wasn't motivated to pay the bills in a timely manner, and late fines were routine. I realized that by paying the bills before the due dates, I could save Richard money on the excess charges alone. When he upgraded the store's cash register and gave the old one to his friend Jeff Ginsburg, Jeff discovered $200 in cash and $300 in uncashed checks wedged into the back behind the tray.

I became manager and took on more responsibility, focusing on organization and public relations. I had Richard erect a sign—a giant record—that was perpendicular to the street, so people driving by took more notice. I got more of my writer friends to trade in their promotional records. The record companies gave these sample records to writers with the intention that they review them and to DJs and programmers with the hope that they play them on the radio. They didn't like the idea that so many of these recipients traded in or sold these records to one of the many used record stores, such as Rhino, that were able to resell them. A customer who bought a promo instead of buying a new copy deprived the label of profits and the artist of royalties. To my fellow writers and me—who were paid poorly—this was a way to supplement our incomes. Because the practice was so common, the labels probably should have been more vigilant about disseminating this free product.

My friends David Goldman and Justin Pierce were taking an evening class from David Geffen at UCLA. On the night they invited me to join them, music attorney Lee Phillips was the guest speaker. I saw Geffen before the class started and introduced myself, not mentioning Rhino. Toward the end, one of the students asked, "How can a store like Rhino legally sell promotional records?" Geffen's short answer was, "They can't, and we're going to get them." I was unnerved, sinking lower in my seat. But nothing happened. In California, the first-sale doctrine stipulated, in short, that there were no restrictions—as it related to records—for an owner to sell an item he owned.

I should also mention that in some cases where money was needed to buy cocaine or other drugs to give to a radio programmer in exchange for playing a record, such a transaction couldn't be entered into a company expense account. A label promo man would then requisition records, which were later sold to a store for untraceable cash. Unfortunately, Rhino attracted comparatively few promos. Most went to Aron's. As a result of my experience at the store, years later when we were dispensing promos at our label, I tried to limit the number we made available. Still, it used to infuriate me when I heard that there were quantities at some stores, no doubt sold by people who worked for our distributor.

Richard erected a new sign: *WELCOME WHEREHOUSE & RECORD CO. SPIES (please show your security ID for special discount)*. It wasn't the result of drug-induced paranoia: Rhino was under surveillance. Not only were record companies sending in spies to look for promos, so did the Wherehouse Records store in Westwood Village. As a result, the Wherehouse Records fifty-store chain initiated a lawsuit against Rhino for selling new releases below cost. The Unfair Practices Act was enacted to protect small stores from the better-funded corporations who could undercut them and drive them out of business. In a twist, Wherehouse Records attempted to use it against Rhino. Owing to Rhino's return privilege with City One-Stop, Richard was able to bring in a small quantity of new records at a lower price. The case was settled out of court. Because of the press coverage I was able to get, most notably Heather Harris's piece in the *L.A. Free Press*, more people became aware of Rhino and sales increased. As a result of the scrutiny, bootlegs were phased out.

I ran a few ads in the UCLA *Daily Bruin*, and even tried one in the University High School paper, but they didn't seem to generate much interest. One that ran in an October 1974 issue of the *Daily Bruin* posed a unique challenge for fans to vote for their preference of two acts by buying the new, live triple album from Emerson, Lake & Palmer, *Welcome Back, My Friends . . .* for $6.98, or any of the Steppenwolf albums we had in the bargain bin for 20¢. The ad billed it as *Steppenwolf vs. ELP! The Battle of the Century*. We had prizes: tickets, posters, and *Autographed pictures of your favorite stars (Autographed by us, of course.)* Despite the price disparity, ELP won the challenge.

For writers who still thought going to Westwood was inconvenient, I went to their apartments to buy records, a service other stores didn't offer. I also had Richard carry more new releases. He got rid of the cable spools and had more racks installed. The stock grew to the point where Rhino was known for having the best selection of jazz west of the Rockies, excellent used and cutout selections, a rock collector's bin, and an in-depth catalogue of new releases. We were an early supporter of reggae and punk. The store's gross sales doubled in each of the first two years I was manager.

Lee Kaplan's preference for occasionally wearing a Japanese kimono to work reflected his pretensions as a teen. Although he was a fan of the Electric Light Orchestra and had rock ambitions as a bass guitarist, he was into the most obscure improvised music and became head of the one-man jazz department. His ordering was inspired, but the market for acts he championed, such as the Art Ensemble of Chicago, remained limited. He used his connections to supply the store with albums privately pressed by Sun Ra in Philadelphia, ones for which the keyboardist and/or his band members had created unique collaged artworks or drawings as the covers.

Lee also secured a source in New York where we could buy Jamaican pressings of reggae artists. We were the first ones to have them in Los Angeles, although the orders we received from these ganja-affected distributors were frequently a mishmash. While most of the records in a shipment were the titles we had ordered, some were ones they threw in that they thought we should have, and others seemed like ones they were simply trying to get rid of. Jamaican records were poorly pressed, often pockmarked, and some-times even included off-center labels that covered over the actual grooves. Not only were there "no returns" for the unwanted or defective pressings, but shipments were only sent via UPS C.O.D.—usually without advance notice—which presented problems if they showed up on a day when we didn't have enough cash in the till.

The combined musical knowledge of Rhino's staff (Richard, Lee, Jeff, and me) could probably have trounced that of any record store in the world. Jeff Gold and Lee Kaplan were mainstays of the store, but since Lee was at UCLA and Jeff at USC, their presence was limited to after school, Saturdays, and during the summer. Despite the occasional flare-up of ado-lescent attitude, it was hard to fire them. They knew their music and often worked when it wasn't their shift and they weren't getting paid.

Mark Leviton was living with his girlfriend in Claremont, an expanded college community an hour's drive east of Los Angeles. His unrealized plans to earn a living writing fiction were further aggravated by a summer of many smoggy, hundred-degree days in an un-air-conditioned house. He approached me about opening a Rhino store in Claremont for them to run. As there was no record store in town, it wasn't hard to convince Richard.

Rhino Claremont opened in September 1974 in a reconverted house on West Second Street, with the original hitching ring for horses affixed to a tree in front. Mark and his now-wife, Linda, bought a small metal box to use instead of a cash register, which seemed too much for their modest goals and wouldn't have fit the small store anyway. Richard sprang for a couple hundred t-shirts to give away on opening day. Wanting to be realistic, he advised Mark and Linda not to get their hopes up too high. He recounted his lonely days when the Westwood store first opened and the times he took out his frustration on whoever did manage to wander in.

On the first day, Mark and Linda were overwhelmed by the onslaught. I had to make a run from Westwood with a carload of records to restock the store. When the dust cleared, the small metal box had taken in $1,300, which was a little more than the Westwood store grossed in a whole week. The weekly sales tally settled in at $3,000 during the school year, giving us at the flagship store, an inferiority complex.

While the humor displayed in the new store couldn't compete with Westwood's, the musical reverence was similar. In responding to its community's needs, Rhino Claremont became more of a folk venue than the Westwood store, and resident musicians David Lindley, Chris Darrow, and Jackson Browne were customers. Windham Hill founder Will Ackerman came in and offered Mark an in-store play copy of his first album if he'd buy five of the few hundred he'd pressed. Mark liked the album and was soon selling dozens each week. The feminist label Olivia sold well, as did obscure artists like Honk (*Five Summer Stories*) and Hawaiian band Kalapana. Other than selling an impressive amount of folk music titles, the store's customer interests were very similar to Westwood's.

Each morning I called Mark in Claremont and took his order for product over the phone, which was cheaper than having him call City One-Stop directly. Then I called City and recited both our orders, usually speaking to Howard Kaylan's brother Alan, whom I knew from high school. Sometimes I picked up the order before I opened the store, sometimes Richard got it if he was in the neighborhood. UPS shipped Claremont's order. Every morning I deposited the previous day's receipts and got change at the nearby California Overseas Bank.

To the uninitiated, the incomprehensible assault of hand-lettered signs and disfigured promotional posters could have been as disorienting as being in the maze at a house of mirrors. A more thoughtful first-time visitor might think, "Are these guys serious, or what?" But at both stores relationships developed between Rhino staff and customers who "got it." The Westwood store was a fun place to hang out, and some consumers reasoned that if they were spending so much time at Rhino anyway, they might as well work there. Championship Vinyl, the store depicted in Nick Hornby's 1995 novel *High Fidelity*—and the movie on which it was based—captured much of what Rhino was like, except that our staffers weren't as condescending.

One customer, Mark Felsot, put it this way: "I felt more comfortable at Rhino than in my own bedroom." Rhino was a real experience for the record junkie, and many of the customers were as colorful as the surroundings. Al Johnson and his friend Ken traveled forty miles to Rhino every Saturday. The crazy pair sprawled on the floor and barricaded themselves with the hundreds of albums they selected from the bargain bins. After spending hours in the store, they narrowed their mess and bought about 20 percent of the total, with no record costing more than a quarter. Years later, Johnson distinguished himself by penning a number of songs on Ricky Lee Jones' first album, as well as working as an electrical engineer.

The "Guy Who Asked Too Many Questions" was harmless enough, but his barrage necessitated Richard limiting him to three queries a visit. He was a nice guy though, so when he came in he'd say, "How ya doin'?" Richard would respond, flinging his finger in the air, "That's one!" Even worse was the gold chain-wearing Italian film student from USC. Every visit he sequentially held up a dozen albums and grunted, "Iz zis good?"

Again, he was a nice guy, but totally oblivious of his behavior. Obnoxious customers often discovered themselves posted on Rhino's "Worst Customer List." Usually it didn't deter their presence or demeanor.

Some customers were so offensive that Richard instituted a "Banned from the Store" policy. Steve Sandemeyer, an overweight jazz aficionado with dandruff sprinkling his greasy hair, would habitually sidle up to a much younger girl in the rock section and have no compunction in trying to chat her up. After ignoring a few warnings, Richard, half-yelling and half-laughing at the absurdity, threw him out. Another banned jazz fan tried to talk Richard into merely suspending him, "like they do in basketball." A black man wearing a dashiki came into the store and amassed a stack of thirty albums. He was on his way out when I stopped him, and told him he had to pay for them. His indignation flared. He slammed the albums on the counter and said, "You want me to pay for these!" Angrily swearing, he reached into his pocket and hurled coins at the back wall. After a handful of volleys, he walked out of the store with no records.

One obnoxious visitor, who hung out in the store for hours on end, never buying anything, became Rhino's mascot. Wild Man Fischer (real name Larry) was discovered by Frank Zappa in 1968 singing songs on the Sunset Strip for a dime. He boasted an impassioned, emotionally bare, ragged delivery, and a repertoire of childlike songs. His love for rock 'n' roll and a belief that he would one day make it big added to his absurd charm. Zappa produced a remarkable double-album portrait, *An Evening with Wildman Fischer*. I first saw him around this time walking through the UCLA campus wearing one flip-flop on his right foot, with the other bare.

Even though his album sold only twelve thousand copies, everybody at Rhino owned one. When Wild Man visited other stores, often he was asked to leave. At Rhino he was acknowledged as a talent. His presence was wearing, including his incessant cycle of self-serving queries: "Am I better than Captain Beefheart? Do you think I'm funnier than Bob Hope? Do I sing better than Frank Sinatra?" In appreciation, he made up a song about our store, which we pressed into a single to give away to our customers.

Tim Doherty was typical of how the ardent Rhino fan related to the store: "My first impression was how the music I was reading about in

Cream, Who Put the Bomp and *New York Rocker,* came to life in the store. They weren't championing the hit artists of the day, but ones like Sparks, the Quick, and the Dictators. You could rely on the staff's recommendations that a record was good. Not only was the store a fun place to be, it was a place for information and to meet others who were into the same music. You'd go in on a Monday and Gary Stewart would be talking about who was on *Rodney On the Roq* [Rodney Bingenheimer's radio show on KROQ] the previous night."

Just because somebody rarely made a purchase, didn't mean that we couldn't establish a friendly relationship. Bill Leibowitz, an accountant by training, became an executive working for the real estate company that managed the Motown office building in Hollywood. He was a great fan of rock 'n' roll, a nice guy, and we enjoyed talking to him. He realized a life-long dream when he opened the Golden Apple Comics store on Melrose Avenue. A yo-yo champ when he was a kid, he did much to spread the culture of yo-yos and comics throughout the city.

There was magnanimity about Richard. He once loaned money to a teenage customer, holding his headphones as collateral. One Christmas Eve Richard leaped on the city bus that stopped by Rhino, dispensed record albums to all the riders, and leaped off at the next stop.

I was envious of Tower Records where celebrities shopped and bought lots of records. We could have used the business. Tower had regular visits from Brian Wilson, David Bowie, and Elton John, who bought so many records they allowed him to shop after hours. We had Russell Morris, and he didn't even buy anything. Ten years before *Crocodile Dundee,* when Australian accents were less common in America, Russell Morris came in to sell the promo records he had received from his label, RCA. Sometimes he sent his beautiful, petite wife, whose name was Paula, but who pronounced it "Poola." With their charming accents, they were always welcome. I felt sorry for him. He had had five big hits in his native Australia, but here he was struggling. Singer Nicolette Larson, who was signed to Warner Brothers, sold some albums she had received from them. She was always friendly, with an engaging smile.

One day in March 1975, Bob Emmer, who was head of West Coast publicity for Atlantic Records, brought the Pretty Things by the store.

The English band had a new album out, *Silk Torpedo*, on Led Zeppelin's Atlantic-distributed Swan Song imprint. Bob wasn't bringing them by to encourage sales with a meet-and-greet; it was an act of desperation. Even though *Silk Torpedo* was a fine album, he had difficulty in setting up interviews with the group. He called the store to see if Steve Rosen and I would do him a favor and interview them, and I said to bring them by. We didn't have time to come up with much in the way of insightful questions. Singer Phil Maye and bassist Jack Green seemed confused by the cramped, backroom setting—with abandoned tire—where we conducted the interview. Green had previously played in T. Rex and was a Wild Man Fischer fan. Neither of us wrote an article about the visit.

As the business grew there was more of an opportunity to give jobs to our friends. It didn't always work out. I met Steve Rosen on the rock writers' circuit, and we became friends. He was a good guitarist and fashioned himself after Deep Purple's Ritchie Blackmore. I was happy to give him a job at the store, but when we increased his responsibilities to opening up—so I could pick up records downtown—he had difficulty showing up on time, and I had to fire him. I believe it affected our friendship.

One day, a group of kids barreled into the store as though they were being chased by a rival gang in *West Side Story*. They had long hair, leather jackets, and were generally rough around the edges. They looked intimidating to me. They asked us to stock their new punk fanzine, *Back Door Man*, on consignment. Richard, without hesitation, said "Sure." "Phast Phreddie" Patterson and his crew were all from LA's South Bay. They were passionate about the local scene and were fans of Iggy Pop and Blue Oyster Cult.

Some industry professionals were regular customers, but not many. Pete Rugolo lived in the area. He had been a jazz arranger—mostly for big bands, but also for Miles Davis—and now he was composing and arranging for TV. He used Rhino as his library, looking for arranging ideas. Film editors Kent Beyda and Mark Goldblatt, both working for New World Pictures, bought not only for their own interests but to get ideas for the movies they were editing.

One afternoon, teenage jazz fanatic Don Lucoff brought jazz musician Rahsaan Roland Kirk by the store. Kirk wasn't happy to be there, and he presciently lambasted the staff for accidentally playing tenor saxophonist Sonny Rollins' newly-arrived *Live in Japan* album at the wrong speed on the turntable. The previous record had been a 45 rpm single, and the setting hadn't been changed back to 33 1/3 rpm to accommodate the long player. As the Rollins' track was actually a slow ballad, the faster tempo version (seemingly played on an alto!) didn't seem out of place to anybody but Rahsaan Roland Kirk.

In the 2010 film *The Runaways*, Kristen Stewart played Joan Jett, but with her natural good looks she was a dead ringer for the fourteen-year-old Kari Krome, the girl who set the project in motion. Kari used to come into the store accompanied by a much older woman who didn't appear to be her mother; I had heard that she was a lesbian. She was very shy. At the July 3, 1975, Alice Cooper party at the Palladium, she approached producer Kim Fowley with the idea of starting an all-girl band and enlisted Joan Larkin—later Joan Jett—to join. Ultimately Kari became estranged from the project because she couldn't sing and was too young. Though it was originally conceived as a vehicle for her songs, she was relegated to a handful of co-songwriting credits.

Fowley invited me to see the Runaways' first public showcase on September 12, 1975, in Phast Phreddie's parents' sunken living room in north Torrance. Joan Jett played guitar, Sandy West played drums, and Micki Steele played bass. I liked the concept, but they weren't very good. It was only a month or two prior to this that I met Joan at the Continental Hyatt House, leaning on a post in the lobby. I went there with Toby Mamis to interview Suzi Quatro. Toby was Suzi's publicist at the time. Joan took the bus in from West Covina to get a glimpse of her idol. Toby could have ignored her, but he was considerate, to the point of introducing me to this young fan.

Buddy Miles had been a formidable talent as a drummer and soul singer, initially as a member of the Electric Flag, and then with his own band. He had one big-selling album, *Them Changes*, in 1970. Richard used to sneak into the Whisky a Go-Go to see him play. By the time he released his first album for Casablanca, *More Miles Per Gallon* in August 1975, his poor career moves had severely tarnished his integrity. For having titled his previous album *Booger Bear*, he had become something of a joke, even to Richard. It was with that sense of playfulness—not a respect for his current endeavor—that we decorated the store to enter a display contest for the new album. In the photo we submitted, Richard, Jeff, Lee, and I all wore masks of Buddy's face that we cut out from the marketing poster. We won a motor scooter that was sold and the money split among us. I don't recall that we moved that many of Buddy's album—I mean, at a retail price.

In March of the next year Buddy released his subsequent album, *Bicentennial Gathering of the Tribes*, featuring a cover portrait of him wearing an Indian headdress. Richard and Jeff had their photo taken with Buddy at a promotional meet-and-greet at City One-Stop. The next day Jeff saw him at Tower Records and had him write an autograph to Richard, as "Booger Bear." In his later years, Buddy's career was resurrected as the singer on the California Raisins commercials.

The Nuart Theater in West Los Angeles was among the first movie houses to program limited runs of films, mostly changing its program daily. The theater was best known for its weekly midnight showings of *The Rocky Horror Picture Show*. The screenings cultivated an audience, many of whom dressed up like characters from the movie and interacted with the actors on the screen. Richard came up with the idea to mirror their monthly calendar with one that would highlight different promotional days at the store. I responded to Richard's lead and contributed where I could. It was our most ambitious promotion, and he was able to get record company advertising money to supplement the calendar we produced which spanned from April 1 to May 15, 1976.

It's difficult to assess how effective the special days were for drumming up business. Some, like Reggae Day—which included an in-store performance—didn't attract any more customers. Nor did Mother's Day, in which our mothers manned the checkout counter. Still, enough days were successful that we did the promotion again in the fall of the following year. A sampling of days:

Those who excel academically often get rewards. Richard, an academic underachiever himself, wanted to balance that with "C" Student Day: *In honor of all the underachievers in this world, anyone bringing in a report card showing his grade average was "C" or below will receive a free album. Report cards can be from any year, and skillful forgeries will qualify.*

The typical record store was staffed by low-key, hippie-garbed clerks. For Salesman Day, Richard, Lee, and I slicked ourselves up with matching seersucker jackets that Richard had picked up at a thrift store and wore "Wherehouse Records" name tags. In the manner of aggressive hi-fi salesmen, we were overly solicitous in approaching our customers. As part of the day, we had the Hassle the Salesman Contest: *Ever wanna get back at us for only giving you 5 cents in trade on the first Mama's and Papa's LP? Have you been fuming ever since we ran out of Steve Martin's album? This is your day, go ahead and hassle us. Best hassler wins a prize. (Sadists, don't be left out.)*

It's one thing to rebel against the constraints of a job or an employer, but what are you rebelling against when you are the business owner? Richard and I were both fans of Monty Python's Flying Circus. At the store we stocked cutouts of their first two albums and promoted them to our customers. After the series started airing on the local PBS station we sold impressive numbers of those as well as the new *Matching Tie and Handkerchief* album. The Pythons were a new influence on our humor. We transposed their bit about the furniture salesman who puts a bag over his head and yells when a customer mentions "mattress." We tried it twice with Richard shouting "Whoop Whoop!" to a trigger word, but the customers didn't seem to notice the aberrant behavior.

Sometimes Richard's actions bordered the obnoxious. He hung a noose around the neck of a cardboard standup of John Denver to express how he felt about his music. After closing hour, Richard often answered the phone and impersonated a long, absurd, automatic phone message—including the beep—and waited to see if the customer had lasted the duration. When the Rhino softball team played the opening day of the 1976 Hollywood Showbiz League against the team from *Happy Days* (which included Ron Howard and Henry Winkler), there were no planned opening day ceremonies, like in professional baseball. We Rhinos arranged ourselves along the third bass line and played the National Anthem on kazoos. For the opening pitch Richard substituted the softball with a grapefruit that was painted white. The first batter for Happy Days swung at the fat pitch and splattered the grapefruit, to our amusement.

Obviously the goal was for Rhino to be considered as much more than a typical record store. More than anything else, an atmosphere prevailed that music was to be taken seriously, even if it was presented in a fun manner. The Ramones first came to the store in August 1976 and made a point of visiting when they were in town. Rather than punk or hard rock, as suggested by their image, I was surprised that their purchases were usually of '60s artists like Herman's Hermits and the Lovin' Spoonful.

In London in September 1976, I went to a cutout dealer and bought a few hundred albums, as well as buying the first Stiff Records to be sold in a US store. When I returned, Richard made a big deal of surprising me with a listening booth he had installed. Listening booths were a feature of many record stores in the '50s and '60s, but had largely died out by the '70s. They provided a small area where one or two people could listen to a demonstration record before deciding to buy a new copy. Ours was a little larger than a phone booth, but with tall Plexiglas walls, it looked more like a dunk tank. It was a novel idea, but the turntable kept breaking, so I don't know if it actually paid for itself.

In January 1977 we hired Gary Stewart. Compared to Jeff and Lee, Gary was a novice, but he was eager to learn and had a great attitude. As a high school student he was disenchanted with the music played on Top 40 radio. That void was filled when he was exposed to great artists of the '60s—"like the Animals, Herman's Hermits, and Otis Redding"—from listening to oldies radio and reading *Phonograph Record Magazine* and *Bomp*. As a young consumer he asked good questions, bought the records we recommended, and was always welcomed. "There was an aloofness that pervaded the store that I really liked," he observed. "The people there had a sense of being in the know, and the more time I spent in the store, I felt I had that as well, even though I didn't understand what I was in the know about." Gary was also attending Cal State Northridge and working part-time at McDonald's.

The stock often reflected Richard's penchant for taking a stance. He refused to carry Barbra Streisand's *A Star is Born* soundtrack album because Columbia Records had raised the list price by $2, from $6.98 to $8.98. Even though his profit would have been more, he tried to discourage customers from endorsing the price hike, reasoning that if these pricing experiments succeeded, all new records would be unnecessarily more expensive. Of course, explanatory posters accompanied these positions.

In August 1977 we temporarily relocated the store to 10461 Santa Monica Boulevard next to a McDonald's, while a new building was being constructed on the site of the old one. The new location was a building owned by and split with Carmine's Restaurant. Our space had formerly been a clothing store, and we made use of the changing rooms—sans partitions—for our listening booth and a new magazine rack. At three each afternoon, the aroma of sautéed garlic and onions permeated our back room as the cooks next door prepared the evening meals. Sometimes we saw actor James Caan pull up to the front in his sports car. Curiously, on a number of Monday evenings when the restaurant was closed, black Cadillacs and town cars bearing New Jersey and New York plates filled the parking lot.

After school started in September the kids from Concord High School a block away spent their breaks in the store. It was a small, progressive, liberal arts school that catered to mostly sensitive, bored rich kids. Among the handful of regulars was David Crouch, a nice guy who seemed more interested in what we were doing than the others. A few months after he graduated, Richard and I hired him to work at the Rhino label.

McDonald's management was upset because our customers occasionally parked in their lot. Rather than attempting to work things out agreeably, the by-the-book management became antagonistic. Richard responded by lampooning their Ronald McDonald clown character, having Jeff Ginsburg assume a considerably more perverse looking clown with a curly red wig, rhino horn, and placard identifying him as *Rhino McDino*. Taking a break during a Rhino promotion, McDino entered McDonald's to quench his thirst, but was refused service. Richard responded to McDonald's further uptight seriousness by painting a mural of our new McDino mascot on the side of the building that faced McDonald's lot. It parodied the hamburger chain's numerical claims of hamburgers purchased by stating how many records we had moved: "Over 300,000 sold."

Maybe it was being next to McDonald's, but we had more visits from celebrities—although I don't recall anybody coming in more than once. One afternoon when I returned to the store during a slow afternoon, someone who looked like Bryan Ferry was perusing the bins. Jeff Gold and the other employees were sitting behind the counter, nonchalant. As Jeff was a big Roxy Music fan, I reasoned that it couldn't be him. After he purchased his records and left, I remarked that the customer looked like Bryan Ferry. When Jeff said it was, I couldn't believe he didn't talk to him. Bryan was apparently so shy that he had a short guy with him who whipped up to the counter and asked questions like where Jack Nitzche's *Lonely Surfer* album was, and then rushed back to tell Bryan. They whispered to each other. After snaring that one, Bryan sent his man over to the counter to ask where the first Neil Young album was, etc. "I guess he didn't feel like talking," Jeff said. Alice Cooper and Burton Cummings came in, separately, looking for out-of-print Jimi Hendrix and Traffic albums. Steely Dan's Donald Fagen asked for albums by jazz pianist Lennie Tristano.

One ex-rock star who came in more than once—and I wished he hadn't—was Sky Saxon, the ex-lead singer of the Seeds. I had been a fan of his LA band, which was best known for its 1967 Top 40 hit "Pushin' Too Hard." I ran into him at the Troubadour in 1971. Saxon looked and sounded like comedian Jerry Lewis: he had a handsome, fuller face with a cleft chin and a distinct, nasal singing voice. When I met him he still had his rock-star good looks. I tried to set up a concert for him and his group at UCLA, but he wasn't together enough to make it happen. When he came into the store seven years later, he was a different person. With his long, stringy hair, he looked twenty years older than he was, reminding me of the Old Witch from *Tales of the Crypt*. In slow, burned-out hippie patter, he explained that he was now called "Sunlight" (his real name was Richard Marsh) and had been living in a commune in Hawaii. He collected packs of dogs because D-O-G spelled backwards was G-O-D. He was flogging his new record, "Beautiful Stars," a twelve-inch single pressed on red vinyl. I bought some just to get rid of him.

At a subsequent visit, he introduced us to his manager, "Flashlight" (real name: Jeff Gruber), an obviously sleazy, Igor-type of character. A few years later Gruber hoodwinked Richard into compiling a box of Rhino promos to be picked up for the Troggs' lead singer, Reg Presley, who he said was in town. Weeks later he tried to pull the scam again, but I answered the phone this time. I could tell the "Reg Presley" who was calling had a fake

English accent—I had spent time with Presley years earlier and knew what he sounded like. I shined Gruber—I mean, Flashlight—on.

The most beautiful girl I had ever seen—close up—walked into the store with her boyfriend. The fantasy I was developing quickly evaporated when she asked for a 1972 album by the Addrisi Brothers, *We've Got to Get It On Again*, revealing her lack of taste. Anna Bjornsdottir was from Iceland. She left her phone number, but I wasn't able to find the album for her. Later, when I saw that she had a small part in *More American Graffiti*, I reasoned that's why she was in town.

I came up with the idea that we should picket the store in order to get media coverage. Businesses are usually picketed by disgruntled employees or their union in a dispute over labor policies or compensation. In this case, we employees picketed in front of the store, proclaiming that our customers were unfair to us because we didn't have enough of them. The media didn't bite. Years later we tried the same stunt when we picketed record stores (with their permission) to *Save the LP*, in an effort to gain attention for the rapidly declining vinyl format. The media didn't bite that time, either.

From the time I first met him, Richard always had a beard. For Halloween he, Fark, and Joe Morris (actually Joe Blustein) shaved half of their respective beards before making the party circuit. No one believed the half beards were real. When Richard was back at the store, now fully shaved, no one recognized him. He never grew another beard, nor did his friends.

In November 1977 we kicked off another Calendar of Events, which ran through December. Most of the theme days were different. Unemployed People's Day reflected the economy of the time: *Down and out, need a job, don't know where your next record is coming from? Cast the blues aside, Rhino is here to help out. No, we can't give you a job. But we will be giving you a free record. Just bring in your unemployment card and we will give you a free record by an unemployed rock group.* During Thanksgiving week we sold our "turkey" albums for forty cents a pound.

Previously we had in-store appearances from radio DJ Rodney Bingenheimer and producer Kim Fowley. Fowley's night was particularly entertaining. He took charge by sticking the microphone in front of the amplifier, generating painful feedback to get the crowd's attention, and calling Rhino's customers "assholes." We brought him back for an encore. With more space, we were able to accommodate more fans, so we had more guests: singer Peter Noone (Herman's Hermits), producer Mike Chapman, and Wild Man Fischer. Writer Richard Meltzer, who penned this chapter's epigraph, climaxed the performance with his band Vom by pouring cockroaches onto his head, which he failed to retrieve prior to leaving.

On Saturday, December 10, UK pub band Eddie and the Hot Rods pulled up to the front of the store on a flatbed truck for a prearranged live performance. Their UK hit from that past summer, "Do Anything You Wanna Do," was among my favorite records of the year. Island Records A&R man and ex-rock star Spencer Davis joined them on guitar for a cover of Bob Seger's "Get Out of Denver." They were in town playing the Whisky. Unfortunately, not many people turned up to see them play at Rhino.

The Beverly Hills outpost of the German label Ariola Records wanted to get into the punk game and formed an imprint called Zombie Records. The first release was a record I produced, "Punk Rock Christmas" by the Ravers. Richard got a Christmas tree to display in the window, which we decorated with the single's picture sleeves, each attached by a safety pin. Pat Smear (real name: Georg Ruthenberg), the guitarist of the Germs, came in and commenced to spit on the tree display, apparently resenting what he saw as the commercial exploitation of the punk scene, or expressing his frustration that the Germs couldn't get signed. Being totally insensitive to the pain he must have been suffering, I threw him out. Months later at the new store, Lee threw him out again—this time with fellow Germ Darby Crash—for spitting on our window.

Jeff Gold had introduced me to Bruce Gary, a record collector who always seemed to be hustling for gigs as a drummer. Based on the local airplay that "Punk Rock Christmas" was receiving, Bruce came into the back room and offered his services as a drummer together with ex-Cream bassist Jack Bruce, "for scale," for an upcoming recording project. It was tempting, but I had nothing planned.

Richard and I released our first album on the Rhino Records label, *Wildmania* by Wild Man Fischer, in January 1978. We had previously released a number of singles, but an LP marked a bigger commitment. Initial sales were good enough to encourage us to plan more albums. Throughout the year, while I was still in charge of managing the store, more of my time went into working on our label releases. Putting the records together, and in some cases making new recordings in the studio, was more creatively stimulating for Richard and me than running a record store.

We grew comfortable with having more room than in our previous building. Our problems with McDonald's notwithstanding, we considered not moving back, but Carmine wanted the option of expanding his restaurant into the space and only wanted to make Rhino's occupation temporary. McDonald's threatened legal action over the Rhino McDino mural on the building, so Richard painted it over, but only after we had moved back to Westwood Boulevard into the new building in April 1978.

Lee arranged to import pressings from Japan, which music fans coveted—even at high prices—because they sounded better than their American counterparts and had elaborate packaging. Usually the enclosed lyric sheets contained numerous amusing errors. Some albums hadn't been issued in the United States, such as recent Sony releases by Miles Davis—live titles, *Pangea* and *Agharta*—and live albums by Cheap Trick and Santana, and the Runaways on Mercury. We sold sixty copies of *Cheap Trick at Budokan*. Its success encouraged the group's US label, Epic, to manufacture the album in the States. It spawned the group's first hit single "I Want You to Want Me" and sold better than any other album released throughout their career.

Even as a teen, Jeff Gold amassed a formidable Jimi Hendrix vinyl collection. He brought to the store the expertise of the collectors market and, with Lee, had the knowledge to identify what European import albums we should carry. We stocked imports from the UK Virgin label, as well as European progressive groups like Neu!, Gong, and Tangerine Dream. When closing on Saturday nights, Jeff played a 45 of Booker T. and the MG's "Green Onions" at a 33 1/3 speed to clear the store of lingering customers.

You had to be smart to do your job at Rhino. In assessing used or promotional albums that were traded in, you had to be as sharp as a bond salesman or insurance actuary. You wanted to pay top dollar—more than the stores in Hollywood—to entice customers to make the trip to Westwood. But if you guessed wrong too many times—if you overpaid—the store failed to make a profit. You had to be aware of all the new releases, as well as all the albums of the sixties and seventies—and then some—and in an age before the personal computer, all in your head. And you had to know when tastes changed. In 1976 *Frampton Comes Alive!* was the top selling record of the year. Less than three years later, it was the top traded-in record of the year. Nobody wanted it, even at bargain bin prices. There were twenty-five used copies sitting on a shelf in the back room.

We enjoyed recommending obscure records to our clientele. Whether an album was worthwhile was not necessarily reflected by its sales, and good records fell through the cracks. Among our favorites: Tommy Hoehn's *Losing You To Sleep*, Godfrey Daniel's *Take a Sad Song . . .*, David Werner's *Whiz Kid*, Big Star's first two records, and albums by Elliott Murphy, Zuider Zee, Van Dyke Parks, Michael Roether, and The Moon (featuring ex-Beach Boy David Marks). The jazz department, which was responsible for 40 percent of Rhino's total stock, boasted old releases on Pacific Jazz, 1500-series Blue Note, and Ken Nordine's *Word Jazz*.

We stocked a lot of independently pressed records that we recommended to our customers, the best example being Devo's first two singles. We promoted them and sold close to four hundred, much more than any other store. We sold so many of professional wrestler Freddie Blassie's *King of Men* EP that we made a deal to issue it on our new Rhino label. Rory Johnston was Sex Pistols' manager Malcolm McLaren's West Coast representative. He brought the Clash's Mick Jones into the new store, but only after I promised to give Jones free records.

Nels Cline, a guitarist friend of Lee's, joined him in the jazz department. He heard Will Ackerman playing his new record on the radio. Cline liked it and contacted Will, but had to convince him to sell the store a box of twenty-five. Will expressed his doubts because he didn't think Rhino could sell that many. He sent the box anyway. Rhino became the first store in LA to stock the record, and that initial box sold out in less than a week.

Cline developed a friendship with jazz customer George Winston, who was then employed as a deliveryman for Larry Flint Publications' *Hustler* and *Chic*. He had been a stride piano practitioner, but was no longer active. Nels encouraged George to resume playing and later introduced him to Ackerman. One day George wanted to get Nels' opinion on a tape "a friend" of his had recently recorded. Nels replied that it was "the most boring music he had ever heard." George revealed that it was, in fact, he himself performing what was to be his debut Windham Hill album, *Autumn*, which became the tiny label's breakout success. George went on to become the best-selling instrumentalist of his day. Despite his success, George shuns the spotlight: "It's like I'm in the Rhino listening booth, and I'm having this terrible dream . . ."

In part because of the success of Rhino Claremont, I had suggested we open more stores. If we had a couple more, we would have sufficient enough business to be able to buy directly from the major labels, paying less per record than buying from a middle-man, or one-stop, as we had been doing. Richard thought two more stores would mean more investment and more potential headaches; plus he would have to find an honest and capable manager for each.

Year in, year out, the store kept getting better. It achieved a level far beyond anything Richard Foos imagined when he opened the original store. Richard Meltzer's article in *Coast* magazine was titled "Best Damned Record Store in California." Ray Coleman's column from America in the English music weekly *Melody Maker* said, "This place is amazing!" The accolades were nice, and the business generated enough for a hippie like Richard to live on, but Richard was no longer interested in retail.

In 1978 he hired a business broker to sell the store. The buyer, Steve Ferber, had sold a magazine stand and was looking for a subsequent business. He was a pipe-smoking hippie and reggae fan. He asked me to stay on to manage the store, and was willing to give me a slight increase over what Richard had paid me, but I declined. Richard and I were moving on at the end of the year, as cofounders of the Rhino Records label.

CHAPTER 2

The Rhino Label Part One

The Independent Years

We're on a mission from God.

—Elwood Blues, the Blues Brothers

Because Richard, Jeff, and I had Wild Man's album, he felt accepted—and loved—when he visited the Rhino store. In appreciation, he made up a song about us, "Go to Rhino Records":

Go to Rhino Records on Westwood Boulevard
They have nice people there
They'll show you where the records are
Where are the records?
They're over there, they're all over the place

Go to Rhino Records on Westwood Boulevard
You can get Herb Alpert and Jackie Lomax for 40¢*
Da doot, da dooo!

*(selections from our bargain bin)

I called up Jeff Gold and told him to get to the store with his hand-held cassette recorder. We captured two takes of Wild Man bellowing his song in the back room. We gave Jeff "producer" credit. Richard and I decided to release it as a single. Because I had done this before with my band, I showed Richard the procedure.

But first we needed a "B" side. We wrote "Rhino, The Place to Go" with lyrics that celebrated how much our store was better than our competitors. For the recording, I sang, Richard played bass, Steve Rosen played guitar, and his brother Mick played drums. The other stores, rather than being offended, were amused that they were mentioned on a record, as amateurish as the performance was. We pressed 500 singles and gave them away to our customers as a gift in 1975.

I told Bill Stout about our release, and he offered to design a Rhino Records logo. It was a 1950s greaser-looking man-rhino with a pimply, teenage complexion and a record around his horn. I loved it. I designed the label to look like the well-organized one used by A&M Records, and we chose yellow: it was the best color as a background for black text, it was Richard's favorite color, and it was the color of the coolest US label, Epic Records (for whom the Yardbirds, Hollies, Dave Clark Five, Jeff Beck Group, and Donovan had recorded in the 1960s).

Our single found its way to England where BBC DJ John Peel took a fancy to it and played it on his radio show. That's when we pressed up an additional thousand to sell. It was so well liked and so novel that his listeners voted it into his Festive Fifty for 1976, placing it at #48. Led Zeppelin's "Stairway to Heaven" topped the list.

This first single, which could be described as "novelty," set the tone for many of Rhino's early releases. Richard and I related to the fun and outrageousness of rock 'n' roll, from cartoonish characters like Little Richard and Jerry Lee Lewis, to the humor of Frank Zappa and the Mothers of Invention. The comedy we heard on the radio and on records greatly influenced us. Among the pleasures of listening to Top 40 radio in the 1950s and 1960s were the novelty records—as they were called—that became hits. David Seville, an actor who changed his name from Ross Bagdasarian, topped the charts with "Witch Doctor" in 1958. Its appeal was the unique sound of voices that were sped up in the recording. He used a similar approach, this time with harmonies, for Alvin and the Chipmunks. Decades before their animated cartoon shows of the early 1960s and 1980s, and the smash hit movies of the last few years, Seville achieved success with two top ten Chipmunk hits over a six-month period in the late 1950s.

Also in the '50s we liked Sheb Wooley's "The Purple People Eater" and Homer & Jethro's "The Battle of Kookamunga," which parodied Johnny Horton's serious "Battle of New Orleans" into a teenage, summer camp setting. There were hits in the '60s as well, like Napoleon XIV's "They're Coming to Take Me Away, Ha-Haaa!" which made it to number three. It featured a hysterical vocalist and manic effects in a comedic reflection of the country's newfound interest in psychology. Radio playlists constricted in the 1970s, however, and subsequently deprived listeners the joy of hearing novelty records as part of the Top 40.

The early 1960s also saw a reaction to post-World War II conservatism with more self-expression proliferating in big-selling comedy albums, mostly recorded performances in clubs by Bill Cosby, Bob Newhart, Woody Allen, Jose Jimenez (a character of Bill Dana's), and Carl Reiner and Mel Brooks with their 2000 Year Old Man. Lenny Bruce made a big impact on me, but not until his recordings were reissued in the early 1970s. This evolved into more produced, studio recorded albums by the Firesign Theatre and others.

Over the next year we experimented with various types of singles, testing this new market for independently pressed records. In 1976 we established a new label, Big 7 Inch Records, inspired by Bull Moose Jackson's double-entendre song "Big Ten Inch Record." Ten inches was the diameter of a 78 rpm record; seven inches, 45 rpm. We thought that competing record stores would not stock a record that would remind buyers of the Rhino store. We realized the Rhino imprint was not a problem when Bomp Records distributed our first two singles to Tower Records.

We released an intended comeback effort by Roky Erickson. Roky, Rhino's second artist to have spent time in a mental institution, was leader of the 1960s psychedelic band the Thirteenth Floor Elevators. They never had a Top 40 hit, but were familiar from the track "You're Gonna Miss Me" on Elektra's *Nuggets* compilation album. Two Rhino customers, Greg Turner and Steve Besser, contacted Jeff Gold and the three of them ventured north to San Anselmo, near San Francisco, to help with the process. (Greg became a member of the Angry Samoans, whose 1982 album, *Back from Samoa*, was graded an "A" by noted critic Robert Christgau—and later, a college math professor.)

It was a harrowing experience. Jeff called the store frantically on more than one occasion. It seemed that the trio's main purpose was to keep Roky occupied while his band recorded the instrumental backing, and then deliver him to the studio later to perform his vocals. They took him to an International House of Pancakes, and tipped the waitress generously to make sure the meal lasted at least four hours. Roky was a big fan of obscure horror movies and talked endlessly about such films as *They Saved Hitler's Brain*. In their company, Roky felt comfortable enough to admit that he was really an alien, and that aliens were going to take over the world. Then the situation degenerated when Roky smeared blueberry syrup over his face. The next day they chose another restaurant, one that attracted an older, conservative crowd. Roky stood up and commenced to sing a song he made up on the spot: "President Ford is a square queen!"

The two songs turned out well, but the record sold only 2,000 copies when it was released in early 1977. While manning the counter one afternoon, I received a call from London. Virgin Records wanted to license our recording for Europe. We were familiar with Virgin because we sold import copies of their stable of progressive rock artists like Mike Oldfield, Tangerine Dream, and Gong. I couldn't understand how Erickson's record would fit in, but I made the deal. It was our first international license.

I should point out that the number we used for Roky's single, RNOR 002, had been used previously. Richard had devised a "Become a Rock Star" promotion at the store in which the winner would be able to record a song and have it released on the budding Rhino label. Richard produced the single by Chris & the Contraband. Although it sounded amateurish, I thought he did a good job. Chris sounded like pop singer Linda Ronstadt. We pressed up the record, but Chris didn't like the result and had us destroy them. The record is Rhino's rarest, and only a few people know of its existence.

It was fun making singles, but they didn't sell that well. I thought we needed to step up and release our first album, by Wild Man Fischer. At that time Wild Man was attending Dodgers games, sitting in the left-field pavilion. He had a built-in audience and sang between innings, which is where we recorded him for part of the album. It was hard to believe, but young kids stood in line to have him sign a baseball. We titled it

Wildmania, borrowing the term from *Beatlemania*, which was concocted to describe the frenzy of Beatles fans in the 1960s.

With the release of *Wildmania* in January 1978, we formalized the label as 50/50 partners. It was only right that Richard should be the president because he started the store and was the oldest, if only by a year. What was I going to be titled? "Vice president" would only have put me in a lesser position. From my London visits, I learned that the head of an English company was usually the managing director, as they didn't have presidents. For example, Mickie Most headed up Rak Records, the label he owned, and his title was "Managing Director." If it worked for him, it could work for me. Although it was unheard of for a company to have both, nobody ever asked me about the competing titles.

There were three labels that most inspired me in wanting to form a company. The Beatles' Apple Records paved the way for artists owning labels. In their initial advertising campaign they implied that an artist could come in off the street and be heard, possibly be signed by Apple, and have hits. I liked that open policy, and I even made a deal with someone who came in off the street. Frank Zappa—along with his manager Herb Cohen—formed another artist-owned label, Bizarre Records. By signing Wild Man Fischer, Captain Beefheart, and the GTOs, he showed us that a label could embrace unconventional, if not outright bizarre, talent. Jac Holzman created Elektra where artistry was prioritized over commercial potential. His acts included the Doors, Love, Tim Buckley, Judy Collins, and the Paul Butterfield Blues Band. Whether or not we could follow in these labels' footprints was beside the point. They forged our aspirations.

In October we released an EP (*Extended Play*, fewer songs than an LP, or album) by the Turtles, the 1960s rock group best known for "Happy Together." We wanted to take advantage of the picture disc craze. Picture discs pressed clear vinyl on top of a photo. Because of the layered process, the sound wasn't as good as on standard pressings. The appeal was the visual—it almost didn't matter what was recorded on the disc. Our Turtles EP was comprised of a popular album track, "Surfer Dan," and three psychedelic recordings that were deemed too extreme to have been releasable. Even though the songs were mostly new—albeit ten years old—it was our first release of older masters.

Our sales totaled $90,000 in our first year of releasing albums, and Richard was sufficiently encouraged—and bored with retail—for us to grow the label in its own location. We had benefitted from radio play on a limited number of stations, including KROQ in Los Angeles, that resulted in some impressive sales within our first year. It was even more of an accomplishment as it was the last big sales year before a recession hit the industry, and we couldn't get records manufactured for a month because the major labels—with their own plants at capacity—monopolized the independent presses. Paul Rappaport estimated that if our Temple City Kazoo Orchestra EP hadn't been back ordered when it was most in demand, we would have sold more than 100,000 instead of only 14,000.

In January 1979 Richard sold the store and we moved to a warehouse space on Pico Boulevard east of Barrington Avenue next to a massage parlor. It had previously been a youth gym and had a dilapidated, mosquito-ridden pool behind it. My friend Todd Schneider and his brother, David, had rented it and named it Changes with designs of opening a nightclub, but they only used it as a rehearsal space.

The previous year I had auditioned Martha Davies there. The original Motels had broken up and I wanted to take her into the studio to record a single. I changed "All the Wrong Girls Like Me," which Mark Leviton and I had written to be Peter Noone's comeback hit—but which he rejected—to suit her gender. I also had her sing "Strange Movies," an obscure Troggs' single sung from the point of view of someone watching a porno movie. Having seen her perform with the first group of Motels at the Whisky, during which she provocatively swayed in a short skirt and fishnet stockings, I thought it fit her sexual image. With a small nose and rosebud mouth, she looked like a beautiful, silent-screen vamp, like Clara Bow or Theda Bara.

She sang both songs well and said she wanted to proceed, but she failed to attend the next two practices, so I abandoned the project. I thought she might have felt uncomfortable with "Strange Movies," although she didn't express it. Much later she told me that it was probably her alcoholism that explained her behavior, even though I saw no symptoms. She even showed up to the audition with her two young daughters in tow. As a consolation, I was able to license "Counting" for our 1978 LA bands compilation, *Saturday Night Pogo*, marking the Motels debut on vinyl.

Richard had the only enclosed office, beneath the stairs, with poor lighting and threadbare carpet. I had no such luxury. My office was on the second floor landing, partially separated from the adjoining cubicles. The second floor lacked air-conditioning, ventilation, and airflow, and got extremely hot in the summer. There was one stereo in the whole building, on the first floor. Anytime anyone wanted us to hear a demo tape, we had to listen to it amidst the activity in the shipping department. Much as I thought it would be cool to be the only record company that had a pool (we could invite visitors to "bring your swimsuit"), we needed the space for parking and filled it in.

Until business grew to the point where we could take salaries, I was paid from Richard's small wholesale business, which was independent of the label. We also benefitted from a warehouse employee to stock and ship our records. For a paging system we used the microphone and bass amp from my band days. When we had our warehouse sales I made announcements in a voice impersonating TV show host Ed Sullivan.

One day, our first label employee Chaz Austin's humor turned to exasperation when he paged Richard after fielding another phone call from one of his friends: "Hey Richard, don't your friends have normal names?" Their nicknames seemed straight out of a Dick Tracy comic strip: Bowl (Pete Parks), Circles (John Robinson), Fark (John Farkash), Menk (Ron Kahn), Eppy (Alan Epstein), Fox (Richard Weinstein).

My attitude was always to do whatever it takes. I thought the lavatory was disgusting: the urinals and toilets that we, and our guests, used. My parents didn't have a maid or use a cleaning woman; my mom did all her own cleaning. Not having had that experience, it didn't occur to me that we could have hired a cleaning crew to solve the problem. When even Chaz refused to clean, I did it myself. In a similar situation, Richard was cleverer than I. When our regular trash collectors stopped coming—they said we owed them money, Richard said we were paid up—Richard boxed up our trash and sent it to them by UPS.

One evening when I visited Mike Chapman in the recording studio, he floated a concept that I had never considered before. During a lull, he postulated, "I could have been anything I wanted to be. I could have been a doctor or a lawyer, but I chose to be a record producer." It dawned on me that I could do that, too. I could be anything I wanted to be. Richard and I never had a boss telling us that we couldn't do something or that we weren't experienced or smart enough. As we divvied up the functions required by a record company, Chapman's belief had taken root. As our shoestring budget couldn't provide for much in the way of support staff, I never thought that I couldn't apply at least some competency to a task.

Among all the functions of a record company, we each took the ones that were most natural to us. Richard: manufacturing, dealing with the distributors; Harold: publicity, royalties accounting, cover design. We both initiated ideas for projects and produced them in the studio. I did radio promotion, then Richard tried it, and then it was back to me. Richard initially did the bookkeeping, and then I took over. For accounting royalties, I wrote down the amounts from our sales invoices on graph paper, and then added up the totals manually. I did each record twice. If I got the same number, I went on to the next one. If I didn't, I added it again until I arrived at the same number a second time. I tallied royalties in this manner for our first seven years. From time to time a recipient had a question, but I was never challenged.

While we did hire designers for our album covers, not every project could justify the expense, so I designed many. I hadn't taken design classes, but I knew what looked good. Quite often I adapted a design from another album cover. I opted for simple designs, often using a large photo for the front cover similar to British albums in the sixties, and copy a layout for the reverse. I penciled it out and took it to the graphics house a few blocks away. I tried to use Bill Stout more, but few of our releases could merit his fee. At times he was commissioned to design artwork for a project that wasn't selected, which he allowed us to use at a cut-rate. A typical example was the illustration he created for a poster for the movie *Fast Times at Ridgemont High*, which we used for one of our *The History of Surf Music* volumes. Even though our funds were limited, we produced attractive covers. Budget label Pickwick International, a much better financed company, bought high school student art for fifty dollars for their covers.

We were unaware of it at the time, but this was a great experience in learning about all the different areas of a record company. In my discussions with a product manager, A&R manager, or publicist at a major label, they were very knowledgeable in their fields, but considerably less so in others. Because the late 1970s saw such a major boon to record sales, the massive profits hid the excesses of the time—some fueled by the popularity of cocaine use in the music industry—and perpetuated indulgent practices. Because neither of us had worked full time for a label, we never acquired those habits. In a few cases where we hired an employee who had worked at a major label, we noticed a lack of self-restraint.

The most difficult area for us was radio. Record sales were generated when listeners heard a record with enough frequency to determine they liked it and wanted to buy it. In a utopian world, radio stations would play the best music for their formats and not play what they deemed substandard. I think most listeners think that a station makes up its playlist from what its listeners like by tallying requests on its phone lines. Many stations also based their selections on illegal payments filtered to them by the labels, a practice often referred to as payola. Ethically we would not have participated, but we couldn't compete against the other labels that were much better funded than we were. Even when we could get friendly programmers to talk to us on the phone, they often told us they liked our records but then wouldn't play them. College radio was more open, but didn't seem to generate enough sales for us to see a difference.

The best example of this practice was Los Angeles radio play for Pink Floyd's *The Wall*. The double album was released in December 1979 and was an immediate success, but three of the key radio stations failed to add the single, "Another Brick in the Wall Part II." After a few weeks, Columbia Records provided money to the independent promotion men it hired to make the payments to the stations. Not surprisingly, they all added the single to their playlists in the same week.

As a Los Angeles-based company, I thought it was important for us to support the local music scene. I was greatly disappointed that even those bands with large followings—who made good records—were not added to the playlists of the local stations who felt no similar need to support local talent. As a consequence, most lost money for us, making it difficult to continue recording bands such as the Pop, Weirdos, and the Naughty Sweeties. Freddy Moore, the lead singer and guitarist with the Nu Kats, came to the office for meetings accompanied by his teenage fiancé, who was dressed like a Southern belle in a frilly skirt and petticoat. Demi Moore—need I say it, the popular actress—cowrote the best song on the EP with Freddy, and made her acting debut on our low-budget promotional video.

We were just winging it. There was no strategy. Our releases in the second year mirrored those in the first. We felt they would do better because we allocated our profits to improve the production, and we had more distributors carrying our line. In the short time that had passed, radio playlists became more restricted and programmers were less inclined to play our product.

A case in point was the money and effort we lavished on the follow-up to our biggest selling record of the previous year by the Temple City Kazoo Orchestra. The Kazoos Brothers' *Some Kazoos*—the Rolling Stones' latest album was titled *Some Girls*—was our ploy to take advantage of the newfound popularity of the Blues Brothers, characters created by John Belushi and Dan Aykroyd on *Saturday Night Live*. This time we recorded in an actual studio—albeit a low-budget one—and spent time trying to get it right: breaking down the songs we covered, like Sam & Dave's "Soul Man," to transpose the instruments to kazoo—a real learning experience in understanding musical arrangement—and recording parts by slowing down or speeding up the tape, as need be (e.g., a kazoo recorded when the tape had been sped up more approximates the lower range of a bass guitar when played at normal speed). We splurged for a color photo session and a cover designer. Among our subtle jokes, the back cover listed the recording sessions as having taken place February 28 through 30.

We were asked to appear on *The Dinah Shore Show*—for no money. I didn't have a star complex, but compared with our appearance on *The Mike Douglas Show*—also for no money—we were on poverty row. For Douglas, we were placed in a large waiting room stocked with drinks and a crudités platter. Across the hall was vocal group Tavares—nice guys who expressed a curiosity in our kazoos. Tom Knapp, who worked at City One-Stop and was enlisted to flesh out our orchestra, didn't let the prospect that he was to blow on a kazoo instead of playing a real instrument stop him from stepping into the shoes of a real rock star like Keith Richards by swigging from his own pint of whisky, to the embarrassment of the rest of us. Gary Myrick and David Dennard, who made a real case for rock legitimacy as members of the recently signed Figures, joined us for the taping and had no trouble behaving civilly.

For *Dinah*, we were relegated to a small room that was more like a hastily constructed lean-to without enough seats for our slimmed-down combo, and no amenities. On camera, Richard commented to Dinah about how impressed he was at how well her studio audience had played the kazoos we furnished them with to accompany our musical entrance: "I don't recall seeing any of them at our kazoo school," he feigned. Neither our appearance on Dinah's show nor the success of *The Blues Brothers* feature film months later moved records. The Kazoos Brothers EP sold about 25 percent of what the Temple City Kazoo Orchestra's had, losing money in the process.

By mid-year 1979, our business was so anemic I wasn't sure the company would be able to survive. I asked Mike Chapman and Nicky Chinn, independently of each other, if they would hire me to be the A&R (Artists & Repertoire) person at their new company, Dreamland Records. Fortunately, they declined, saying they would do it themselves. Despite Chapman's momentum as America's hottest record producer, Dreamland failed, losing millions of dollars, and was gone two years later.

From the money we had banked from our first year, we had some funds to license recordings from the major labels. One desire we had in forming our company was to reissue the out-of-print records we had loved growing up. The majors were letting a great deal of these recordings languish in their vaults as they focused on big selling titles by contemporary acts like Fleetwood Mac. My ex-editor at the *Daily Bruin* (and bass player on my band's first two singles) Jim Bickhart worked at Warner Special Products (WSP) and licensed us a *Best of Allan Sherman*. We paid WSP a $3,000 advance against future royalties earned from sales. As Allan Sherman records had been out of print for years, Warner Brothers looked at the income generated from Rhino's compilation as extra profits.

Sherman was an anomaly for a pop singer. He looked like a cross between a swarthy Venice gondolier and an over-sized curb sitter bellowing for handouts from an outdoor meat market, and possessed a voice as moving as a deadpan teamster trainee's. As a young comedy writer, he created the long-running TV show *I've Got a Secret*. He sang his parody songs at Hollywood parties for fun until TV show host Steve Allen pushed him to record them. Unlike the romantic pop songs of the early sixties, Sherman's uniquely reflected the suburban growth and petty materialism of the flexing middle class. Sherman only had one big hit. The melody for "Hello Muddah, Hello Faddah!" was from Ponchielli's "Dance of the Hours"—which was familiar from its use in Walt Disney's *Fantasia*— and the lyrics that of a kid's diary of summer camp. More importantly, Sherman popularized the concept of replacing the lyrics of well-known songs with humorous, incongruous ones. He was a big influence on both of us. We later recorded modern day equivalents like "Walk on the Kosher Side," which took Lou Reed's song of transexuality, "Walk On the Wild Side," into a commentary on Jewish assimilation. "Weird Al" Yankovic carries Sherman's banner today.

Our first proper rock reissue was done for perverse reasons. The Barbarians were a run-of-the-mill garage band from Boston whose name was kept alive from having a track on the *Nuggets* compilation. They hold the distinction of being the only unknown band in the 1964 concert film *T.A.M.I. Show*—alongside the Rolling Stones, James Brown, Chuck Berry, and other stars. They were memorable because their drummer, Moulty, played with a hook on his left arm. Producer Doug Morris, later the head of Atlantic Records, took a common phrase addressed to young men who sported Beatles-styled hair, "Are You A Boy Or Are You A Girl," and wrote a song with his brother that became a regional hit for the Barbarians.

Following a Rolling Stones tour in 1979, group members Ron Wood and Keith Richards took to the road again to play twenty dates fronting the New Barbarians. As the group didn't have a record out, we thought that a reissue of the 1960s Barbarians would confuse fans, resulting in sales. Did we really believe that? No, or course not, but we were hopeful. Mostly, we took pleasure in the absurdity of our intention. As the Barbarians album was long out of print, I called Laurie Records and made a deal for Rhino to reissue it. Laurie was beyond its hit years, but had enjoyed a nice run with the Chiffons, Dion and the Belmonts, and Gerry and the Pacemakers.

I concocted a Barbarians' Fan Club headquartered in Luxembourg. I called world traveler Peter Noone to have him make up a name that sounded like someone who lived there. I wrote the liner notes as *Joe Doissy*, in the mode of a foreign fan who misunderstood the merits of the American group. If the tone of the liner notes wasn't a tip off, the unnecessary diagram that we included identifying the four band members would have been. Rather than a numerical sequence of 1, 2, 3, 4, we used 2, 3b, 5a, 6c. To give the album even more importance, I came up with the pretentious sounding *Golden Archive Series* so this could be presented as part of an ongoing *very important series*. Our ploy didn't work. We sold only 5,000 copies, but the album was profitable.

In September "Weird Al" came to see me. He had recorded a parody of the Knack's hit "My Sharona" in a lavatory at his school, Cal Poly San Luis Obispo, where he was an architecture major. "My Bologna" was a popular track on Dr. Demento's radio show. I told Al I was interested, and suggested issuing the record to look like a package of bologna, with the record a lunchmeat picture disc. I never heard back from him. As Capitol Records issued the Knack's records and was a "major label," he made his deal with them. It would have been a priority for us. Capitol released it to placate the Knack. The record never charted.

In conjunction with KROQ and DJ Jed the Fish, we issued an album of the winners of the station's Devotees contest. KROQ received over 400 tapes from people playing in Devo's style, but the finalists were so marginal, Richard went into the studio and recorded a cover of Merle Haggard's "Okie from Muskogee" as the *Bakersfield Boogie Boys*, to bolster the quality of the album. That track proved so popular that Richard and I produced an EP with the fabricated group—to few sales.

I made a deal with the Firesign Theatre to issue an EP from the five segments they produced for a proposed radio series based on their popular private eye character Nick Danger. Our sales in 1979 were $130,000, but our expenses vastly increased. We were headed for a loss, but 10,000 Firesign Theatre EPs and 8,000 *Devotees* LPs were enough to bring us close to breaking even. We realized that we were likely to have few records selling 10,000, so we had to release more albums, with the assumption that most would be profitable and that the aggregate would help us build the business. In our first two years, we averaged nine releases. In the following two, we upped it to eighteen.

Our coffers were also bolstered by the few thousand dollars we received for the rights to issue the Temple City Kazoo Orchestra and Gefilte Joe & the Fish in Germany. Peter Schimmelfennig's formula to success was signing East German rock bands to his Pool Records label and selling them to West Germans. Handsome, strapping, charming, and German, it made no sense to us how he could appreciate the humor of the early Rhino novelty releases. He and his cohorts wined and dined Richard and me at Dar Maghreb, a Moroccan restaurant in Hollywood. How could we resist? We were happy to take his money, but saner heads prevailed and he never issued our product. I ran into Peter again in October 1990 at a reception at UCLA's Royce Hall after the screening of a restored *Metropolis*. He was shepherding the (German) DEFA Symphony Orchestra that provided the film's live soundtrack on its tour of America.

Dr. Demento (Barry Hansen) had a long-running, syndicated radio show composed of comedy and novelty recordings. He encouraged listeners to submit their own recordings and played the more interesting ones on the show. He even played my band's first record, "Nose Job." His biggest discovery was "Weird Al" Yankovic. Because Richard and I loved novelty records, and because *Circus Royale*, the sequel to our second album, *Rhino Royale*, only sold a disappointing 5,000 records, we thought we'd see how many more sales Demento could attract with his audience. *Dementia Royale* (see, we even kept the theme), released in February 1980, moved 14,000 albums in its first two years.

I met Paul Almond when he was an attorney on staff at Warner Brothers Records, through my friend David Berson. Paul left Warner Brothers to get into the film business, working for Roger Corman at New World Pictures. The first deal we did together was for the soundtrack to *The Brood*, a horror movie directed by David Cronenberg. Because composer Howard Shore had conducted the orchestra in Canada—it was cheaper than doing so in the United States—I thought we wouldn't be subject to American musicians' union reuse payments. What that meant was, for example, if New World paid the orchestra members a total of $10,000 for the recording for the movie, Rhino would have to pay the same amount again—even though no new recording was made—solely because the music was being used for a second purpose, in this case a soundtrack album. The reuse payment made it too expensive for our limited budget, so we passed. Reuse payments were not a problem with *Battle Beyond the Stars*, which became Rhino's first soundtrack release, in September 1980. The film and score were derivative of *Star Wars*, although it has the distinction of being composer James Horner's first soundtrack album. Horner soon became a major composer and conductor, with the two highest grossing films of all time, *Titanic* and *Avatar*, among his credits.

We soon discovered that it wasn't cost effective to pay a lawyer to negotiate contracts for the small amount of records we sold, so I took that over. The "standard" licensing agreements from the major labels usually contained unreasonable or inapplicable clauses that I had to scrutinize and change or delete. It was a game; the label used those who signed off on these as leverage to its advantage later. Paul pointed out that lawyers are paid to construct contracts—which will produce potential profits—but rarely paid to edit them, or make them easier to read, because that activity will not lead to the potential profit of a deal. The one he created for New World Pictures was well written and succinct, and there was nothing devious about it. More than anything else, it gave me respect for Paul and his integrity and furthered our friendship. More practically, I took his form, retyped it with a few changes, and used it as Rhino's standard contract for many years.

Seymour Stein, President of Sire Records, came to see me on the third Monday of November 1980, wanting to license "Fish Heads" by Barnes & Barnes, a top-rated request on Dr. Demento's radio show. It was an unusually hot day as Seymour joined me upstairs in my windowless cubical. He was wearing a wool suit, but had dispensed with his tie. With his profuse sweating and unsuccessful attempts at blotting with a hankie, it was clear he was uncomfortable.

I had been looking forward to meeting Seymour because he was a music guy. More than anybody else in the States, he promoted new wave with his signings of the Ramones, Talking Heads, and Richard Hell and the Voidoids. Sire had even reissued Elektra's *Nuggets* album. As Rhino was a small label, I could identify with his stinginess. The first Ramones album cost only $6,400 to record. His artists didn't sell that well and Sire wasn't considered a success, but as a Warner-distributed label it was much better funded than Rhino.

As Seymour attempted to charm me with his stuttering speech, I was almost insulted that he wasn't offering any advance against royalties to license "Fish Heads." We certainly could have used the money, if he had. On his way out he noticed a couple of albums on the shelf among our non-Rhino wholesale stock. There were two volumes of recordings from Buddy Holly's appearances on radio shows. Seymour asked for two sets and promised to send us some Sire albums in exchange. Months later I called Seymour's office a couple of times to remind him, but didn't receive a check or records for the Holly LPs.

A few months into 1981, I noticed that Richard wasn't around much. I was doing all of the work on most of our releases. One day when Richard was in, I asked him why. He told me that he and Chuck Rose—a friend whose family owned the 35-store Rose Records chain based in Chicago— had started up Sounds Good, a one-stop in Chatsworth. It felt to me like he was giving up on our label by withdrawing into another business. I would have felt differently about it if he had been upfront in telling me about his intentions. I don't know whether he wanted to avoid the confrontation or whether he was just neglectful. As partners in the record label, a reasonable expectation was that the workload would be split fairly evenly. I didn't like it, but I carried on. Richard had nothing to do with the majority of the eighteen records we released that year, the major exception being the Richie Valens box set that we worked on together.

Having built a strong following where he was referred to as "The Little Richard of the San Fernando Valley," Richie Valens is best known for his hits "La Bamba" and "Donna," and for perishing in the same plane crash that claimed Buddy Holly and The Big Bopper in February 1959. While at the store, I took note of the box sets that were beginning to be issued from Europe on rock pioneers like Holly and Gene Vincent. Our *History of Richie Valens* was the first retrospective box released in the United States. For the booklet, Richard went to Pacoima Jr. High School and copied a yearbook photo of Valens (actually Richard Valenzuela). We also included an unpublished photo from the crash site. One of the three discs, *Live at Pacoima Jr. High*, was then going for $100 on the collectors market. Live recordings of rock 'n' roll performers were rare in the 1950s, and this primitive one was accomplished with a Dictaphone, a device commonly used in an office to aid with dictation. To promote it, I had Louis Barron construct a twelve-inch single that combined "La Bamba" with "C'mon Let's Go"—speeding up the former and slowing down the later—to attempt to get play in dance clubs. Barron and his wife were responsible for the first electronic film score, 1956's *Forbidden Planet*.

Not too long after Danny Sugerman published his coauthored biography on the Doors' Jim Morrison, *No One Here Gets Out Alive*, he brought to us two new artist projects. The Zippers was a band from the South Bay produced by the Doors' keyboardist Ray Manzarek, whom Danny managed. Bebe Buell, a Cover Girl model, was known for her relationship with Todd Rundgren, for having been a *Playboy* centerfold, and much later as the mom and manager of actress Liv Tyler. She was passionate about rock and collected famous musicians for boyfriends as others would their records: Steven Tyler, Elvis Costello, Rod Stewart. For her EP, she solicited help from members of the Cars and Rick Derringer's band. Despite the talent, an inspired selection of cover songs, and the first wrap-around poster cover issued in the United States, sales were less than 5,000. Danny was one of the few people who could foresee our potential. He recommended that Manzarek invest in Rhino. Other than giving up a portion of ownership of our company, I was so unsophisticated I couldn't think of a way we could have spent the money, so I declined.

There were other labels I admired that started up around the same time as Rhino. In September 1981, Jay Clem at Ralph Records in San Francisco gave me a tour of his offices. Ralph primarily existed to release albums by the Residents, an avant-garde rock band whose members wore large eyeball masks to conceal their identities. In addition to the offices, the complex included a recording studio, a darkroom, and a basement area with sets to film promotional videos. The offices were messy, but I was impressed that so much was accommodated in-house. If it was up to me, and if Rhino had the budget, I would have copied their setup.

I liked a good number of the artists on England's Stiff Records, including Nick Lowe, Wreckless Eric, Elvis Costello, and Rachel Sweet. I thought we were clever and funny, but Stiff had us beat, both in terms of graphics and image. Their wittiness started with their wry name, Stiff, which referred to a record that failed to chart well. It extended with the prefixes used to identify the numbers of their singles, *BUY*, and to slogans such as "Round Records for Square People" and "Where the Fun Never Sets." Ten years later, after we licensed them an album by Phranc for which they never paid us, I came up with another slogan for them: "I got Stiffed by Stiff!" Soon after, they went out of business.

There wasn't much of a lesson learned, more one observed. Be yourself and go with your strengths. Don't try to be a Stiff or a Ralph. The difficulty we experienced in selling new artists and novelty records made us realize that we should focus on reissues. It was a great time for us as we were able to release best-of albums by a number of artists whose records we bought when we were growing up: the Turtles, Monkees, Box Tops, Troggs, and Spencer Davis Group. Some of our reissues sounded so good, it was like hearing them for the first time. In a couple of cases, as with the Beau Brummels and the Everly Brothers, we discovered that we were the first ones to use the first generation masters. Sitting in front of my stereo speakers, listening to the test pressings, left me enthralled.

It was difficult to produce a compilation composed of hits by various artists because one had to license from numerous labels. Local disc jockey Art Laboe introduced the format with *Oldies But Goodies* in 1959. He had been smooching with a girl on his living room couch when one of the 45s he had stacked on his record player kept repeating because the subsequent record failed to drop properly. His annoyed girlfriend said something like, "Art, why don't you put all of those hits on an LP?" The first volume of *Oldies But Goodies* sold extremely well, staying on *Billboard*'s album chart for over three years, and more followed, all on Laboe's Original Sound Records.

This perpetuated a culture where non-current hits were seen as passé. They were lumped together as Oldies but Goodies, with DJs and others playing on high school nostalgia with *Do-you-remember-when* reminiscences. Songwriter Paul Politi keyed off the success of LaBoe's LP and wrote "Those Oldies But Goodies (Remind Me of You)." Vocal group Little Caesar & the Romans—whose visual gimmick was wearing togas during their performances—hit the top ten with it in 1961. They broke up a year later, in part because of an argument between two members who each considered himself Little Caesar.

I always thought music should be judged on its own merits, as a living, breathing thing. Music can be effective to a listener, no matter what era it was created in, as the work of Beethoven, Mozart, and others are considered today. During the Monkees revival in the mid-eighties, young kids were exposed to the music and bought the records because they enjoyed what they heard, even though it might have been created before they were born. When movie fans were moved by the song that played over the opening credits of *Pulp Fiction*, they were reacting to the visceral quality of the instrumental, rather than realizing or caring that Dick Dale's "Miserlou" had been recorded thirty years previously. So my goal at Rhino was not only to make the hits available again to those who wanted to hear them, but to turn people on to the great music of the past that they may never have heard.

By contrast, the major labels that held the rights to older hits were focused on breaking new artists, with the successful ones bringing in large amounts of money to sustain their operations. Older recordings, if they were issued at all, were compiled into albums with the goal of spending the least amount of money possible to maximize the income from these slower-selling titles.

We were the first company to take the position that this music was important and deserved to be reissued with quality in mind—which was a standard I forged for Rhino. That meant trolling for rare photographs for the album jacket, writing fact-filled liner notes for the back cover, and in some cases, issuing a record that sounded better than the original release, as exemplified by our very first best-of albums by Allan Sherman and Love. I was able to get deals with top mastering studios—Artisan and Precision Lacquer—by utilizing time slots that hadn't been booked by their more lucrative clients. Mastering is the process whereby the music as recorded on tape is transferred to another medium, such as an album lacquer from which a stamper is made to press the record.

Bob Marin was an eccentric who never used his kitchen at home because he didn't want to get it dirty. With a bowl hairstyle—actually a wig—he looked like John Fogerty from Creedence Clearwater Revival.

I first met him in the Rhino store days, when he pulled up to the back parking lot in his Plymouth Valiant. The trunk was full of Island Records promotional albums that Bob wanted to sell us. Although his car was con-servative—not what one would think a music guy would drive—Marin kept it in pristine condition. Years later he splurged on a reproduction of a flamboyant Auburn Chord convertible.

As with a lot of salesmen, he was engaging and friendly, but often lacking in knowledge of what he was selling. This came to light shortly before we dismissed him as our sales rep—he declined our offer to be an employee, preferring to remain independent so he could represent more companies—when he failed to realize that the titles and covers of our new band compilations were parodies: *Saturday Night Pogo* for *Saturday Night Fever*, the best-selling album of 1978, and *L. A. IN* for *ALIEN*, the hit movie of 1979.

Gary Stewart took over Marin's sales tasks in August 1981 despite only having sold records to individual consumers in the store. Gary's office was in an open area with asbestos bags—or some other insula-tion—hung precariously close to his head. He sat in a kitchen chair in front of a heavy, metal desk with one side bashed in and a drawer that wouldn't open, and had meetings with guests on a moth-eaten sofa. Despite the impoverished surroundings, he was thrilled to be working for an actual record label.

Chuck Rose recommended Brian Schuman, who joined us shortly thereafter, and anchored our warehouse. As a further example of our penny-pinching (literally), Brian and Gary, with modest grumbles, walked to the office supply warehouse next door to use their Xerox machine for ten cents a copy.

My contract drafting was soon tested in small claims court. In 1971 John Lee Hooker and Canned Heat had sold a lot of records with their album *Hooker 'N Heat*. Ten years later, Howard B. Wolf brought us an album he produced of Hooker and Heat performing at the local Fox Venice Theatre. He was a bit older than us and dressed in an expensive, hippie style: designer jeans, leather fedora, hand-tooled leather briefcase. He was smart and charming, and came across as a hippie capitalist. He had credibility for having been Jefferson Airplane's publisher, and impressed us in revealing that his new girlfriend, Nancy Lee Andrews, was Ringo's recently spurned ex-fiancé.

The album had barely been released when Wolf surprised us by suing us in small claims court. He thought he should have been paid royalties even though we were still recouping the advance we had paid him. As he told me, it was cheaper for him to file the suit than to have paid a lawyer to interpret the clause for him. As he had also filed a small claims action against a store for bedding he had purchased, he conveniently scheduled our case before his other one. I was steamed that Richard and I had to disrupt our day to travel all the way downtown to appear. As I had drafted the agreement, I represented our side to the judge. It was a music contract, it dealt with copyrights, it was out of his league. He postponed judgment until he could consult a judge who was more knowledgeable. As Richard and I left the courtroom, Wolf was hauling out his bedding from the plastic bags he brought. The judgment came in the mail two weeks later, in our favor. Wolf was so likable it was hard for me to stay angry with him. As a result of his impatience to get paid, I negotiated a royalty buyout. As the album eventually racked up more than 40,000 units, the additional profits we made more than compensated for our court appearance.

In January 1982 I was encouraged to attend the yearly record business convention in Cannes, known as MIDEM (Marche International du Disque et de l'Edition Musicale). Flying with Bob Marin, we got off to a rocky start. As we cleared customs in Paris, he shooed me away. He barely made the flight to Nice; he was shaking as he made his way to his seat. He had been detained because a customs agent had found a vial in his suitcase with traces of cocaine. How stupid could he have been! The first day of the convention I woke up late. Marin had already left our room and didn't bother to wake me. I was jetlagged, but made my way to the Palais where the convention was held.

Unlike in previous years, there were few major labels. At this point, it was mostly publishers. Over the next few days I made the rounds and met with a number of labels, few of which were familiar with Rhino. They seemed more interested in selling their masters than in buying.

The highlights for me were taking in a couple of live performances with Toby Mamis. Alice Cooper wasn't in the best vocal form when he ran through selections of his newest album, *Special Forces*, which included a cover of Love's "Seven and Seven Is." He did have a superb guitarist in his band, Mike Pinera, whom I had met when he was in the Iron Butterfly. A new act called Cheetah showcased two attractive, hard-rocking women in the mold of AC/DC—both acts produced by ex-Easybeats Harry Vanda and George Young. Toby and I went backstage afterwards, and I was thrilled to meet George Young—the Easybeats had been one of my favorite groups—and his brother George Alexander (Alexander Young), who had been a member of Grapefruit. I also reconnected with Tom Evans, the bass player from Badfinger, who had been hired to back up Cheetah. He seemed happy to see me and invited me to visit him in England.

One evening at the Carlton Hotel bar, I ran into Seymour Stein and needled him about owing us money. He glanced uncomfortably my way and then disappeared into the throng. I felt he was a music executive who could identify with our passion, who could have been an ally, with whom we could have made deals. But in revealing himself to be too cheap to even honor a fifteen dollar debt, it might have cost him more in the long run. Because Sire hadn't performed that well, Warner Brothers took over full ownership. He received a half-point royalty on acts he signed to the label and then kvetched about it being too low after Madonna hit big. His kvetching was successful; his royalty was increased.

I met Martin Mills, the head of UK Beggars Banquet, who wanted to release Spirit's *Potatoland* and a unique-to-the-UK Rhino sampler I titled *Dr. Rhino and Mr. Hyde* that paired one side of novelty with another of new artists. We concluded the deal in London, where he was nice enough to invite me to his house for dinner. I didn't visit Tom Evans. Because of a strike the trains were running inconsistently, and I didn't want to risk being stranded in Surrey.

At the end of March, the annual NARM convention (National Association of Record Merchandisers) was held nearby at the Century Plaza Hotel. Because of the registration fee, we weren't planning on going. An attendee from out of town was visiting our offices, and we took note of the badge, which was printed on green stock. We got a similar colored paper, Xeroxed his badge, and placed it in the same style plastic holder. To encounter less scrutiny, Richard and I entered the exhibit area by walking into the lower level through the hotel's delivery entrance. We were only at the convention a little more than an hour. It made us realize that we had to be more a part of our industry. Initially we attended the smaller NAIRD convention (National Association of Independent Record Distributors) before we became yearly (paying) participants of NARM. Four years later the NARM convention was back at the Century Plaza Hotel. The Wherehouse chain distributed copies of the *Los Angeles Times* Sunday *Calendar* magazine, which happened to have Richard and me on the cover, in a feature on Rhino.

Marin was ahead of the curve when it came to anticipating the public's interest in the new CD (compact disc) format. He convinced Richard to start an import company, Sounds Good Imports, in the fall of 1982. For the most part only classical music CDs were available, which Bob imported from Germany and Japan. Around this time he introduced us to Brett Gurewitz, who produced some twelve-inch promotional singles for us. Gurewitz played guitar for Bad Religion and had just formed his own label, Epitaph Records.

Richard had taken the concept of the successful parking lot sales we had at the store and relocated it to the building the label shared with Richard's wholesale businesses and a company he was part owner of, the Thinking Cap Company, which sold hats affixed with patches of philosophers' names. Because vigilance over selling bootlegs was slight, there wasn't much concern over the number of titles that were among the thousands of albums offered for sale, but overall, they represented a small portion. An undercover officer had attended the November 1982 weekend sale, bought bootlegs as evidence, and came away with the impression that we were a manufacturer or distributor. Consequently, on the following Monday morning, we were raided by a large number of LAPD officers who swarmed into our building—from both the front and rear entrances—supported by two semi-trailer trucks that barreled into our parking lot.

The police officers didn't have a feel for what was, and what was not, a bootleg. Quite a number of albums that were seized—like *Rock Steady with Flo & Eddie* on Epiphany Records—were not. One man took crime-scene photographs, including that of an Electric Prunes album propped up in my office that was for my personal use. One officer searching Richard's file cabinet uncovered a baggie of marijuana. Never knowing Richard to be a pot smoker, I later asked him about it. He said that he had forgotten about it—it was at least four years old. When the officer in charge realized their miscalculation, he dismissed half of his men, along with one of the semis. The other was loaded with so few boxes, they could have easily fit inside of a mid-size sedan.

I was emotionally drained and dispirited that Monday afternoon. The Rhino label was rolling. Our sales were projected to increase by 50 percent over the previous year. What was going to happen now? Would I be able to make the payments on the house I had bought earlier in the year? Even though our label wasn't at fault, with Richard as co-owner, our licensing from other companies could have been in jeopardy if they thought Rhino was also manufacturing bootleg albums. Eli Okun at CBS Special Products advised Richard to initiate meetings with the major labels we licensed from and put the infraction in context, which he did. The case was settled three years later, with Richard and Bob Marin pleading "no contest" with the Los Angeles City Attorney's office, and each fined $12,500 on two counts of selling bootlegs.

In the spring of 1983 we moved into a larger building, the former headquarters of San Remo Shoes, at the corner of 12th and Olympic in Santa Monica. I was looking forward to walking the mile to the beach during my lunch break. How often did I go? Never. With Brian and Gary, two warehousemen, a receptionist, and an office manager/bookkeeper—Diane Temkin, who later married Brian—we were now eight, and on our way to generating a million dollars in sales.

Seeing how well Marin sold CDs gave us the confidence to release our initial titles, although it was hard to get them manufactured as the majors also readied their product. In 1984 we released greatest hits CDs by the Turtles and Jerry Lee Lewis, and one by the Firesign Theatre—the first spoken word CD—beating a few major labels to the market. Little did we anticipate at the time how music fans would take to these cute little discs. I was surprised that so many people replaced their records with newly released CDs. As a consequence of that and the effectiveness of MTV in marketing new artists, the industry's sales boosted to new heights.

While this new medium had many positive qualities, I thought vinyl records sounded better. I did a few comparisons. My main criticism was that vocals sounded warmer on vinyl. This was, in part, because CDs didn't reproduce the full musical performance, but sampled it at various points and then created the music in between. In January 1985 we hired Bill Inglot, one of Gary's friends, who had been instrumental in compiling our Monkees rarities albums. Bill took over mastering fulltime and set a standard for reissues within the industry.

Our records were distributed by a number of independent companies throughout the United States. In the early days of rock 'n' roll, the independents were the primary labels. Sun (Elvis), Specialty (Little Richard), Del Fi (Richie Valens), and Atlantic (Drifters) were all distributed by independent companies. In the 1960s, White Whale (The Turtles), Kama Sutra (Lovin' Spoonful), Roulette (Tommy James and the Shondells), and Dunhill (Mamas and Papas, Grass Roots) were similarly distributed. As the decade progressed, the major labels sniffed the success of rock and got in on the action. However, the indie network remained strong throughout the 1970s with Motown, A&M, Chrysalis, and Arista. But in the 1980s those, too, moved to the majors, and the effectiveness of the indies diminished. Retailers, naturally, gave the major labels higher priority: they had bigger-selling artists, larger advertising budgets, and were more apt to get paid before the independent distributors.

It was not uncommon for the indie distributors to be delinquent in paying their Rhino bills, which they invariably did, but only after many phone calls. As a consequence, it was hard to plan around not knowing when we would be paid. In the past, because we were fiscally conservative and practical, and had no need to siphon money from the business to fund expensive habits, money had never been a problem.

While the independent distributors used by Rhino had their share of fine salespeople, coordination was extremely difficult. For instance, when the Beat Farmers were touring with the Blasters in Colorado, their engaging performances resulted in significant album sales. Rhino's distributor in that area hadn't paid us for months, so we didn't ship any further orders, hoping that would motivate them into paying. Consequently, we didn't sell all the records that we could have. As Rhino's sales grew, the money that was owed to us by distributors increased, and we had to take out our first bank loan in 1984. This meant that we had to incur an additional expense—interest on our loan.

On Saturday, June 22, 1985, my date Stephanie and I were killing time at the Hollywood Palladium between acts on a triple bill of the Unforgiven, the Blasters, and the Beat Farmers. I ran into the *L.A. Times* music critic, Robert Hilburn. Although I had written for Hilburn in my freelance days, he had given Rhino scant coverage through the years. At the Palladium he asked me questions about how we were able to get the masters for our packages. More specifically, he was nearly incredulous that the owners of Sun Records entrusted to us the sacred recordings of, say, Jerry Lee Lewis. I explained to him that in many cases, the labels didn't have the product out, or didn't feel our higher-priced packages would compete with theirs. I told him how we went about licensing the songs. He said he wanted to write a feature on us. When I didn't hear from him, I thought his interest had waned. It took him almost six months to contact us again and schedule an interview. Given how unenthusiastic he had been previously, I was surprised at how well the article turned out. It was the cover story of the *Times Calendar* magazine for March 9, 1986.

Our CD sales were increasing, but now that more labels were issuing their own, we experienced difficulty in getting them manufactured. As we were growing, we were frustrated and stymied by the independent distributors. We could have used the help of one of the bigger companies, but the majors weren't interested in Rhino because our business was too small and we didn't have hits. Zach Horowitz, a young lawyer at CBS Records with whom I'd become friendly, submitted a proposal to his company, but they declined distributing us. If we wanted to grow, it was clear we needed to make a deal with one of the major labels, but we didn't know if it was possible.

C H A P T E R   3

The Albert Einstein of the Record Business

My Partner Richard Foos

It wasn't that early, around ten o'clock, when I visited Richard at home for the first time. It was September 21, 1973, and I was flying to London in a few hours. I wanted Richard to have the pristine stack of promotional albums I had been saving for him so he would have a small but potent supply to bolster the stock of the record store he was to open in a few weeks. One of his roommates answered the door at his suburban house in West Los Angeles. Richard was still asleep. When he trudged into the living room minutes later, his gut was busting out of a t-shirt two sizes too small, and he was scratching his right buttock inside of the only other article of clothing he was wearing, his Fruit of the Loom underwear.

*   *   *

Eighteen months before, I was leafing through the bootleg albums that were on sale at Lewin's Record Paradise on Hollywood Boulevard. In the 1960s the store was important because it was the only one in the area that stocked English imports. The original Beatles and Rolling Stones albums released in England were coveted because they had additional songs and different covers than their American counterparts. Only later were the imports also valued for their superior sound. By the early 1970s, with the Beatles having

51

broken up, and with the same albums now being issued on both sides of the Atlantic, the store was a shadow of itself, reduced to selling bootlegs. When I commented on the high prices to a fellow shopper, he alerted me to a guy who had a record concession in Santa Monica who not only had lower prices but also took records in trade.

Apollo Electronics stood at 315 Broadway across from a vacant parking lot. Richard was friendly with the son of the owner and made an arrangement to rent space in the store to sell mostly used albums. Whenever I came to shop or sell my promotional albums—Richard paid better than Aron's Records in Hollywood—there were usually no other customers.

I instantly liked him. He was low-key, but friendly. At times he seemed clueless, and I felt I had to help him where I could. After he opened the Rhino Records store, I encouraged my fellow rock writers to make the trek from Hollywood to Westwood to trade in their records with him.

Had Albert Einstein grown up in an affluent suburb of Pittsburgh and been attracted to absurdist humor and rock 'n' roll instead of math and physics, he might have been similar to Richard Foos. Like the disheveled, absent-minded professor—always thinking, with his head in the clouds—Richard could be forgetful and neglectful. A creative thinker who made up his own games—and changed the rules of existing ones—he was like a missing character from the *Seinfeld* TV show.

Richard came over to my apartment with one of his roommates, Pete Parks. Pete had returned from a camping trip during which his girlfriend had drowned. Richard brought Pete over so he could make a recording of the tribute song he had written to present to her parents. Given the solemnity, and that I didn't know Pete, I felt very uncomfortable. My feeling only increased as I endured take after take of Pete coarsely bellowing "Jodie!" I was relieved when they left. Pete had eaten half of an orange, but left the remains and juice splattered on my kitchen counter. I couldn't imagine the song giving her parents any comfort.

What also struck me that day was that Pete kept calling Richard "Mack." Usually someone referred to with that sobriquet has a surname prefixed with "Mac" or "Mc" and is of Irish or Scottish extraction. Richard looked neither. When I asked him, he told me it referred to Mack Trucks because he came from Truckee, a small town in Northern California near the Nevada border. It wasn't until years later that I learned that Richard wasn't from Truckee at all.

Richard Foos was born in New York City in 1949. His family soon moved to Pittsburgh where, as a preteen, he acquired a taste for early 1960s rock 'n' roll. The first record he bought was Joe Jones' "You Talk Too Much," and the first record he "went crazy over" was local group the Marcels' "Blue Moon." The first album he bought was the Four Seasons' *Sherry*. Every Friday night he listened to the new Top 40 countdown on radio station KQV, rooting for his favorite records to make it to number one. Richard was a big fan of Lou Christie, who had four top twenty hits, including the astonishing "Lightnin' Strikes." "He grew up in my neighborhood," recalled Richard. "I was a friend of a girl who had once been to his house. Until I got into the record business, that's the closest I'd ever come to meeting a rock star." (Richard and I had lunch with Lou when he sang on one of our albums. Meeting him was a highlight for both of us.)

In 1963 one of his best friends became immersed in listening to black music. Initially Richard found the style too foreign, but after a while he acquired a taste for it, furthered by the soul records he heard on Porky Chedwick's show on WAMO. He became so passionate about this once alien music that he began to scrounge around junk stores to find rare Rhythm & Blues (R&B) records. As few whites were fans of non-mainstream black music, it became a way for him to express his individuality and nonconformity. At the same time, he became aware of the plight of black Americans and empathized with their cause.

Interestingly enough, Richard didn't go back to check out the rock 'n' roll greats of the previous decade until he had been exposed to the material via cover versions released during the mid-sixties British Invasion. Richard preferred harder sounding groups like the Rolling Stones and Animals, and mentions the Yardbirds as his favorite rock band of the period. As he matured, his understanding of black social issues increased and he became more radical in his political views.

One of Richard's best friends was a Beach Boys fanatic, and together they listened to the hit singles and album cuts. The Southern California that the Beach Boys conveyed to Richard was of a dreamland where everyone had blond hair, was beautiful, and hung out all day at the beach living a very liberating life. This fantasy contrasted sharply with Pittsburgh's drabness and a routine of hanging out at the local pool hall. When his father was offered a job as vice president of the Los Angeles May Company department stores, necessitating a move to Southern California, Richard anticipated paradise.

When he showed up for his first day as a senior at Beverly Hills High, he was shocked. He'd carefully dressed up Brooks Brothers for style, as he'd heard that Californians were sartorial trendsetters. What he faced was a student body of unattractive teenagers (the beautiful celebrity kids were probably sequestered in private schools), sporting torn Cords, blue deck tennis shoes, and pocket t-shirts. Even more disappointing, the kids weren't as hip as those in Pittsburgh; they lacked the street orientation. Still, the weather was pleasant, there were more radio stations that played rock, and more local music TV shows like *Boss City* and *The Lloyd Thaxton Show*. The DJs were more charismatic and the programming often more adventurous (e.g., Stones' Weekends).

Richard's interest in music and black social issues increased. Once he and his friends went to a black music lineup at the Shrine Auditorium. One of Richard's missions was to turn his peers onto the hip R&B music he experienced in Pittsburgh. They were the only white people that they could see. The show was sold out and they couldn't get in, but Richard encountered an advocate of the Black Power political movement who talked to him for three hours outside the auditorium.

The next step in being a music fan was to pick up an instrument and learn how to play. Richard was able to fake competence on the bass guitar and joined Larry Parker (later proprietor of a well-known Beverly Hills diner) in a series of bands. Sometimes they practiced after hours in a USC sociology department conference room. In addition to the usual wedding and Bar Mitzvah gigs, their most adventurous musical endeavor placed the duo as the only white musicians in an otherwise all-black blues band. Their strong desire to taste some blues roots led them to an all-black after-hours club in South Central LA, playing for a small audience that appeared to include hookers and pimps. Afraid for their safety, Larry's grandmother sent along a bodyguard—a cook at his Uncle's deli—to watch over the band. On a good night, Richard recalled, he made five dollars.

Much of what shaped his sense of humor was the absurdity of growing up in a highly structured environment. His wit was sharpened by the peculiarly East Coast ritual of *cutting contests*. These exchanges were best documented by comedian Gabriel Kaplan in his "Up Your Hole With a Mellow Roll" routine, in which he described the fierce one-upmanship in trying to creatively put the other down: "I've heard your father is a skin diver for Roto Rooter." He was also inspired by Alan Abel's book *Confessions of a Hoaxer*. It was while in college—he attended Whittier, USC, and San Fernando Valley State—that Richard acquired the nickname "Gimmick," later shortened to "Mack," because he was always coming up with something. He was thought of as the type of person who would do anything for a practical joke.

Some of Richard's behavior fell into the category of sub-petty theft. His guide was Abbie Hoffman's best seller from 1971, *Steal This Book*, which advocated rebelling against the establishment. He and his friends avoided buying tickets to see movies by walking backwards into theaters from the exits. Sometimes they departed restaurants without paying for their meals.

Richard coached the Little League baseball team on which his younger brother, Garson, played. He attempted to motivate the lethargic players by festooning the dugout with *Playboy* magazine centerfolds. Major League pitcher Jim Bouton had published *Ball Four*, a candid look at baseball behind the scenes. Inspired, Richard wrote fictionalized, outrageous exploits of his team, and had Circles sell *Who Do They Ball For?* to the parents in the stands for ten cents. Once he even placed Fark in the outfield. Even though he wore a uniform, Fark was in his early twenties and sported a beard and long hair. He lasted half an inning before the umpire noticed him and had him ejected.

Richard's first attempt at record retail was Mojo Records, a proposed door-to-door record delivery service he formed with Circles who had acquired fifty promotional albums from a friend of his father's. Rather than make them part of his collection, he and Richard decided to use their booty to trade for records they could sell for full value. They advertised their service in an ad in the *L.A. Free Press*, but nobody responded. Next they randomly called people listed in the phone directory to tell them about their company. Finally a customer called back. But the effort it took Richard and Circles to track down the obscure classical recording, traipsing around to six stores and then trading records for it, all for five dollars, diminished their enthusiasm.

After graduating from San Fernando Valley State College with a sociology degree, Richard opted for community work in South Central Los Angeles. For a time he ran the Free Store, where anyone who had an unemployment card could take home an item that had been donated.

Being a hard-core record fan, Richard continued to seek bargains and obscurities at swap meets. At La Mirada, a reappropriated drive-in theater, he saw a dealer selling hundreds of albums, more records than he had ever seen outside of a store. When he asked, the dealer candidly admitted that he got the whole stack from Aron's for a mere three dollars. Richard thought he could do the same.

Needing a way to supplement his meager community work income, he moved into the space at Apollo. In addition to records from his own collection, Richard creamed Aron's (and other stores) bargain bins when they opened, knowing he could resell these used records for a profit. Richard's out-of-the-way concession became a stop for collectors: delighting them with grossly under-valued collector's items, but frustrating them because he wrote the price with a Marks-A-Lot right on the LP covers. I remember purchasing Little Eva's *Locomotion* album for thirty-five cents (then worth thirty dollars), and Jeff Gold recalls a Beatles MGM album priced at fifty cents (worth fifty dollars). When Jeff noticed a few copies of David Bowie's American debut album (on Deram), he asked Richard if there were any in back stock he could purchase. Richard sold him what he wanted at a nice four dollar mark-up. Gold says they were worth about $100 each.

Around this time Richard had a "record review" column in the small, local newspaper *The Venice Beachhead*. Instead of record reviews, "Politidiscs" acted as a showcase for Richard's *Mad* magazine-like writing. In a typical column he commented that Bob Dylan's new *Dylan* album was too commercial and so over-produced that it would have been rejected as programming by the Muzak company. He then devoted the bulk of his column to provide the "rumored" lyrics and spoken dialogue of Dylan's commercial for Coke, rewritten (by Richard) from his song "Just Like a Woman."

Although Richard's father's background was in retail—on a higher, chain level—Richard didn't have the driving acumen in this area. Establishing a record store was merely an outgrowth of the Free Store and Apollo experiences. When he opened the Rhino store a mile south of UCLA, he assumed, incorrectly as it turned out, that the students would be clamoring for a cheap record store.

Richard needed to express himself humorously outside of Rhino. He wrote fake issues of the UCLA *Daily Bruin* that were distributed on campus on a day when the real paper wasn't published. The issue was complete with major stories, such as "UCLA Students To Be Bussed." An advertisement for the "Charles C. Koalsin [sic] Cheat Method—Successfully Used at West Point and the Air Force Academy" promised to raise grade point averages by one whole point. The Crime and Punishment section reported the following: the arrest of Armand Biceps, star of the UCLA weight lifting team for shoplifting—actually lifting a shop and moving it to a new location; the discovery of the body of Nicholas Simpson, who had been missing for three years and consequently racked up an F average because he had failed to file a withdrawal notice; and the detailed report of the mysterious theft of an economy sized bar of Ivory soap from the men's shower. Listings for UCLA's Experimental College included classes on Famous Chinese Launderers, Proper Kidnapping Etiquette, and How to Avoid Giving to Charities Without Guilt.

Richard teamed with Joe Morris, Robbie Robinson, and (briefly) Robin Cleary in *The Snickers Comedy Hour*, a Sunday night show that aired in the mid-seventies on the then weak-signaled KCRW, a national public broadcasting station based in Santa Monica. It was conceived to feature an hour's worth of newly written and recorded comedy. With a few songs slated for the first show, Richard asked me to supply the vocals. I impersonated Bob Dylan on "Stuck Inside of L.A. in a Place Called Malibu" (with new lyrics about him living in the beach town) and Dracula on Beach Boys parody "Give Your Death to the World." I became a member of the group. The show was like an American version of *Monty Python's Flying Circus*.

Snickers proved to be a valuable training ground for our later exploits into writing and recording novelty records for Rhino. One better-realized skit was "The Ed Sullivan Invasion Caper," during which a town is taken over by numerous (TV host) Ed Sullivans in a similar manner to *Invasion of the Body Snatchers*.

Ultimately, writing and producing an hour's worth of comedy (later a half hour) every week—part time—became too taxing and the show ended. Some original *Snickers* bits were incorporated into early Rhino albums. Richard and Joe then teamed up for *Sneakin' Back*, a show that interspersed oldies with new comedy and satire. During a tribute to the "late" early-sixties teen idol Dion, an impersonator phoned in as his mother, crying that her son wasn't dead.

To the embarrassment of his neighbors (if not his parents) on Maple Drive in affluent Beverly Hills, Richard always seemed to be driving a dirty vehicle with a bashed-in passenger door. Initially it was a red Dodge Dart. Not long after he opened the store he bought a yellow Ford van that soon gathered a layer of dust and a bashed-in passenger door. It could have been the subject of a horror movie like *Christine*, the 1958 Plymouth Fury from Stephen King's novel. The interior of the van was like the Bermuda Triangle—objects kept disappearing into it. It was almost an unspoken consequence that a certain number of objects were to be sacrificed to the van in exchange for having gotten a deal on the purchase price. One night, for a joke, Richard and a few of his friends dressed in suits and went to Lawry's Prime Rib, a gourmet restaurant on La Cienega's Restaurant Row in Beverly Hills. They emerged from the battered, yellow wreck, much to the surprise of the valet parkers.

Like his van, Richard always seemed to need a hosing down. From zipping around town hustling for deals to pricing records in the dangerously cramped, non-air-conditioned back room of the store, the swirl of dirt and dust slowly orbiting his frame recalled the "Pig Pen" character from *Peanuts*.

As creative as Richard was, and as much as his mind was working, he could be neglectful when it came to practical matters. Was it forgetfulness or laziness that transformed his pool into a swamp, or the rotting food in his small refrigerator into a science project? It was probably more forgetfulness when Richard failed to inform me when he changed the alarm code at the Rhino store. I usually opened, and I had to endure the alarm ringing until I could contact him for the revised code. The scenario repeated a couple of years later at our first label office.

Richard carried a fat wallet. It wasn't so much that it was stuffed with currency, it was a matter that more odd papers and cards went in than came out. It was referred to as the "exploding wallet," because often when Richard opened it, objects flew out. Richard was forced to reform when his chiropractor informed him that the pain he was experiencing was because his back was out of alignment from sitting on the thick wallet in his right back pocket. It's almost as if the producers of *Seinfeld* got wind of Richard's indisposition and, many years later, turned it into a George Costanza side plot on 1998's "The Reverse Peephole" episode.

Guidance counselors in high school and college rarely get to know a student well enough to make apt suggestions. Had I been Richard's, with the knowledge of having worked with him for twenty-seven years, I would have felt his aptitude was best suited to be a contributing writer on a comedy TV show. He didn't have the discipline to write scripts, but could have excelled at coming up with humorous scenarios and comedic lines. Richard had an interest in psychology, and even took two classes from *Billy Jack* movie director, actor, and writer Tom Laughlin in Jungian psychology. At times when we discussed employees, he had a quick grasp of their psychological makeup. I think he could have been a good psychological therapist or a speechwriter. As the president of the label, a couple of times a year he gave a speech to the company. While he was always uncomfortable and lacked rhythm, his speeches were effective because they were so well composed.

When I approached Richard about making more of a commitment to expanding the label, it wasn't as if he had any insight that it would be successful or, as competent as I had proven myself in the record store, that he thought I had the knowledge to make it a success. I think it was more that he thought it would be fun, that he wanted to support my desire, and that he was responding to his gambling nature. It was a roll of the dice. Through the years Richard backed friends in numerous other businesses, but none were successful.

In the early 1980s the industry experienced a sales slump. Executives placed the blame on kids who spent their money at video game parlors and on music fans who borrowed albums from friends to make cassette tape copies. Because the industry failed to acknowledge the obvious reason—the decline in the quality of the music—Richard wrote a facetious letter-to-the-editor that was published in *Billboard* magazine in July 1982. He identified the main culprits as those who shared their records with others, pointing out that listening to music was "a personal experience meant only for the individual purchasing the LP." He advocated an industry-wide campaign with the slogan "Music is a personal experience, don't share it." In subsequent weeks there were a number of replies to the magazine from people who took his letter seriously.

I didn't have the same proclivity for practical jokes as Richard. Nonetheless I perpetrated one on him. *Man on the Flying Trapeze* is a movie from 1935 starring W. C. Fields, whose character could find any requested document in his overstuffed and messy rolltop desk. Richard's desk at Rhino was like that: papers everywhere, boxes on the floor. When Richard went out of town, I organized his desk, neatened up the room, and hung an elaborately framed photo on the wall of his previously messy room. My effort, or the humor of it, failed to generate a smile upon Richard's return.

Richard was a big fan of professional wrestling, more the ludicrous personas than the skill. He even got his friends to send him videotapes of wrestlers from other parts of the country. He showed me one, which turned out to be among our favorites. El Ejecutivo, from Argentina, walked briskly down the aisle towards the ring wearing a businessman's suit and hat, carrying a briefcase and umbrella in one hand and smoking a cigar with the other. He gives instructions to his secretary, who's holding a phone and books. Right up until the match begins against a Genghis Khan replete with costume, he dictates notes to his secretary who has set up a makeshift office on the apron of the ring. During the match he brushes his suit off, looks at his watch as though he has an upcoming appointment, and gives instructions to his secretary who also fields phone calls.

In sports, Richard was like a magician. In tennis, he twisted his body around and sliced a serve that broke four feet away from his opponent. In addition to his spins on the basketball court, his eyes gave no clue to his next move. Soon after the Minneapolis Lakers moved to Los Angeles in 1960, they established a formidable team led by Jerry West and Elgin Baylor, who are both in the Basketball Hall of Fame. Baylor was more influential since many young basketball fans, including me, copied his balletic moves. He was the first player whose style incorporated a number of spin shots and fancy moves, including the hanging jump shot. His body went in one direction as he shot in the opposite. As Pittsburgh didn't have an NBA team, Richard hadn't seen Baylor play until he moved to Beverly Hills, after which he also adopted Baylor's style.

In many ways, 1983's *Big Daddy* was an album that best defined a Rhino release: it was fun, spirited, creative rock 'n' roll, it was roots music, and it was novelty. In truth, the idea of arranging contemporary pop songs in 1950s styles had been done previously. The album that inspired the project was a 1972 release, *Take a Sad Song . . .* Godfrey Daniel, the artist, was a pseudonym for producer Andy Solomon, who appropriated W. C. Fields' minced oath. Although Richard, I, and Big Daddy's Bob Wayne learned of this record independently of each other, it was Richard's love of 1950s rock 'n' roll that produced a new recording that improved on the concept.

Wayne, also a connoisseur of 1950s music, contacted the members of his former oldies band, Big Daddy, to record the album. He and Richard came up with the arrangements. Highlights included an authentic Everly Brothers impersonation of Rick James' "Superfreak," and a stunning a cappella rendition of "Eye of the Tiger," the theme from *Rocky*. Rather than have the album released in a cheesy, K-Tel-like, 1980s hits done 1950s-style package, I came up with the concept that explained Big Daddy's style.

Richard wrote an extensive story for the liner notes—a prime example of his creativity and imagination—which we packaged to look like an article from a *National Enquirer* type tabloid. The story explained that when the members were young teens, they were on a USO tour of Southeast Asia. They were captured by the Pathet Lao and held captive for twenty-four years before they were released. Back home, all their American references were from the 1950s, including their musical ones.

During their debriefing, an official felt sorry for them and got them sheet music of contemporary hits so they could learn new songs. They worked up the only arrangements they knew, 1950s rock 'n' roll, which explained the songs on the record. Richard's writing was convincing, except when he integrated his jokes, like when he reported that as a rock 'n' roll band, they "were held in such low regard by the rest of the performers, they had to ride behind the main tour bus in an ox cart."

A natural for a feature film, Richard and I collaborated on expanding the story, which we optioned to New World Pictures. With New World's skimpy budget, I had difficulty finding a writer who I thought could turn in a funny script. One exception was Dan Waters, whose screenplay for New World's upcoming *Heathers* I thought had the goods. I met with Waters—who later wrote *Batman Returns*—but he wasn't interested. I allowed our option to expire rather than waste New World's money.

In the summer of 1984 Bruce Springsteen had his biggest hit with "Dancing in the Dark" and his biggest-selling album with *Born in the U.S.A.* Big Daddy fleshed out the melody by arranging the song in the style of Pat Boone. The joke was that an artist of high integrity (Springsteen) was covered by one who was perceived as having low musical integrity (Boone). In the spring of 1985 our record climbed into the top twenty in England, but the label, Making Waves, went out of business and we didn't get paid.

Richard and I loved Big Daddy, and we funded four albums with them, including a twenty-fifth anniversary tribute to the Beatles' *Sgt. Pepper*. In order to try to get them attention, I came up with the idea of having them act in their story—and perform a set afterwards—in a small theater. We launched *Stranded in the Jungle* in the spring of 1991 at the Groundlings Theater on Melrose Avenue. The Wednesday performances were well-attended, but the novelty of a rock 'n' roll band launching a dramatic production to promote their album didn't get the media response I was hoping for.

Members of Bid Daddy helped out on a number of our projects, including masquerading as the Benzedrine Monks of Santo Domonica. In 1994 *Chant*, a rerelease of a twenty-year-old album of Gregorian chants by the Benedictine Monks of Santo Domingo de Silos, became a phenomenon, selling three million copies in the United States. Our parody, *Chantmania*, was an EP of chanted rock songs that included "Losing My Religion" and "(Theme from) The Monkees"—"Hey, hey, we're the Monks . . ." It sold 43,000 copies.

One of Richard's passions was the doo-wop vocal group sound from the fifties and early sixties. He championed a 4-CD box set compiled by Bob Hyde and Walter DeVenne, justifying the expense by keeping the costs down. He didn't even spring for color photographs to be used in the packaging. He planned to sell it only through mail order because he didn't think there would be a broader market. Much to everyone's surprise, owing to a series of televised doo-wop revival shows on PBS, it became a top seller, racking up over 250,000 boxes sold.

Richard is married to Shari Famous, a talented comedian and singer who we had used on a few of our early recordings. Over the last ten years of our Rhino partnership, even though our families didn't socialize much, I was pleased that our wives liked each other and our daughters enjoyed playing together.

CHAPTER 4

Mr. Perfect

You're perfect.

—Stephanie Nemeth to Harold Bronson on June 26, 1985,
moments before she dumped him

My mom should have been a movie actress—if her Orthodox Jewish mother had allowed her. She was beautiful, at times compared to Lana Turner. She was outgoing and had a daffy personality. She could have been an attractive comedienne like Joan Blondell, Gracie Allen, or Goldie Hawn. Her parents emigrated from Russia, met in the United States, and raised their family in Jersey City. Her father was a gambler who made small portions of bathtub whiskey during Prohibition. He owned a small taxi company that went bust in the Great Depression. He made more money than he lost as a gambler, bought a bus for one of his three sons to drive, and a small clothing store for the family to run. The few times I visited my grandparents and uncles in West New York, New Jersey, they were warm and loving. This was in contrast to my father's family, who was emotionally cold, and not in the least interested in me.

My mother loved people, talked to anyone, and made her living mostly as a waitress prior to marrying my dad. Despite the daffiness I experienced, there were flashes of intelligence. During World War II, when women entered the workforce as young men were drafted into the military, at Western Electric she was awarded a certificate and singled out during a company meeting for suggesting a mechanical improvement on a machine that was injuring users.

My father's parents had both emigrated from Romania. He grew up in Los Angeles, in the West Adams district. He remembered playing in the large bowl of the Los Angeles Memorial Coliseum prior to construction, when he was nine years old. My paternal grandfather was one of the cheapest individuals who ever lived. Even though he owned two apartment buildings, I rarely received a gift from him. Once he gave me a plastic toy car that had twine attached to it so it could be pulled. A departed tenant had left it in a vacated apartment. This parsimony rubbed off on my dad, but less so, and then later on me, albeit watered down. This proved to be invaluable in the first few years of the Rhino label as we struggled for profitability.

My dad took a commercial course in high school and didn't see a need to go to college. He was working as a bookkeeper for the American Terrazzo Company in the Mojave Desert when he had enough of the heat and quit, failing to realize the impact the Great Depression would have on securing another job. As a result, he went into the wholesale produce business, first with his brother-in-law—that went bust—and then by himself. He had mostly restaurants as accounts. While working with him one day I met Bob Cobb, the co-owner of the Brown Derby restaurant who concocted the Cobb Salad. My dad woke up in the wee hours of the morning, drove his truck to the produce market downtown, and bought whatever he needed to deliver to his customers that day. He didn't like it, but he did it to earn money to support his family.

At times I thought it would be nice to have a father who worked in an office and had normal work hours and vacation time. While I gleaned a responsible work ethic from him, I also realized that, unlike him, it was important for me to work at something I liked. Although I didn't realize it at the time, having a role model who had his own business made me feel comfortable with having my own business—not that his was particularly successful. When he was squeezed out by the competition, he got a job working for the post office. He liked the idea of being a mailman because of the exercise and the fresh air, but had to settle for working in the weight room downtown. He said it was the best job he ever had. He liked the paid vacations, which he never had as the proprietor of a one-man business. He worked there for fourteen years until his vision deteriorated so much that he couldn't drive to work any longer.

By contemporary standards my parents had a good marriage, but it wasn't one that I wanted. They were opposites. I believe that people with opposite personality traits are drawn together to, subconsciously, complement the traits they lack. In my parents' marriage, there were rarely fights, just bickering. My mom was an extrovert who liked people; my dad was an introvert who didn't. As I was growing up, their friends were few and far between. Their marriage gave me a benchmark on which to improve.

My mother was very loving and overly complimentary. My father was as parsimonious with money as he was with praise. I never received much praise as a young adult and have always had difficulty accepting it when it came. My judgment was good, but I also had a non-obsessive need to be right most of the time. As a result, in the early years of Rhino, when building the business was difficult, I was prone to blame others. This came to a head when Gary Stewart and Brian Schuman called for a meeting, which Richard also attended. They expressed themselves. It hurt, but they made their point, and I changed.

I don't think much was passed onto me by my parents that I could point to professionally. It's not like Paul Simon, Paul McCartney, Pete Townshend, and Elvis Costello, successful music artists whose fathers were bandleaders. If anything, my parents' advice of "save a little, spend a little" translated into a guide that helped Rhino to build in the early days. In establishing a new business, proprietors will often spring for new furniture or classy offices to project a veneer of success. For Richard and me, our office was initially stocked with thrift store and castoff furniture in order to have more money to put into our product.

I grew up in Westchester, the Los Angeles suburb that includes the Los Angeles International Airport. Bean fields gave way to tracts of modest housing to accommodate the postwar demand. Because of the proximity to the airport, quite a number of aerospace companies, like Hughes Aircraft and Northrop, were located nearby. In October 1957 the Soviet Union launched Sputnik, the first artificial satellite to orbit the Earth. The US government accelerated its program to catch up, resulting in an expansion of the related businesses in the area. As a result, many engineers and college graduates moved to Westchester. As parents, they were smarter than average, and so were their kids. In two of the three years I attended Westchester High School, we placed tops academically among the city's high schools. Westchester was devoutly conservative, had no teen nightclubs of its own, and was so far out of the happening Hollywood area (twelve miles) as to strip it of all means of convenience to acquire that hipness comfortably. In the early 1970s, Westchester's potency was severely sapped as funding for the aerospace industry diminished. Nice tract homes were demolished when the airport expanded to accommodate larger jets—ruining a nice community.

My parents weren't interested in the arts or culture. They didn't read books or respond to art. They weren't interested in the theater, classical music, or poetry. As a family, we did go to the movies. My mom cooked, cleaned house, and enjoyed daily outings visiting the neighborhood stores. She chain-smoked, drank coffee continually, and chatted endlessly. My dad enjoyed keeping up with current events by reading the afternoon newspaper. What we did have was television. As a family, we were heavy on the comedies that proliferated in the 1950s: Sid Caesar's *Your Show of Shows*, *The Ernie Kovacs Show*, *The Jackie Gleason Show*, *The Steve Allen Show*, and Groucho Marx's *You Bet Your Life*. The latter was more of a quiz show, and I responded to and absorbed the factual answers to the point where, at an early age, I was able to do better than most of the TV contestants.

At age ten I became a fan of *The Twilight Zone*. I watched it by myself late at night, in the dark, which could be unnerving. It was a novelty watching old movies on TV instead of in a theater. Horror movies of the post-World War II period were low budget and, after their initial run in second-rate theaters and drive-ins, ended up on our local *Chiller Theater*. Their popularity among kids spawned magazines like *Famous Monsters*.

There was another show that programmed Sherlock Holmes movies. The re-exposure of these older films revived interest even though they were decades old. For kids or teens, it was not nostalgia or yearning for a previous era, but a response to what they experienced regardless of when the movies were produced. The Three Stooges became so popular that fan clubs sprang up, and the reconstituted trio was enlisted to star in three new movies, which weren't very good. The new phenomenon of Head

Shops—which catered to the new drug culture—sold new posters of old movie stars Humphrey Bogart, W. C. Fields, Jean Paul Belmondo, and the Marx Brothers.

As soldiers returned from their service in World War II, and as the country returned to normal, a large number of babies were born. Decades later those who were born during this period were labeled "baby boomers." This resulted in a large youth culture which had its greatest impact in the growth of rock 'n' roll, the first music that was marketed to appeal to teenagers.

We didn't listen to much music in my house. Sunday mornings were an exception. While my mom prepared a scrumptious breakfast of pancakes and eggs, we listened to 78 rpm records. These were ten-inch records made from fragile shellac that revolved 78 times per minute (rpm) on the turntable. By the mid-1950s they were already dying out in favor of the less fragile and smaller seven-inch vinyl records which played at 45 rpm. Because longer programs that played on a number of 78 rpm discs were housed in a book with sleeves like a photo album, the multidisc set was called a record album. That name stuck when the longer playing time could be accommodated on one twelve-inch disc that played at 33 1/3 rpm.

We listened to pop songs of the 1940s and 1950s, such as "Fascination" by Jane Morgan ('57), and even the rhythm & blues of Ella Mae Morse performing "Down the Road Apiece" ('52). But it was the novelty records that I liked the most: "Smoke! Smoke! Smoke! (That Cigarette)" by Tex Williams, "Pico and Sepulveda" by Felix Figueroa, "I'm My Own Grandpa" by Lonzo and Oscar, and "I'm My Own Grandmaw" by Jo Stafford (all '47). I particularly responded to the Jewish humor of Mickey Katz, who parodied songs like "Witch Doctor," making it "K'nish Doctor," and to Stan Freberg's "St. George and the Dragonet," his Christmas-themed parody of the *Dragnet* detective TV show.

I was a little too young to relate to rock 'n' roll, which seemed too sexually oriented to me at the time. The first record I bought was a 45 of "The Battle of New Orleans" by Johnny Horton, a number one hit in 1959 about the War of 1812. History was awash on TV during this time. Coming out of the tumultuous War, people wanted distraction and escape in their entertainment rather than reality. While game shows proliferated, most of the diversion was offered in historical settings.

Despite how unappealing the American Western is to contemporary audiences, when I was a kid it was prevalent. *Gunsmoke* and *Bonanza* were the most popular and longest running, but there were over fifty other western TV shows, including *Have Gun Will Travel, The Rebel, Sugar Foot, Maverick, Zorro, Wyatt Earp,* and *The Cisco Kid.* Among the more popular series shown on *The Wonderful World of Disney* were ones that combined the western with historical figures: Davy Crockett, The Swamp Fox, Elfego Baca. Older cowboy film stars, like Roy Rodgers, Gene Autry, and Hopalong Cassidy experienced a revival as their movies were shown on TV.

Westerns were popular in feature films as well, with John Wayne being the most popular film star in the world largely from starring in Westerns. Low-budget productions filmed in Spain and Italy, and later referred to as *Spaghetti Westerns*, aimed to make modest profits from a genre that seemed on its last legs in the mid-sixties, but became minor hits. The star of these was Clint Eastwood, who found it difficult to reestablish himself after a six-year run starring in *Rawhide.*

Shows from other historical settings were common. Ones based on World War II became hits, whether serious, like *Rat Patrol* and *Combat,* or comedic, like *Hogan's Heroes* and *McHale's Navy. The Roaring Twenties* and *Margie* took place in the 1920s.

With families being reintegrated after the war and others being started, family comedies proliferated. I watched most of them: *The Danny Thomas Show, The Life of Riley, Leave It to Beaver, Father Knows Best, Bachelor Father, My Three Sons, The Real McCoys.* The family life as depicted in a series such as *The Donna Reed Show* was so appealing that it made me wish my mom were Donna Reed. The show with the longest duration, *The Adventures of Ozzie and Harriet,* launched the career of their son, Ricky Nelson, whose music I liked. I also watched programs starring animals: *Lassie, Rin Tin Tin,* and *Circus Boy* (which starred future Monkee Micky Dolenz billed as Mickey Braddock.) Despite the weekly situations presented, and the conflicts that dramas needed, these shows instilled positive family values.

In addition to history, I was drawn to the many sources of comedy: sitcoms on TV (*Sgt. Bilko* and *Car 54, Where Are You?*); older films on TV starring the Marx Brothers, the Three Stooges, the Bowery Boys, Laurel and Hardy, Buster Keaton, and W.C. Fields; new films starring Dean Martin and Jerry Lewis.

The second record I bought was comedic. "Itsy Bitsy Teenie Weenie Yellow Polka-Dot Bikini" by Brian Hyland topped the charts in the summer of 1960. I only occasionally bought a record prior to the Beatles, but I did hear records on the radio that I liked.

The next summer my mom and I visited her family in West New York, New Jersey. The hits I enjoyed listening to on the radio were "Pretty Little Angel Eyes" by Curtis Lee (an astonishingly arranged record) and "Hello Mary Lou" by Ricky Nelson. In 1962 I liked "Little Red Rented Rowboat" by Joe Dowell and "Old River" by Walter Brennan. The next year it was "Surfin' Safari" by the Beach Boys and "Surf City" by Jan and Dean. My two favorite artists of the pre-Beatles era were Buddy Holly and the Coasters, although I didn't buy their records until years later.

The reason I bought so few records was because I spent my meager allowance on baseball cards and baseball magazines. Baseball was much more interesting to me than popular music. I enjoyed playing the game, but soon realized that my ability was only average. More to the point, I loved collecting baseball cards even before the Dodgers moved from Brooklyn to Los Angeles for the 1958 season. Jackie Robinson, having been a star for the Dodgers in Brooklyn, made a big impression on me as the first Negro to break the color barrier in the major leagues. Seeing *The Jackie Robinson Story* movie on TV gave me a perspective on race relations that I didn't experience growing up in a white community.

My main link to the sport was through the cards and baseball magazines. I went to only one or two games a year and, for the first few years, there was little baseball on TV. A local station only broadcast eleven Dodgers games a season, all against the rival Giants in San Francisco. At that time the only nationally broadcast games were the All Star games and the World Series. I was so hard up for baseball that in the winter of 1959 I regularly watched games that were televised from Cuba because each team had a few major leaguers on its roster.

My interest in history gave me a desire to learn about the greats of decades past. I bought hardcover books, like the excellent anthology *Baseball's Greatest Players* and *Babe Ruth*, and paperbacks of contemporary greats Willie Mays, Stan Musial, and Ted Williams published by *Sport Magazine*.

My passion for the history of the game even brought me a small windfall when I was thirteen. Bennie the Fan hosted a local show prior to the Los Angeles Angels televised games. I submitted a postcard to be a contestant. I received a call on a Friday afternoon inquiring if I was going to be home the following afternoon, as my postcard was going to be near the top of the fishbowl, and they wanted to check that if my card were drawn, I would be home to answer the call. I wasn't assured that they were going to call me, so I watched the show alone.

I was up to speed in knowing the contemporary players and the greats from history, but when they called me and displayed a photo of a player from the past, it wasn't one with whom I was familiar. It looked a bit like the much older Angels' General Manager Fred Haney, and that was my guess. I won a McCullough outdoor motor for the boat I didn't have. We sold it for over a hundred dollars.

I was much more of a Dodgers fan, and in 1963 the club fielded the best lineup in Los Angeles history, with Sandy Koufax, Don Drysdale, and Tommy Davis. While I listened to and watched as many games as I could, through their winning of the World Series, my interest in collecting baseball cards diminished and I gave up halfway through the season. It coincided with my interest in girls, and girls weren't into baseball.

When I was in junior high I had a young science teacher who exposed his students to science fiction. My next-door neighbor also recommended authors. Their enthusiasm, and the many genre films that were produced to appeal to teens, made me a science fiction fan. I enjoyed reading Ray Bradbury, Alfred Bestar, George Orwell, and Jules Verne. I got further into it and mail ordered "true stories" of alien encounters and Hans Holzer's books on ghosts.

As far as becoming interested in music, my first exposure to the Beatles was from a photo on the large button a classmate wore to school in anticipation of their performance on *The Ed Sullivan Show*. With their hair combed over their foreheads, they all looked like Moe Howard from the Three Stooges to me. I was intrigued by their performance, but not sold. The sound through the TV was muted and dull. Hearing their records on the radio was a different story: they were exhilarating. I was hooked and bought every single and album.

In press conferences and interviews the Beatles came across as witty, which was unique among pop music performers. Compared to the Beatles, the members of any number of other groups I may have heard interviewed, like the Beach Boys or Four Seasons, came across as dull. I found out that it wasn't the Three Stooges who were an influence on the Beatles, but the Goons, a comedy trio that included Peter Sellers, who had a long running radio show on the BBC. The Beatles sense of humor made them even more appealing and is best displayed in their first film, *A Hard Day's Night.*

I became a fan of the other British groups that followed in their wake: the Rolling Stones, Dave Clark Five, Herman's Hermits, the Kinks, the Zombies, and later the Who and the Yardbirds. The lead singer of Herman's Hermits, Peter Noone, who was only two and a half years older than I, was the only one who was as personable as the Beatles.

The primary appeal to me was the records, not the personalities of the musicians. In interviews the Rolling Stones always came across as disinterested. As intelligent as Mick Jagger's musical contributions appear to make him, in interviews he never seemed interesting. The Dave Clark Five in their movie *Having a Wild Weekend* didn't project well as personalities or actors, nor did Gerry and the Pacemakers in their movie *Ferry Cross the Mersey.*

When the American groups got up to speed and formed Beatles-styled combos, I was on board. The first group to have a hit was San Francisco's the Beau Brummels, with "Laugh Laugh." I bought their records and those by the Byrds, Turtles, Lovin' Spoonful, Paul Revere and the Raiders, and later the Doors and Love. While I was inspired by the rock groups of the era, I remembered liking most of the Top 40—including Motown and songs by smooth singers like Mel Carter and Dean Martin.

It was the music I responded to, not the fandom. I didn't buy the teen magazines, which were the only news source for pop music until *Rolling*

Stone appeared a few years later. The teen magazines focused on personality, life style, and romance, while *Rolling Stone* was concerned with the music and the process.

Although neither of my parents had gone to college, it was always a goal of mine, and UCLA was the natural choice and the top academic university in the area. In high school I probably should have been an art major, but I couldn't think of how to apply it. I never thought of myself as Mr. Perfect, and I wasn't the type of student who studied excessively in order to get perfect grades. I was in the honors program for math and science, not because I was particularly interested in those fields, but because I thought the school's hardest major would better prepare me for the rigors of college. Some people look back at high school as the best time of their lives. For me it was a stepping-stone to college.

When I entered UCLA in September 1968, I was intending to be a lawyer. My favorite subject had been history, but as I didn't want to teach, I couldn't figure out what to do with a history major professionally. As there was no pre-law major, the counselor recommended political science. It was while reading one of the textbooks for a class in international relations—reading a page four times and still not retaining the information—that I realized political science wasn't for me. I also didn't feel strongly enough about being a lawyer to spend an additional three years in law school to get a degree.

In the spring quarter I went to the office of UCLA's newspaper, the *Daily Bruin*, to inquire about writing record reviews. I was told to see John Mendelsohn, the paper's music editor. His writing in the *Daily Bruin*— and in *Rolling Stone*—was exceptional, and his taste was exquisite. He was my first editor and gave me some tips. I was so motivated to improve my writing that I analyzed better written reviews to learn the craft. Although I didn't realize the significance at the time, writing for the *Bruin* was my window into the record business.

When I started UCLA, I never considered joining a fraternity. To a rock fan like me, it sounded passé, the rituals and hazing of another time. Yet I had close to that camaraderie with the writers in the entertainment section of the *Daily Bruin*. The cubicles didn't resemble a clubhouse, but it was a place to hang out, to make phone calls, or to write up a story between classes. I often went to shows with Jim Bickhart, Mark Leviton, and movie reviewer Stan Berkowitz.

Since I wasn't paid for my submissions, I had the freedom to write whatever I wanted, which included retrospectives on bands I liked. Most of the rock artists that were popular prior to the existence of late sixties music magazines like *Rolling Stone*, were never the subjects of a serious history or commentary. Coverage in typical teen-appealing magazines like *Teen, 16,* and *Tiger Beat*, were concerned with more superficial topics like the artist's favorite colors, TV shows, or clothes, and included overly familiar responses like, "Girls who wear short skirts and not too much make-up" to questions such as, "What type of girls do you like?" The Yardbirds, Manfred Mann, Herman's Hermits and the Move were sixties bands on which I wrote the first semi-scholarly features.

I expanded to writing for *Rolling Stone, L.A. Free Press, L.A. Times,* and various rock magazines. It sure beat washing dishes or working as a market box boy for extra money—both of which I had done—plus I received free records and concert tickets. I got to know the publicists at the Hollywood based labels and learned about the functions of a record company. I wasn't interested in writing about artists whose music I didn't like, which meant that I turned down assignments, even if they paid.

Sometimes I even got to interview performers from my favorite bands. In November 1969 I conducted my first interview, with Maurice Gibb of the Bee Gees. Because I hadn't done one before, I didn't own a cassette machine, so I lugged my heavy reel-to-reel tape recorder up to the publicist's office on Sunset Boulevard. When I entered, Maurice's wife, the singer Lulu, zipped past me on the way to an afternoon of shopping. I found that I had to share my time with a plump young woman who was writing this for her mimeographed, eight-page newsletter. Her mother took photos and made a snide remark about Lulu.

Maurice (pronounced Morris) was a little guy, thin-boned, with a receding hairline and a fringed beard. I found him friendly and charming. He drank a beer. Although he was the first rock star I met, I wasn't enthralled, nor did I feel anointed. It was enjoyable to spend time with him and learn about his career. But there was also a disquieting element. As it was my first interview, my sensibility was still unformed. I couldn't understand why he was making claims that I sensed were untrue. Was he forever in pop star mode, where he had to fabricate outrageous tidbits to get into the gossip columns? But I was a representative of an august journal! He said he had played bass on two songs on *Abbey Road*, which had been released the previous month; that he was pleased that "Something," the single off the album, was a big hit because he had played the lead guitar on it; and that he had written a song with Eric Clapton and George Harrison. Why would Paul McCartney have permitted somebody else to play bass on a Beatles record? Why would George Harrison not have played lead guitar on the song he wrote and sang? Could Maurice have been delirious and really believed what he told me? I wasn't experienced or confident enough to have challenged him, and I left those assertions out of my article.

On January 2, 1970, I sent a letter to CBS Records' A&R department in New York expressing my idea to compile a comprehensive best of the Yardbirds, who had recorded for Epic. I had a title, "The World's First Super Group," a song list, and a suggestion for the cover art. I was informed that I first had to submit my idea to CBS's legal department. It took a couple of exchanges before they permitted me to submit it to A&R. Twelve months later, A&R's Don Ellis informed me that, my suggestion notwithstanding, they had no plans to produce such a reissue. I didn't receive a comment on the viability of the project, or any of the specifics. It was more like a standard-language legal letter to protect the rights of CBS. Even though I didn't realize it at the time, this early interest in revisiting a musical artist's career planted the seed for Rhino releasing reissues almost ten years later.

At UCLA I was most drawn to psychology and film classes. In order for a psychology major to be meaningful, it had to entail post-graduate studies. I liked the classes, but didn't feel strongly about committing to the major. By the time I realized I wanted to learn more about film, I didn't think I would be accepted to the much-in-demand program. The more obvious major for me, journalism, was one UCLA didn't offer. I concocted a major of mostly psychology, sociology, and film classes. I found a professor who gave her approval and named it "Sociology in the Media," with which I graduated in 1972.

My senior year I was the campus rep for CBS Records. The company's more familiar labels were Columbia and Epic. I excelled at getting records added to the campus radio station, putting on concerts, composing and placing ads in the basketball program, and promoting product at the four Westwood Village record stores. Despite my impressive track record, CBS didn't hire me after graduating, nor did any of the other record companies. As much as the record business was populated by wild and creative personalities, much of it was staid. Only years later did Paul Rappaport, who hired me for the part-time position, speculate on why CBS didn't offer me a job: "You liked to stretch the envelope and you had a strong personality. I remember suggesting that you tone down your Redbone ad, that the CBS-types would think it's too wild. They would wonder if they would be able to mold you to what they wanted done."

Almost a year after graduating, I finally got a job, a four-month placement as a US passport agent. Four days a week I was at my desk checking over applications and documentation that were mailed in by various post offices. Saturdays I joined others behind the counter dealing directly with the public. With no real supervisor on duty, I pushed the "jacket" dress requirement. The previous fall while in London, I had purchased a thin, purple satin jacket with exaggerated lapels in the manner of glam rock star Marc Bolan. I paired that with a large bow tie in the style of the Kinks' Ray Davies. Other times I donned a Civil War marching band coat—with tails—that I had picked up at the MGM Studio warehouse sale. There were no reprimands or negative comments from the acting supervisor and surprisingly few comments from the public. My stint as a passport agent provided an income, but I knew a straight job was not one in which I would feel comfortable or thrive.

I have always responded to throwaway lines, one-liners, and asides: short phrases that are incidental to the focus of the main content. There's a scene in *A Hard Day's Night* where the Beatles are sitting in a train coach. John Lennon picks up a bottle of Coca-Cola and sniffs from the top. I didn't realize until I saw the film the third time—in my twenties—that he was referring to cocaine. (Until 1904 the soda was made with the drug.) Or on the live side of Flo & Eddie's *Illegal, Immoral and Fattening* album, Howard Kaylan (Eddie) keys off the piano player's noodling with

"All my friends in Tulsa," impersonating Oklahoman Leon Russell, who was popular at the time.

In the introduction to the *Mystery Science Theater 3000* TV show, one of the robot characters, Tom Servo, says, "Hello there," in the same manner that Irish singer Val Doonican is impersonated in the Bonzo Dog Band's "The Intro and the Outro." The appeal of these comments probably started with me viewing Marx Brothers movies on TV. *The Rocky and Bullwinkle Show* incorporated the style, as did *The Simpsons* decades later. *Mad* magazine did the same thing, with its background gags and later, *MAD Marginals*, drawings outside the edge of the frame.

In a similar spirit, I took an Epic Records biography for the Hollies that was so generally written, I did little more than substitute my band's name for the Hollies when retyping it, and passed it off as our bio. When we played a noontime concert at UCLA's Ackerman Union Grand Ballroom, I had Justin Pierce introduce us with the same "Ladies and Gentlemen, it's all about to happen . . ." that opened the Rolling Stones' live album *Get Yer Ya-Yas Out,* and also had guitarist Bill Pique recite the same line Mick uttered during the concert about busting a button on his trousers and that they might fall down. It was funny, or at least amusing to anybody who made the connection. And to those who didn't, it was just part of the show.

On the last day of my job at the discount department store Fedco, where I worked as a sacker, I changed my nametag to read "Pete Townshend." Nobody commented on my name change, or that it was the same as the guitarist of the Who. When I reviewed soul singer Willie Henderson for *Cash Box* magazine, in a performance at the Playboy Club, I referred to Henderson as being "late of Pablo Fanque's Fair." That wasn't his previous engagement, but a reference to the Beatles' lyric in the *Sgt. Pepper's* song "Being For the Benefit of Mr. Kite."

On occasion I amused myself similarly at Rhino—whether anybody noticed or not. Every year we took a company photo that was featured on the back of our yearly calendar and catalog. Every year I wore a red shirt. I was waiting for someone to mention it before I would change shirts. Only prior to my last photo session did someone, Sharon Foster, our head of human resources, ask me about it. I had worn it for eight straight photos.

For the last one, I wore a white dress shirt with a large clock face on the front. I pointed to the clock, inferring that my time was up at the company.

The Beatles led the charge of what became known as the *British Invasion*, but no one had compiled a comprehensive overview of that mid-sixties period. I loved the music and wanted to produce such a series. I couldn't hope to get tracks by the Beatles or Rolling Stones—although any buyer of the series should already have albums by those artists—and I was frustrated by those who turned us down on other artists. Even though we had been referred to in the press as "the Smithsonian of the music business," and our product was of a high quality, it didn't mean that the other labels valued our commitment to the preservation of rock history. ABKCO controlled the Rolling Stones, but also Herman's Hermits, Marianne Faithful, and the early Animals' hits, and had a policy of not licensing to other record companies so people had to buy their own product. PolyGram initially declined to license us their artists—the Bee Gees, Cream, Dusty Springfield, Eric Burdon & the Animals, the Mindbenders, and Them—but later agreed for our second set of releases.

We were distributed by Capitol Records, so it was hard for them to refuse our request for the artists they controlled: Gerry & the Pacemakers, Freddie & the Dreamers, Billy J. Kramer & the Dakotas, Manfred Mann, Peter & Gordon, the Hollies, and the Spencer Davis Group. Other artists that were part of the initial four albums included the Kinks, Yardbirds, Searchers, Zombies, and Troggs. Released in 1988, sales of *The British Invasion: The History of British Rock* averaged 60,000. Even though the next set of five were equally as good, having been issued three years later, totals were half of the first release. The series wasn't definitive but we did manage to include one Beatles hit, "Ain't She Sweet."

The Rutles was a 1978 TV special that parodied the Beatles segment of a British documentary on pop music, *All You Need Is Love*, which provided inspiration for the show's UK title: *All You Need Is Cash*. Monty Python's Eric Idle wrote and codirected the mockumentary. Neil Innes, who had been a member of the Bonzo Dog Band and had written songs for Monty Python, composed and produced the music. It was almost like hearing a new Beatles album. Even though the TV special only managed low ratings, the album was on the chart for nine weeks.

I arranged for Rhino to license it for CD and included extra tracks that Bill Inglot discovered in the tape vault that were part of the special's soundtrack but not on the original LP. As part of the process I enjoyed getting to know Neil. He was so good with melody in capturing the feel of songs from the sixties that I asked him to write for the Monkees' reunion album we were planning, but he never got around to it. I felt gratified that not only could we give the fans the six extra songs on the CD, but that I could send Neil a check for $35,000 for the publishing on those songs, as his regular royalty payments had been absorbed by the black hole of the production company. We sold 80,000 albums.

After Stephanie Nemeth's short, first marriage—to someone else—she became my wife on April 1, 1990. I chose the date because it was easy to remember and, as it was April Fools' Day, to fly in the face of those who say it's foolish to get married. We've been married for over twenty years. We have a good life with two wonderful children. Since getting to know her, she's always been my favorite person.

CHAPTER 5

Unsung Heroes

Artists are crazy. When you're winning, you keep going.
It's like throwing dice, when you're winning, you don't stop.

—Mickie Most, producer, September 22, 1972

In the summer after my junior year of high school, I attended a dance at Pacific Palisades High School. I wasn't familiar with the band, the Boston Tea Party, but was impressed at how good they were: musically, vocally, their presence, and song selection. I later heard their records, which in no way compared to how impressive they were live. It occurred to me that not everybody who was good becomes successful. I felt the same way when, a few years later, I saw the Fountain of Youth play at a dance in the gym at Loyola Marymount University. They were so good that, even as a trio, they were able to convincingly capture the Beatles' "I Am the Walrus." The following are some of Rhino's artists that had the goods to be successful, but ultimately weren't.

THE TWISTERS

The Twisters were my favorite club band. When I was looking for a band to produce, Mark Volman told me to check them out. They had the songs, they played well together, and they were visually exciting. Their front man was good-looking, in the suave manner of Brian Ferry, and he was English, a novelty among bands in Southern California. The quintet was from the blue collar South Bay where their extreme popularity at the Sweetwater was akin to the Beatles at Liverpool's Cavern. One of their songs, "Vampire Bat," inspired their fans to choreograph a dance to match the music. Because singer Michael Wainwright had been in touch with what was happening in England, he was quick to incorporate flourishes from Dr. Feelgood and the Police, the latter by way of a reggae arrangement of the Supremes' "Where Did Our Love Go." Initially they were eager and responsive. When I casually suggested they clean up their appearance, get rid of their hippie mustaches and cut their long hair to approximate the look of a new wave act, they did it. Paul Wexler finagled spec time at The Band's studio—I don't mean Big Pink—Shangri La in Malibu. He and I produced a couple of songs with them, which were released on Rhino compilations. Other suggestions I made were beyond their collective grasp. Months later they signed with two guys who had music biz credentials.

Aaron Russo parlayed his management of Bette Midler into producing her first feature film, *The Rose*, which was very successful. With a career as a film producer looming—he also produced *Trading Places*—I couldn't understand why he and music producer Paul Rothchild wanted to use their cachet to launch a new wave label to extract a big advance from one of the major companies. In the short term, the opportunistic pair signed new wave artists to manage. I don't think it was because they related to or loved the music, and their ambitions for a label never panned out. As managers of the Twisters, they did some good for them: they got them a better booking agent, sprung for some ads, and Rothchild produced them in the studio. But nothing happened, and Russo lost interest as his film career blossomed.

Bill Gazeki, who engineered The *Rose* soundtrack, produced six tracks with the Twisters but couldn't get them signed either. I made a deal with the group and with Gazeki to release those tracks as an EP. Their subsequent managers wanted to limit sales to California so that the group wouldn't be overexposed when their, ahem, major label album was released, so we agreed to sell the record only in California. I felt that the group had a large enough local following that our release would be profitable.

Their fans bought close to 4,000 records, and *The Twisters* entered (industry trade magazine) *Record World's* January 1981 album chart, thereby earning it the distinction of Rhino's first charting record. Unfortunately, the group's vision was limited, and their management's was equally near-sighted. Rhino's national distributors were clamoring for its first charting record, but we couldn't sell it to them. I appealed to the managers, but they were steadfast. Needless to say, the record soon fell off the chart and the momentum created for the band totally disappeared.

The Twisters never signed to a major label. Two years later an album was finally released on The Goods Records, a vanity label that was distributed by MCA. The cover qualified as among the worst ever for a rock band; there were no photos of the members on the jacket, nor were their names listed. A year later, they broke up.

I kept in touch with Wainwright and the Twisters' road manager, Geoff Hagins, and produced a couple of songs with Wainwright's subsequent band, Fun the mental, in 1983. The project lost steam when keyboardist and versatile instrumentalist Mike Lardie was able to realize his dream of being a rock star by joining Great White. Years later I wanted to include a track on a Rhino compilation album, but Lardie had lost the master tape. He had engineered the session at the studio where he worked, and mixed the multitrack tape to a DAT (Digital Audio Tape) cassette, instead of a two-track analogue tape, as was customary.

BARNES & BARNES

Robert Haimer and Bill Mumy (a child actor best known from the TV series *Lost in Space*) were childhood friends who went new wave as Barnes & Barnes. A song recorded in Bill's home studio, "Fish Heads," achieved massive popularity on Dr. Demento's radio show. Their artistic enclave of supporters, mostly transplants from Texas, included Bill Paxton, who considered himself more of a guerilla filmmaker than an actor, and Rocky Schenck. They teamed to produce a "Fish Heads" video. LA radio station KROQ played the song, *Saturday Night Live* aired their video, and ex-Doors manager Bill Siddons—Robert was a big Doors fan—promised to get them a record deal. Given the attention, Bill and Robert thought they could be the next Devo or Wall of Voodoo. We released their first album, *Voobaha*, in 1980, and a handful more through the years.

While their home recordings were well produced and arranged, they were a little too weird, and they suffered from not having been recorded in a professional studio. That and Robert's refusal to play live hindered their career more than their talent. If a major label had signed and nurtured them, they could have sold much more than what they were able to do on Rhino. In using an example from cinema, David Lynch's weird *Eraserhead* initially played to a cult audience. When he got backing from a major studio, he excelled as a talented director. I had Barnes & Barnes produce a number of records for us, and they always delivered artistically, if not commercially.

JULIE BROWN

When we were originally sent a copy of a privately pressed twelve-inch single, "I Like 'em Big and Stupid" by Julie Brown, we passed. Richard and I didn't think the song was that good, and the cover photo looked like a housewife in her late twenties trying to cash in on the rock scene. Only later, when we heard the B-side, "The Homecoming Queen's Got a Gun," and met Julie, revamped with a new wave style, did we agree to sign her. We hit it off with her and her producer/husband Terrence McNally. We had them record three additional songs to qualify releasing the record as an EP, and shoot a new cover to reflect how Julie currently looked. We insisted she record one of her demos, "'Cause I'm a Blonde," which became the second most popular song on the record. Richard had her write a song, "Queen of Pleasure," for the new dance single he was recording with movie icon Mamie Van Doren. On their own, they produced an inspired and funny video of "Homecoming Queen" to match the cleverness of the lyrics.

The EP was released in October 1984. Dr. Demento jumped on the record right away, and then KROQ and some other stations. By February we had gotten enough airplay and sales to make the *Billboard* album chart. Warner Brothers Pictures signed her to develop another of the songs, "Earth Girls Are Easy," into a feature film. It was at this time that Julie's momentum started to unravel. Julie and Terrence thought Rhino's continuing promotion would overexpose other songs on the record, like "Earth Girls," rendering them old songs when heard in the film. Because Warner

Brothers Pictures was producing the movie, a Warner Music label, Sire, signed her as a recording artist. In order to limit her exposure, Sire told MTV not to play the video. But that's not what MTV told us. They cited Julie's shooting spree, despite the video being comedic. MTV made no justification to Rhino for why they had played the Rolling Stones' "Under Cover of Night" video where the violence was more realistically portrayed. We were incensed at Sire's intrusion, but as a small label, we didn't have any influence with MTV. During the seven weeks it was on *Billboard*'s chart, MTV played the video once.

Record producer Mickie Most's words of wisdom have resonated with me since I interviewed him for *Rolling Stone*: when you have momentum, you keep it going. His point was that you can never guarantee that the next thing you do will be successful. When you're fortunate enough to have a shot at a hit record, you do all you can to make it happen, rather than putting on the breaks, which happened here. We didn't want to stand in the way of Julie's career moves, so we cooperated and let Warner buy us out of our deal with Julie. If we had done otherwise, we would not have had the cooperation of the artist on the current project, or for any in the future. The right strategy would have been for us to continue to market Julie's record, but we gave in to the artist's wishes. At 57,000 copies, it was by far Rhino's biggest selling record to date, but we could have sold so much more if the plug wasn't pulled.

I had to negotiate with Julie and Terrence's lawyer, Jody Graham, who I found exceedingly unpleasant and unreasonably demanding. It was the first time I had dealt with a lawyer whose professional personality was so repulsive. I cringed every time I had to talk to her on the phone. Still, I completed the deal. I thought there's no way I want to deal with her again, making me realize that an artist's lawyer or representative could hamper a business relationship.

The momentum we helped create with Julie totally dissipated. After twelve script rewrites, Warner Brothers passed, and the film project transferred to De Laurentiis Entertainment. During the interim, interest in Julie had cooled to the extent that the starring role she had been expecting went to Geena Davis, and she had to settle on a supporting one. MTV hired an English VJ (video jockey) who also went by the name Julie Brown. With *her* popularity, Rhino started receiving orders—which we couldn't fulfill—from store buyers who thought the more visible MTV star was the singer of Rhino's record. Late in 1987, Sire released Julie's album, *Trapped in the Body of a White Girl*—which included two of Rhino's songs—but it flopped, as did the *Earth Girls Are Easy* movie, which debuted in theaters in May 1989.

We liked Julie and Terrence, and had intermittent relationships with both after they divorced. Julie continued to act. In 1992 she produced, wrote, and starred in *Medusa: Dare to Be Truthful*, a funny parody of Madonna's documentary. In 1998 she starred in Rhino Films' first released feature, *Plump Fiction*, a parody of *Pulp Fiction*. I thought Julie had the talent to be a star, but it was not to be.

DADDY MAXFIELD

Louis Maxfield (real name Naktin) was among the best guitarists in the city, but few people outside of the neighborhood kids knew about him. He was like Jimmy Page—even looked a bit like him, except for Page's wavy hair—but he was better. Page was more dexterous as a guitarist, but Louis came up with better melodies and hooks in his songwriting.

In 1967, when Louis was in high school, his band, the Looking Glasses—which included John Branca, who later became a top music business attorney and deal maker—released a single on a small label that got enough airplay on local radio that the band performed on the TV show *Groovy*. It was a brief, exciting few weeks, but the record never charted. In his subsequent musical endeavors, Louis got just enough encouragement to believe that the brass ring was within his grasp. The next year his group, now called Odyssey, recorded a single for White Whale—the company that released the Turtles' hits. Two years later he was part of another White Whale release, this time a studio group called Shake that attempted to get a hit with "Two of Us," a song the Beatles hadn't issued as a single from their new *Let It Be* album.

Louis met singer Graham Daddy, and the next year they signed a publishing deal with Frank Zappa's company, Bizarre. In 1972 they took some recordings they had made to London. Pye Records liked "Rave 'n'

Rock," had them rework it, and released it as a Daddy Maxfield single to some dance club play. Back in the States, they signed a publishing deal with RCA Records, who managed to get two sides of theirs released as a single on United Artists in 1976.

I met Louis when he lived with his parents and brother upstairs from Justin Pierce in the Fairfax district. Louis, Graham, and I wrote a few songs together—my lyrics, their music—which turned out great. Through the years they helped out on some Rhino novelty songs, and I used Louis as much as I could for recording sessions. They were good enough to make it, but success was always elusive. Sometimes their behavior worked against them.

THE RAVERS

It was June 1977, and I was roasting by the pool at the Sahara Hotel in Las Vegas. I was there to interview comedian George Carlin for the *Los Angeles Times* and to cover his performance that evening in the hotel's Congo Room. While lounging by the pool, the 100-degree heat must have got to me as I started writing a Christmas song about the new punk rock movement. I imagined how the Christmas season would change if punk became popular and wrote the lyrics on the back of a *Newsweek* magazine I was reading. One line purposely reflected the stupidity of the singer: "All those Christmas trees swinging safety pins from their leaves." Of course, Christmas trees are pines, which have needles, not leaves. I was friendly with Pat Siciliano, who was West Coast head of publicity for Epic Records. He had expressed an interest in learning how to produce a record, and I offered to find a project for us to produce together. He said he could get Epic to pay for it.

I had Louis and Graham write the music for "It's Gonna Be a Punk Rock Christmas." It was convenient to use their band for the recording, which, in addition to Graham on lead vocals and Louis on guitar, included David Dennard on bass and Mike Campbell on drums. As they were all in their later twenties, they couldn't relate to this obnoxious music coming from England.

I called Siciliano numerous times to tell him we were ready, but he never picked up the phone or returned any of my calls. I didn't have much money, but I felt so strongly about what we were doing, I shelled out $600 to record the song and the B-side, a comparable version of "Silent Night." The studio was located across from Grauman's Chinese Theatre on the third floor of a seedy office building. It was run by a guy named Gary who assumed an Eastern name, Ganapati, and transformed his look with robes and long fingernails.

As Daddy Maxfield, by name, didn't want to be associated with the record, I came up with the Ravers, after the English slang of someone who goes mad in a rock 'n' roll context, as expressed in the lyrics of the Small Faces' "Lazy Sunday." Three companies were interested. I would have liked to sign with Warner Brothers Records, who ultimately didn't make a formal offer. David Berson said something interesting to me—that Warner would prefer to have made a deal on a record they didn't completely believe in rather than turning it down and see it become a hit elsewhere. They would have paid an advance on a record in order to avoid the embarrassment if they showed poor judgment in turning down a hit.

I first met Gerry Hoff when he headed the Moody Blues' Threshold Records in the United States. When that imprint closed its doors, he became West Coast head of A&R for the parent label, Mercury Records. He was interested, but instead signed a weird group from Cleveland, Pere Ubu, to kick start Mercury's new punk label, Blank Records. Scott Shannon had excelled in the world of radio, but now he was head of A&R for Ariola. He wanted to get into the punk game as well. He made a deal for the Ravers record to launch the new Zombie Records imprint.

The record received impressive airplay in LA and in other parts of the country, yet failed to become a hit. Although initially Graham and Louis were repelled by the new punk sensibility, the airplay made them reassess their situation. They manifested newfound punk identities and marched up to Ariola to make demands from Jay Lasker, the president. I was the only one who had interacted with the label—I had only met Lasker briefly—and Louis and Graham didn't run their plan by me. I was surprised to get a phone call that afternoon from Shannon, who said that if I wanted to make another record for the company, I needed to get a new group. What could they have done, I wondered. I was shuddering; they might have blown my relationship.

Louis and Graham had been accompanied by two striking women, Graham's wife and her friend. Graham adopted an aggressive, cockney tone and demanded that Ariola book them into the Whisky to play and make up promotional t-shirts and 8x10 publicity photos. Lasker and Shannon reeled at their lack of diplomacy and the threat to their pocketbook.

Why did they do it? Louis later said that they thought they could be as big as David Bowie or Led Zeppelin and that fueled their bluster. I felt betrayed by their move, which also put my deal in jeopardy. Initially Shannon said that the Ravers were off the label. I didn't speak to them for well over a year after the incident.

I replaced Daddy Maxfield with Atom, a band Todd Schneider managed. During the recording at Studio Sound Recorders, Shannon dropped by and wanted to take a dinner break with his engineer buddy from Nashville, Jack Stack-A-Track, who he was able to scrape up work for by sticking him on our session. I had asked Jack what he had done previously that prepared him to work our rock session, and he replied that he had been recording bird calls for *National Geographic*. The buddies dined in the elegance of the French restaurant next door. Shannon asked me to join them, but I chose to work, utilizing the assistant engineer. Shannon said he'd bring me dinner. It said a lot about Shannon that he brought me back not the French repast I was expecting, but a burger and fries from McDonald's.

Shannon came across as slick and pompous, one of those guys who tries to pass themselves off as knowing more than they do. He wasn't much of a record executive, either, but he knew his music. I was surprised to discover that two of my favorite obscure records of the time, "Dirty Pictures" by Radio Stars and *I Like Your Style*, the first solo album by Hot Chocolate's Tony Wilson, were also on his personal playlist.

"I love it. Let's put it out next week," said Shannon, of the Ravers' second recording session: his suggestion of a cover of the Honeycombs' "Have I the Right" backed with "Rich Kids," a Leviton-Bronson original that would have made the *Guinness Book of Records* as the first punk record to utilize string arrangements, if there had been such a category. Zombie's other releases, produced by Shannon and Stack-A-Track for *Dazzle-Em Productions*, fared less successfully than "Punk Rock Christmas." The plug was pulled on the punk experiment, and the second Ravers' single was never released. I bought back the four masters and issued them on Rhino as a twelve-inch EP, on "Red and Green Christmas vinyl."

Shannon went back to radio, and built a significant career as a program director and on-air personality. When Richard and I were on a Rhino promotional tour in September 1999, he welcomed us as guests on his morning show on New York's WPLJ.

I had Louis help out on the Monkees 1987 new recordings, from which he established a professional relationship with the producer Roger Bechirian. It took David Dennard about a year to embrace the new music, which he did by becoming the bass player in Gary Myrick and the Figures. Dennard did many sessions for us, as well.

MOGAN DAVID AND HIS WINOS

My band, Mogan David and His Winos, was a loose affair formed during high school to pass the time during summer vacation. We never considered performing for anybody. We amused ourselves by hearing how we sounded butchering the hits of the day as recorded on my reel-to-reel tape recorder. Some of us could play instruments; others could not. The name Mogan David and His Winos—with the spelling changed from that of the Mogen David Wine Corp to avoid getting sued—was inspired by those crazy band names of the psychedelic era, such as Jefferson Airplane and the Strawberry Alarm Clock.

After high school we had summer jobs and the band concept was abandoned. On a summer afternoon following my sophomore year at college, I invited guitarist Jon Kellerman and bassist Jim Bickhart, both fellow writers from the *Daily Bruin*, to join me and Tom Matye—the Winos' pianist from high school, now also at UCLA—for an afternoon of recording in the Matye family living room. A high school friend whose drumming I admired decided not to honor his commitment to participate, but did loan me his kit, so I played drums even though I hadn't previously. I wasn't able to coordinate the bass drum pedal, so there was no bass drum on the recording.

We recorded a song I always liked from *Mad* magazine, "Nose Job." Rather than the doo-wop arrangement of the original, I fashioned ours more like the Rolling Stones, singing the comedic lyrics deadpan, with a drawl in the manner of Mick Jagger. The B-side, "The Big War," was inspired by a Zombies' song, and was written by Tom and me. I placed an order with Rainbo Records in Hollywood. The label name I chose was Kosher Records.

One day Paul Rappaport came into the *Daily Bruin* office and introduced himself as the campus rep for CBS Records. We became friends. With his facial hair and frizzy mop, Paul looked like Fleetwood Mac's Peter Green, but he played guitar more like the Rolling Stones' Keith Richards, which meant that he also referenced Chuck Berry. He had a true rock spirit, which was confirmed when he was kicked out of high school, twice: once for wearing knee-high boots, just like Paul Revere and the Raiders did, and once for combing his hair down over his forehead, the length approaching the look of the Beatles. Paul had once been in a band that played the Hullabaloo club in Hollywood. He thought of himself as a blues guitarist, and considered himself a *feel player*, which meant that he could communicate emotionally, but he lacked the discipline to learn musical signature and nomenclature, as the "F" he received on his Music 1 test confirmed.

Paul heard "Nose Job" on the UCLA radio station, KLA, and loved it. He ordered twenty copies from me. He didn't pay in cash, but in promos. Because Jon Kellerman was immersed in graduate school, I asked Paul to fill his slot for the recording of the next Winos' single. "When I agreed to join the Winos, I was reticent," said Paul. "In other bands I had been in, there was a seriousness about practicing for a gig or getting good enough to get a record deal. I found that attitude lacking in the Winos; it was about playing to have fun." Paul's style was perfect, plus he played the same make of guitar as Kellerman, a Gibson Melody Maker.

I met Mark Leviton the previous year when as a freshman he came into the *Daily Bruin* office to inquire about writing for the entertainment section. The few of us who were there were impressed when he told us that he had published a record review in *Rolling Stone* when he was still in high school. In addition to liking all the bands of the British Invasion, Mark and I bonded over our mutual appreciation of Frank Zappa, the Firesign Theatre, and private detective novelist Raymond Chandler. He didn't look like a wannabe rock star. He had short, crinkly hair and a beard, and he wore glasses. When I visited him during the summer at his home in Northridge, he impressed me by being able to play the entirety of the Who's *Tommy* solely by himself on guitar. He was quite a sight to see, sitting on his bed, pin wheeling his right arm in Townshend fashion as he blasted through the rock opera on his Herb Ellis model Gibson guitar. His voice lacked dynamics, but it was in tune, and he displayed a real rhythmic feel with his playing. He joined the Winos and we wrote the next single together.

The band's apex occurred on May 31, 1973, when we played a free noon concert at UCLA's Ackerman Union Grand Ballroom. It was the same stage on which Procol Harum, Deep Purple, Alice Cooper, and Carole King had played. Paul was the only stellar player, but even he could be flaky. "Train Kept A-Rollin'" is a song most rock fans know, but was never a hit. Originally performed by Tiny Bradshaw and his jump-blues swing band in the early 1950s, it was transformed into rockabilly by Johnny Burnette and the Rock 'n' Roll Trio. That's where the Yardbirds heard it, and they recorded it on their *Having a Rave Up* album. In 1974 Aerosmith recorded it for their *Get Your Wings* album. The main hook of the song is an irresistible throbbing rhythm, which Paul refused to play when the Winos performed it, robbing the song of its primarily appeal. We ended our set with Paul walking off the stage with a watermelon on his shoulder, just like Alvin Lee in the *Woodstock* movie.

We also recorded two songs for a proposed third single release: a heavy metal styled arrangement of the Leiber-Stoller song "Love Potion Number 9," and an original composition, "Beauty Queen." On the latter song Paul engaged me in an hour-long discussion on whether we should, or shouldn't, use maracas. It was our best recording to date and showed real progress. However, neither our progress nor our potential were recognized by the industry.

I compiled an album of our old and new tracks and a handful of songs recorded on cassette from our performance in Shelly and Nikki

Heber's backyard. I copied the elaborate presentation of the Who's *Live at Leeds* album. In their package they had reprints of items from their history, like rejection letters and income sheets. In ours, we made fun of ourselves by including a copy of Paul's failed music test and the two ads I did featuring Mark and me plugging Columbia product, among other items. I titled it *Savage Young Winos* as a joke. With the initial success of the Beatles, a dubious record company released a flimsy album of eight songs where the Beatles were primarily used as a backup band to singer Tony Sheridan. It was titled *Savage Young Beatles*, and it featured an early photo of the group wearing leather jackets. I borrowed leather jackets from Michael Ochs to approximate the Beatles look for our group photo and copied the album design. We pressed up less than a thousand copies. In a poor move and despite my warning, Paul responded to the overly enthusiastic husband of a coworker and shipped the bulk of his share to France and was never paid.

At the time, record companies were more interested in singer/song-writers and disco artists, not a 1960s influenced rock band. I would not have evaluated us as being good enough to make it, but we were better than the punk bands that proliferated in the late 1970s. If I had been prescient, a more fitting name for the band would have been the Record Executives. We didn't make it as a rock band, which resulted in a detour-free route for three of us to excel as high-level executives in the business.

When Paul Rappaport was initially offered the position of college rep, he wasn't that enthused, but it set him on a course that would give meaning to his professional life. He was offered a full-time job in the promotion department, but after a couple of years he was disenchanted with "working for the man." The world of record companies, the ones who made the records he bought, seemed fake, populated by "hey babe," insincere, older promotion guys. He was going to quit. At the end of a company event, as people were trailing out, he approached the special guest, singer Tony Bennett, and expressed his frustration. Tony commiserated, telling Paul, "Sometimes the business is fucked up," then inspiring him with: "You have to be yourself, but be the best *you*, you can be."

Paul stayed the course, exercised more of his ideas, and rose to Vice President of Artist Development, being so well considered that he survived numerous company purges to rack up a remarkable 33 1/3 years at Columbia Records. He got to work with one of his heroes, Keith Richards, when Columbia distributed the Rolling Stones' label. He was so well thought of by Pink Floyd that they invited him to play guitar during the encore at one of their concerts. In July 1989, at the London Arena, he traded licks with Dave Gilmore during "Run Like Hell."

Mark Leviton worked at Warner Brothers licensing division, Warner Special Products, for twenty-five years, rising to vice president of the division. Jim Bickhart was employed as a writer for A&M Records and Warner Brothers Records, then as Mark's predecessor at Warner Special Products, before opting for a career in city government, most recently in the offices of Los Angeles mayor Antonio Villaraigosa. I, of course, was managing director of Rhino, in addition to cofounder of the label.

Al Albert, the Winos 1973 drummer, didn't work in the record business, but he also became a VP, with Clairmont Camera, a company that rents cameras and other equipment for film and TV production. Jonathan Kellerman transitioned from child psychology into a successful career as a best-selling author of murder mysteries.

Twenty years after our UCLA performance, I resurrected the Winos for a reunion. We recorded two songs over a weekend: "I'm an Adult Now" was a cover of a particularly apt song by the Pursuit of Happiness that voiced the dilemma of rockers aging. "Cover Girl," a song Mark and I composed in the 1970s, was consistent with other songs we wrote that expressed the frustration we felt with unapproachable girls. We considered it the best song we had written. More importantly, after not having played together for twenty years, our sound was remarkably intact: meaning we had an identifiable sound, which wasn't always easy for an artist to achieve. It reminded me of a rehearsal I attended of a Yardbirds reunion in June 1983. The original singer, Keith Relf, had passed away, and none of their celebrated original guitarists were there, but, remarkably, the rhythm section of Chris Dreja (guitar), Paul Samwell-Smith (bass), and Jim McCarty (drums) sounded just like it did in the 1960s. It made me appreciate the concept of chemistry in a band; the emotional quality that infused their playing was the same as individuals as it was as an ensemble. And the same could have been said about Mogan David and His Winos.

CHAPTER 6

Turtlemania!

The Story of America's Beatles

Among all the artists Rhino was to reissue, none was more important than the Turtles. It wasn't just the opportunity to mine the group's rich but neglected catalogue, it was also that the remaining original Turtles, Howard Kaylan and Mark Volman, were early supporters of ours and participants in Rhino projects throughout our twenty-four years at the label. They were so culturally in synch with Richard and me, that they would have been prime candidates to join our board of directors, if we had one.

That the Turtles came from my hometown made it all the more reso-nant. I'd first heard about the group from a classmate at an Orville Wright Jr. High sports night (dance) who declared the Crossfires—the progenitor of the Turtles—the best band he'd ever seen. I soon found out more about them from playing *Risk* at Harvey Portz's home. Harvey was the younger brother of the group's bass player, Chuck, who was making a bass with a body in the shape of an Iron Cross in the family garage.

In its own way, the Los Angeles suburb of Westchester was close to idyllic in the mid-1960s. While the far from affluent community had to contend with the increasing roar of the newest jets taking off from the Los Angeles International Airport, it was, to use Frank Zappa's description of the fictitious Centerville, "A real nice place to raise your kids up." In their first year as the Turtles, the band burned up local radio with their first three singles. "It Ain't Me Babe," "Let Me Be," and "You Baby" all hit the top ten.

I loved the Turtles music. I knew a couple of their younger brothers and had a little more insight that made me appreciate their records all the more. I thought their records were consistently the best produced of any American rock band of the sixties. They played well as an ensemble, their harmonies were spot on, and they were blessed with an exceptional lead singer in Howard Kaylan (and later, a superb drummer in Johny Barbata). They were unique in their ability to capture the sound of their records live, and for the humor in their stage personality. Only later, when I interviewed Howard Kaylan in August 1971 for a *Rolling Stone* feature, did I realize that they also had great stories—from starting out as a local surf band to being the first rock group to play at the White House.

Howard (né Kaplan) distinguished himself as the best singer of Westchester High School's award-winning A Cappella Choir. His status in choir and as a top student didn't mean that he and his pal, Mark Volman, could repress their natural humor and behavior in choir. The director, Robert Wood, called them into his office numerous times trying to reason with them to behave, since all the other kids looked up to them. But Howard and Mark were bitten by rock 'n' roll: they fronted the area's best band, the Crossfires. In Howard's first semester in high school, he described himself as "socially less than a potato." By the next semester, after having joined the band, he felt like he had become a local teen idol.

The Crossfires' reputation as the South Bay's best band owed itself to some extent to winning Battle of the Bands contests. The members started as an instrumental surf band—odd, because most were in choir—initially as the Night Riders. In the early 1960s surfers adopted the German Iron Cross, which is why the group changed its name to the Crossfires. Initially surfers wore this World War II decoration, passed on by their fathers, as a group-defining, antiestablishment symbol. The image was popularized by custom car designer and artist Ed "Big Daddy" Roth, who sold various by-products, including medallions and decals, and by *Surfer* magazine artist Rick Griffin.

In 1962 the hardest dance music of the time evolved out of Dick Dale's concept of the surfer stomp: searing guitar solos over a pounding rhythm section. The Crossfires covered records by Dale, the Surfaris, the Rhythm Rockers, and the Lively Ones. Al Nichol was the most musically gifted in the band. He had the best record collection and was the one who helped the others with the arrangements. He was one of the city's very best surf guitarists.

Al, Howard (on tenor sax), and Chuck Portz (on bass) were all in Westchester High's A Cappella Choir. Mark Volman was in Choir as well, but initially he was a fan of the group, who danced wildly in front of the stage when they played. He asked Howard if he could join. "I was always attracted to funny people," said Howard, during an interview I conducted for a 1991 documentary on the Turtles, from which most of the quotations in this chapter are derived. "I thought the band could use this guy, could use a little levity, because it was not a happy band. It was a band that was concentrating on the music, on getting it right. Having Mark in the band would make it fun."

In February 1963 Howard, Chuck, and Al took a lunchtime meeting with Mark at the school cafeteria to discuss adding Mark to the band, although no one knew what his role would be. Don Murray, the drummer, wasn't present because he attended Morningside High in Inglewood, seven miles away. The Crossfires still largely played instrumentals because, in Howard's assessment, "You couldn't stomp to singing." Mark was hired to help set up the equipment and sing a couple of songs with the group, but Al didn't want to pay him.

Howard: "The first night he's on the job, we're playing a UCLA fraternity. The frat boys are preparing the evening's drink—Hawaiian punch, any liquor they can get, dry ice—in a galvanized tub, and it's foaming. They called it Red Death, and we had a few of them. Mark falls down these steep stairs with the drums, and he's laughing his head off." Because of that, and other clumsy incidents, Mark acquired the nickname "Bumbling Idiot." When Mark's father learned that he was only making five dollars a night while the others were getting seventeen, he bought his son an alto sax so he would be on equal footing as a contributing instrumentalist.

In most rock bands it's assumed that the singer is the leader or the spokesman because he's the one who's primarily engaging the audience. "Mark and I were never the leaders of the band in name," Howard clarified. "Our earliest business cards for the Crossfires had two phone numbers on them: Al Nichol's and Don Murray's. Mark and I were never considered the leaders because we really weren't musicians. To be a musician in the band meant that you had to play an instrument and know chord changes. We were sax players, we were singers, we were comics. We didn't have that skill. In the rest of the members' eyes, our position was diminished. It was like, 'Here's the band [the other four guys], and here's these two guys.'"

With Mark in the band, they added more vocal numbers, initially R&B songs like "Kansas City," "Money," and "Justine." When the Beatles and the other groups of the British Invasion hit the charts, the Crossfires impressed their fans by being able to reproduce those records' vocal harmonies. Rhythm guitarist Jim Tucker, from Aviation High in Redondo Beach, completed the lineup. In early 1965, the group appeared on the local TV show *9th Street West* lip-synching their "One Potato, Two Potato" single. They autographed a potato to give away. When asked where they were from, Chuck thoughtlessly said, "Los Angeles 45" (the postal code) rather than the more identifiable "Westchester."

Enthusiastic fans of the group from high school formed the Chunky Club and flocked to see the group play. A subset, calling themselves the Spoon Men, brought spoons and ladles to the dances. A male member aimed his spoon towards his partner's vagina, motioned in a digging and scooping manner, and then brought the spoon before his face and pretended to drink the imaginary contents. This behavior caused them to get thrown out of dances. Coupled with the band's manner of substituting their own lewd lyrics in songs like Ray Charles' "What'd I Say," the Crossfires were banned from playing in the area by the Westchester Women's Club after they had received a copy of a police report. As a consequence the band could also no longer play the Westport Beach Club, the Masonic Lodge, and the Moose Lodge. This was a blow to them as it was money out of their pockets. As a result, in May1965, the Crossfires found themselves at a crossroads.

In high school Howard did well enough academically to be selected class valedictorian and to be awarded a scholarship to UCLA, but he went primarily to appease his parents and squandered his freshman year. At an early age he wanted to be a recording artist. He ripped the labels off of 45s and wrote "Howard Kaylan" on them, the name he assumed at eighteen. He spent too much time with his show on the little-heard campus radio station where he regularly interviewed Mark in the guise of various English rock stars traveling through town. "Van Morrison, my cousin from Ireland," got the most listener calls. The Crossfires were all enrolled in college, except for Mark, who was still in high school. Howard was the only one at a top university.

As winners of the Revelaire Club's Battle of the Bands contest, the Crossfires played regularly on Friday and Saturday nights at the Redondo Beach nightclub, earning $120 a night split six ways. Usually they played their own sets, but at times they also backed up vocal groups like the Coasters, Righteous Brothers, and Sonny and Cher. Al and Don were now married. Al had a child and Don had one on the way, and they needed to make more money. With no momentum or interest—the two singles the group had recorded failed to become hits—it was agreed that the band would break up.

After a set, they were about to climb the stairs to the club's office to submit their resignation, but the two owners got to them first. Reb Foster was a popular LA DJ who booked the acts. His cousin, Bill Utley, took care of the business. They brought the Crossfires to their office for a meeting with two men who were starting a new label. The resignation was quickly pocketed. Lee Lasseff and Ted Feigin had worked as record promotion men, for Liberty and London, respectively. They didn't have a name for their label yet, but wanted to sign the Crossfires. They were impressed with the band's cover of the Byrds' (Bob Dylan-penned) "Mr. Tambourine Man," which was then in the top ten. Al had recently purchased a twelve-string guitar so he could get the same sound as on the record. Lee and Ted thought that folk rock would be big, and they wanted the group to record another of Bob Dylan's songs to release as their debut single.

It was nice to have the interest, but realistically, this wasn't an offer from one of the established labels. The new label was named White Whale because Ted Feigin loved *Moby Dick*. He named the publishing company

Ishmael after the book's protagonist sailor, and a later publishing company, Pequod, after the whaling ship. Lee and Ted's interest was a way for the band members to postpone giving up the rock 'n' roll dream and assuming adult responsibilities.

In a subsequent meeting at the club, Reb and Bill offered to be the group's managers. The bandmates were too naïve to question them. Reb thought they needed a new name, not one linked to the passé surfing craze. The band suggested the Half Dozen and the Six Pack. Reb didn't think those would work if, say, a member left the band and wasn't replaced. He suggested the Turtles; it was an animal name, like the Byrds. He thought the "tles"—also in the Beatles—sounded British, and that they would have more appeal if record buyers thought they were a new British band. The group went along with it, but weren't fond of the name. They thought Reb was making fun of the way they looked, that they were slow and clunky. (It was also a name that was strongly considered for the group that became the Monkees.) The next weekend when the Crossfires announced their name change, they were booed at the club.

In keeping with Lee and Ted's interest in "Mr. Tambourine Man," Howard chose Dylan's "It Ain't Me Babe," and suggested the band record it in a style similar to that of the Zombies. Los Angeles' four major pop stations added the record to their playlists in mid-July. A few weeks later it hit the national charts. On August 7, when the record was in the top ten locally, the Turtles played their first big show as one of the opening acts for Herman's Hermits at the Rose Bowl, which drew 35,000 kids. A few days later they played with the Hermits in San Diego. In San Francisco for their third appearance with the Hermits—at the Civic Auditorium—they were turned away from the Fairmont Hotel, where they had reservations, because of their uncommonly long hair. Utley was able to extract $200 from the hotel manager before making accommodations elsewhere.

The Turtles flew out of Los Angeles on Sunday, August 15, to join the Dick Clark Caravan of Stars. As the plane soared, they saw the smoke from the burning buildings in the Watts Riots. They would be joining Tom Jones, Peter and Gordon, the Shirelles, Brian Hyland, Ronnie Dove, Billie Jo Royal, and Mel Carter.

They checked in at the Hilton in Chicago prior to the Caravan's arrival. Most of the hotel guests were attending the Veterans of Foreign Wars convention. The number of troops joining the war in Vietnam was escalating. The longhaired Turtles rankled these vets and were stared at everywhere they went in the hotel. One veteran scornfully told them, "I lost my arm defending you!"

Chuck almost got into a fight with them: "These VFW guys surrounded us and called us 'slime' and 'sluts,' and told us when they were done drinking that night they'd come back down and shoot us." The Turtles were among the few American longhaired rock bands with a hit on the charts, and much of the country wasn't comfortable with the new hairstyles. They were spat upon, called "girls," and sworn at.

Al walked to the park across the street to take it all in. He wanted to take a picture of the hotel, of his hotel room, of the Chicago skyline. He got mugged. That night at McCormick Place, the Turtles played their two songs in the show. They were the only longhaired band on the tour. All of the other acts used the tour backup band, Jimmy Ford and the Executives. Three of its members later formed Chicago. The Turtles were paid $2,000 a week.

Upon boarding the Caravan bus the next day, Mark and Howard were feeling particularly appreciated, as their seating assignments were in the hip area, in the back of the bus. They sat next to the two biggest stars on the tour: Howard was next to Gordon Waller of Peter and Gordon, Mark was behind him next to Tom Jones. Jones had recently been in the top ten with "It's Not Unusual." British Invasion exponents Peter and Gordon had six Top 30 hits, including a number one the previous summer with "A World Without Love." Significantly more girls had congregated outside of their windows than the others. The girls were flush with excitement. Tom was talking to the exhilarated girls outside, but they couldn't hear him through the glass window. As Tom stroked himself, he said, "Oh, you love me darlin'. You'd love to suck on Wendell, wouldn't you? Oh, he's gettin' a rise out of you, there." It wasn't hard for Howard to guess what Wendell was.

Brian Hyland, a clean-looking teen idol who had last been in the top ten three years prior to this with "Sealed With a Kiss," passed on advice about the girls congregating outside of the bus. He told the newcomers to pay more attention to the straight-faced girls in the back pretending not to be fans, as they were the ones more willing to have sex than the smiling ones up front.

As the bus got rolling to the next show in Nashville, these showbiz vets gave them the lay of the land. It was a great feeling, like being at camp. To save money, the Caravan stayed in hotels every other evening, which meant that the alternating nights were spent sleeping on the bus. Howard and Mark revised their opinion of the nice-guy tour director when they learned from Gordon and Tom that, as bigger stars, they would sleep stretched out on their seats, which meant that Howard and Mark ended up sleeping on the floor below. At night, on the floor, they waved to each other.

All the Turtles were shocked at the uninhibited behavior of the people on the tour, especially the interracial coupling. Peter Asher, Gordon Waller, and Tom Jones' manager Gordon Mills were having affairs with three of the black girls in the Shirelles. Ronnie, a large black man who was the Shirelles' road manager, presented the Turtles with their first exposure to a homosexual. Ronnie was good at breaking the tension. He had a riding crop that he used to flick. Howard: "He'd address Mark, 'Hey, Sophie Tucker, you there with the hair and the belly.' Snap! 'Sit down, Honey.' Snap! Snap!" Sophie Tucker—who was fat—was billed as the Last of the Red-Hot Mamas and was one of the most popular singers from earlier in the century.

"He was always saying, 'Don't get grand on us,'" Mark said. "Meaning, don't let it go to your head. It was a nice way of reminding us to keep our newfound success in perspective. Between leaving the theater and getting to the bus, we would have to be guarded because the girls were constantly ripping at our clothes. We were surrogates for the Beatles. He'd say, 'They're even chasing Sophie Tucker tonight!'"

After a show in Connecticut, Jim Tucker wasn't so lucky. "Some girls pushed me over an embankment and I landed on a park lawn," he recollected. "The next thing I knew I was lying on my back, my shirt was ripped, my pants were down around my knees, and a girl was running up the street with my guitar."

The Turtles became friends with Mel Carter, a good-looking black gospel singer turned pop crooner who was high on the charts with "Hold

Me, Thrill Me, Kiss Me." "I went to a predominantly white restaurant with Mel Carter in Alabama," said Chuck. "A 70-year-old man picked up his plate of beef, mashed potatoes, and gravy and threw it at us. It went down Mel's front. We were called 'White Niggers.' The cops came and took us away."

The Turtles had wanted to appear hip, so they had told Mel that they had smoked marijuana. When the Crossfires played in Hollywood, they tried to enhance their appeal by announcing from the stage, "We are hot because we smoke pot!" But they didn't. After a show in Syracuse, New York, Howard, Mark, Don, and Al joined Mel in his hotel room. Mel filled his pipe from what must have been a pound of grass held in a large plastic bag. He passed his pipe to them, but he could see they weren't inhaling properly. "I'm going to give you the super toke," he said, "to make sure you get high." He took a large hit from his pipe, exhaled into each of their mouths, and then clamped his hand over each of their faces to make sure they kept it in. After some coughing, they got the hang of it. He shared with them the tricks of the trade, like wedging a towel into the bottom of the door to the hallway and burning Aqua Velva aftershave in an ashtray to disguise the smell.

Back in their room, the Turtles shared new sensations like excited kids. They sampled different sodas and candies. They adjusted the color knobs on the TV set they were watching to distort the picture. Without the others realizing it, Al made his way outside and onto the third-story ledge where he knocked on their windows and on those of other guests. The Turtles quickly realized that they wanted to be in that state all of the time, but they had to be discreet.

While members of hit rock acts were pulling in much more than an average wage, few were making the big bucks, as Bill Utley explained: "The Turtles bridged a couple of eras. When they started only the Beatles were making big money, because prior to the Beatles, the groups weren't paid that much. I used to put the Beach Boys, Jan & Dean and groups like that on stage for $200 a night. The Righteous Brothers were an expensive act at $300 a night. The Turtles were part of the vanguard of developing the concert business. But there weren't $40,000 dates. The goal at the time was to bring the Turtles up to $750 a night."

On top of that, there was the belief that rock music played by musicians with Beatle-styled hair was a fad. Even the Beatles didn't think their success would last. As early as 1965, Ringo was contemplating opening a chain of ladies hair salons after "the bubble burst." Utley's approach was to make hay while the sun shined, which meant that the Turtles worked. It was also good exposure for selling records. "Our lives were taken from us like we were public property," said Chuck. "We just went and went and went, one tour after another. When we were in town, we were recording. It drained everybody."

After another multi-act bus tour, Wrap Up '65, the group took to the road, Utley often losing his way behind the wheel of a station wagon pulling a U-Haul trailer. They went out for six-week stints, mostly to the Midwest, playing in small bars and dilapidated dance halls that were equipped for big bands but not rock 'n' roll groups. They shared double hotel rooms. The group made between $600 and $800 a night, and were sometimes expected to provide three hours of music. On many nights, after packing their gear, they had to drive hundreds of miles to the next gig.

"Because of our long hair we suffered a lot of indignity, especially in the South and Midwest where people were very conservative," said Don. "They saw longhairs on TV, but it was a different matter when they came to their town where all the kids had crew cuts. We stood out real bad. We went into restaurants and the whole place would go silent, and they would stare at us."

White Whale had an impressive launch, selling 550,000 copies of the "It Ain't Me Babe" single. The Turtles success caused them to be lumped into the folk rock genre. Folk singers Woody Guthrie and Pete Seeger inspired Bob Dylan and other performers of the early 1960s folk boom. Many of their songs were concerned with political or social topics, providing a template for the folk rock, or protest rock movement in 1965/1966.

The "folk rock" label originally applied to the Byrds after they hit with "Mr. Tambourine Man." It described a Beatles-styled rock band performing an arrangement of what was originally an acoustic folk song with electric guitars. Bob Dylan preceded the Turtles into the charts with "Like a Rolling Stone." Sonny and Cher's music was similarly characterized. The Turtles needed another folk rock hit and met with P. F. Sloan, a musical prodigy who had been performing on hit records and producing and writing hits while still in his teens. For a time he was labeled the "West Coast Dylan" before he flamed out in 1967.

At Hollywood's Crescendo Tiger's Tail where the band was rehearsing for their evening performance, Sloan presented the Turtles with a few songs. They thought the lyrics of "Eve of Destruction" were too extreme and passed. (After Barry McGuire's version topped the charts, they recorded it for their debut album, which sold an impressive 100,000 copies.) Instead, the Turtles chose "Let Me Be," an expression of sullen adolescent independence, which barely made it into the national Top 30. Even though the group recorded more tracks that fit comfortably in this genre—Howard rose to the occasion by penning "House of Pain"—their commitment wasn't genuine.

The Crossfires had always been a fun band. During one of their original songs, "Dr. Jekyll and Mr. Hyde," Mark donned a monster mask and ran through the crowd. As white, middle-class boys, they had difficulty identifying with protest songs, and guessing correctly that the genre was waning, opted for a pop rock sound similar to New York's Lovin' Spoonful. Sloan provided the song for their new direction as well, with "You Baby." To complement this shift, White Whale had them jettison their grungy, Rolling Stones-look for the *You Baby* album cover. The Turtles wore sport jackets, ties, and turtlenecks and were each embraced by a youthful model.

One reason to go to college was to have a deferment from being drafted in the military. As full-time rock stars, the Turtles no longer had that reprieve. Around the time "You Baby" was released, Howard and Mark were ordered to report to the draft board. Before the Selective Service Administration wised up, it was easier to avoid being drafted for military service, but it still took a great deal of effort. Herb Cohen was a distant cousin of Howard's who managed folk clubs and performers. For many years he was Frank Zappa's manager. Howard met Herb at Frank's house— Frank was out of town—to seek ways they could prepare themselves for their physical and mental examinations. Howard and Mark implemented many of the suggestions, which included taking a lot of drugs, not sleeping, and refraining from bathing. All of the Turtles, in their own ways, avoided serving—as did a majority of those Americans in hit rock bands.

By the time the Turtles played the Phone Booth in New York in March of 1966, "You Baby" had risen to number two on LA's top radio stations, but hadn't yet made the charts in New York. One night Bob Dylan was seated in the front row, wearing dark sunglasses and a polka dot shirt. The Turtles ended their set with "It Ain't Me Babe." Afterwards they were paraded past his table to meet him. "Bob was bent over, almost comatose," according to Howard. "We were shocked at his condition. When it came to my turn, Bob said, 'I really liked that last song you did. It had a nice ring to it.'" Before Howard could respond, Bob passed out into his plate of pasta.

Don was the first to exhibit the effects of the pressure they were feeling. He had an artistic nature and was more sensitive than the others. In addition, both he and Al were married with kids but unable to resist the lure of their willing female fans, which added to the tension he was experiencing. Years before Led Zeppelin and the Who set the standard for hotel room demolition, the Turtles came under scrutiny when, during a domestic argument, Don's wife heaved a lamp through the window of the Fremont Hotel room to the street below. Coupled with Chuck's transgression of prowling the lobby in his bare feet, the Turtles were banned from appearing in Las Vegas, and rock groups became unwelcome performers at the downtown showrooms for many years.

During this period Don described himself as going "berserk." He became paranoid. There was an episode in the car on the way to Philadelphia. Sitting in the front seat, he accused Mark of staring at the back of his head, and then accused all the band members of looking at him, saying that they were all against him. Hours later, during a run through at Jerry Blavat's TV show, *The Discophonic Scene*, he turned on Jim Tucker and both had to be restrained from fighting.

At the end of May, the Turtles were in the middle of a session at Western Recorders when Don quit the band. "There were a number of reasons why I left the band," he said. "There were the undercurrents of all the wives and girlfriends pressuring us about whether or not we were sleeping with groupies. There was the road weariness of all the dives we were playing in. For my own self, I always felt a pressure of trying to lift anything we did on record up to a higher artistic quality."

Don also cited the friction between Al and Howard over the songwriting. In the Crossfires, Al was the dominant writer, composing mostly surf instrumentals. In the Turtles, Lee and Ted favored Howard's compositions. On the first two Turtles' albums, Howard had seven songwriting credits to Al's one. Howard was also the writer on three of the Turtles' first four single B-sides.

I met with Don on a number of occasions and found him intelligent and friendly. Some of the things he said made me think that there was still the residue of the mental state that Howard and Mark had referred to. "When we got to the 'You Baby' record a lot of things happened that did a lot of damage to me personally," Don said. "I had been working on a syncopated style of playing drums, and I wanted to use this beat on 'You Baby.' It did end up on the record, but I had to go through a lot of grief. The writer P. F. Sloan came to our rehearsal, listened to the way we were playing the song and told us that it was no good, that he had a track already recorded with the Mamas and Papas singing. He could merely erase their vocals and put ours on.

"I said, 'Nobody's playing the drums for me.' He said, 'Hal Blaine is on the track and he's the greatest drummer in the world.' He got furious and stormed out. Lee and Ted said, 'Nice going Murray, that's your songwriter, now what are you going to do?' The record was a big hit on the West Coast, but only got to seventeen on the *Cash Box* chart because it didn't get much airplay on the East Coast. Lee and Ted told me, 'It's because the kids on the East Coast don't like the way you play drums.' It changed everything for me. I started thinking I was a lousy drummer, that I was holding the band back. I started getting nuts about it, and it ate on me." Interestingly enough, when I conducted the interviews for the Turtles' documentary, both Sloan and producer Bones Howe also took credit for coming up with the drum arrangement.

The Turtles didn't want to see Don go. He was the cutest and most English-looking of the group, and he resembled Paul McCartney. Whatever teen appeal they had diminished when he left. "Playing as the Crossfires was the best time we ever had together," Don recalled. "We double-dated, we rehearsed once or twice a week. We couldn't get enough of trying new things, of hoping and dreaming together. We were very close. When we started doing the road shows as the Turtles, we were together so much that when we got back to Los Angeles in between tours, we'd never even see each other."

Don departed before it was apparent that the Turtles' fourth single was a flop. Lee and Ted wanted the Turtles to record a group-composed song so they could reap the extra income from the publishing. It would take more than a master detective to discover why as unlikely a song as "Grim Reaper of Love" was chosen to follow the poppy "You Baby." The droning raga would have been well suited to the soundtrack of an Indian horror movie. Chuck and Al wrote it after a gig in Oregon. Al had just acquired a Coral Electric Sitar, a guitar configured to approximate the sound of the Indian instrument. It's an interesting record, and was selected probably because it was the band's best composition at the time.

Gene Clark, who had been the primary vocalist and songwriter in the Byrds, told drummer Johny Barbata about the job opening. Like the Turtles, Johny had started out in a surf band, the Sentinals. Unlike Don Murray, he wasn't much to look at. His audition for the Turtles was so impressive that they knew right away he would be an asset. In addition to being an astute technician, Barbata played with flair, twirling his drumsticks. Coupled with Mark's tambourine acrobatics, the Turtles amped up their showmanship.

Chuck was the next to leave. His reasons echoed Don's: "In high school with the Night Riders and the Crossfires, and even in the first year and a half with the Turtles, we were really a happy group. We did a lot of things together. But then the demand on our time caught up with us. We could never get away from each other, and we never had enough time for ourselves. I left because I no longer felt part of the group off-stage, and if I wasn't part of them off-stage, I couldn't be part of them on-stage. It was a result of everything we were doing. I was stressed out."

By early October the group's fifth single, "Outside Chance" (composed by Warren Zevon), hadn't even made the Top 100, and Chuck threw in the towel. Mark and Howard pointed out that Chuck's departure was amiable. He wanted to go back to college and get involved in a catering business. They also thought that Johny's assertive drumming might have challenged Chuck's ability. At the time most hit rock bands relied on session players to provide the instrumental backing while recording, but not the respected Turtles.

The Turtles didn't get the recognition for their musical chops, but they were solid. "I went to one recording date, for 'Let Me Be,' and I was very impressed with them," P. F. Sloan said. "The bass sound particularly was great, different from any of the groups I had heard before. Their electric guitar sounds were unique, they were really exciting, much more so than other groups of the time."

Bill Utley was also complimentary: "Chuck Portz put down a good, heavy bass line. He used to hit those strings like he was shooting arrows. I thought Don Murray was an excellent drummer. Jim Tucker was a good-looking guy who did a good job of playing rhythm guitar. I had a lot of other groups approach me and want to know how the Turtles got their sound, but they couldn't duplicate it, even with more musicians."

Howard Kaylan may well have been the best singer in an American rock band of the period. His exceptional voice impressed Robert Wood, his high school choir teacher, who remembered decades later Howard's soliloquy from the school's presentation of Rodgers and Hammerstein's *Carousel*. As a non-player, Mark Volman's importance might not have been apparent. He provided a high harmony, similar to the roles that David Crosby furnished in the Byrds and Graham Nash in the Hollies. (Although Nash strummed a guitar live, mostly it was unamplified.) Mark's humorous antics contributed substantially to the group's unique personality.

As much as Chip Douglas—formerly with Gene Clark's group—was an apt replacement on bass, with Don and Chuck gone, the Turtles were transitioning from the tight and familiar high school band they once were into a business enterprise, into a profession. The Turtles attempted to get back to the "You Baby" sound with "Can I Get to Know You Better," their third single composed by P. F. Sloan and Steve Barri. Despite being a superb record, it was the group's third flop in a row.

The Turtles pushed Lee and Ted to make a deal with Koppelman-Rubin and Associates, the production company that had been successful at sustaining a string of seven straight top ten hits for the Lovin' Spoonful. The producers assigned the unproven Joe Wissert to oversee the recording of the group's next single, "Happy Together." The song was composed by

Alan Gordon and Garry Bonner, who had been members of the Magicians, an unsuccessful Greenwich Village band signed to Koppelman-Rubin. "Happy Together" had been making the rounds and had been turned down by other artists, but the Turtles liked it.

"It was just a simple, scratchy demonstration record," Howard said, "singing accompanied by a guitar and somebody keeping time by slapping his thighs. The publishing company flew the writers out to Los Angeles to play the song for us, and it sounded exactly the same as the demo, except for the scratches." The Turtles made it a part of their live set, and as they played it they made adjustments in the arrangement. Chip had a lot to do with it, helping to arrange the vocals, brass, and woodwinds during the recording in mid-December.

Chip's involvement was no secret, and when the Turtles performed at the Whisky A Go-Go in Hollywood later that month, Mike Nesmith approached him about being the Monkees' next producer even though he hadn't produced before. In the Turtles, Chip was making $150 a week. Nesmith promised him a payday of over $100,000 for their next album. Chip had already started working with the Monkees when he left the Turtles in early February 1967, shortly after appearing with the group on *The Smothers Brothers Comedy Hour* TV show. His place was filled by Jim Pons, the bass player in the Leaves, a group best known for their hit "Hey Joe." The Turtles immediately liked him: he was low-key, warm, and friendly. Pons' first recording session was in early March for "She'd Rather Be With Me."

Jim Pons encouraged a spiritual consciousness in the band. He led discussions on the philosophy of self-discovery and leading a spiritual life, as well as on such topics as psychedelic drugs, Eastern religions, Scientology, and transcendental meditation. Pons also brought an element of diplomacy to the Turtles in dealing with White Whale. On tour, Pons whiled away the hours making collages of photos cut from pornographic magazines. "Being in the Turtles was a strange coexistence of the spiritual and the hedonistic," he noted.

"Happy Together" knocked the Beatles' "Penny Lane" out of the number one slot on March 25, 1967, and remained there for three weeks. It was climbing the chart in Britain when a tour was planned for early June. "Happy Together" made it to number twelve in Britain, which pleased the

Turtles primarily because that meant that the Beatles had probably heard their record. They still had not met their idols, although Howard and Jim came close.

On the evening of August 28, 1966, after the Turtles performance at the Whisky, Howard drove Jim and his housemate, ex-Beach Boy David Marks, to a party for the Beatles at their rented house on Curson Terrace in the Hollywood Hills. In the traffic crawl outside the house, Marks talked back to a policeman, causing the car to be searched. The police claimed they found a marijuana roach and some seeds in the trunk of Howard's two-day-old Pontiac GTO. In the 1960s possession of marijuana was considered a felony offense. Howard claimed the marijuana was planted, but all three were arrested, missed the party, and spent an anxious night in jail.

The Turtles arrived at Kennedy Airport late in the evening on May 30, 1967, after having played a Memorial Day weekend at the Steel Pier in Atlantic City where circus act Antalek's Chimps opened for them. They were exhausted. Although their flight wasn't for seven hours, Utley wouldn't pay for hotel rooms and insisted they sleep on seats in the lounge. Howard had words with Bill, whose temper flared. He swore at Howard, called him "ungrateful," and slammed him up against the glass window.

They flew to London on an Air India flight that Howard swears permitted live chickens as part of the carry-on baggage. They were met at the airport by Allan McDougall, their publicist. He took them to see Steve Sanders, an American photographer who had been a roadie for the Mamas and Papas and was now living in London. He served them tea. The night before, John Lennon had used a red ink pen to draw a picture of a girl on Steve's wall. The Turtles were so excited that Lennon had just been there that they posed for pictures with the signed illustration.

They made a round of the hip clubs and ended up at the Speakeasy, arriving after midnight. The Beatles had spent the evening in De Lane Lea Recording Studios working on "It's All Too Much," a track that appeared on the *Yellow Submarine* soundtrack. Paul McCartney, John Lennon, and Ringo Starr were ensconced in the primo booth by the time the Turtles showed up and were introduced to them. To the Turtles, the Beatles were acting strange, as though they were on LSD. Paul was crawling underneath tables taking pictures up girls' dresses. Jim Pons was so transfixed watching John Lennon nod back and forth into the flame of a candle on the table that it took him a while to realize that he was sitting next to Paul. John Lennon was known to insult people, especially when he was drunk, and Jim Tucker took the brunt of his barbs. Brian Jones introduced Howard to Jimi Hendrix. The two drank cognac and ate spinach omelets, but the unfamiliar combination was too much for Howard, who threw up on Jimi.

It was a whirlwind: a handful of club and ballroom dates, press interviews, radio and TV appearances, and clothes shopping. Their UK label, Decca Records, hosted a press reception for them with Jeff Beck and Lulu in attendance. Allan took them to the flat he shared with Graham Nash. Allan also did publicity for Graham's group the Hollies. Graham enthralled them by playing an advance tape of the Beatles' new album, *Sgt. Pepper's Lonely Hearts Club Band*. Howard encapsulated the trip: "It was all we imagined London to be, but more so. Donovan was at Graham Nash's house sitting on a rug with incense burning and big hookah pipes and hash all over the place. Stoned gypsy girls were twirling around in tie-died dresses and lace curtains." Jim Pons was more succinct: "The Beatles telling me they liked my records. How much better can it get?"

A combination of jet lag, little sleep, and smoking hash lowered their resistance, and both Jim Tucker and Howard became ill, resulting in a number of commitments being cancelled. On Sunday, June 4, the Turtles played a good show at the Speakeasy. Mark remembered Jimi wearing the "eye coat" that later appeared on the cover of his debut American album. The Rolling Stones' Brian Jones, a known blues fanatic, told the Turtles how much he liked their California harmony sound. He took still photos and filmed their appearance with his movie camera. Also in attendance: Peter and Gordon, members of the Who, Moody Blues, and Procol Harum. As a result of their visibility in Britain, "She'd Rather Be With Me" rose to number four on the UK charts. Jimi Hendrix commented on the single in *Melody Maker*: "They don't need all these instruments, because their voices sound very good."

Jim Tucker: "I played my last job in England. We were always on the road, we were always recording, we didn't have very much of our own free time. When I was on the road, all I ever thought about was coming back and being with my friends. I didn't care for the English food. I lived on chips [French fries] and avocados. Howard and I got sick and were both flat on our backs. I woke up one morning and was feeling better, walked over to the window, and realized how tired I was, that I didn't want to do this any longer." When members of the Turtles arrived at the airport to return to the States, they were surprised to see Jim Tucker taking an earlier flight back to Los Angeles with Reb Foster.

Howard and Mark attributed Tucker leaving the band to his realization that the Beatles weren't gods, that they did stupid things just like they did. They both described Tucker as having "flipped out." Howard was more specific: "He saw his idols crumble before his eyes." It also may have been that as music evolved, as a rhythm guitarist, he wasn't involved creatively as much as the others. Even though the Turtles had a number one hit, much of the time they were still playing in dumpy clubs.

When the group landed in Florida to fulfill two weeks of contracted dates, they were disoriented. They hadn't slept, and they had gone from the cold of London to humidity and temperatures in the high eighties. There was also the emotional impact of not knowing what happened to Tucker. They were told he was sick, that he needed some time off. The issue of his future with the group wasn't discussed. The group had to perform the remaining dates as a quintet. Because Al wasn't a flashy lead guitarist, he didn't get recognition for his playing. He was so skilled as a rhythm player that he was aptly able to cover Jim Tucker's parts as well as his own, and the Turtles never replaced Tucker.

With Tucker gone, not only did the group lose their second best looking member—next to Murray—but another link to the high school band that they had been. The next two singles made the top twenty. "You Know What I Mean" and "She's My Girl" were composed by Bonner and Gordon and produced by Joe Wissert. Interestingly, the four Bonner and Gordon hits were about imagined or dreamed relationships, not ones actually experienced. "She's My Girl," which Don Murray considered the best record the Turtles ever made, was deemed a disappointment when it only managed to get to 14 on *Billboard's* chart. The Turtles turned down Bonner and Gordon's "Celebrity Ball," a song that became a hit for Three Dog Night in 1970 as "Celebrate."

Koppelman-Rubin extracted a big cut for providing their production services. The Turtles, now more popular than ever and flexing their worth, were whining about wanting to produce themselves. Lee and Ted thought it would be a good idea to unburden themselves of Koppelman-Rubin and give the Turtles a shot.

"To some extent there was an ongoing crisis of identity with the Turtles," noted Bill Utley. "If the Turtles had been comfortable with who and what they were, I think they could have been even bigger." There was something charming about the Turtles dedication to the Beatles. They had their own sound, they were making great records, they had a slew of hits—but they wanted to be the Beatles.

It started in the Crossfires days, when they grew their hair long. After a show they went to a coffee shop or bowling alley and affected English accents. They knew they couldn't pass off being the Beatles, who were too well known, but they could be a less visible group like Gerry and the Pacemakers or the Dave Clark Five. They knew all their names and enjoyed the surprised reaction from waitresses who thought their customers were celebrities. People asked them for their autographs, and they got free drinks. The group knew what to order, too, confusing their server by requesting "white tea with a bickie [a biscuit, or cookie] on the side so we can dunk it."

In August 1966, when the Turtles found themselves in Miami with a few days off, they went to the Bahamas and explored the island by motorbike looking for the locations where the Beatles filmed *Help!* Their mentality became, "If the Beatles can do it, so can we." A month later when the Beatles' *Revolver* was released, they purchased a portable record player in order to listen to it. To get as close into the Beatles' mindset as possible, they took the drugs they imagined the Beatles had. They draped scarves over the hotel room lamps, lit incense, turned the TV set to a snow pattern, and congregated into a group circle.

Later, when the Beatles formed their own label, Apple, the Turtles formed Blimp. When the Beatles opened the Apple Boutique, the Turtles rented the building that formerly housed Thee Experience nightclub so their wives could open their own clothing store. The impact of the Beatles' *Sgt. Pepper's* album pushed them into creating psychedelic recordings, commencing with sessions booked early in January 1968.

"We were such lovers of the Beatles," said Howard, "and the way they were able to walk the line and have hit records and still release concept albums, that we wanted our next album to be a concept album big time." Many of their peers were making music that got played on the more album-oriented FM radio. "Because we were having hits, our records were not considered serious music," Howard reasoned. "They were thought of as bubble gum music, and we didn't see any way out from being considered AM for the rest of our lives."

As much as 1967 was a big year for the Turtles, it was also a big year for the Doors, who had opened for the Turtles the previous year. The Turtles took note that the credit for writing, arranging, and performing the songs was attributed to "The Doors." With the Turtles lineup in place a year now, the members were feeling very democratic and adopted the Doors model. "We wanted to minimize our egos," Howard said. "We wanted to go for a harmonious group feeling."

In the unlikely setting of Chess Studios in Chicago, the group sat in lotus positions on Indian rugs. Incense was lit, drugs consumed, and Indian instruments appropriated: Al grasped the sitar, Howard the tamboura, and Jim the sarod. At times Jim even thought he was the Walrus, just like John Lennon in *Magical Mystery Tour*. By the time the Turtles added the voices from a cobbled together choir of thirty kids on one of the three songs, they actually believed they had tapped into the energy of the cosmos. Despite how they were feeling, the result, while interesting, was deemed unreleasable by White Whale.

"Sound Asleep," the one Turtles-produced track issued as a single, included real and manufactured sound effects, like quaking ducks, an orchestra of sawing logs, and a falling tree. Hidden in the mix was a sax playing "Oh Beautiful" and the Turtles singing "Waiting for the Robert E. Lee." In mid-March 1968 it had reached its highest point on *Billboard's* Hot 100, a commercial failure at 57. Oddly enough, a German language version, "Dondolo" by Rex Gildo, made the German top ten a year later.

On Thursday, April 4, the Turtles flew from Los Angeles to Chicago to start another tour, enjoying the fruits of success. The Turtles' hits compilation, *Golden Greats*, had recently hit the top ten and was on the way to achieving gold record status (sales of 500,000). "We were living the fat life," Howard recalled. "We took two floors at the Astor Tower, the same hotel where the Beatles stayed. We all had suites. The rooms were decorated in chrome, velvet and smoked glass. We had a white grand piano in the living room. We had food sent up from Maxim's de Paris, which was in the basement. We had our own plane, a DC-3, and our two 24-hour limo drivers, Doc and George, waiting downstairs for us." At their peak, the Turtles made between $3,500 and $5,000 a night.

That evening Martin Luther King, Jr. was assassinated. Because of the riots the following day, Friday evening's attendance at the Cheetah Club was down. A thousand fans showed up, but three thousand had been expected. Howard and other members of the Turtles unwound by watching stag films. The next night's show was cancelled, which was just as well since Howard was sick.

As if the social turmoil wasn't enough, the Turtles were recoiling from the pressure of having the heads of their label clamoring for another song like "Happy Together." On the outside the Turtles were these Happy Together guys—the purveyors of fun-spirited romantic pop songs—but inside they wanted to be artistic and creative. Feeling vulnerable on all sides, Howard retreated to his bedroom, sipped the chicken soup he had delivered from Mr. Chicken, and poured his anxiety into composing a parody of "Happy Together." He copied the structure, inverted the melody, and exaggerated the teenage lyrics: "Gee I think you're swell . . . you're fab and gear, etcetera . . . I think I love you Elenore Freebish." (Fab gear, already passé by 1968, was an expression used by the Beatles and other members of the British Invasion to refer to fabulous clothes.) He hoped Lee and Ted would find the effort so ridiculous, they would admit their folly and permit the Turtles to continue to follow in the Beatles' psychedelic footsteps. But they didn't get the joke, nor did record buyers.

Chip Douglas thought the melody was so strong, he convinced Howard to tone down the lyrics for the recording. Any insincerity remaining in the revised lyrics was obscured by Howard's tender vocal and Chip's fine production. "Elenore" is the band's second best remembered and only self-composed hit, and was also the first hit to feature a moog synthesizer. It reached number six in the United States, and the top ten in England, Canada, Australia, and New Zealand, where it was number one.

In Britain, unlike in America, music fans preferred their own homegrown artists, which meant that American rock bands had few hits. With three big hits in Britain, the Turtles fared better than other American bands like the Byrds, Lovin' Spoonful, Paul Revere & the Raiders, the Rascals, and Tommy James and the Shondells.

While the Turtles' self-produced foray into psychedelia wasn't fruitful, they were able to realize their concept album, *The Turtles Present the Battle of the Bands*. They went back to their roots, and created a different act to represent each of the songs on the album. They looked upon it as their *Sgt. Pepper's*. "The Beatles presented a variety show, 'Come on in, folks, here's the show!' We did that," said Mark. "It has an introduction song like theirs, 'Tonight, the Battle of the Bands,' and it fades into a harp which was our way of showing that this album was drug induced." Few rock artists had followed with a Beatles-like concept album when *The Battle of the Bands* was released in November 1968, and none with an intended sense of humor.

Like the Beatles, the Turtles lived life on the road in a band cocoon, and concocted their own shared expressions, which resulted in the chanted "I'm Chief Kamanawanalea" (i.e. "come on, I wanna lay ya"). The songs weren't all satirical and goofy. The album's closer, "Earth Anthem," was a serious song about ecology. The album contained two stellar tracks. Like "Elenore," "You Showed Me" climbed to number six on *Billboard's* chart, and benefitted from an accident. The Jim McGuinn-Gene Clark composition was recorded by the Byrds prior to their first hit, but never released. From having played in Gene Clark's subsequent band, Chip knew the song. When he played it for the Turtles for them to consider recording, the bellows on his pump organ was broken, which meant that he could only play the up-tempo song at a slow speed. The song's beauty and appeal was immediate to the Turtles, and they recorded it—at the lower tempo. The album only managed to get to 128 on *Billboard's* album chart, adding to the Turtles' frustration that White Whale could only effectively sell singles and not the album format that was now garnering respect among musicians and music fans.

"I'm Chief Kamanawanalea" was a showcase for their drummer, Johny Barbata. "On his best days, he was one of the greatest humans alive," said Mark. "He would be funny and sing along to records with us. When we were at photo sessions he'd keep telling us, 'Give 'em that knowing acid look.' But he was also an egomaniac who was always berating the rest of the members of the band, especially Howard and me. He said we should lose weight, that we should dress better, that I should cut my hair. He felt we could be bigger if we weren't slobs, if we cleaned up our appearance. Johny was always a good guy, but it was a side of his we didn't like. It got so that the rest of the members wouldn't ride with him to the gigs. He was in one car with one of our road managers, and we were in the other."

Despite Johny's encouragement, Mark and Howard's collective weight grew to where it proved to be a liability in one daytime college performance. Cafeteria tables were braced together to form a makeshift stage, and Mark's jumping caused it to implode. Johny Barbata: "It was just like in a cartoon, where the blanket goes into a hole in the floor and everything gets sucked in. The music was still playing, and Howard and Mark climbed out, still singing. Mark had a cut on his face. The crowd was laughing and applauding. It was great."

"We started hanging out a lot with Spanky and Our Gang who lived in Chicago," said Howard. "At that time Spanky made a devastating pot punch. Their drummer, John Seiter, became a very good friend of ours. We became so tight with him that our drummer wouldn't even come around. Johny was very important to the Turtles, but we got tired of his goading, so we eased him out." Johny was also looking to better himself. Returning to Los Angeles, he played the drums on albums by Dave Mason and Ry Cooder before joining Crosby, Stills, Nash & Young.

Spanky and Our Gang's music was similar to the Turtles, but they had fewer hits. They only had one top ten record, "Sunday Will Never Be the Same." Because of the Gang's clean image, when Seiter joined they nicknamed him "the Chief" to explain his very long hair—he wasn't Indian.

The group's producer used studio musicians on their records. "We were offering Seiter a chance to play on our records, to be one-fifth of the group, to participate in the writing and the producing and the touring," said Howard. "It was an offer he couldn't refuse. We looked upon the Turtles as a family, and a feeling of friendship and camaraderie was more important than the music we played. John Seiter is a wonderful human being, a real good soul singer and stuff, but he was never the drummer that Johny Barbata was. He was hired because he fit in so well that it was like he was already family." When Seiter joined in February 1969, the Turtles were in the top ten with "You Showed Me."

A renewed feeling of brotherhood permeated the new lineup. It was common for the band members to congregate in the middle of their tour bus and, after having smoked some grass, to collectively chant. This was not merely a ten-minute exercise, but one that often went on for hours. The various members settled into their own notes, and droning harmonies elevated the experience to an even higher plane.

No longer brash, impressionable teens, but world-wise adults in their early twenties, the search for a more valid identity compelled them to reject the former "slick Hollywood production" they were accustomed to in favor of a more artful approach. Collectively the Turtles had not heard a better rock album than *The Kinks Are the Village Green Preservation Society*. The album failed to chart on either side of the Atlantic when originally released in late 1968, but within a few years it was considered a classic, ranked at 252 in a 2003 poll of top albums conducted by *Rolling Stone*. The next best thing to being the Kinks, they reasoned, was to be produced by head-Kink Ray Davies himself—however far-fetched the fantasy was, as Ray hadn't produced anybody but the Kinks. The Turtles were in St. John's, Newfoundland, Canada, to play at the Memorial University. Because they were the farthest east and closest to England that they would be, they called Ray and introduced themselves over the telephone. Much to their surprise, he agreed to produce them.

It was an odd weekend for the Turtles. The local hotels were booked, so the band was separated—for the first time. Mark and Howard shared rooms on the third floor of a frat house. Whether it was the drugs they had taken, or the strong Newfoundland Screech they had downed, they swear the place was haunted. They worked on their new concept album. "A number of the soldiers who returned home from Vietnam told us they would be alone at night in the jungle and find comfort in the 'imagine me and you' lyrics, and envisioned being happy together with their girlfriends back home," Howard explained.

In thinking about the soldiers in Vietnam, they came up with a work about a returning quadriplegic who learns that it's not what he has, but what's in his heart that's important. The concept was titled "Stump Boy": "Stump Boy dun-dun-dun-dunt, he has no arms, he has no legs, he has nowhere to go now." Only one track was completed, the potent "We Ain't Gonna Party No More," which graced the B-side of a later Turtles single. "Youth in Asia," another song, was recorded by Flo & Eddie in 1975.

The Turtles considered Ray Davies to be one of the reigning geniuses of pop music, and there was so much idol worship on their part, they even wrote songs in the Kinks style. Ray had other reasons for coming to Los Angeles: he wanted to check up on why Warner Brothers Records was neglecting the Kinks, and he looked forward to the respite from his shaky marriage. He arrived in mid-April 1969 for a week of recording.

The Turtles were already wrestling with their unhip image when their management office received a hand-engraved invitation for the group to perform at the White House at Tricia Nixon's Masked Ball on May 10. They were aware that the president's youngest daughter had cited the group as her favorite in a magazine interview. The band wasn't aligned with the politics of President Nixon's administration and was inclined to reject the offer. Their managers presented a more reasonable context: they explained that it wasn't political, it was comparable to performing before the Queen of England, and they should do it because they were Americans.

Like so many of the Turtles' episodes, it gravitated toward the surreal. Tour manager Carlos Bernal: "We arrived the night before with the equipment. The Secret Service guys were not familiar with instrument cases, so during the inspection when they came to the trap case—the one that contained the snare drum and assorted smaller items like drum sticks and pedals—they turned it upside down, which set off the combination metronome/tuner. When they heard the rapid ticking, they thought it was a bomb and they all jumped back. They put us up against a wall. As they opened the trap case, the high pitch of the tuner went off and everybody hit the dirt. They took the device inside the White House. Ten minutes later they came back with it. It was soaking wet and the front plate had been peeled off. The next day we received a White House check for the cost."

The Turtles were met at the airport, and each member was sequestered in his own chauffeured car with an American flag flying on the front. When they arrived at the White House, each Turtle was escorted to a holding lounge and given his own dossier to hold for security clearance. Afterward, they had the freedom to wander throughout the White House, as long as they didn't go upstairs to the living quarters. They were given the Lincoln Library for a dressing room, and they prepared for the evening like they would any other, by snorting cocaine. According to Mark, "It was a fun party, they treated us nice, and the food was good. There were about 450 young adults, lots of Congressmen's and Ambassadors' kids, and boy were they wrecked." Mark was, too: he fell off the small stage five times and almost got into a fight with Pat Nugent when he hit on his wife, President Lyndon Johnson's youngest daughter Luci.

Tricia glowed with the genuine charm of a Cinderella. Her hand-held mask sparkled with crystals. She was dating the recently elected Congressman from northern Los Angeles County, Barry Goldwater, Jr. Mark told him that he voted for him, but he hadn't. The men were in tuxedos, the women in gowns. In order to make their (small) statement, the Turtles wore non-matching coats, and scarves instead of bow ties.

Inside the ballroom kids distributed SDS literature, which was a surprise as the Students for a Democratic Society was the most prominent and progressive left-wing activist organization, one at odds with the Nixon administration. The Temptations were also on the bill. That the Turtles were the first rock band to perform at the White House was overlooked at the time. Tricia sent each member of the Turtles a hand written thank-you note and a photo of the event. The Turtles' co-manager, Jeff Wald, positioned his wife, singer Helen Reddy, in the center of the photo. She was two years away from her first hit record.

The Turtles were enough of a hit that one of the guests, the daughter from one of the heads of US Steel, asked them to play at a society party in Burlingame, California. It was there that Howard went "mental." The Turtles played through five of the group's biggest hits to almost no response. The guests were so caught up in socializing they gave scant attention to the music. Problems the Turtles were experiencing had been festering for a long time. Boom! Howard broke loose and heaved chairs, lounges, and umbrellas into the pool. Mark made an effort to cover for him, explaining it as part of the act. It was obvious that Howard's actions had spoken for the whole band, but the others contained themselves. The set was cut short so that Howard could recompose. He quit the group then. He stayed home and took a lot of drugs.

"I never looked at myself as head of the band," said Howard. "I always gave way to Al's superior musical knowledge, or to a group vote of any kind. In the early days Chuck Portz used to call me the King Penguin because I strutted around the stage and the rehearsal halls like I knew what was happening, and everybody else better keep it down. But it was strictly a façade. In the Turtle years I felt quite helpless and alone. I was singing and fronting the band, but *that* was the band. I think probably deep down, psychologically, I knew that physically I had no business being there because I wasn't good looking enough to be on the cover of a teen magazine like Peter Noone [Herman's Hermits] or Mark Lindsay [Paul Revere & the Raiders]. I tried to make up for it in other ways, like singing my ass off."

The "democracy" in the Turtles reached its peak with their new album. This was due to the collective response to business pressures and the fact that Howard had recently rejoined the band after having quit in an uncharacteristic squabble. With Howard gone, the rest of the members opted to continue sharing lead vocals, an opportunity they were not ready to give up when Howard returned. This diffused one of the strengths of the group—Howard's voice—and that in the instance where they exist, the Howard-sung demos are more effective. Recording with Davies resumed on June 24. While the *Turtle Soup* title was inevitable, on the LP it turned out to be appropriate as the vocal diversity represented a true bouillabaisse.

The members were overly sensitive about the orchestral backing of their hits overshadowing their contribution as musicians. They were looking for more of an ensemble sound, similar to the *Village Green* Kinks. Without having conveyed this to Davies, Ray had prepared for an orchestra accompaniment similar to their 1967 hits. Consequently, they had Ray re-mix the album to the point where arranger Ray Pohlman's orchestrations were in the background. That not only served to dilute their effectiveness, but to defeat the purpose of involving Davies in the first place. Despite some fine recordings, it was their worst selling album since 1966's *You Baby*.

Though the Turtles' albums usually didn't get recognized for their artistic merit, British writer Tom Hibbert's definitive reference book, *The Perfect Collection*, referred to *Turtle Soup* as "one of the five very best albums of the Sixties." While this stance is certainly a subjective one, it was indeed a very special album for the Turtles, and it also ended up being the last album the group ever completed.

The Turtles still used Chicago as a Midwest hub, but with the hits having dried up they could no longer afford the Astor Tower. They now shared double rooms at the Lake Shore Drive Holiday Inn. Gone was their private plane. They now traveled in two Ford station wagons. Had there been a hit single when the album was released in late October 1969, there probably would have been more fortitude to survive the various problems that were confronting the group.

As a consequence of the influence of marijuana on the members' judgment, these otherwise smart individuals weren't as sharp as they should have been when it came to taking care of business. They were very trusting of those in their inner circle, and were not too scrutinizing when they were presented with documents to sign. A case in point was their trusted road manager Dave Krambeck. Looking for a way to improve his position, towards the end of 1967 Krambeck schemed to take over the management of the Turtles, a move that resulted in the group having eight managers in a little over two years, and a slow unraveling of their career.

Originally Bill Utley (1) traveled with the Turtles. He then hired Krambeck to be the group's road manager. Krambeck told the Turtles that Utley was screwing them over. By this time they were tired of Utley's paternalism and his demanding tour schedule, and were inclined to believe Krambeck. Krambeck told Utley that the group didn't like him and didn't want him to be their manager any longer. He colluded with White Whale, who were more than willing to get rid of the shrewd Utley in favor of someone—Krambeck—they could manipulate. Krambeck (2) worked out an agreement to buy the Turtles out of their current management contract for $250,000. He then got the Turtles to sign off on getting an advance from White Whale to make the initial $50,000 installment to Reb Foster Associates. Krambeck was in way over his head. Unbeknownst to the band, he sold half of his management of the Turtles to a New York firm, Martin Philips Management (3), for $13,000. Krambeck told them the contract was with a new talent agency. He soon missed the second installment payment to Reb Foster, and disappeared to Mexico with $27,000 of the Turtles road earnings and, temporarily, with Jim Pons' wife. What followed was a succession of road managers who became the group's manager: Rick Soderlind (4) and Charlie Galvin (5), who had married Spanky.

Because of the missed payment, Reb Foster Associates initiated a lawsuit against the Turtles for $2,500,000. Michael Philips Management also initiated a lawsuit for commissions of $85,000. Soderlind recommended attorney Rosalie Morton to sort things out. The Turtles thought they needed clearer heads to make sense of what was going on, so they cut out peyote (mescaline), magic mushrooms (psilocybin), and THC (tetrahydrocannabinol) from their regular drug regimen.

Initially the Turtles thought Morton was great. She was very protective of them and became their de facto manager. She arranged for them to hire a business management company that collected a fee of 5 percent of their earnings. She suggested that they stop hiring their friends to manage them and get a "class organization." She recommended Campbell-Silver-Cosby (6).

Roy Silver managed TV star Bill Cosby, then in production on *The Bill Cosby Show* for NBC. At the time, Bruce Post Campbell was producing a movie. The company also had a record label, Tetragrammaton, for which Deep Purple recorded their first three albums. The Turtles met with Roy Silver and liked him a lot, so they signed. It soon became apparent that Roy didn't have the time to manage the Turtles, so he assigned them to others at the firm. Within months Bill Cosby left, and the Turtles did shortly thereafter, preferring to go with two of the managers they had worked with, Jeff Wald and Ron DeBlasio (7), who broke away and started their own company.

Rosalie Morton revealed herself to be a loose cannon. She launched a costly and aggressive legal strategy that Mark and Howard said "ruined our career." Carlos Bernal estimated that they were on the road 80 percent of the time: "We'd be out on the road for three or four weeks, and come home for a week or less. Sometimes we only had enough time to change our clothes, turn in the money, and get new contracts before we had to leave again." But while they were home, their time was compromised further when members of the Turtles had to sit in depositions. Morton handled one of the cases and handed off the other to a novice attorney. Then she gave her case to an associate when she ran for Los Angeles County prosecutor. In this position she had a long career, but it was not without controversy. She was accused of misconduct numerous times and had been suspended. In one case, California Supreme Court Justice Kathryn Werdegar wrote: "Morton's actions, at times childish and unprofessional, and at other times outrageous and unethical, betrayed her trust as a public prosecutor. Her methods were deceptive and reprehensible."

The pressures mounted: the two lawsuits, a demanding touring schedule, Lee and Ted pushing the Turtles to record a more radio-friendly record that could be a hit, and there was strong evidence that White Whale hadn't paid the group all that it should have. During one six-month period, an audit revealed that the Turtles had been shorted by $160,000. They were bleeding money.

When the Turtles got to know Jeff Wald better, they realized they didn't like his personality. In January 1970, they set up a meeting with Bill Utley, the best manager they ever had. Reb Foster Associates was now big, representing Steppenwolf and Three Dog Night, the latter of whom benefitted from the initial Turtles' payment which was used to buy their equipment. Utley agreed to manage them again, and threw out the lawsuit. The Turtles then settled with Michael Philips Management by paying them $25,000. Without hits, their status declined to where they were opening up on bills headlined by Three Dog Night and Steppenwolf. Utley wanted to clean the Turtles up, told them to cut their hair and dress better. They bristled at his comments even though it was good advice.

Jerry Yester, who had worked with the Lovin' Spoonful, was slated to produce the Turtles' sixth album. The collective, we-are-all-brothers feeling had faded. The only songs submitted by the group that Lee and Ted liked were the ones written by Howard and Mark. There was tension as Al, Jim, and John attempted to infuse their concepts on Howard's and Mark's songs in order to qualify for shared songwriting credits—rather than to consider whether their ideas were what was best for the Turtles' music. Howard and Mark, with Yester's support, asserted their proprietary. Howard: "A lot of our energies were stifled during that time because you'd start to write a song, you'd bring it to the rest of the guys, and they would throw in their two-cents, and it would come out being written by the Turtles, but it wasn't anything close to the way you envisioned it. It's sort of a testimony to Mark and me that we were able to get ourselves even heard above all that democratic junk, because it really had a debilitating effect on most of the material." The in-studio resentment and outside pressures built to such a point that, in early May, the group called it quits.

"It wasn't just the pressure we were experiencing from the record label, now it was the band," Howard said. "We were growing apart. Al and Jim were trying to take the group in a country direction, which I wasn't in favor of. Because we had set ourselves up as a democracy, we were hearing, 'How come Howard's and Mark's songs are being selected by White Whale and ours aren't? That's not right.' You're right it's not right. We should be writing the songs and you guys should be history. So we broke up the band."

With most creative artists, their first, or first and second albums tend to be their best because they have had years to write their material before recording. Atypically, as the Turtles matured, their albums kept getting better. It seems likely that had the album tentatively titled *Shell Shock* been finished, it would have been the group's best.

Howard: "When we told our attorney, he said, 'Boy, are you guys stupid.' He explained that we were signed to White Whale not only as the band the Turtles, but as individuals, so we couldn't use our own names." At the time the Turtles broke up, fourteen people were on the payroll (down from twenty-two). They owed $45,000. The Turtles' suit against White Whale for unpaid royalties wasn't settled until 1974, at which time Howard and Mark, the only remaining members, were awarded a small amount of money and ownership of the Turtles' masters.

Within weeks following the dissolution of the band, Mark and Howard found themselves in Frank Zappa's new lineup of the Mothers of Invention. In the "Relevant Quotes" section of the liner notes to the

Mothers of Invention's first album, 1966's *Freak Out!*, "A noted L.A. Disc Jockey" (actually Reb Foster) is quoted as saying, "I'd like to clean you boys up a bit and mold you. I believe I could make you as big as the Turtles." When Jim Pons joined eight months later, three-fifths of the Turtles were now in the Mothers. In a not totally satisfying way, the Turtles of AM radio were now accepted by FM radio, except it was Frank's band and they received no royalties from sales of the records.

During a concert in London, Frank was seriously injured when a fan pulled him off the stage into the orchestra pit. Needing to work, most of the band members continued with Howard and Mark. As they were prevented from calling themselves the Turtles, they used The Phlorescent Leech and Eddie for their debut album on Reprise Records. It was a nickname for the Turtles' roadies, Carlos Bernal and Dennis Jones. Howard: "Carlos always asked for things: 'Can I have a cigarette; can I borrow five bucks; hey, give me the keys to your car.' He dressed flamboyantly, with an Afghan coat and scarf, and he had bushy hair. We named him the Phlorescent Leech."

Mark: "Dennis Jones was the president of his frat house at Cal State Northridge. He had short hair and wore a letterman's jacket. He looked like an Eddie, so we called him 'Eddie.' They both played guitar, and when we were thinking of producing other acts for Blimp, we were going to make an album called 'The Phlorescent Leech and Eddie' starring Carlos Bernal and Dennis Jones."

For subsequent albums—one more for Reprise, two for Columbia—they shortened their name to Flo & Eddie (Mark is Flo and Howard is Eddie). The albums were good, but none sold well enough to have made *Billboard*'s Top 200 LP chart. *The Rolling Stone Record Guide* even gave *Illegal, Immoral, and Fattening* four stars. Subsequently, Mark and Howard complained of a sinus problem: "Nobody wants to sign us." Over the next ten years they were involved with numerous projects, and then revived the Turtles (they were the only original members) for a consistent slate of dates on a yearly basis.

As Mark matured, he took more of an interest in the Turtles' business affairs. In 1992 the one-time high school class clown enrolled in college at the age of forty-five. He became the class valedictorian, graduating magna cum laude in Communications at Loyola Marymount University, and was accepted into the honor society. Two years later, in 1999, he achieved his master's degree in Film Studies and Screenwriting. An inspiration to us all, Professor Flo, as he is now sometimes called, teaches classes on screenwriting and the music business at Belmont University in Tennessee, where he is an assistant professor.

It was the Turtles that set it all in motion: "I was not pegged to be a success in adult life," Mark reflected. "Being in the band taught me about commitment and responsibility. It taught me about getting up off the ground at the lowest points, and trying to get back to the top. It taught me about humility, and how to deal with people in our most successful times so I wouldn't be thought of as somebody who relied on their success for friendship, and for anything other than it being work. I learned the ethics of work."

*   *   *

I saw Flo & Eddie play more than any other act, first on August 7, 1971, with the Mothers of Invention at UCLA's Pauley Pavilion. I loved their songs and the creative way they integrated humor into their set. On occasion I wrote an article on them, and a friendship developed. When I told them about the record label Richard and I were forming in the back room of our record store, they were supportive, and licensed us a handful of unreleased tracks from the psychedelic sessions to issue a Turtles picture disc. I paid them an advance of $1,100. It was a thrill for me to have the Turtles on a Rhino release, as unconventional as it was. I hoped that we could build our label to the point where we could do justice releasing the entire Turtles oeuvre.

In working on subsequent projects with them, I got to know them better, and got more of an understanding of how creative and funny they were offstage. I had many enjoyable times hanging out with Howard and Mark, hearing their marvelous stories told with insight and humor, and creating projects together. Visiting with them was like being a guest on "Anything Can Happen Day" on *The Mickey Mouse Club*. They were in a reggae phase where they played reggae cassettes, smoked ganja, and sprinkled the conversation with "Ya, mon!" (They even recorded an album in

Jamaica, at Tuff Gong Studios in 1981.) Then it was electronic music, nodding along to Kraftwerk. Sometimes it was work related: composing and recording soundtracks in the studio for kids' TV specials with The Care Bears and Strawberry Shortcake, or writing a TV pilot while working out of their office at Miss Universe. It's hard to imagine, but Howard and Mark escorted the Miss Teen and Miss USA contestants during the taping of the shows.

I overhauled the Turtles catalogue: improved the song selection on their original albums, added liner notes, created the two albums that should have been released but weren't, and reimagined the *Battle of the Bands* package. Howard and I re-mixed the multitrack tapes to restore the presence of Ray Davies' orchestration for Rhino's 1986 rerelease of *Turtle Soup*. I also improved the sequencing. Did we believe it would sell? No, and it only sold three thousand. We did it in service to the art.

The first extensive interviews I did with Mark and Howard were for the booklet that accompanied the three-record set, *The History of Flo & Eddie and the Turtles*. The album included the Westchester High A Capella Choir (with four members of the band) singing the school alma mater, the better Turtles' records that weren't on their *Greatest Hits*, Flo & Eddie tracks, rarities, and a recreation of their imaginative radio show. It was a fun and informative package.

On record the Turtles were pristine, polished, and accomplished. Back in their hotel rooms when they needed to let off steam and relax, they became the Rhythm Butchers. They took drugs, rotated whatever instruments were handy, and butchered pop classics of the day, all recorded on a cassette machine. Knowing that sales would be modest, we pressed up seven-inch EPs in a limited-edition series. We thought we'd keep it to a thousand, but the last few only sold in the low hundreds. Mark and Howard signed the first volume, and Jim Pons, the second. From 1980 to 1986 we released seven volumes. Howard and Mark were so into the project, they made up satin Rhythm Butchers jackets with our names on the front. More EPs were planned, but the weak sales made us less interested and we weren't motivated to complete the last five volumes. The point was made. As our *Greatest Hits* album(s) sold over 300,000 copies, there was more than enough profit to absorb whatever we lost on some of the projects, like the Rhythm Butchers.

During the Turtles days, Howard and Mark wished the group had an outstanding lead guitarist like Jeff Beck in the Yardbirds. When the Yardbirds broke up in 1968, drummer Jim McCarty and vocalist Keith Relf formed a group, Together, because they wanted to go in a musical direction like the Turtles. I thought of realizing their one-time desires by combining the relevant elements of each group. As the Yardbirds (except for Relf, who died in 1976) played well when they reunited to record as the Box of Frogs in 1984 (with Beck on three songs), I thought of flying Howard and Mark over to London to record an album with the remaining members: Beck, McCarty, bassist Paul Samwell-Smith, and rhythm guitarist Chris Dreja. It took some persuasion to convince Samwell-Smith, who preferred producing to playing bass. (He had produced the two Box of Frogs LPs, as well as successful albums by Cat Stevens and Jethro Tull.) During my phone conversation with him, when I was in London in September 1987, he expressed his frustration regarding Jeff Beck: "Sometimes he showed up for a session; other times he wouldn't." Because this would have been an expensive endeavor for us, I didn't want to risk our finances if Beck was unreliable, and didn't proceed further.

From having produced a few feature films, in 2000 I wanted to make a Turtles movie based on the dinner Howard had with Jimi Hendrix when the Turtles visited London in 1967. I thought it would be a much more manageable period in which to set a movie than one that spanned their career. I had Howard write the screenplay because of his gift for humor and dialogue, and so that it would be faithful to the events he experienced. Bill Fishman, who had directed a number of Monkees videos for us, was the director. For a low budget feature it turned out well, but no company wanted to distribute such a period piece without any stars. Billy Bob Thornton loved it and recommended it to Bob Weinstein at Dimension/Miramax, but we never heard from him. Noted music producer Brooks Arthur felt similarly, and arranged a screening for Adam Sandler, who told me it was "excellent . . . but not comedic enough" to put through his deal at Sony. So, *My Dinner With Jimi* (inspired by the 1981 feature *My Dinner With Andre*) came out on DVD and didn't come close to recouping the money Richard and I had invested. It was gratifying to have heard from a number of people, like the Bee Gees' Barry Gibb, about how well we recreated the era.

The professional relationship I had with Howard and Mark spanned the full twenty-four years I was at the label. As enjoyable and creatively stimulating working with them was, seeing how well they worked together provided a role model for me in my partnership with Richard. As friends since high school, their business relationship has lasted over fifty years.

The Rhino Label Part Two

The Capitol Years

*Harold and Richard had the audacity to create a
significant record label and a large catalog of products,
all of which were the creations and dreams of
other people and other record companies.*

—Dan Davis, Capitol Records executive, in jest, 1989

I was in a meeting room in an industrial park in Norcross, a suburb
of Atlanta. "How many of you have seen the new issue of *Newsweek?*"
Nobody raised a hand. This was not a good sign. There was a photo of
Richard and me accompanying a full-page article on Rhino. I didn't ask
the question because I was craving the recognition or attention, although
one might have thought differently had they seen me saunter around the
terminal at JFK Airport the previous afternoon with a copy in my left
hand or noticed, hours later, how many times I glanced at the priest at the
end of my row on the flight to Atlanta, until the moment he flipped past
the page bearing my picture in the copy he was reading. I arrived in New
York on October 2, 1985, from London, and it was the first time I was
able to see the new issue.

We had recently completed our distribution deal with Capitol Records,
and a number of us were visiting the branch sales offices to introduce ourselves and make short presentations. That the southern branch salesmen
weren't readers of *Newsweek*, and that none of their cronies alerted them
to the article about the music biz, was a reflection of their lack of worldli-
ness. After my presentation, Jerry Brackenridge, the head of the branch,

invited me to stay for lunch, which meant reaching my hand into a paper bucket to pull out pieces of fried chicken. As I chomped away, I would have felt more welcomed if someone had approached me with a comment like, "I really like your label," but no one did.

*   *   *

Stephen Powers, who had done some consulting for us, owned a small folk music label, Mountain Railroad Records. He got a job in the A&R department of Capitol Records and recommended us to his superiors for distribution. Record companies were still rebuilding after the recession in the early 1980s. As a result, Capitol was looking to bolster its profits and market share. The company would benefit from us in a number of ways: by taking a distribution fee on every record, by earning licensing fees, and from a markup on those records manufactured for us.

Unlike the other major labels, there were few Jews working at Capitol, and we had heard that the executives might have been anti-Semitic. Capitol had a good ol' boy culture, heavy on sports viewing. There was also a dearth of women executives. Despite our reservations, we had no alternative if we wanted to improve our distribution, so we proceeded to make a deal. It was later reported in *Billboard* that marketing vice president Walter Lee was named in a suit by a promotion exec who claimed that Lee "abused him" with a three-foot-long cattle prod, poking him repeatedly in the forearm, telling him "You're dog meat. Go back to your stall."

I contacted Bob Gibson, one of rock's most respected publicists, whom I had known in my rock writing days. Bob always impressed me as being smart and having an understanding of the business. He recommended we hire lawyer Jay Cooper to represent us as he had negotiated Tina Turner's recent signing to Capitol, and was familiar with their contracts and manner of negotiating. Jay did a decent job, and it didn't seem like it took him that long to make changes to Capitol's contract.

We didn't hire outside lawyers much. I negotiated most of the contracts myself, but I had no experience with a distribution agreement. In order to avoid the shock of receiving Cooper's legal bill, Richard and I calculated what we thought was the *most* he would charge us. Richard put the bill on my desk and wrote at the top, "Read it and Weep." The bill was for two and a half times the amount we had calculated: it totaled $27,000. There was no hourly computation. We asked Jay about it. He said he made his calculation based on the deal, as that's the way he did business. It was our first experience with the ethics of music business lawyers, and not our last. Jay did not divulge, up front, that he did not charge on an hourly basis, as most lawyers do, and he did not reveal how he calculated what to charge, and therefore his estimate of what our bill would be. He further justified his charge by saying that it included any work that was needed if there were problems with the agreement. He agreed to shave four thousand off, so Richard felt we should pay it because we didn't want to alienate him if we needed him in the future.

The change took effect in October 1985. Capitol's distribution was nation-wide, and they were contracted to pay us at the end of every month. It took well over a year following the change for us to receive the majority of the money due from our prior distributors, and some money was never collected.

For our first meeting with Don Zimmermann, the president of Capitol Records, Richard and I presented ourselves at the Capitol Tower in Hollywood wearing suits and ties. Don was unshaven and dressed casually: jeans, a loose-fitting pull-over shirt, and tennis shoes with no socks. We felt like country bumpkins dressed in out-of-place, ill-fitting suits. Next we saw the manager in charge of manufacturing. His small office looked more like a hunting club: wood paneling, green carpet, and wooden ducks. Welcome to the record business.

Despite our reservations that the Capitol guys seemed conservative, we got to know them and like them, especially national sales director Joe McFadden, president of sales Joe Mansfield, and vice presidents Dan Davis, Dennis White, and David Kronemyer. Similar to the Warner Music Group's sales division WEA, their distribution wing was named CEMA, from the first letters of the primary owned labels: Capitol, EMI, Manhattan (jazz), and Angel (classical).

Bob Cahill was a real find. Sharon Foster, our head of human resources, had worked with Bob at Integrity Entertainment Corp. (the Wherehouse Records chain) and thought he would be a good head of sales even though he had no direct experience dealing with accounts. Because we couldn't compete with the salaries the major labels were paying, our goal was to identify those who had potential, even if they lacked experience. Cahill was a man of many quirks who gave off a frenetic energy. He looked like the younger, goofy brother of movie villain Richard Widmark (*Kiss of Death*) when he played psychotic characters: the same manic grin, the same blond hair, and the same high forehead. Bob tried to look hip, with a shark's tooth dangling from his left ear, but the black plastic rims of his spectacles seemed out of place, and his thinning hair pulled back into a ponytail only made him look like he had had a cheap facelift. When he was excited, he bobbed and weaved in his office chair like a Jack-in-the-box on a spring.

After Cahill got to know Capitol's regional sales staff, we had him provide an assessment for us. As in any organization, some people were more effective than others. The South was an underperforming area for us, so he provided this overview of branch manager Jerry Brackenridge:

This is a man very paranoid about keeping his job, whose main focus is meeting his monthly quotas as dictated by the Capitol Tower. He will respond only to positive feedback, and views any negatives presented as personal attacks directed at himself and his staff. Classic big fish in a small pond syndrome; he thinks he deserves a lot of respect for being where he is for so long. He's an absolute dictator of Capitol staff in the southeast who motivates by intimidation. Acts only as administrator of branch activities, and has as little contact as possible with his account base. Doesn't work catalog product at all, ours or his. In short, an overly sensitive good 'ol boy suffering from job burnout.

Quality was one of the hallmarks by which we defined our company. We put more money and time into our reissues than other labels, resulting in records that were more satisfying to our consumers. Because cassette tapes were mass-produced at a high copying speed, they didn't sound as good as vinyl records. It took some convincing on Capitol's part to encourage us to manufacture in this format. Their reasoning was that some customers preferred the portability of cassettes, and some retailers wanted to sell them. They were right. Our vinyl always sold much more than our cassettes, but the cassettes added to our sales.

There was an important point that Jay Cooper overlooked in our contract. In most wholesale businesses, goods are sold to retailers one-way, which means they can't be returned. But returns are routine in the record business. It's often hard to predict if a new record will become a hit. Often, in anticipation of success, a label will ship a large number of records so a store won't run out if it becomes a hit and sells. If it flops, the records will be sent back to the label. Sometimes product is shipped because the label hopes that retailers will get excited and want to promote an album that appears to be a success. Sometimes this can backfire. The soundtrack from the 1978 film *Sgt. Pepper's Lonely Hearts Club Band* experienced hundreds of thousands of returns, as did a compilation of comedic moments from *The Tonight Show*.

Even though we were not in the hits business, and not subject to those kinds of returns, the Capitol contract put their company in first position regarding a lean on our assets in case they had so many returns on our product that we ended up owing them money. The stigma that 100 percent of the records we ship could be returned to us also made it difficult to obtain a bank loan. A bank loaning us money would want to be in a first position if Rhino experienced financial difficulty, so it would be paid back before any other creditor. But as Capitol was in the first position to be paid back, it made any loan to us riskier for the bank, so they were reluctant unless we got that point amended. Jay Cooper had overlooked this in the security agreement. It took some time, but we got Capitol to agree to put their company in a secondary position to any bank loan.

As much as people liked our logo character, which we named *Rocky Rhino*, we received complaints about the pimples and threatening expression. Our art director, Don Brown, thought that Rocky should move past his teen look and elected to clean up his rough skin. I had Scott Shaw, an artist Bill Stout recommended, create an alternative standing Rocky logo in a position copied from sixties label Parrot (which released records by Them and the Zombies). Don devised a new typeface for the company name inspired by another of my favorite sixties labels, Immediate Records. Immediate was an independent company cofounded by the Rolling Stones manager, Andrew Loog Oldham. It had noteworthy artists—Small Faces, the Nice, Amen Corner—hip graphics, and clever slogans such as "Happy to be a part of the industry of human happiness."

Billy Vera and the Beaters generated Rhino's only US hit. With a recording career stretching back to the 1960s, Billy Vera (born William McCord) made some headway as a songwriter and artist, but had failed to break into the Top 30. Richard regularly saw his band play around town, so Billy felt comfortable approaching him about reissuing the album he had released in 1981 that was now out of print. Because so many of his fans had requested it, Billy told Richard that he wouldn't lose money. Richard turned the project over to Rhino's head of A&R, Gary Stewart, to work with Billy on creating *By Request*, a new compilation from the two Alfa Records albums, featuring live recordings at the Roxy Theatre in West Hollywood. Billy rerecorded one of those songs, "At This Moment," at the request of the producers of the top-rated TV show *Family Ties*.

It was a song that almost didn't survive being dropped into the wastebasket. When Billy was thirty-three, he met a beautiful, twenty-year-old woman. On their first date she told him about breaking up with her boyfriend. Billy wrote a song from her boyfriend's perspective, but he couldn't figure out a way to finish it. In most cases he would have thrown it away, but this time he didn't. He dated that girl, but it wasn't until she dumped him a year later that he knew how the song should end. Alfa had originally released Billy's recording as a single, but it only got up to number 79 on the *Billboard* chart.

Our reissue was selling moderately, certainly in line with Billy's projections. The producers used the song again on *Family Ties*, this time on back-to-back episodes when the main characters Alex (Michael J. Fox) and Ellen (Tracy Pollan) were having difficulties with their romance. Fans referred to it as *Alex and Ellen's theme song*, and that exposure made the record a hit. Rhino's young marketing and sales force rose to the occasion and the record hit the top of the charts in January 1987—all without having to spend any money paying independent promoters, a questionable and very costly practice that the labels felt they had to support. We could have sold more, but one of Brackenridge's sales guys, one of the two who covered Florida, didn't know that Vera's hit was one his company distributed.

In early 1987, as "At This Moment" ascended the charts, I placed a call to Seymour Stein—with whom I hadn't spoken since that encounter at MIDEM—to see if he had any suggestions on which companies would be good to license the record to in foreign territories. Seymour was known for his knowledge of the international market. When his secretary told him I was on the line, I could hear him ask her, "Is he calling about the money I owe him?" He took the call. I told him that's not why I phoned, but he wasn't much help.

At the end of January I attended MIDEM again, since I was in charge of licensing the album to other countries. Unlike my previous time at the convention, I could set up as many meetings as I wanted, as it was rare for somebody to have a record that was currently number one in America available for licensing. The biggest advance I was offered was from Fanfare Records in England, whose head of A&R, Simon Cowell— later of *American Idol* and *X Factor*—loved the record.

Prior to his hit rejuvenating his recording career, the forty-two-year-old Vera was scraping together a living: a trickle of songwriting royalties, infrequent acting jobs, and club dates with his band. He said, "I don't know what I would have done if it weren't for Rhino." Fox and Pollan married in real life, after which Fox said they couldn't get on a dance floor anywhere in the world without the song being played by a DJ or band. The album sold well enough for the RIAA to certify it a gold album. Customarily, a framed award would be sent to the artist and to the record company. In gratitude for our company-wide success, Richard and I bought gold records for all of our employees.

Dennis White, who made our distribution deal and was a supporter of our label, told us about imminent changes at Capitol. They were bringing in Joe Smith to head the label. Smith had built his reputation growing Warner Brothers Records with Mo Ostin. He was a legendary figure to me. I became familiar with the Warner execs from reading the label's clever in-house *Circular* magazine (with contributions from John Mendelsohn and Jim Bickhart). Joe was affable, a raconteur. He introduced himself to me backstage when the Faces played the Long Beach Arena in July 1971. I don't know if he thought I was a member of the band, or merely responded to the Jethro Tull English-styled t-shirt I wore that Warner had given away as part of a promotion.

Joe fared less well when he next ran Elektra/Asylum. The label lost $27 million in his last two years as chairman. Dennis said the decision to bring in Joe was based on his relations with successful acts, which he could then lure over to Capitol.

Joe's office at Capitol was more befitting a basketball executive than a record company president. There were framed photos of Lakers players displayed around the room, but nothing that showed any interest in music. Joe was a courtside season ticket holder to the Lakers' games. We had a meeting during which I was expecting Joe to congratulate us on having had our biggest sales month, but it never came. As we were leaving, I mentioned it to him, and he responded that he had known, but I don't think he'd been aware. Despite White's expectation, the only big name signing Joe made was ex-Warner act the Doobie Brothers. Capitol revived their flagging career, but only had one big-selling album with them.

We didn't get off to a good start with Joe. Not long after he became president he signed Billy Vera. Neither Joe nor the other execs at Capitol had the courtesy to discuss this with us or to consider that we might have wanted to sign Billy to a new deal ourselves. Billy didn't tell us, either. Even though we didn't have Billy signed as an artist to Rhino, it felt as though Capitol, our distributor, had stolen Billy away from us. They even provided some icing on the cake by getting Billy a star on the Hollywood Walk of Fame, right in front of the Capitol Tower. Joe claimed that he hadn't been at the label long enough to have been aware of our relationship.

There were other problems. Rhino had, potentially, two new albums that could compete with Vera's Capitol debut. One was a soundtrack for the Blake Edward's film *Blind Date*, which featured three of Billy's songs, and we also could have released the other Alfa Records tracks. We worked things out, but neither side prospered. *Blind Date*, despite starring Bruce Willis and Kim Basinger, fared only modestly at the box office. Our soundtrack made *Billboard's* album chart for one week; Capitol's album didn't even chart. We felt marginalized by the incident.

That ruffling of our feathers notwithstanding, we were doing well. In 1986, our first full year distributed by CEMA, our sales doubled. Our reissues sold consistently, and we had a significant number of sales as Billy and the Beaters went up the charts. Most of all we benefitted from the Monkees revival, charting with six of our Monkees albums. Along with Arista's *Greatest Hits*, the Monkees matched Led Zeppelin and U2 in having had seven albums charting concurrently on *Billboard's* Top Pop

Albums chart in the 1980s. We sold 150,000 copies each of the Monkees' first two albums.

In 1987 our sales nearly doubled again, to over $14 million. Billy and the Beaters and a newly recorded album by the Monkees were our best sellers. We also benefitted from a licensing deal I made for the Bearsville catalogue, of which Todd Rundgren and Foghat were the biggest selling artists. In October we were able to hire our first in-house attorney, my friend Bob Emmer. We now had a staff of fifty.

Richard and I went to an antique advertising fair at the Pasadena Civic Center. We were surprised to see a couple of vendors selling newly made 78 rpm records of older hits. It was clear these were unlicensed bootlegs copied from records. Richard had a vintage jukebox and explained that these machines only played 78s. A collector could retool his machine to play 45s—which were available to purchase—but then the value of his jukebox would decrease. We decided to produce a proper set that sounded good, unlike these bootleg recordings, or the worn 78s a collector found at swap meets and thrift stores. *Jukebox Classics* included fifty hits on twenty-five discs in a box. Although we only sold a little more than a thousand, it was profitable because the list price was high at $125. This odd item befuddled the CEMA salesmen. It sold well enough that we followed it up two years later, and then a third box in 1993 of masters from the Atlantic catalogue.

Richard encouraged inclusiveness, which resulted in employees feeling more connected to the company. He had employees who would otherwise not be credited on an album added in the *thank you* sections even if their contributions were nil. The fallout was too many meetings and, at times, a too-many-cooks-spoil-the-broth lack of effectiveness.

I had a number of ideas for our tenth anniversary, but many were stalled by the committee process. Jeff Gold, now working at A&M Records, produced a twenty-fifth anniversary book for them, and I was looking to make one for us. It never happened. Our anniversary party was held at the Santa Monica Pier on November 12, 1987. It was a good one, complete with a roving doo-wop group and rides on the Ferris wheel. I was able to entice enough celebrities to have attracted a multipage feature in *Mojo* magazine, had it existed at the time: Arthur Lee and Bryan MacLean

(Love), Howard Kaylan and Mark Volman (the Turtles), Ron and Russell Mael (Sparks), Spencer Davis, Greg Kihn, Walter Egan, Billy Vera, Gloria Jones and her son Rolan Bolan, and the Firesign Theatre. The primary reason for putting effort and expense into an anniversary is to benefit from the press and media exposure, while the celebration is secondary. I was disappointed that we got no TV coverage or notable print articles.

In late December we moved to a much larger building in Santa Monica, formerly a machine shop, with depressions in the concrete floor where equipment had been extracted. There was lots of room to build offices, and parking spaces for seventy cars. Unlike our previous location, there were two restaurants we could walk to, and in an example of being decades ahead of a trend, there was a semi-gourmet food truck that stopped in front of our loading dock across the alley from where architect Frank Gehry had his offices.

In recognition of our tenth anniversary we asked the city of Los Angeles to proclaim a Rhino Records Day, which they designated on February 29, 1988. We rented a bus, and Richard and I, Flo & Eddie, Billy Vera, Dr. Demento, and a number of our employees made it to the mayor's office for the ceremony. Even though Mayor Tom Bradley signed the proclamation, he wasn't there, nor was the deputy mayor. In the presentation room the wind quickly dissipated from our sails. The sole newsman anchoring the area, an old-time photographer with an inch of ash oozing from the end of his cigarette, took note of our arrival. With sagging eyelids and an overall defeated look that recalled the cartoon dog Droopy, he halfway rose from the bench where he was sitting before he decided that we weren't worthy enough to merit a few snaps for the *Los Angeles Times*. A lower member of the mayor's staff made the presentation.

At a party at director Bill Fishman's house, I met Catherine Hardwicke, who impressed me with her intelligence and creativity. She is best known as the director of *Twilight* and *Thirteen*, but she was then a production designer, most recently on the short-lived *New Monkees* TV show. Rhino owned a small truck that we took to the set in Valencia and came away with a few abandoned items: a couple of plastic cacti and a chair covered in plastic leaves. The fish-tank coffee table had already been taken. I had Catherine redesign our lobby into a (Rhino) safari motif. A year later, after Richard and I bought back into the Rhino store, I had her design the expansion.

Because we were growing as a company, Richard and I needed to learn more about managing our employees. Neither of us were natural or charismatic leaders. We were more like introverted scientists tinkering on projects in the lab. We loved music, we loved putting together the records we put out, we had a feel for business, but we had no experience and no training to manage a rapidly growing staff. We had both read *How to Win Friends and Influence People* by Dale Carnegie when we were in our teens. Rereading that book helped us. Carnegie recommends refraining from criticizing and to express appreciation for others' efforts. Richard turned me on to Tom Peters' *In Search of Excellence* (cowritten with Robert Waterman, Jr.). Some of the ideas we had already adopted, like getting feedback from our customers, which we had done even in the store days. Some we were in the process of finding out, like emphasizing our strengths, our reissues. Others we embraced, like considering employees as assets of the company and not micromanaging them.

I had heard about the culture of employment in Japan, where employees were considered part of a family, where they had their jobs until they retired. I liked that concept. While I wanted to cut good deals for Rhino, and wanted us to make a good profit, profit wasn't my main goal. I thought the product—with support from the organization—would naturally drive profits. I wanted anyone who had a job to be productive and contribute, and I liked the idea of having motivated employees. I thought it benefitted the company in the long run.

Compared to other businesses—even ones in the desired entertainment industry—working at Rhino was like floating through the good-vibes atmosphere in a Donovan song. Even though we had a lot of motivated employees, Richard and I were surprised at how many seemed to be angry or bitter. For many, it was their first real job, and they didn't have anything to compare their good fortune to. Those who had worked for other record companies valued their experience at Rhino, feeling that they were part of the company, not merely employees. We both would have preferred a more intimate work force of thirty or so, but we couldn't stand in the way of progress.

Richard, more easily than I, grasped the structural and human resources needs of the company. We both were open to contributions from other employees. Marc Bolan (Rolan's father) had expressed to me that he didn't care where an idea came from. He gave an example of a taxi driver who happened to be in the recording studio making a suggestion. He said that if it were a good one, he would adopt it. It made sense to me. As most of our employees would presumably be into music, we wanted them to feel that they could express themselves. If they felt they could participate, they would be more motivated. A case in point was our *Golden Throats* series, a cousin to film's *Golden Turkey*, the so-bad-it's-good concept. Two guys in our warehouse, Gary Petersen and Pat Serchio, amused themselves by challenging each other to find the worst recordings by celebrities, the best-known example being William Shatner's overly dramatic reading of the Beatles' "Lucy in the Sky with Diamonds." They brought the idea to us and we allowed them to compile an album. The first one was released in May 1988 and sold 57,000.

In April 1987 Gene Simmons (of the band Kiss) made a presentation at our marketing meeting. He and I had become friendly. He was one of three people to contact me after our article appeared in *Newsweek*, in response to my comment that we wanted to produce movies. We developed a project together. He was at Rhino to pitch us on backing him in a heavy metal label. The genre had been sweeping the nation, to the point where even the most mediocre of bands were selling. It seemed like a good idea, but, as we found out later, we were behind the curve.

In our discussion after Gene's departure, Bob Cahill expressed that he didn't think his name added much value. He reasoned that since Gene had shown no exercise of taste in his professional life, why did we need him when we could do it ourselves? Richard and I weren't into the music, but we felt that we needed to acknowledge our younger employees' desires to participate in the careers of living, breathing artists, instead of old codgers who might still be on the revival circuit. We liked Cahill, and felt like rewarding both him and the project's other main proponent, Dave Darus, who did a stellar job working the Billy Vera record even though it was his first job in radio promotion.

Starting a heavy metal label wasn't that original of an idea, and while it was questionable that our tight purses would have been able to accommodate Gene, I felt compromised because we had appropriated his idea. To his betterment, he made a deal with RCA Records for Simmons Records—the logo, tellingly, depicted a bag of money. Our label, Rampage, made good use of an alternate—not Rocky—rhinoceros logo. The first of our six newly recorded albums came out in March 1988. Overall the venture lost money for us. We only had one successful release, the first album by Nitro. The image that represents the whole affair to me was when Richard and Bob Emmer were corralled by the group into hearing a preview of their second album played at ear-splitting volume in their van with marijuana smoke spilling out, just like in a Cheech and Chong movie. The group's first album sold 50,000; the second, 11,000.

Back in the store days, Richard would occasionally play a record by the Village People although we weren't disco fans. Their songs were melodic and fun, even though the group—other than lead Victor Willis—didn't sing on their records. In the ensuing years, their hit "Y.M.C.A." had become de rigueur at teen parties. Never mind that the kids are oblivious that the song celebrates a pickup place for young gay men. The vocal group only had three Top 30 hits, and had been off the charts for nine years when PolyGram agreed to license us a greatest hits album. We thought it would sell well, but were surprised at how much. Another of Richard's (sort-of) jokes had turned into a big seller.

While companies tend to flaunt—or even inflate—their success, we purposely tried to downplay ours. We thought it would be best to be below the radar, or else the major labels would take more notice of what we were doing, to our detriment. As royalty payments rolled into our licensors, our impressive sales became apparent. When PolyGram noticed that our *Village People Greatest Hits* had sold so well—ultimately 188,000 copies—they denied our request to extend our three-year license and put out their own hits album. The same thing happened with Stephen Bishop's *Best of Bish*. Also released in 1988, it sold 54,000 and was still selling when MCA Records turned down our renewal so they could issue their own version.

The first time this happened was when Capitol declined our request to extend the rights to our 1984 *Best of the Spencer Davis Group* for the

CD format. We had sold almost 40,000 copies on vinyl and cassette. Capitol, instead, produced their own CD. It wasn't a matter of Capitol considering which company would best serve the music, it was pure economics: Capitol thought they would make more money by releasing their own CD rather than extending the rights to Rhino. There were reasons why our reissues were usually better than any other label's: we grew up with the music and understood its impact, and it was a priority to do a great job and to get it right. As an example, Capitol's *The Best of the Spencer Davis Group* CD (issued in 1987 on the EMI American label) featured a photo on the front that didn't include Stevie Winwood, the lead singer on such hits as "I'm a Man" and "Gimme Some Lovin'." Stevie and his brother Muff left the group in 1967. The photo depicted the subsequent lineup, with only two members of the original band who played on the tracks. For our package I tracked down rare photos, including an impressive shot for the cover. I had Spencer Davis write the liner notes. Actually I assembled them, from an interview I had conducted with him in 1971. I used only his comments, and attributed the notes to him. Our packages always included composer credits, which theirs lacked. Aside from our loss of revenue, as record fans, the displays of incompetence were infuriating.

As a consequence of the major labels being more proprietary, we had to be more creative in general, and in coming up with ideas for compilations featuring many artists. If a label wanted to hold onto their artists for a best of album, they still might license us a hit for one of our compilations. Richard came up with the idea to package hits CDs endorsed by the *Billboard* name, as in *Billboard* magazine, the record industry's main trade publication. While the majors and other labels usually offered their oldies product at budget and midline prices, Rhino's were mostly at full list price. The mass marketing rack jobbers had a problem with that. (Rack jobbers typically provided product to retailers that didn't have their own music buyers, one example being a section in a discount department store.) Despite our quality, they were reluctant to pay more for oldies available at lesser price points. As the racks were responsible for a large number of sales, Richard came up with a lower-priced series we could feel comfortable releasing.

It was also a move to legitimize "the hits" concept. Companies whose brands were familiar from TV advertising, like K-tel, often used versions of hits that had been rerecorded and didn't come close to approximating the original records. In contrast, we were dedicated to using the original hits and making them sound good. We released our first four volumes of *Billboard Top Rock 'n' Roll Hits* in June 1988. It proved to be extremely profitable and became Rhino's best-selling series. Six of our albums qualified for gold records, all of them hits from the '80s.

When I first listened to my import copy of *Five Live Yardbirds*—the only full album the group recorded when Eric Clapton was a member—the playing sounded too fast. I attributed it to the excitement of London's Marquee Club audience or the amphetamines rock groups routinely consumed in 1964, when the live recording was made. But the reason was a simpler one: it was sped up in the mastering. Bill Inglot proved his value once again when he corrected the speed for our May 1988 rerelease.

Also that month Cahill met with representatives from Author Services Incorporated (ASI), the company that licensed L. Ron Hubbard's works. Although best known as the founder of Scientology, Hubbard had started out as a writer of pulp fiction. He had written lyrics for a number of songs based on his best-selling science fiction book series *Mission Earth*. They had Edgar Winter compose the music and produce an album from Hubbard's lyrics. We invited the ASI reps to attend our next marketing meeting, at which point they explained that from their research, they determined that Rhino was the most creative at marketing among all the record companies, and that's why they called us. We couldn't help being flattered and responsive to their proposal. Hubbard's publisher was marketing *Dianetics*, his guide to Scientology, as having sold eight million copies. Cahill thought there could be easily one in ten readers who were so devoted to Hubbard that they would buy our album. One in ten didn't seem unreasonable. If so, that would mean 800,000 albums sold.

Mark Volman was a fan of the books, and assured me that they had nothing to do with Scientology. Despite our high regard for Edgar Winter's musical ability, we were not impressed by the finished product and should have declined, but we were eager for the sales we anticipated, and we liked the people we met with. Richard came up with a great idea, which was to make the first 3-D promotional video. Elvira had performed a low-budget representation that aired on her local TV show, *Elvira's Movie Macabre*. We hired the people she used, and spent $35,000 making it, by far the most we had ever spent on a rock video. Much to our disappointment, the 3-D effect didn't work very well and neither did the video. After consulting with ASI, we didn't circulate the video. As a company we were good about not wasting money, and I felt sick that we received no benefit from that expense. We did market the record, but radio stations weren't interested in playing it. It was released in June 1989 and sales only managed a little more than 15,000, far short of our expectations.

At the video shoot I met Edgar and his wife, and was impressed at how nice they were. Edgar made it a point to tell me that he was no longer a member of the church of Scientology. I thought that as long as we were promoting this new album, we should try to license a "best of." Gary Petersen, a big fan of Winter's who we promoted to assist in the A&R department, compiled the album. Whatever money we lost on *Mission Earth* we more than made up for on *The Edgar Winter Collection*, which sold 80,000.

All of a sudden, independent film companies were contacting us about buying our company. Over the course of a year, we met with the heads of New Line Cinema (*Nightmare on Elm Street*), Carolco (*Rambo, Terminator*), and Atlantic Releasing (*Valley Girl, Teen Wolf*). Independently of each other, they thought that it would be a good idea to own a record company with a consistent revenue stream during periods in which they didn't have any new movies in the theaters. Maybe they all used the same consultant.

In the spring of 1989 we met with Bob Shaye and members of his New Line staff on two occasions. We liked Bob, and saw a similarity to Rhino in how his business developed: from distributor of underground films to success with producing low budget ones. Ultimately, Shaye had second thoughts, owing to his unfamiliarity with the record business. Atlantic Releasing (not affiliated with Atlantic Records) and Carolco soon went bankrupt. New Line was bought by Turner Broadcasting Systems, and later became absorbed by Warner Brothers Pictures.

Although I had met the other three Beatles, briefly—George Harrison told me, "I quite liked your Carl Perkins album"—I had two meetings with Ringo Starr. His best of, *Blast From Your Past*, was one of Capitol's most consistent sellers. After leaving the label, Ringo made five subsequent albums, but the quality didn't approach that of his earlier work. Still, I thought enough fans would want to own a best of volume two, and thought we could compile a decent album from the better tracks of those five. When Ringo expert Risty Alexander and I arrived at Ringo's hotel room at L'Ermitage in Beverly Hills at 5 p.m. on September 2, 1988, Ringo and his wife, Barbara, were preparing to eat their breakfast of cold cereal. While Risty and I waited on the sofa fifteen feet away, I was struck by Ringo's inhospitality. He failed to offer us something to eat, or even a glass of water.

When we conferred, he was congenial but low-key. He showed us the bootlegged *Sgt. Pepper's* t-shirt he wore under a long-sleeve shirt. Barbara, seemingly dissatisfied with the luxury hotel, asked me about the Four Seasons, as if I had stayed there and could offer an assessment. Our second meeting, four months later, was at the Four Seasons. Ringo approved of our track listing, said he would help with the promotion, and suggested a photo for our cover that had been an unused shot for a previous album.

Starr Struck: Best of Ringo Starr Vol. 2 was released in February 1989. Early the following month, I received a letter from Ringo telling us how pleased he was with the finished product. Six months later I heard from Risty, who bumped into Ringo's manager, Hilary Gerrard, at one of Ringo's concerts. Gerrard told him that he was "angry" at Rhino because of our lack of promotion. Irked, I fired off a letter in which I told him what we did, and pointed out that Ringo had done nothing to promote it. He did no interviews and didn't play a single song from the compilation on that summer's inaugural Ringo and His All-Starr Band tour. We did what we could, and in the first nine months of release had moved more copies than *Blast From Your Past*, which sold at a cheaper, midline price. His Capitol album boasted seven top ten hits. Ours had none. We sold 24,000 over the life of the project.

We re-signed with Capitol for another three-year period, and we were able to improve our deal. There were some additional points: one identified specific Capitol artists that we could release compilations on, and another stipulated that Capitol's promotion department had to work a minimum number of our new artists to radio.

One of the reasons we re-signed was that the new head of EMI Music, Joe Smith's boss, was Jim Fifield. He had come from General Mills (breakfast cereals) and CBS/Fox Video, and didn't have any previous record business experience. When he told us that Rhino was one of his two favorite labels—along with blues label Alligator—we thought we now had influence at the top. But his presence didn't really improve our relationship with the company. The only advice we got from him was to abandon signing new artists. Of course he was right, in that they usually lost money.

Fifield was hired with a mandate to increase market share for EMI worldwide: that is, to increase EMI's and Capitol's sales compared to all the other companies in the industry. After a few years Fifield received enormous bonuses—over $10 million in one year—not linked to profitability, but to an increase in market share. As a business owner, I thought any bonus payment not linked to a company's profit was short sighted. More egregiously, in our modern era, top executives often get stock options that they can exercise regardless of a company's profitability. A stock can increase rapidly, an executive can cash in, and then the stock can go down.

Capitol became our partners in purchasing a few catalogues of master recordings, most importantly, Roulette Records. We couldn't fund the entire purchase price, and since we were based in the United States, we made the deal for the rights in North America with Capitol kicking in for the rest of the world. As we were joint venturing on catalogues, and with our sales exceeding our projections, Capitol could have been eyeing us for a larger role. They could have bought Rhino and made our company their reissue division.

Adrian Harewood in our finance department showed me printouts of our inventory indicating that Joe Smith had requisitioned over two hundred of our albums to send to his friends. From my time as a rock writer in my twenties, I saw the liberal disbursements of promotional copies of albums to writers, radio programmers and DJs, and to buyers. Joe, no doubt, was used to allocating whatever he wanted, even if it wasn't for business purposes. But, as the president of the label, when he sent out

Capitol product, Capitol paid for it. When he sent out Rhino product, we paid for it. I didn't think promotional copies were an effective marketing expense, and I tried to limit how many we allocated. I also looked upon our line as having value, and the more promotional copies out there devalued it. Promotional records tended to end up in the used bargain bins of record stores. Having run the Rhino store, Richard and I were all too familiar with the practice. Through an intermediary, we brought our concerns to Joe's attention. He promised not to do it again, but he never reimbursed us for the expense.

In July 1989 we released a double album anthology by the Righteous Brothers, a white soul duo who were best known for the hits "You've Lost That Lovin' Feelin'" and "(You're My) Soul and Inspiration." The album was selling nicely when, a year later, the haunting strains of their version of "Unchained Melody" were featured in the hit movie *Ghost*. It rekindled interest in them and our release flew off the shelves, garnering us a gold record and sales of 335,000.

As Gary Stewart was younger than Richard and me, he brought an added perspective and an appreciation for newer music. He noticed that a lot of hits that he enjoyed listening to on the radio as a teen were not easily available, songs like "Billy, Don't Be a Hero" by Bo Donaldson and the Heywoods, "Na Na Hey Hey Kiss Him Goodbye" by Steam, "In the Summertime" by Mungo Jerry, "Reflections of My Life" by the Marmalade, and "Julie, Do Ya Love Me" by Bobby Sherman. Realizing that these artists were not considered critical favorites and wanting a fun series, Gary, with Garson's input, titled it *Have a Nice Day: Super Hits of the '70s*. The initial four volumes were released in April 1990, with four more a month later. We thought it would be a success but were surprised by how much. The series grew to twenty-five volumes, with half moving over 100,000 copies.

As it relates to the concept of so-bad-it's-good, or so-bad-let's-make-fun-of-it, I launched *The Rhino Awards*. It was inspired by *The Golden Raspberry Awards*, which "awarded" the worst films, filmmakers, and actors of the previous year. The underlying reason was that quite often in the Grammys, as voted on by the recording professionals who are members of the organization NARAS (National Academy of Recording Arts & Sciences), artists of substance are often ignored in favor of those who are ephemeral. This was particularly true in the first ten years or so, when rock artists got the short shrift. A case in point was the disco vocal act A Taste of Honey, who was awarded a Grammy Award for Best New Artist of 1978—over Elvis Costello, the Cars, and Toto—largely on the strength of their fatuous number one hit "Boogie Oogie Oogie." I named our award for worst new artist after them.

I invited the media to attend the presentation on February 19, 1991, a day before the Grammy Awards ceremony, at Canter's Delicatessen. I tabulated the votes submitted by members of the music press, some of whom were presenters at the breakfast event. The winners didn't show, but we had awards made: a wooden rhino painted gold on a wood base with a brass nameplate. Other awards were The Leroy Neiman Award for worst artist (not picked up by Vanilla Ice) and The Carl "Kung Fu Fighting" Douglas Award for most inferior single.

We got good coverage in the local media, TV news, as well as print. As our visibility was rising in the industry, Richard didn't feel we should risk offending a winning executive, so we discontinued it after that first year, point made. Still, there was a direct link between the attitude we expressed in sending up a successful act like Led Zeppelin on our 1978 kazoo record and the Rhino Awards.

In similar spirit I wrote a letter to the RIAA concerning our Billy Vera gold record. The RIAA audits a distributor's sales to determine that, in this case, at least 500,000 albums have been shipped out. But what happens when, as with our album, so many unsold records were returned that net sales dipped below that amount? After a number of weeks without a response, I called the RIAA. The woman I spoke with seemed flummoxed, as no one had ever asked them that before. She said they only certified on records shipped—not sold—and we didn't have to relinquish our gold record awards. The point I made was that just because a record had received gold or platinum status didn't necessarily mean that it truly sold at those levels; tens of thousands—if not hundreds of thousands—of records could have remained unsold. Subsequent sales of Vera's *By Request* were slow, but steady, eventually recouping those deficient sales, and netting at 510,000.

Our sales in 1990 were $32 million, and we were hopeful of hitting $35 million in 1991, at which point we got a reduction in the distribution fee we paid Capitol. We were to vastly exceed that, with $42 million in sales. One of the records that helped to get us there was a reissue of soul singer Betty Wright's 1978 live album. Wright was only seventeen when she recorded her best-known hit, 1971's "Clean Up Woman." *Betty Wright Live* was so well considered by her fans that it sold over 300,000 copies for us.

Another successful release in 1991 came from an uncommon source, the artist himself. Johnny Rivers had a slew of hits, including "Memphis," "Secret Agent Man," and "The Poor Side of Town." He lobbied Richard for a more extensive collection of his work than what was available from Capitol Records. (Most of his hits had been on Imperial, which Capitol owned.) We had our reservations because we didn't see how our double album anthology could compete effectively with Capitol's album. Theirs was available at a midline price (a tier below front line product); ours would cost twice as much. Johnny assured us that it would do well despite the price difference. Because we were distributed by Capitol, and because of Johnny's support, Capitol licensed us the tracks we needed. Johnny was right. *The Johnny Rivers Anthology 1964-1977* sold 155,000 for Rhino.

A stigma we faced was employees who wanted more action, who craved the excitement of working a contemporary artist, rather than being satisfied by Rhino's commitment to preserving and presenting the great music of the past. Cahill excelled at Rhino and was now socialized enough to attract an offer from SBK Records at two and a half times his Rhino salary—even though it was more expensive to live in Manhattan. As a company, we lost something when Cahill departed.

Even more of a disappointment was Toby Mamis. I met him in October 1972 when he was the publicist for the Hollies, whom I interviewed for a feature in *Rolling Stone*. We hit it off immediately. As I got to know Toby, I thought he was the smartest person I had met in the music business. Toby worked for us for four months as a full-time consultant, but his heart wasn't in it. Despite our friendship, his work was uninspired. He left to take a position in management working for Shep Gordon, whose main client was Alice Cooper. Toby was given an opportunity to sign acts to manage and commission. He had a long run in Shep's employ, but never found a hit act to manage. Had Bob and a motivated Toby both stayed at Rhino, presumably the company would have benefitted, as well as their careers and bank accounts. For Richard, Gary, Brian, Garson, myself, and others, we felt as though we were on a mission. Other employees didn't feel the same way and had no qualms about taking jobs with larger companies. Despite the fine work we were doing, and our impressive increases in sales, many thought of us as belonging to the minor leagues.

In the spring of 1991, with a year remaining on our contract, we weren't feeling appreciated by our distributor. Around the time we made our deal with Capitol in 1985, they had signed Heart, a rock band from Seattle fronted by a pair of beautiful sisters. Heart had been very successful, but their sales had declined by the time they signed with Capitol. The company did a great job, not only reviving them, but also selling more albums than they had previously. With their albums averaging three million each, Capitol made a lot of money from the act. Typically a label in that situation would be responsive to a big moneymaker like Heart. Capitol's profits from Rhino's sales were comparable—over six million in 1991. (The money Capitol made from Rhino was all without risk. For a new artist, Capitol furnished recording costs, an advance of royalties that might not be earned back, tour support, and costly allocations for marketing and radio promotion.)

By comparison, we felt slighted. Capitol's radio department failed to promote the two projects we gave them, breaching that provision in the agreement. We were supposed to have been able to reissue a small number of Capitol's artists. These were not big selling ones, like the Beach Boys—but the Classics IV, the Raspberries, Canned Heat, and others. Capitol knowingly breached this provision, so they could reissue them on their own label. We hadn't known it at the time, but Smith and Fifield had their eyes on bigger game. With a mandate to increase market share, within the year Capitol/EMI bought Virgin Records for $957 million and the other half of Chrysalis Records they didn't already own. Smith didn't give Rhino much consideration. Nobody thought we would leave.

Had Capitol treated us right, we could have easily re-signed with them. We also felt that given the inconsistencies in their sales department, we could improve our distribution with another company. We had a few meetings with other labels, but there wasn't much enthusiasm. Randy Friedman set up a lunch for us with Mo Ostin. Mo seemed more interested in asking us about Joe Smith than in learning about Rhino.

Richard and I met with a couple of execs from PolyGram. Zach Horowitz was now at MCA Universal, and we met with him and Irving Azoff. The entrance to the wing housing Azoff's office was like entering a bank vault. Of anybody we met, Azoff was the most interested, but MCA had less stature than Capitol. A couple of months later, Azoff was gone. We took a follow-up meeting with his replacement, Al Teller, who opened the meeting with, "So, why are you here?"

John Branca pitched Rhino to Bob Morgado, the Chairman of the Warner Music Group, but he wasn't interested. A few months later, Alan Lenard met with Morgado regarding Warner's interest in buying his client Fantasy Records (whose best-selling artist had been Creedence Clearwater Revival). Morgado asked him that if Warner bought it, what would they do with it, who would they get to run it? Alan knew of our situation and suggested that Morgado could make a deal with Rhino, and then we could manage the Fantasy catalogue. Morgado sent Paul Vidich, his VP of mergers and acquisitions, to meet with Richard and me in July 1991. Branca and his associate, Gary Stiffelman—and much later, Lenard, insinuating himself into the deal—commenced negotiations. (Warner never bought Fantasy.)

The Warner Music Group's policy was that any new company had to come in through one of the original three labels: Warner, Elektra, or Atlantic. As we were based on the West Coast, it made sense for us to come in through Warner Brothers, which was headquartered in Burbank. But Morgado and Ostin were having a minor feud. Morgado looked to Rhino to bolster a floundering Atlantic Records, benefitting label head Doug Morris, with whom he had a good relationship. It wasn't as if Doug was a Rhino fan. He was reluctant and only agreed to the deal when Morgado assured him that the Warner Music Group would absorb any losses from the joint venture. Warner Music Group CFO Jerry Gold put it this way: "It was odd that we had to shove it down Doug's throat."

We weren't used to such extensive and detailed negotiations. It seemed like everything was a big deal. As the owners of our company, Richard and I could do whatever we both agreed upon: we had our own video division, we had produced a TV pilot (for NBC), we published books, we wanted to produce movies, we had an idea for a Rhino-themed restaurant, and we had recently bought back into the Rhino store. In our negotiations, all of these areas had to be discussed, and by a group of lawyers whose specialty was the record business.

We wanted to exclude the Rhino store, but they wanted it part of the joint venture, even though they had no understanding of retail. It was a poor move on their part as they had to absorb significant losses from the store years later. They were also proving difficult with respect to Rhino Films. We would have preferred that it would have been part of the joint venture, but as feature film production was very risky, I couldn't blame them for excluding it. They were fine with Richard and me having those interests in a separate company, but then they balked because of a prior agreement Warner Brothers Pictures had with two Japanese conglomerates, Itochu and Toshiba. If Richard and I, employees of a Time Warner joint-venture company, had a blockbuster hit independently of Warner Brothers, then those companies wouldn't have benefitted from the small percentages they owned.

The negotiations got me so frustrated that during a break I called Zach from the Warner conference room to see if I could rekindle MCA's interest. I thought we should be with a West Coast label—MCA was in Universal City—and with people we knew, like Zach. Zach has many fine qualities, but he is not an entrepreneur or a visionary, so what he suggested was not enough to make me want to abandon our current discussions.

It was imperative that the negotiations include a number of titles from Atlantic's catalogue. Atlantic used that to leverage a 50 percent ownership in Rhino, in addition to a minimal amount of cash, to create a joint venture, as the new Rhino company was referred to. As a result, the catalogues of many of the stellar artists that Atlantic was known for were now under Rhino's management: artists like Aretha Franklin, Otis Redding, the Rascals, the Coasters, and Iron Butterfly. Atlantic did not hand over their better-selling catalogue artists, like Led Zeppelin and Crosby, Stills and Nash. We thought Bobby Darin should have been included on our list, but Atlantic withheld him as a feature film was being contemplated and they didn't want to share the revenue with Rhino. The film, *Beyond the Sea*, wasn't released until 2004. Richard had our finance department work up some numbers from ones Atlantic had supplied and estimated that those masters were bringing in a profit of $4 million a year to Atlantic, with a shrinking revenue stream.

Henry Droz, the president of WEA, hosted a dinner in the WEA conference room in Burbank. WEA's senior execs welcomed a handful of our senior staff. It was catered by Val's, an upscale restaurant, and was the best meal I ever had. It was a warm and classy welcome, beyond any gesture we had received from Capitol.

In 1956 Dickie Goodman and Bill Buchanan introduced a form of novelty record called *break-in* with their hit "The Flying Saucer." It consisted of a comedic narrative, such as a radio newsman reporting on an invasion from outer space with snippets of recent hit records punctuating the story. Inspired by that form, Richard concocted our advance release cassettes—circulated to salesmen so they could become familiar with the next month's releases—to incorporate stories rather than merely a series of songs on a tape. They were quite imaginative.

For our final tape for our September 1991 releases, I came up with an idea based on an obscure doo-wop record we now owned as part of our Roulette Records purchase. Prior to becoming a record executive, Joe Smith was a popular DJ in Boston. Hoping to get a hit, the Valentines vocal group recorded a song about him, "Joe Smith." Our storyline consisted of Joe (voiced by ex-Conception Corporation member Ira Miller) calling Richard to tell him about a great record he wanted Rhino to put out, only to be interrupted by Richard telling Joe about our new releases and playing segments. After a few phone calls, Richard is ready to listen, at which point Joe plays "Joe Smith." I thought it was well executed, but we got little feedback from the CEMA salesmen. The only response I got from Joe was when he asked me who impersonated him.

Joe, who never had much time for us, who never invited us to lunch or to sit with him courtside at a Lakers game, who would have swatted us off his shoulder like a bothersome gnat if others were not watching, in early September drove the fourteen miles to Rhino—the only time he had visited us—to attempt to charm us. Unbeknownst to Joe, we had already signed our deal with Atlantic. We reiterated our reasons for leaving. His gesture was too little, too late. Unfortunately, we never had the opportunity to work with Joe when he was at the height of his game, at Warner Brothers.

The Monkees

Bigger Than the Beatles

You and me, we're odd ducks.

—Mike Nesmith to Harold Bronson, November 22, 1995

"This face! This face!" Davy Jones expressed his frustration as we sat in a booth at Canter's Delicatessen in July 1999, waiting for our breakfast order to arrive. The second woman in less than ten minutes had approached our table to tell him how much of a fan she was. I got the impression that in exchange for the inconvenience of being recognized and approached in public thirty years after his popularity had peaked, Davy expected a fee. Davy was always under financial pressure. Once he left a long message on my voice mail. It was not pleasant listening to his anger intensify as he expressed the opinion that we should be paying the Monkees a higher royalty rate. As much as I was put off by his tone, I couldn't help but be amused when he calmed himself at the end to tell me to "have a nice day."

It's not that he wasn't making good money performing throughout the country. It's that he had a poor grasp of business and the added burden of alimony. Davy had walked the few blocks to Canter's. He was staying with his girlfriend, Gillian Holt, to whom I introduced him. She had been with comedian Bill Maher backstage after the Monkees' performance at the Universal Amphitheater. I was talking to Bill when she pulled me aside and asked me to introduce her to the much older Davy. She ended up with a part as the Princess in the Monkees' TV special *Hey, Hey, It's the Monkees.*

I first met Davy in 1976, when he was promoting an album and tour as a member of Dolenz, Jones, Boyce & Hart. I was surprised to discover that even though he had made millions of dollars as a Monkee, a little more than five years after the group dissolved, he was driving a battered, yellow Volkswagen Bug.

*   *   *

In 1969 Warner Brothers mounted a campaign to reinvigorate the commercially anemic Kinks. The "God Save the Kinks" campaign, spearheaded by John Mendelsohn, was very successful in calling attention to the group and selling records. "Rhino Saves the Monkees," in spirit if not in name, could describe the company-wide commitment in mining the group's catalogue and helping to resurrect their career. It didn't matter that the Monkees were never hip. It was as though watching the TV show caused a gene to mutate, making Gary Stewart, Bill Inglot, Andrew Sandoval, and me lifelong fans. Even blues hound Richard Foos watched most of the shows the first season. That passion resulted in remarkable products and a unique marketing strategy unequaled in the music industry.

The first anyone had heard of the Monkees was in September 1966, when there was a big marketing push promoting their new TV show. As a sixteen year old, I wasn't enamored with their debut single, "Last Train to Clarksville," and I was skeptical of a formal TV show about a rock group with a silly name like the Monkees. After real, legitimate rock groups like the Beatles, Byrds, and Turtles, how could you take the Monkees seriously?

The idea originated with Bob Rafelson, who came up with it in 1962 when the TV show would have been about a then-in-vogue folk group. The Beatles had successfully enhanced their persona in two feature films, *A Hard Day's Night* and *Help!,* providing a template for *The Monkees* TV show.

Despite my reservations, when the show aired, I was immediately hooked and watched every week. The Beatles' last tour ended two weeks before the show's debut. Subsequently, the Beatles preferred to spend more time sequestered in their recording studio and were considerably less visible. Into this void stepped the Monkees, who provided an apt, and in many ways better, substitute. As much as the Beatles' individual personalities distinguished them from other pop performers when they arrived on the scene, the Monkees were even more personable, charismatic, and funny. Of course, as actors on a TV show, they had writers. The Monkees benefitted from great songs, knowledgeable producers, unlimited recording studio time, and the best facilities and backup instrumentalists available. The whole combination produced great records—singles as well as album tracks—and that's why interest in their music remains decades later.

At the time *The Monkees* TV show was being cast, Davy was already signed to Screen Gems, a subsidiary of Columbia Pictures TV. He was a true asset. In a period when British rock bands ruled the US charts, he was the only British member of the group. He looked a bit like Paul McCartney and oozed personality. Another British band, Herman's Hermits, actually sold more singles than the Beatles in 1965, with hits like "Mrs. Brown You've Got a Lovely Daughter" and "I'm Henry VIII, I Am." The members were from Manchester, as was Davy Jones, who replaced Hermits lead singer Peter Noone on the covers of the teen magazines. When Noone finally got around to viewing the TV show when it aired later in Britain, he said of Davy, "He does me better than me."

Having appeared on Broadway in *Oliver!*, he projected very well and was physically adept, including dancing. He was the best looking of the four Monkees and quickly became the romantic heartthrob, his five foot three height notwithstanding. Because he embodied that role so well, Micky Dolenz became the comedian. Davy was actually funnier. Possessed of a warm, charming singing voice, one would be hard-pressed to come up with a more effective romantic singer for teenage girls at the time. Consequently, he appeared on the most covers of the teen magazines. His fame was so pervasive, that it caused an up-and-coming London singer, one who had already released a handful of flop singles, to abandon his birth name David Jones—becoming David Bowie.

The TV show didn't have a big budget, but worked because of the scripted humor, the actors' personalities, and the music, which was featured in each show. It wasn't because of the story lines. Many of the episodes mined genres that had been used many times before in TV and movies. The stories included hillbillies, private detectives, spies, ghosts, cowboys, pirates, society snobs, boxers, and a mad scientist. So did the Bowery Boys, in their low-budget comedies in the 1940s and 1950s.

The high quality of the records is the primary reason for the continued interest in the Monkees as a group. They benefited from Don Kirshner's stable of top writers who were signed to Screen Gems, including Gerry Goffin and Carole King ("Pleasant Valley Sunday"), Neil Diamond ("I'm a Believer"), and Tommy Boyce and Bobby Hart ("Valleri"). The production was perfect, and at times, inspired. And the Monkees successfully conveyed their personalities in their vocals, an asset not lost on producer Jeff Barry. "When I produced Micky singing 'I'm a Believer,' I was struck by how differently he sang from anybody I had worked with before," he said. "With most singers the words are vehicles for the notes, but Micky, being an actor, added an extra, dramatic quality."

The problem that developed was an issue of musical integrity as rock musicians strived for more artistry and for more respect. Although hired to act on a TV show, the Monkees were chosen for their musical ability. The demands of filming a weekly series made it difficult for the Monkees to provide the instrumentation for their records, and resentment brewed. Similar to other shows on the air at the time, *The Monkees* totaled fifty-eight episodes over two seasons. Currently, network shows are only required to produce twenty-two shows to satisfy a season's schedule.

Their first two albums sold five million apiece, featuring only the Monkees' voices and not their instrumental performances. Originally the producers hadn't expected them to play, but as the first season progressed, the Monkees asserted their desire to play as they had originally intended. However, the project's music supervisor, Don Kirshner, didn't feel the need to revise his successful formula. Nesmith and Tork, who considered themselves musicians primarily, were frustrated and alienated by the recording process. However, they were naively unaware that many top rock bands of the day—Paul Revere & the Raiders, Herman's Hermits, the Association, and the Beach Boys, among them—invariably used studio musicians to record their instrumental backing tracks. Those groups might have played on their first few albums, but by 1966 it was studio players. Although a group like the Turtles played on all of their recordings, there was no distinction, because the fans didn't know. Peter Noone provided a perspective: "For us, it was primarily a financial decision. We made most of our money on the road. So it cost us money to be in the studio learning and recording the songs. We were fortunate to have the talents of Jimmy Page, John Paul Jones and other studio musicians to record our backing tracks."

Mike Nesmith expressed his frustration that the Monkees were prevented from playing on their records to the *Saturday Evening Post* magazine, which ran the story in January 1967. As I wasn't a reader of that magazine, the controversy escaped me. I saw the Monkees playing instruments on the show and on the cover of their first album. It never occurred to me that they didn't provide the backing for their records.

Having outsold the Beatles on their first two albums, the producers didn't want to jeopardize their franchise. When Kirshner refused to alter his production mode, he was fired. He sued and received a settlement. The Monkees were permitted to play on their records and had more input in the song selection. Did the records suffer musically? No. Sales of the subsequent albums declined by half, and who's to say that wouldn't have happened anyway?

Of equal importance to the music was the TV show. Producer /director Bob Rafelson, influenced by France's new wave cinematic style, bettered his Beatles model in creating a TV series that ran circles around other shows airing at the time. Its quality and innovation didn't go unnoticed. The show garnered two Emmy awards in its first season.

When the Beatles emerged in March, they seemed to have aged forty years. In the promo films for "Strawberry Fields Forever" and "Penny Lane," they looked like sedated granddads in turn-of-the-century clothes. George sprouted a beard, the others, mustaches. As potent as the record was, it was also strange, and the Turtles' "Happy Together" knocked the Beatles out of the top slot after only one week. The popularity of the vibrant and youthful Monkees was uncontested: four of their albums made it to number one in 1967. The TV show continued until it ran its natural course and came to an end after two seasons.

Davy loved horses and fantasized that he could have been a professional jockey. But there was no indication from his teen years as a rider that he could have been successful. In his teens Davy had become a star acting in London's West End production of *Oliver!* playing the Artful Dodger. The production moved to Broadway where he was nominated for a Tony Award. As a consequence, Davy always felt more at ease with theater people, with the socializing after the shows, than he did later with the rock scene. As the sixties evolved, drugs held more prominence in the culture and more influence in the creative process, but Davy never felt comfortable with the emerging hippie and drug culture, or psychedelic music.

After the Monkees, Davy worked where he could: solo dates, TV guest appearances, and theater, but to little acclaim. He signed a record contract with Bell Records, but charted no higher than fifty-two with "Rainy Jane" in June 1971.

I think all the members were shocked at how their extreme popularity dwindled when the TV series was no more. Rather than the Monkees appreciating what they accomplished as an ensemble, and the fortune they reaped, and how that residual good will had bolstered their earning power in subsequent decades, they looked upon that experience as having prevented them from being taken seriously in their subsequent ventures. In the two years of the show's first run, the Monkees were so popular, it's easy to see how the members were blindsided into thinking there would be a demand for them after the series was off the air.

When the Monkees were allowed to play their own instruments and function as a band for the recording of their third album, *Headquarters*, Peter was in his element. He played bass, guitar, banjo, and keyboards. Davy and Micky, being less instrumentally adept, were less inclined to commit the time and effort in subsequent recordings. With filming TV shows and playing concert dates, the time devoted to recording *Headquarters* was an additional burden to be avoided in the future. Peter wanted to be in a band, recording and touring. When he realized that wasn't going to happen again with the Monkees, he became disenchanted and left.

Peter did form a band, Peter Tork and/or Release, and recorded, but nothing was finished. As with the Monkees, he suffered from a lack of confidence, and enough focus to complete his songs. While in the Monkees, his songs did get occasional recognition. He co-composed a song the TV producers selected to accompany the end credits during the second season. The two songs he wrote for *Head* fit the movie perfectly. Peter preferred a drug-infused hippie lifestyle, which meant that others used his house as a crash pad and took advantage of his generosity. It was a fourteen-room house previously owned by TV star Wally Cox. When Peter's Monkees money was spent, he sold the house to Stephen Stills, who had recommended Peter for the role.

Mike Nesmith was the second among the Monkees to leave the project. Although he gave up the guarantee of a salary as being a member of the group, his songwriting royalties from Monkees recordings meant that he made substantially more money than any of the others. The show's producers didn't believe in Mike's songs—didn't think they could become hits—but included them on the albums to placate him. They didn't know what they had.

One song they rejected, "Different Drum," became the first big hit for Linda Ronstadt, as a member of the Stone Poneys in late 1967. The first hit album for the Nitty Gritty Dirt Band, *Uncle Charlie & His Dog Teddy*, leads off with Mike's song "Some of Shelley's Blues," with another, "Propinquity," later in the lineup. A couple of months after the last Monkees single (just Davy and Micky) barely made it into *Billboard's* Hot 100, Mike graced the top twenty with "Joanne," the debut release of his new ensemble, the First National Band. That was to be his only Top 40 hit performing a song he had composed.

Mike was the first Monkee I met, in May 1971. I started contributing to a local arts magazine, *Coast*, that appealed primarily to those interested in listening to music on their upscale stereo systems. Although reruns of *The Monkees* were relegated to Saturday mornings, editor Jim Martin—who, atypically for Los Angeles, wore a cowboy hat—learned that the network was receiving over a thousand fan letters a week. He assigned me to write a feature on the group for the magazine's upcoming rock music issue.

I interviewed Mike at the Screen Gems Publishing office on Sunset Boulevard in Hollywood. Mike was smart and surprisingly candid. He complimented Peter Tork on his musical chops and intelligence, but made it clear that he never liked him. Putting his comment in perspective, he then revealed that he didn't like his mother, even though he considered her a "nice lady." He estimated that there were forty Monkees recordings that had never been released.

Mike's TV character was more mature, more of the adult. As a tall Texan, he could have been President Lyndon B. Johnson's errant son. With the Monkees he played guitar, sang the occasional lead vocal, and quickly established himself as the group's best songwriter. He was such a fan of country and western music that he, inappropriately, infused this style into the recordings, unintentionally creating the country-rock hybrid.

I saw him play a few times, and visited him backstage when he appeared at a free noontime concert at UCLA's Ackerman Union Grand Ballroom in February 1972. Bob Chorush, a likeable eccentric who headed *Rolling Stone*'s Los Angeles office, invited me to join him on a visit to Mike's home. Mike was disaffected by how little the success of the Monkees' records had to do with the integrity of the music, and he considered his earnings tainted money he didn't deserve. As a consequence, he squandered most of it. He had to vacate his large house off of Mulholland Drive, and relocated his family to a San Fernando Valley tract house he originally bought for his chauffeur. Mike's wife, Phyllis, was a proponent for the legislation to legalize marijuana.

In 1973 Mike made a deal with Elektra Records for a new country label. He signed and produced artists with the intention of using local talent to create an identifiable scene, similar to Nashville or Bakersfield. I liked the concept and visited Countryside Studios, a house that Mike had partly converted into a recording studio. As Mike and I sat talking in the kitchen, a large plate of hot, greasy bacon was placed on the table. As he was eating, I thought it inhospitable that he didn't offer me any—which I would have declined—or even something to drink. He was touting Countryside's new artist, Garland Frady. Garland was a regular performer at Los Angeles' top country music club, The Palomino. I thought Countryside was a noble attempt, but the few records that were released didn't sell well enough to sustain the label.

I met Micky shortly after Mike, when I interviewed him for the same *Coast* magazine article. He had been a child star with the popular *Circus Boy* TV series, which I watched as a kid. In subsequent years—before being cast in *The Monkees*—he suffered the indignity of being sent on auditions for kid roles even though he was well into his teens. With few acting jobs coming his way, Micky studied to be an architect at Trade Tech College.

Micky was a much better actor than he ever got credit for, and an exceptionally versatile singer. He's smart, like an absent-minded professor, and his hobby is quantum physics. With the Monkees he was attracted to the potential of the Moog synthesizer, and had the third one in the country. An underachiever as a songwriter, he scored the Monkees' second biggest hit in Britain with "Randy Scouse Git" (aka "Alternate Title"), which was not released as a single in the United States. Micky has been prone to toss off *The Monkees* as a mere TV show about a rock band, equating his role as a drummer to that of Spock on another well-known TV series: "Leonard Nimoy wasn't really a Vulcan, but he played one on *Star Trek*."

To put the impact of the music in perspective, he recounted a story of a fan who approached him after a Monkees concert. The young girl was bewildered by the seriousness of Micky's new protest song, "Mommy and Daddy," which dealt with the plight of the American Indian. "She had tears in her eyes as she walked up to me and asked why we didn't record any of the good old songs you can dance to," he recollected. "I realized what had happened and what the Monkees were all about. They were what a first-grade teacher is to a child learning math. You can't teach a kid to multiply until you teach him to add. The reason the Monkees were so successful was because we filled a gap. The Beatles and all the other groups were trying to appeal to a sophisticated audience. Nobody was playing to the kids. We gave them something to listen to."

Micky also realized that the Monkees had a larger social significance because they brought long hair into the living room: "Up until then anyone with long hair was thought to be a doper or hippie hoodlum. Even though the Beatles wore long hair, their comments about acid and politics gave it a negative connotation. The kids said, 'See the Monkees, they just wanna laugh and have fun and play.' It then became difficult for the parents to deny them: 'Well, alright, if the Monkees do it, it's okay.'"

TV show, rock band, cultural phenomenon—the Monkees were all of these, but much more, and therein lies the confusion about how they are considered. In the first place, *The Monkees* was a TV show. Although they were acting in fictitious stories, Micky Dolenz, Davy Jones, Michael Nesmith, and Peter Tork were essentially playing themselves and using their own names in the series. They were chosen, in part, because they had musical ability. Hired to play a rock band, they actually became a rock band. They toured and even recorded a couple of albums, performing as a self-contained unit.

After the Monkees, Micky recorded some singles, but never made the charts. He showed a flair for directing, but only managed a few low-budget commercials for local merchants, like Jeans West. It was years later, when he was living in England with his second wife, that he was able to work as a director. Unlike the others, he still had his money. His mother had invested it wisely, buying properties along the Sunset Strip, which sustained his life style for many years.

When I met Peter Tork in the mid-1970s, it was because we were both team representatives in the Hollywood Showbiz Softball League. At the time he was teaching music at a small private school. I was representing the Rhinos. He was representing the Hollywood Vampires, which in prior years had included Alice Cooper and Mark Volman. The Rhinos and the Happy Days team were the nice guys of the league, compared to the overly competitive other teams that were composed of aggressive New Yorkers.

*   *   *

Around the time Rhino formed, the only Monkees album in stores was a hits compilation. With so little of their music available, it was a personal goal to reissue their recordings. In 1980 Capitol Records released the Beatles' album *Rarities*. Bill Inglot, Gary Stewart, and I felt there were enough tracks to compose a similar album from the Monkees' catalogue, and I made a licensing deal with Artista Records. In 1974 Columbia Pictures hired Clive Davis to consolidate their recorded labels—the Monkees recorded for Colgems Records—into a company he named Arista, after a high school honor society of which he'd been a member. Quite often in business a company with the same name won't necessarily be an affiliate of another; in many cases ownership is different. Columbia Pictures was not affiliated with Columbia Records. The record label was part of CBS (Columbia Broadcasting System).

EMI Records owned the British label Columbia Records, for whom the Yardbirds recorded.

In 1982 we released a compilation of rarities titled *Monkee Business*—after a Marx Brothers movie—in a picture disc format. (Queen had named two of their albums after Marx Brothers titles.) It sold well enough to justify the release of a subsequent album, *Monkee Flips* (a wrestling term), two years later. By the end of the 1980s, those two albums had sold about 50,000 each. I had forged a good relationship with Roy Lott, head of business affairs at Arista, and had licensed subsequent, non-Monkees product, a *Best of the Box Tops* and rereleases of the three albums by Nazz, Todd Rundgren's first recorded group.

Bert Schneider, coproducer of *The Monkees*, took note. He came to see me and we made a deal to license two albums of tracks that had never before been released, the tracks Mike Nesmith had mentioned to me in 1971. He claimed that neither Columbia Pictures nor Arista owned the unreleased tracks. Arista had done extremely well with their Monkees best of, to the point where they issued a subsequent volume, but they had no interest in rereleasing the original albums, which I arranged for us to do.

In February 1986, MTV programmed a twenty-two-and-a-half-hour marathon of all *The Monkees* TV episodes. It was so well received that MTV did it again, and then scheduled the shows as part of its daily programming, thus sparking a revival of interest in the Monkees. David Fishof, primarily an agent for NFL players, had staged revival tours of sixties acts in the previous two years, which gave him the experience needed to launch The Monkees Twentieth Anniversary Reunion Tour later that year. The initial dates were well in line with Fishof's previous Happy Together tours, but the demand became so great that some later concerts had the group drawing well in stadiums. In order to do it again the following year, he needed an extra element: a newly recorded album by the Monkees.

On March 23, 1987, Richard and I met Micky Dolenz and David Fishof for dinner at Nick's Fish Market in West Hollywood to discuss Rhino's interest in recording a new Monkees album. Fishof had baited us for many months and then disappeared to see if he could make a deal with one of the majors. It didn't happen, and time was rapidly approaching to prepare for the Monkees' tour. So he and Dolenz sat with the heads of the label that had been responsible for reissuing the entire Monkees catalog, resulting in six of those original albums recharting on *Billboard* the previous fall. At that meeting, Micky explained that the Monkees should be viewed more like the Marx Brothers than a rock group. Given their 1986 success, he envisioned a yearly tour, film, and record for the Monkees.

There was not much time to deliberate. We had to negotiate a deal, select a producer, choose a recording studio, and hire musicians. Close to a hundred songs had to be sifted through. Although Mike Nesmith was not part of the tour, I had solicited his participation in recording the album. I didn't think he'd be interested, and he declined. Considering Rhino's success with the catalog, and a desire to make Monkees fans everywhere happy with a new album, Richard and I plunged ahead, knowing full well it would be Rhino's biggest financial commitment up to that time.

The Monkees hadn't recorded an album of new material since Dolenz and Jones joined their ex-producers/songwriters Tommy Boyce and Bobby Hart for a tour and poor-selling album in the mid-1970s. It sold only 17,000 copies. Although the Monkees' best records embraced many styles, their sound was that of a rock band playing great songs. In the mid-1980s, most successful rock producers busied themselves with heavy metal and synthesized rock. I thought the Monkees needed someone who combined great pop sensibilities with a natural feel for the appealing rawness of rock 'n' roll.

I considered a broad range of producers, including Mitchell Froom (Crowded House), David Kahne (Bangles), and Jim Valence (Bryan Adams' lyricist). Some weren't available, like our first choice, Nick Lowe, who had distinguished himself not only as a producer of Elvis Costello and Graham Parker, but also as a solo artist ("Cruel To Be Kind") and as a member of Rockpile ("Teacher Teacher"). Some, like Lowe's Rockpile cohort Dave Edmunds, weren't interested. Others, like Jimmy Iovine (Tom Petty), were too expensive. The best available choice seemed to be Roger Bechirian, whose producer credits included Nick Lowe, Elvis Costello, and Squeeze. Davy disagreed with the choice, preferring a bigger name. He requested Quincy Jones.

Everybody pitched in the best songs they could find, and a consensus was achieved. The Monkees interact like brothers. There is affection toward one another, some competition, and occasional arguments. Add in the women—Davy's then-wife told me that he was going to be bigger than Bruce Springsteen, while Micky ignored his own impeccable taste in songs and deferred to his then-wife's preferences—and you had constantly changing opinions. At one point, Peter was going to play on the entire album and Micky on part of it. In the end Peter only managed to provide the guitar on one track. There was one song that Roger and I didn't think was worthwhile: Davy was so insistent that we record "(I'll) Love You Forever," which he wrote, he would not fly over to record his vocals until we had recorded the backing track. Lou Naktin produced the basic track, and the song turned out okay.

Recording commenced on May 20 at Cherokee Studios in Hollywood. Other artists who recorded at the complex during the sessions included Dolly Parton, Elton John, and the New Monkees. (*New Monkees* was a syndicated TV show spurred by the renewed popularity of the original group. The actors who starred in the new production, seemingly embarrassed by their close proximity to the genuine Monkees, placed a pseudonym on their door.) Louis Naktin was enlisted to provide a roster of crack local musicians to record the instrumental backing tracks.

With all the Monkees in town, Richard and I met them on June 9 at the house Micky and his family rented in Beverly Hills. After our discussion about the album, Peter casually sat at a keyboard and played part of a Bach concerto. During the evening I came to realize that Davy was naturally the funniest—not Micky, as he was portrayed in the show. The funniest moment came when Davy hid in the narrow storage space to the right of the fireplace, and then opened the door, jokingly trying to scare us.

I picked "(I'd Go The) Whole Wide World" as a vehicle for Davy's English charm. The song, written and performed by Wreckless Eric, had been a stellar single in the early days of Stiff Records. Davy didn't like the song and expressed his disinterest in recording previously released material. Micky did like it, however, and sang it, but it was less effective without Davy's accent. "Heart And Soul," the LP's first single, was penned by a pair of British songwriters discovered by Bechirian. It was Micky's favorite song on the album, and he sang it. David Fishof contributed "Don't Bring Me Down," which was written by Tommy James (the Shondells).

As they rode their tour bus back from rehearsal, Micky lashed out "POOL IT!" at his fellow Monkees to quell a heated exchange. He paused, and the others snickered. He had meant to say, "Cool it," but the malapropism took hold, and the album had a title.

In trying to appeal to contemporary tastes, Bechirian produced a more polished album than we were anticipating. We were surprised that the Monkees didn't care to sing backup on each other's lead vocal tracks, and then realized that they hadn't sung backup that often on their original recordings. Nonetheless, the Monkees made the album they wanted to make and were happy with *Pool It!*

With Fishof boasting of his MTV connections, we launched our most ambitious marketing plan to date. Preacher Ewing and Bill Fishman (the latter best known for the film *Tape Heads*, which was produced by Nesmith) produced a creative, funny video for "Heart And Soul." We were counting on MTV to play the video, but as much as MTV were Monkees supporters the previous year, they abandoned the group in 1987. One issue was the Monkees cancelling their performance at an MTV Super Bowl party earlier in the year. Davy claimed he hadn't agreed to do it. Fishof substituted the Turtles, but then charged MTV for their services. Even though Monkees fans made "Heart And Soul" one of the channel's ten most-requested videos, MTV execs refused to air it.

Despite the quality of the single, most radio stations didn't want to play a new record by any group perceived as 1960s has-beens. That same shortsighted mentality plagued the first Bee Gees single to be issued in four years. "You Win Again," released around the same time, fared only slightly better than "Heart And Soul" in the States, even though it was a number one hit around the world. In addition, shortly before the release of the Monkees' single, British group T'Pau scored on the American charts with a hit also titled "Heart And Soul."

We scrambled and managed some airings and a highly successful promotion on the Nickelodeon channel. Although viewers of the *Nick Rocks* show voted "Heart And Soul" their favorite video of the year, the cable channel was considerably less influential in 1987 than in subsequent years.

Without the MTV support we were expecting, our hope for a gold record was dashed. "Heart And Soul" labored to 87 on *Billboard*'s Hot 100, and *Pool It!* sold 125,000 copies. (In anticipation of a bigger selling album, we had shipped 200,000.) Although disappointing, it was Rhino's biggest-selling original production. Compared to other Monkees' albums, in its original release *Pool It!* out-sold all that came after 1968's *The Birds, The Bees & The Monkees*.

I would have thought that our valiant effort would have further cemented our relationship with the Monkees. It may have, but that didn't mean that they weren't prone to act in their selfish best interests. As part of the new album deal, we were supposed to distribute the live album the group had produced to sell on their tour. Micky's wife, Davy's wife, and Peter's girlfriend thought they could get a better deal from someone else and the three Monkees reneged. No other deal materialized.

*   *   *

I liked what Mike had recorded with the First National Band, but the project was not considered a success. He told me that the most he sold of any of the albums he released on RCA Records in the 1970s was 35,000. In 1989 I made a deal with him to release the best of his post-Monkees recordings on two compilation albums: *The Older Stuff* and *The Newer Stuff* (from his Pacific Arts albums).

Rafelson and Schneider settled a suit with Sony (who had bought Columbia Pictures), which gave them back most of the rights and catalogue of *The Monkees*. Sony only retained TV broadcast and syndication rights. Schneider and his partners wanted to sell those rights and approached Rhino. I was surprised he didn't call me directly; I thought we had a bit of a relationship. I like to think it was because I was such a good negotiator that he had his lawyer contact Richard, but it could have been because Ira Herzog had previously dealt with Richard. They wanted $4 million, and the amount didn't seem to be negotiable. I hadn't experienced a deal that I couldn't finesse and was in a lesser position because it hadn't been presented to me first. That was more money than we had.

I met with Mike at his office in West LA. Because his company distributed home videos, I thought I could team up with him to buy the rights: Rhino would take the audio and Pacific Arts would take the video. I expressed to him that I thought a box set of all the shows would do well. This wasn't the first time we had discussed collaborating. Towards the end of 1989 Mike approached me about merging our companies. Ultimately, he bowed out of the copurchase because he felt he didn't want to have to deal with the other Monkees coming to him for royalties.

We made a deal whereby we took the rights for North America, with Warner Music International kicking in a third of the purchase price for the rest of the world. Bob and Bert signed the contract at our office in January 1994.

Being a fan of an artist and their music inspired me to come up with creative ideas and negotiate the deals to make the projects come to fruition, and the Monkees were the best example of that. As owners we could do what we wanted, rather than being limited as licensees on previous product. I informed the Monkees of our plans and involved them where it was appropriate.

The Monkees afforded a unique, cumulative marketing opportunity, whereby coordinated releases and events can generate more impact than isolated ones. I forged a plan to have a significant Monkees event every few months to sustain renewed interest in the group. The first was to make an event out of awarding them new multiplatinum awards for sales of their original albums. In the sixties the RIAA only certified gold awards: one million sales for a single and 500,000 for an album. As the industry grew, awards were created for platinum—one million albums— and multiplatinum.

Using songwriter/producer Bobby Hart's royalty statements, I was able to get the RIAA to confirm sales of the group's first five albums of fifteen million: five million for their first two, two million for their next two, and one million for their fifth album. On January 5, 1995, I presented framed awards to each of the Monkees at West Hollywood's Hard Rock Cafe (the first one in the United States, and the third one overall). As a rare Monkees reunion of all four members, we got extensive media coverage.

In October 1995 we released our *Deluxe Limited-Edition Box Set* of their TV series and *The Monkees Greatest Hits* album, the latter of which benefitted from a TV advertised mail order campaign. I met with Mike towards the end of November at Santa Monica restaurant DC3 to discuss our plans to celebrate (market) the Monkees' thirtieth anniversary. Mike had been receiving royalties from his mother's invention of Liquid Paper, which had provided him with a nice lifestyle as well as financing his modestly-selling artistic pursuits, but those were running out. As a result, he was more financially motivated to consider recording a new album and touring with the others as part of the anniversary.

The concept for the new record was to revisit the spirit of the group's 1967 album *Headquarters*, which was really the only one on which the four Monkees played. This time out it would be just the four of them— playing, composing, and producing—an arrangement that inspired the title *Justus*. Not only did it refer to *just us*, as the only credited musicians, but also to *justice*, from having been deprived from playing on their very first two albums.

The recording commenced in June 1996, prior to Micky, Davy, and Peter starting their summer tour. I thought the album, released in October 1996, turned out well. There wasn't one bad song on it, but there wasn't anything that sounded like a hit single. I would have liked to have heard more from Mike, who only contributed one new song as a composer. Coinciding with the album's release was *Hey, Hey, We're the Monkees*, a book I put together in order to have visibility in bookstores, as well as a CD-ROM (compact disc read-only memory).

I wanted to get exposure in the new area of computer programs. Other artists, such as the Rolling Stones and David Bowie, had been subjects of CD-ROMs, but development and production costs were too significant for Rhino. I made the deal with Paul Atkinson, the guitarist for the Zombies, who was working at a new company, nu.millennia. I became friendly with Paul after meeting him at Mike Chapman's house when he was head of West Coast A&R for RCA Records. The *Hey, Hey, We're the Monkees* CD-ROM also came out in October.

In January 1997 the Disney Channel premiered a documentary I coproduced, *Hey, Hey, We're the Monkees*. The next month ABC aired *Hey, Hey, It's the Monkees*, an hour-long TV special written and directed by Michael Nesmith. It was meant to be a new episode of the TV show, but failed to capture the spirit or humor of the original, and earned poor ratings.

What made the Monkees' anticipated anniversary tour special was Mike's participation. But after the first leg in England, he couldn't put up with Davy any longer and opted out of the American dates. As the group—minus Mike—had toured the previous year, the reunion lost luster, and sales of our new album suffered considerably. The 63,000 albums we sold was comparable to other older artists releasing albums around that time, like the Kinks and Cheap Trick, but it could have been so much more. In 1999 Mike's Pacific Arts settled a suit with PBS, whose video his company had distributed, resulting in a large windfall, which meant that he wouldn't have the financial need to work with the Monkees.

My ambitions included producing a feature film and a cartoon series. The Beatles' animated series ran on ABC in the sixties. Many baby boomers also thought there had been one for the Monkees, but there hadn't. Jeff DeGrandis was an enthusiastic Monkees (and Beatles) fan who directed and produced animation. I came up with a series of story lines, he created illustrations, and we made the rounds of the animation studios, but there was little interest. With the Monkees providing their own voices, their middle-aged looks would not be a factor. Film Roman, an animation production company that provided the visuals for *The Simpsons*, wanted to own its own show and made an initial offer, but our differences were not resolved. I was able to realize a docudrama, *Daydream Believers' The Monkees Story*, which aired as a ninety-minute TV movie on VH1 in June 2000.

From having been a fan who looked up to these guys, to getting to meet and converse with them as an eager music journalist, it was great to be able to realize product that was creative and of a high quality. Once we got up to speed with our releases, their Rhino royalties markedly increased. Prior to Rhino's ownership, they were each making about $8,000 a year. During my time at the label, it averaged $60,000. After we recouped our purchase price, we increased their royalty rate further. When Rhino's *The Monkees Greatest Hits* turned gold—it sold over 650,000—the Monkees received another framed award from us.

But I was also relegated to an authority figure, more like that of a school principal in dealing with the Monkees. In that respect, I stepped into the position that Bob Rafelson and Bert Schneider had occupied. Even though our ownership was new, I felt as though the Monkees still carried nearly thirty years of residual resentment into our relationship. I had no illusions that I would hang out with them and be their best friend, but I was surprised how rarely they expressed their gratitude for all the good things we did.

At the time *The Monkees* was cast, most rock musicians were antiestablishment. They defied convention by growing their hair long, wearing outrageous outfits, and shunning routine employment, and many broke the law by consuming marijuana and other drugs. Likewise, the Monkees were not compliant individuals. Mike was the most defiant. He punched a hole into the wall of Don Kirshner's suite at the Beverly Hills Hotel when Kirshner refused to let the Monkees play on their own records. Davy Jones marketed Davy Jones glasses until the producers told him to stop because they held those rights. On the first day of filming the Monkees' feature film *Head*, all but Peter Tork struck by failing to report.

Such behavior could be identified even twenty years later. Arista wanted the (three) Monkees to record new tracks that they could add to their best of album to coincide with the 1986 tour. "That Was Then, This Is Now" became a top twenty hit, but Davy didn't like the deal so he wasn't on it. When it was performed as part of the tour, Davy preferred to leave the stage rather than sing backup vocals. On that tour Davy attacked a Coca-Cola machine backstage, angry that the Monkees had to pay Columbia Pictures a small percentage for using the Monkees name and trademark. The Coca-Cola Company owned Columbia Pictures at the time. Although Davy was the most responsive to the fans, when irritated he could also alienate them.

At the Monkees' June 20, 1996, performance at the Universal Amphitheatre, Davy thanked me from the stage as I was sitting in the audience. I was touched by the gesture of appreciation. It was the first time I had been thanked in that manner. I developed a nice rapport with Micky, and he's the only one that I see, socially, on occasion. But even he can feel resentful. He was the lead singer on most of the Monkees' hits, and even on the ones that the others don't play or sing on, he still only gets one-fourth of the royalty.

When I heard that Davy had died in February 2012, I was shocked and puzzled because he had always seemed so healthy. I had seen him only once since I left Rhino. It was mid-November 2008, and it was a curious exchange: I approached him outside the Egyptian Theater, where the American Cinematheque was presenting a program of original *The Monkees* episodes accompanied by rare commercials and outtakes (assembled by Andrew Sandoval) and a screening of *Head*. He looked good, fit, and tan, and I told him so. Rather than responding similarly, or even inquiring what I'd been up to, he rattled off his performing schedule the next few weeks, seeming to equate the demand for his services as a reflection of his self-worth at the age of sixty-two. Of course, I'd heard the routine before.

Mogan David and His Winos
(L-R): Paul Rappaport, Bill Pique, Mark Osterstock, Harold, Al Albert (1973 lineup).

The UCLA *Daily Bruin* entertainment writers— who showed up that day. *Back row:* Jonathan Kellerman, Harold, Bob Elias. *Front row:* Evelyn Renold, Joe Hymson (Spring 1970).

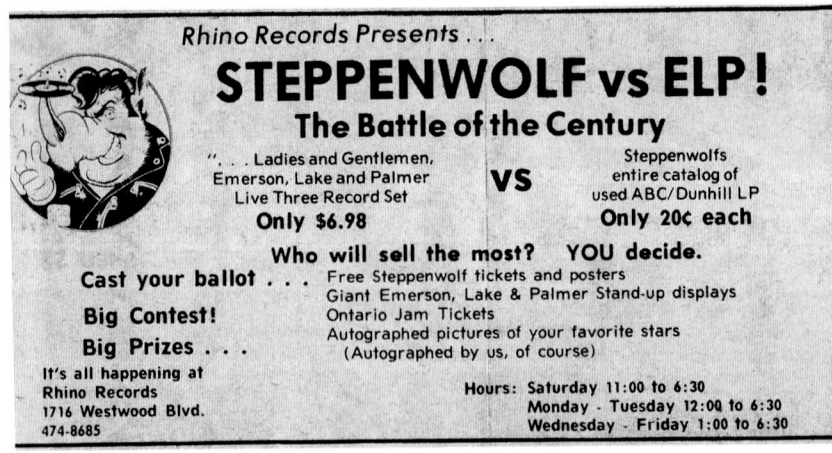

Interviewing Pink Floyd's Rick Wright, August 1974.

Rhino store ad, the UCLA *Daily Bruin*, October 11, 1974.

The Ramones visit Rhino. Joey *(L)* and Johnny flank Harold, February 1977.

Our Spring 1976 store promotional calendar inspired by those of revival movie houses.

The Rhino staff hassle a customer on Salesman Day.
(L-R): Harold, Lee Kaplan, customer Mark Goldblatt, Richard, March 1976.

The Rhino staff pickets the store for lack of customers.
(L-R): Gary Stewart (partially hidden), Jeff Ginsburg as Rhino McDino,
John Farkash, Steve Leibman, Richard, Fall 1977.

Rhino's first LP, January 1978.
Note Richard's head to the right of Wild Man's.

Rhino Records first release, 1975.

Bill Stout's original label artwork
for Rhino Records.

RHINO RECORDS
1716 WESTWOOD BLVD.
LOS ANGELES   90024
474-8685

Agreement between Rhino Records and Mark Volman/Howard Kaylan regarding Rhino's manufacturing a 12" picture disc of the Turtles four songs: The Owl, The Last Thing I Remember, To See the Sun, Surfer Dan

The four songs are leased to Rhino for a two-year period as of the release date. Rhino may not manufacture any more records as of the expiration date, unless Volman/Kaylan grant an extension. Songs are leased to Rhino exclusively for picture disc only.

Rhino agrees to pay Kaylan/Volman an eleven hundred dollar recoupable advance against a royalty of 89¢ per record, to be paid quarterly. Records not to be wholesaled to distributors for more than $ 4.50 per disc. Rhino agrees to press 2,000 records initially. Royalties will be paid on 100 % of the records sold.

Volman/Kaylan hereby verify possession and ownership of photos and masters used.

Volman/Kaylan will receive 25 discs for their promotional use.

Harold Bronson   dated: 9/22/78

Harold Bronson, for Rhino

Mark Volman

Mark Volman

Howard Kaylan

Howard Kaylan

Our first contract to reissue the Turtles.
I think all contracts should be like this, on one page.

The Temple City Kazoo Orchestra performs on *The Mike Douglas Show* with Mike's guests.
Front row: Lee Grant, Mike, Lou "the Hulk" Ferrigno, David Brenner, Cheryl Tiegs.
Back row: Harold, Richard, Frank, David Dennard, Gary Myrick, April 23, 1979.

Promoting Rhino on *Saturday Live*, BBC Radio 1,
flanked by Andy Batten-Foster *(L)* and Richard Skinner, June 11, 1983.

We acknowledged the Olympics coming to L.A. in 1984 with our own vision.

Dr. Demento re-signs with Rhino, November 20, 1984, on the way to going gold with his *20th Anniversary Edition*. The Doc's manager, Jay Levey, is at right.

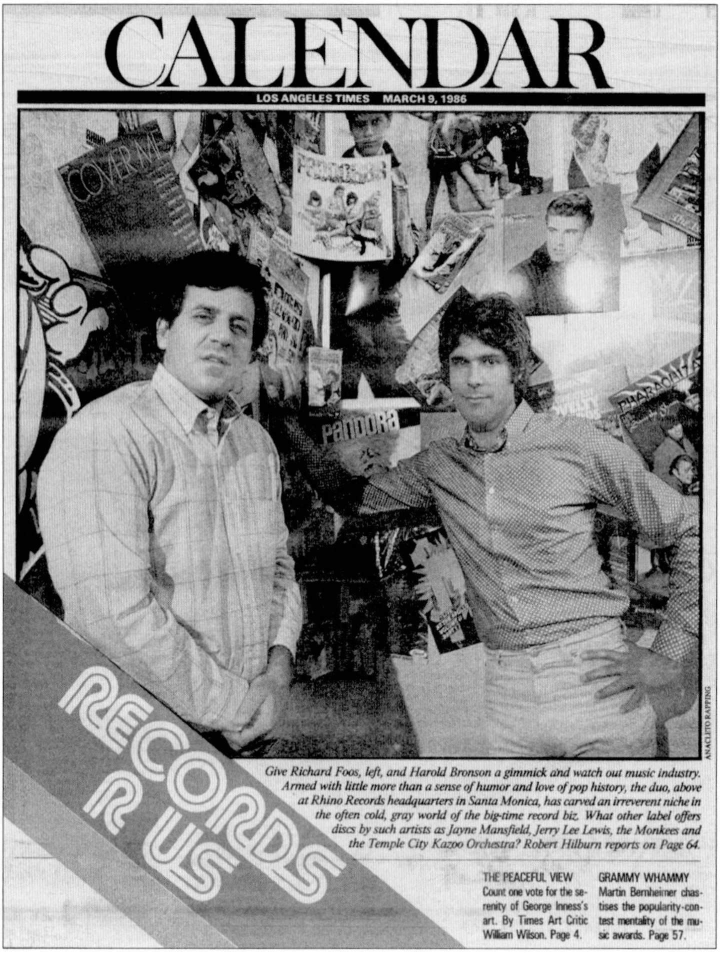

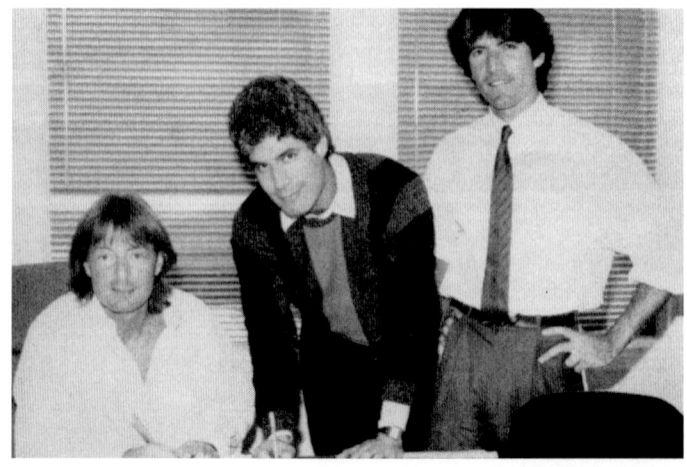

CALENDAR

LOS ANGELES TIMES MARCH 9, 1986

RECORDS R US

Give Richard Foos, left, and Harold Bronson a gimmick and watch out music industry. Armed with little more than a sense of humor and love of pop history, the duo, above at Rhino Records headquarters in Santa Monica, has carved an irreverent niche in the often cold, gray world of the big-time record biz. What other label offers discs by such artists as Jayne Mansfield, Jerry Lee Lewis, the Monkees and the Temple City Kazoo Orchestra? Robert Hilburn reports on Page 64.

ANACLETO RAPPING

THE PEACEFUL VIEW
Count one vote for the serenity of George Inness's art. By Times Art Critic William Wilson. Page 4.

GRAMMY WHAMMY
Martin Bernheimer chastises the popularity-contest mentality of the music awards. Page 57.

Calendar section of *Los Angeles Times*, March 9, 1986.

I sign a mock contract granting Fanfare Records the UK rights for Rhino's Billy Vera album, flanked by Iain Burton *(L)* and Simon Cowell, February 6, 1987.

Rhino's 10th Anniversary Party *(L-R)*: Mark Volman, Arthur Lee, Harold, Howard Kaylan, Santa Monica Pier, November 12, 1987.

Our Sweet Sixteen press photo where we are also identified as the Rhino Brothers, 1994.

Decca throws a press party for the Turtles. *(L-R)*: Jim Tucker, Al Nichol, Jim Pons, Johny Barbata, Mark Volman, Howard Kaylan, London, June 1, 1967.

The Monkees take a break from rehearsing *(L-R)*: Peter Tork, Davy Jones, Micky Dolenz, Mike Nesmith, RCA Victor Studios, Hollywood, June 15, 1966.

Tommy James signs his management contract with Lenny Stogel.
Roulette Records' Morris Levy is at right, September 1966.

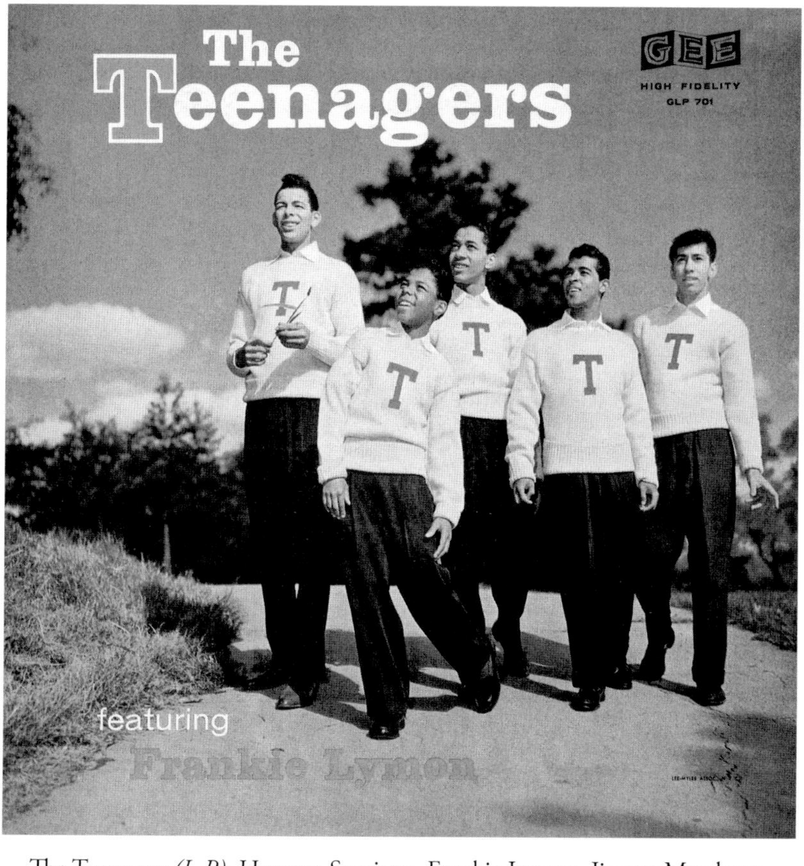

The Teenagers *(L-R)*: Herman Santiago, Frankie Lymon, Jimmy Merchant,
Sherman Garnes, Joe Negroni, 1956.

I gave the Monkees—*(L-R)*: Peter Tork, Davy Jones, Michael Nesmith, Micky Dolenz—platinum record awards in a special presentation at Los Angeles' Hard Rock Café, January 5, 1995.

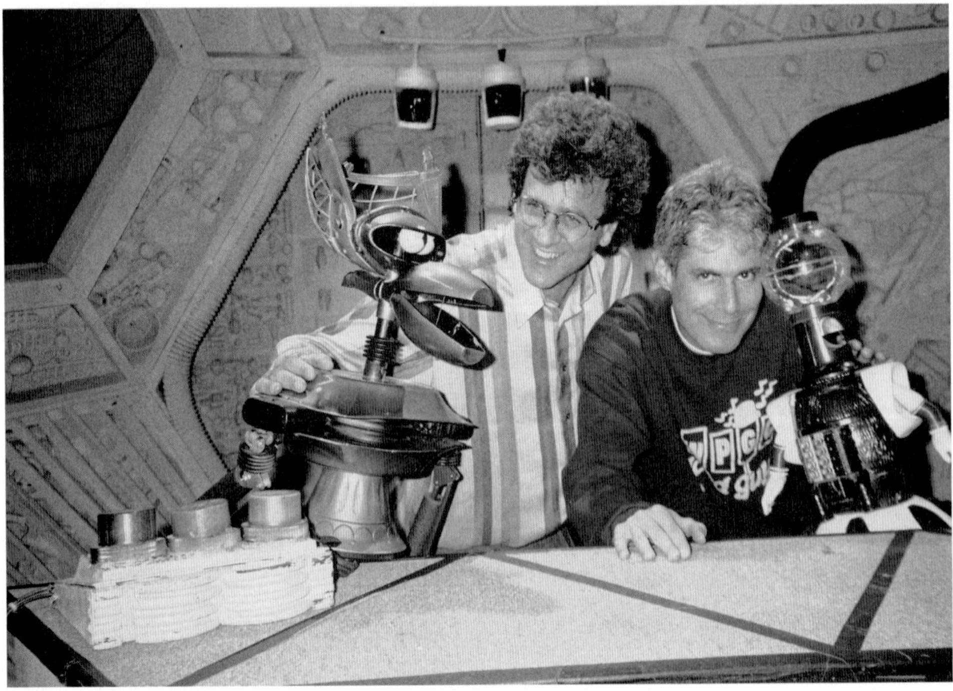

Richard and I visit the Mystery Science Theater 3000 set, flanked by Crow T. Robot *(L)* and Tom Servo, Eden Prairie, Minnesota, October 19, 1994.

Richard and I receive the Governor's Motion Picture Award from Nevada Governor Bob Miller for *Fear & Loathing in Las Vegas,* May 27, 1998.

Rhino signs the Knack.
Back row: Doug Fieger, Harold, co-producer Richard Bosworth, manager Danny Sugerman.
Front row: Terry Bozio, Berton Averre, Prescott Niles, February 12, 1998.

Our 1998 catalogue anticipating the release of Rhino Films' *Fear and Loathing in Las Vegas*.

CHAPTER 9

The Rhino Label
Part Three

The Atlantic Years

It was a disaster: our controller, Gary Gross, had grossly miscalculated our profit for 1992. Instead of making $8 million, we made $800,000, which meant that our profits were half as much as the previous year's. We had been in our joint venture with Atlantic Records for only a year, and not only were our profits down, but our credibility was tarnished. I felt bad about it, but the Atlantic execs were surprisingly understanding. Making it worse was that Richard and I had paid bonuses to our employees—not to ourselves—based on the false numbers. Although we would have been justified in asking for the money back, to do so would have further diminished morale, so we didn't. Because Gross delayed notifying us for many weeks, he had to go.

*   *   *

Atlantic Records was formed in 1947 by Ahmet Ertegun and Herb Abramson. About ten years later Jerry Wexler, essentially, replaced Abramson. Ahmet was a passionate and scholarly jazz fan who later embraced R&B. At the time we came aboard, Ahmet was still at the label, but in a reduced capacity. As a result, we didn't interact with him much.

The first year of our association with Atlantic was getting to know each other, getting acclimated to their corporate way of doing business.

Even though our contract spelled out the artist catalogues we were now in control of, we still had to proceed gingerly. Although we were the ones with the motivation and reputation, there was still some reluctance from certain people at Atlantic. As a compromise, a special logo was concocted, the cumbersome *Rhino Presents Atlantic and Atco Re-masters Series*. It was almost as if the Rhino logo wasn't good enough to stand alone. The Atlantic execs didn't understand the concept of branding. It was especially important for us, as we were a growing company trying to increase awareness of Rhino. Imagine the effect of a well-established logo like Coca-Cola or Virgin being reduced to sharing a small box with two other logos and text? Our egos were in check; releasing the product was the most important thing.

We did extremely well in reinvigorating the Atlantic catalogue—we sold over 100,000 of Aretha Franklin's four-disc box set *Queen of Soul*— but the set that sold exceptionally well was *The John Prine Anthology: Great Days*. Richard and I were fans of Prine from his debut album on Atlantic in 1971. He was the 1970s Bob Dylan: a witty folk singer who championed social causes. After a ten-year run on established labels, he became disenchanted and started his own successful record company. Even though three-quarters of the masters on our anthology were from Atlantic and Asylum—one-quarter from Prine's Oh Boy Records—we weren't required to use the funny hybrid logo. We sold 242,000 copies.

Some corporate policies affected us. Early on we realized that we could get our CDs manufactured for ten cents less per disc than what Warner was charging us. Atlantic wouldn't give us the leeway to go elsewhere. The difference was half a million more dollars to us in the early years, escalating to a million as our business grew. It may have been small change to the Warner Music Group, but not to us. Others policies didn't affect us. For example, as a public company, Time Warner gave into complaining stockholders who were revolted by the extreme messages in certain rap records. The controversy started over "Cop Killer," an Ice-T rap recorded by him and others under the artist name Body Count. The labels were pressured to divest themselves of their lucrative rap artists.

On July 31, 1992, John Lennon and Paul McCartney's one-time favorite singer called me out of the blue. I had never spoken to Harry

Nilsson before. He asked me to call the head of his former label, RCA, to see if they wanted to issue a career spanning anthology—which would have included his better known hits "Everybody's Talkin'," "Without You," and "Coconut"—or if Rhino could do it. I thought it was unusual that he didn't just call RCA himself.

Harry was in a bad way. He was devastated when he learned that his trusted financial advisor had embezzled millions from him, leaving him with $300 in his bank account. Howard Kaylan had called me months earlier. In order to raise Harry's spirits, he wanted to engage him in recording a new album. Howard would produce, and Harry's notable friends, like John Sebastian, Stephen Bishop, and Micky Dolenz, would pitch in. I told him I was on board, but the project never happened. After two calls, Joe Galante called me back and gracelessly told me that RCA would do the anthology, but they didn't. In July 1994 Harry died from heart failure—probably more from a broken heart. RCA issued an anthology the following year.

We organized a company policy on charitable donations and giving back to the community. Contributing to charity was important to Richard's family, and it was also a component of sixties hippie culture. Because my parents didn't have much excess money, it wasn't emphasized in my home. Seeing Richard in action inspired me to develop this area on my own. Gary Stewart introduced us to the Liberty Hill Foundation, which helped us choose organizations that received our cash grants. At Rhino a committee set up a program whereby employees were encouraged to give back to the community by performing community service in exchange for getting time off. We plugged worthwhile organizations in our CD booklets and on our yearly calendar. The organizations benefitted, other companies were moved to set up their own programs after seeing what we had done, and consumers were turned on to charities they might not have otherwise known about.

We had outgrown our space, but still hoped to stay in Santa Monica, even more so after Sony Music moved in a block away. But there didn't seem to be anything suitable. We had a number of meetings with Frederick Smith to relocate to one of his industrial buildings in Culver City, which was to be refashioned by architect Eric Own Moss. As the process was taking more time than we anticipated, we weren't confident the space would be ready in time. We set our sights on a newly completed building on Santa Monica Boulevard, south of Westwood, yards from where silent film comedian Harold Lloyd once had his studio. The Atria West was across the street from where Warner Chappell Music Publishing was ensconced in its sister building. As the entire second floor—36,000 square feet—had been vacant in the year since the building was completed, we were able to negotiate a rent that was workable for us.

Brian Schuman did an exemplary job in using his organizational and design skills in planning our new space with the firm we hired, Beckson Design—with the exception of allocating to Richard a noticeably larger office than mine. As conceived by Beckson, the light and airy interior deviated from a typical linear layout as though a rhino had charged through, knocking offices out of alignment. In one of the hallways there was a sequence of lights that was supposed to recall rhino horns. The main conference room had a large, custom-made table that was in the shape of a rhino horn. It sure looked cool, but it was impractical; the long curve caused some people to disappear from view. The grey color of the fabric chairs represented the color of a rhino's hide. I don't think many people noticed the rhino-inspired touches. We were environmentally conscious, and our reception area floor was made from Syndecrete, a concrete-like composite material made from recycled elements including, in our case, pieces of vinyl records, CDs, and cassettes.

I furnished the lobby in a space age Jetsons style with pieces I acquired from vintage furniture stores Futurama, Off the Wall, Modernica, and the yearly Modernism Show. At Modernica I added an accent piece I'd never seen before, a Weltron 2005 combination turntable and eight-track player that looked like a spaceship hoisted on a pedestal. Richard provided his vintage Coca Cola vending machine, which he had stocked with bottled Rhino Water. After a few months, when the walls still hadn't been addressed, I had old movie posters and our album jackets framed, and hung large photos of rock performers used in the set of our *Billboard* series infomercial. I ordered complementary circus mirrors—one that made you fat, one skinny—to make a walk through a narrow hallway more interesting.

Art's is a popular delicatessen in Studio City. The tagline, "Where every sandwich is a work of Art," was complemented by framed photos of various dishes on the walls. The food looked so appealing in the photos that I contacted the photographer and bought a number from him, ordering as though I would have from a menu: "I'll take the corn beef sandwich, blintzes . . ." It gave our lunchroom a novel look, but didn't reflect the food that was served. We brought in a catered lunch every day that the company subsidized, so it cost an employee only two dollars per meal. In the adjacent room, Richard contributed two pinball machines from his collection, one baseball, the other of the rock group Kiss. We had a small gym, and a meditation room.

I had an idea for a museum-like display in our lobby that featured items from Rhino's history. Rhino, in a traditional sense, didn't have a history: the hit records we reissued were originally on other labels. It was a reaction to those who flaunt their history. In contrast with more legitimate historical displays, our items were mundane. I'm not sure how many people got the joke: just because something is displayed with importance doesn't mean that it is important. A few years later, when Ray Charles showed up to collect his million-dollar check for renewing with us, his manager described to him a jacket of his we had on display—one Richard had picked up years previously in a thrift store for five bucks. Ray thought we deserved better and sent over a flashier one to replace it. It fit me perfectly. Our offices were featured in *Interior Design* magazine and used as a location for the Adam Sandler movie *Airheads*. George Clooney filmed a car commercial for Japan out front.

As I mentioned, when Richard and I moved into our first label location, it was just the two of us and a warehouseman. As our sales increased, we could afford to hire more people. What that meant was that other people were now assuming duties I once had. There were other, newer tasks to oversee owing to the growth of the organization. But this dilution in my duties caused me to meet with Richard and ask for guidance on other things I should be doing. He didn't offer me any ideas in that meeting, or subsequently. It was up to me to redefine my role as the company grew.

I was still making deals and coming up with projects. Much as I wanted to, I couldn't justify the time to produce any of our reissues, but I made suggestions, and on occasion edited or rewrote liner notes. I had established our media licensing (film/TV/commercials), but it didn't appear that we could have increased business enough to hire a full-time employee, so I saved the expense and added revenue to the company by doing it myself. I pursued deals for our home video division.

In the early '90s the concept of branding was in the zeitgeist. For a company like Rhino, it meant that people in general were familiar with our company and logo and, more pointedly, that music buyers were. The next step was to make them aware that we made the highest quality reissues in the market. We hoped that if consumers were considering two or more similar packages, they would buy the Rhino one. Emmer compared Rhino's logo to that of the *Good Housekeeping* "Seal of Approval." In addition to bolstering consumer interest, the increased presence of the brand would make doing business with Rhino more appealing to artists, licensors, and retailers.

The company best at branding was Disney. Walt Disney started out making cartoon shorts and then later produced animated features. The brand was successfully extended into many other areas. It was the standard for me, but by no means a model. Rhino was originally two record stores, and then the record label, and we were conscious of maintaining that identification. Rhino Home Video and Kid Rhino also became established brands in their respective markets.

I took it upon myself to *extend* our brand into other areas, all at no cost to the company or our business. I created a Rhino Books imprint and made book distribution deals with three publishers to get our name and logo presence in book stores. One of the goals of Rhino Films was to get exposure in theaters and on TV. Another was to celebrate the music of our vintage artists by producing docudramas.

With Richard's input, I developed a concept for a Club Rhino restaurant chain. Unlike other theme restaurants, like the Hard Rock Café and Planet Hollywood, ours would have humor. Additionally, I liked the idea of customers being able to order CDs off the menu. Richard and I had meetings with some of the major hotels in Las Vegas. Felix Rappaport, the president of New York New York, had us back for a second meeting, but the others didn't quite get the concept. The main problem was our timing.

The novelty had worn off with theme restaurants. Planet Hollywood had filed for bankruptcy.

Steve Nemeth, my brother-in-law, met one of the owners of the Dodgers minor league team, the San Bernardino Stampede. We were invited to a game, with the intention of renaming the team the Rhinos, and using our logos. It would have increased our merchandising and visibility, not just in San Bernardino but also in the other cities of the Class A California League. While it would have been nice to have seen a team sporting the Rhino logo, I felt that I would have to make a few visits a year to the stadium to check on how it was being used, and I didn't relish the 150-mile round-trip drive. Similarly, Richard looked into forming a Rhinos minor league basketball team to play in the Continental Basketball Association. He and I would have funded it, and we were thinking of placing the team in Santa Barbara or San Diego (formerly the home of the NBA Clippers). Ultimately, we didn't proceed because it didn't seem that there was a way to make money. The league's relationship with the NBA was such that if a stellar player were plucked for one of the major teams, the CBA team would only get a minimal amount of compensation.

One of the more interesting promotional ideas we had was a yearly music trivia contest we promoted with Tower Records, called RMAT (Rhino Musical Aptitude Test). We also co-promoted Retrofest, a one-off pop culture and music festival at the Santa Monica Civic in August 1999. We had a number of acts perform, like Flo & Eddie and the Turtles, Dick Dale, and Berlin, and a number of attractions, but too few people showed up and we lost a lot of money. If it had worked, we could have staged it in numerous cities throughout the summer.

The Monkees was our first property that interested companies in branded merchandise. Because Warner Brothers Pictures had a well-staffed division that handled this area, we offered them the Monkees, but they thought it would bring in too-little revenue to justify their time. I learned the business and made quite a number of deals for common items such as bobble head dolls, bathrobes and pajamas, as well as for expensive, limited edition, band-signed drumheads and lithographs. I made sure the items were made with quality before I approved, and I was sensitive to any issues the members of the Monkees might have had. A few rock artists, such as the Rolling Stones and Grateful Dead, had licensed their name to wine. We were approached to license the Monkees. Knowing that Peter Tork was a member of AA, I spoke to him about the request. We proceeded in licensing a non-alcoholic wine, but it was never produced.

Not every move we made was a successful one. Our decision to enter the kids market at a particular heady management meeting in Oxnard, in June 1990, smacked of hubris, and was a rare misstep. We thought we could be successful in an area we knew nothing about. With a young staff, few of us had children, and that included Richard and me at the time. We weren't interacting with kids, or learning what appealed to them. Raffi, a Canadian singer with a soft tone in the manner of Cat Stevens, sold hundreds of thousands of albums in the kids market, leading those in the music business to perceive that there was a new market for kids' music.

I was designated to oversee the new Kid Rhino imprint and hired one person to head it up. After the first two years, it reported to the A&R department. My initial ideas made sense. One was to compile albums of hits that would appeal to kids. I wanted to record new albums with kid-friendly performers, whose records parents bought when they were younger, and that they might buy for their children. I thought of Donovan, but couldn't get a good phone number for him or a manager. John Sebastian declined, explaining that his voice had deteriorated. My good friend Peter Noone would only agree if I hired the very expensive Phil Ramone to produce. That left Micky Dolenz.

Micky Dolenz Puts You to Sleep was not a commentary on how boring he was, but soothing music intended to relax a child when in bed. It was Kid Rhino's first release in October 1991. Working with Micky was the best experience I had as a producer. He showed up on time, always sang in tune, and possessed a rare ability to sing in any style. Sales were encouraging enough that we followed it up with *Broadway Micky*—much to the chagrin of his fellow Monkee Davy Jones who whined, "Everybody knows I'm the Broadway guy!"

Early on Bob Emmer made a deal to distribute Rabbit Ears, the producer of a high quality animated TV series that paired a familiar actor reading a children's story with a noted musician providing the soundtrack. For example, Robin Williams read *Pecos Bill* with Ry Cooder;

Jack Nicholson read *The Elephant's Child* with Bobby McFerrin. Sales in this initial period were poor. It was clear that we had misjudged the market. It was then I adopted a defensive strategy, one aimed at minimizing losses until we could get a new direction. Emmer inadvertently provided that when he made a deal to issue the songs from Steven Spielberg's new cartoon show *Animaniacs*. The show was wacky and witty, but also with an educational element. The 100,000 we sold of the first album recouped most of the division's losses in that period. It pointed the way to what worked for Kid Rhino. Despite our ambitions, the only releases that had a chance to be successful were ones associated with movies and TV shows.

We contracted with a number of companies that had appealing brands. Among the more successful titles were Nickelodeon's *Blue's Clues* (200,000) and Cartoon Network's *Space Ghost* (83,000). The Fisher-Price and Music for Little People brands didn't work for us. *Space Jam* was a hit movie, pairing basketball great Michael Jordon with Bugs Bunny and other Looney Tunes characters. We sold 175,000 copies of the soundtrack.

Even though at one time Kid Rhino was considered the number two kids label after Disney—a very distant number two—it never made money. The product was lower priced to be affordable to kids. Sometimes we had to absorb the cost of an enclosed toy, or more costly packaging to fit on the racks at toy stores. Also, unlike our catalog business, retail did not look upon kid product as generating sales beyond its initial release.

When a Warner Brothers artist illustrated a 1997 sampler CD for us that depicted Bugs Bunny embracing Kid Rhino, I realized that our junior character had the look—and personality—of a unique cartoon character. I pitched it to Warner Brothers' animation division, but they didn't feel the same way. Kid Rhino lasted longer than it should have, with various personnel taking the helm. Warner Brothers' lack of interest in developing either Rocky Rhino or Kid Rhino as a viable animated character missed the real potential in my mind.

Breaking newly recorded artists was still a problem for us, even with our new relationship. Danny Goldberg was a senior VP at Atlantic, head of A&R for the West Coast office. He has a number of admirable qualities: he's smart, a real music fan, and a champion of liberal causes. He also has a politician's sense of reality, whereby the end is given preference over the means, a trait I discovered when he tried to foist Roger Clinton on us. In a move to get chummy with Roger's brother, president-elect Bill Clinton (or at the very least to be well-positioned at the premier Inaugural Ball, a person in Roger's camp speculated), Danny spent $60,000 having Roger record a cover of Sam Cooke's "A Change Is Gonna Come" with R&B vocal group En Vogue singing backup. When his strategy didn't work, he wanted to wash his hands of the relationship. When the press got wind of the recording, Danny denied that Atlantic had signed him and then came up with an alternative.

He called me and asked, "as a favor," for us to record an album with Roger that Atlantic would pay for. Even if we had been interested, Clinton didn't fit in with our label. A few months later, Richard was able to secure a deal for him with Pyramid Records, a label we distributed. Clinton's original recording was forgotten about. It was a fine performance, but to this day has never been released.

Despite the long odds, there was still a push to record new artists at the company. Our RNA (Rhino New Artists) label failed, so our head of marketing, Chris Tobey, and our A&R Department concocted the Forward imprint. Todd Rundgren wanted to record a new album, and Chris thought he was enough of a prestigious artist to make an impact for Forward's debut. Similar to our contract with Capitol, we had a stipulation that Atlantic's radio promotion department had to work a minimal number of records per year. From overseeing the Bearsville catalogue, I developed a good relationship with Todd's manager, Eric Gardner. Eric wanted confirmation from Atlantic that they would work Todd's record before he made the deal with us. In a conference call, Danny Goldberg assured Eric and me that Atlantic would work the record.

Todd long ago professed boredom with composing the melodic rock songs at which he excelled. His last big selling record (397,000) was 1978's *Hermit of Mink Hollow*. This time out he wanted to revamp himself as a technologically progressive artist named TR-i (Todd Rundgren interactive). The advance and recording cost for Todd to make *New World Order* exceeded $100,000. We spent money on marketing the record, but hadn't seen any effect of Atlantic's radio promotion department. I called Danny to see what had happened. He admitted that it hadn't been worked, and then astonished me when he said that he thought *we only wanted him to tell Eric* that Atlantic was going to work the record so we could sign Todd. *Yeah, Danny*, I thought, *that's why we spent all this money.* The record was over—it was too late to rekindle any interest. In January 1994 Doug Morris appointed Danny president of Atlantic Records.

Colin Reef had been hired to head our finance department. Fairly early on he more than paid for his salary when he noticed that our joint-venture partners were paying us for our product in ninety days, meaning they had our money at their disposal while we had to pay interest to a bank on our $3 million line of credit. He made a case for us being paid on a current basis, just like Virgin Records, a label Atlantic distributed. When they agreed, we no longer had a need for the line of credit.

In the mid-nineties the concept of the superstore took hold. Best Buy, Borders and, to a lesser extent, Circuit City and Barnes & Noble, greatly expanded their stock of deep catalogue. What this meant was that in addition to stocking the hits and the more recent releases by contemporary artists, they were also accommodating older hits and albums. All of those chains were in expansion mode, as was Tower Records, which already was a deep catalogue retailer. Every time a new store was about to open, a large quantity of our product was brought in. As a result, our sales flourished.

Because we were passionately driven, we had the patience to realize our projects. Our *Righteous Brothers Anthology* took six years. Releasing the early recordings of Quiet Riot took ten years. I met Kevin DuBrow at Wong's West nightclub in 1979. He invited me to sit at his booth for a chat, and we both discovered that we were big Steve Marriott fans. Marriott had been the lead singer of the Small Faces and subsequently Humble Pie. We were both in the audience the night Humble Pie played the Whisky in December 1970. We also shared a fondness for other British groups of the period. Kevin had been the lead singer in Quiet Riot, but the group had fallen apart after guitarist Randy Rhoads left to join Ozzy Osbourne's band. At one time they were the heir apparent to Van Halen as the area's most popular heavy metal band. With an enormous local following, the group had sold out venues such as the Starwood, Whisky, and Palomino, but they couldn't get a record deal in the United States. I hadn't seen the original band play, but I borrowed their two albums—which were only released in Japan on CBS Sony—from A&R man Jeff Samuels when I saw them in his office at United Artists Records in 1978. I could see why they didn't get an American deal. The sound on the two albums was thin. Still, Kevin licensed me a track—the first appearance of Quiet Riot on a US record—for our 1980 local bands compilation *Yes Nukes*.

With the accolades Rhoads was getting on tour with Ozzy in the early eighties, I expressed to Kevin an interest in wanting to release the original Quiet Riot material. I also liked his new band, DuBrow, and wanted to sign them to Rhino, but his manager at the time was a flake, and nothing happened. In March 1982, Rhoads was killed in a plane crash, and his notoriety soared. Subsequently, Kevin put together a new band, also called it Quiet Riot, and got a record deal with a label distributed by CBS. On the strength of the band's hit single, a cover of Slade's "Cum On Feel the Noize," in November 1983 Quiet Riot scored the first number one album of the burgeoning heavy metal revival. The band's successive albums each declined in sales from their predecessor, and Kevin quit the band in 1987.

I saw him around this time, and we renewed our discussion about rereleasing the original Quiet Riot records. He had done a test of a song as an example of how the sound could be made more dynamic. One way of doing this was to play an original guitar track through a beefier amplifier and record it in the studio. It took Kevin a few years before he could address the project properly. He and his coproducer did an exemplary job on the album; half of the tracks were from the band's first two LPs, and half were unreleased. But by the time *Quiet Riot: The Randy Rhoads Years* hit the stores in October 1993, interest in both the band and Rhoads had subsided. Had it been released when I first suggested it, in 1982, the album would have sold a multiple of the 50,000 it totaled.

Richard, Gary, and I were a formidable source for ideas of product to release. Yet on the morning of November 2, 1993, our regularly scheduled A&R meeting entered an unwelcomed dimension. Gary led off with suggesting an album by the Gay Men's Chorus of Los Angeles, calling it "Strangers in the Night." How was this a Rhino project? I wondered. Richard then chipped in with "Frank Sinatra Jr.'s Greatest Hits"—except he had no hits. Was I hearing right? I knew it wasn't a hallucination, I hadn't taken any acid, and my office walls were not moving. I checked myself and no, it wasn't a dream, either. It could have been the Twinkie Defense: impaired judgment from eating too much after-Halloween candy. It was like a shift in reality, like the Bizarro World in Superman. The meeting continued with Gary suggesting a box set of feminist songs, and he followed that with a *Hair* (the stage play) tribute album. Richard then had the best idea of the meeting, songs that were on Elvis's jukebox, but it still wasn't a good one.

I wasn't on a power trip, and I didn't enjoy saying "No"—quite the opposite. Still, a person in my position is sowing rejection, in essence: *Your idea isn't good enough.* Anytime we launched a project, it passed through many departments and many hands: legal, to make the deal; A&R, to determine what songs would be on the album; art, for the packaging; sales and marketing; and royalties—no matter how small the revenue. A bad project meant that all of these people had to occupy their time on a money loser at the expense of a title that might have actual potential. I was sensitive to encumbering our employees with an idea that I thought wouldn't justify their efforts and the expense. From these above examples, Gary's liberalism was prone to those who considered themselves marginalized. Richard's emotional makeup included a gambler's roll of the dice, where anything had a chance to be a winner, even long shots. So, in addition to contributing my own ideas—I made no presentations that day—I viewed my role as a mediator. As that November meeting exemplified, sometimes it was difficult to contain my exasperation. I derived no pleasure in being the person most likely to say "No," which also created tension at times.

By the time we made our deal with Atlantic, Ahmet Ertegun seemed to have been slowed by old age. But that didn't stop his drinking. When I was in Hong Kong in April 1999 for the Warner Music Group meetings, Atlantic president Val Azzoli told me a typical story: "After drinking twelve vodkas, Ahmet signed a lounge band at the Grand Hyatt. They showed up on Monday morning, and we paid them off. This would usually happen twice a year." Still, to me, Ahmet was to be respected. So, for example, when he called me and wanted Rhino to issue a CD of a 1973 album by jazz singer and pianist Bobby Short, I didn't reply that it would sell so few CDs that we would lose money on it. It was Ahmet's request, so we did it.

*   *   *

I saw *Pulp Fiction* at an advance screening in New York when we were on a promotional tour for our Sweet Sixteen Anniversary in September 1994. I was so blown away that I plugged it in our interviews. Many months before, I got a call from Karyn Rachtman, the film's music supervisor, who wanted to license Dick Dale's "Miserlou" over the opening credits.

Dick Dale created the style that would be referred to as *surf instrumental*. An avid surfer, he wanted to approximate, musically, the power of the waves he felt when he was on a surfboard. Although "Miserlou" originated as a Greek folk song with Middle Eastern influences, Dick's ferocious arrangement resulted in his best recording. Dick Dale and his band, the Del-Tones, were extremely popular in Southern California in the early 1960s, but their renown was geographically limited because Dick refused to tour so he could be close to his favorite surfing spots. The band's November 1962 record *Surfer's Choice* is regarded as the first surf music album.

Like other instrumental surf groups, when the Beatles hit, their popularity dwindled. Around this time Dick was diagnosed with rectal cancer and given three months to live. An operation was successful and he went to Hawaii to recuperate. He cultivated a menagerie of animals—including a tiger—studied martial arts, and fell in love with his wife, Jeannie, Hawaii's top Tahitian dancer, whom he married shortly after returning to California in 1971. Jeannie encouraged Dick to return to performing, but with her involvement it was more like a Las Vegas lounge act. He started at the bottom and his popularity grew all over again. During the seventies he became very successful in real estate.

In 1981 Bruce Springsteen—and members of his E Street Band—helped to resurrect the career of early sixties rocker Gary U.S. Bonds with a hit single and album. Richard thought that Bruce, and other Dick Dale fans like John Fogerty and ELO's Jeff Lynne, could do the same for Dick. In July, Dick and Jeannie drove to our funky warehouse office in their Rolls Royce, after which we reconvened at a coffee shop. I had met Dick previously, when I covered the Surfer's Stomp revival concert for *Rolling Stone* in August 1973. Paul Rappaport and I went backstage at the Palladium to meet Dick. He was very congenial, and even gave Paul one of his guitar picks—which Paul framed and hung on his office wall.

In his mid-forties, Dick was a handsome and charming man. What I liked most about him was his positive energy and aphorisms. What I liked least about him was his self-centeredness. When he talked, he peculiarly referred to himself in the third person. This could partially be explained because his real name was Richard Monsour. Although he's identified as a pioneer of surf music, when he previously performed country and western music, a DJ thought he should have a more appropriate handle and named him "Dick Dale." Dick and Jeannie had a unique rapport, conversing in a manner that was one or two steps above baby talk. Jeannie, beautiful and voluptuous, sucked on a lollipop.

Dick entertained us with his anecdotes. He once sold out the Los Angeles Memorial Sports Arena (15,000 capacity), leaving thousands of ticketless kids to mill around outside. He had an offer for management from Elvis' manager, Colonel Tom Parker. He gave guitar lessons to a young Jimi Hendrix, who also played guitar left-handed. (In Hendrix's "Third Stone From the Sun," he whispers, "You'll never hear surf music again," which referred to Dick's battle with cancer.) Springsteen sent a limousine for Dick and Jeannie to see him in concert at the Sports Arena—they went, but Dick claimed he was unfamiliar with Springsteen's music.

The album never happened because we couldn't get responses from possible participants. Dick's original records were not available, and there were many fans, like me, who desired them. Dick didn't want them out because he felt those recordings never fully captured the power of his band in concert. In May 1982 I traveled fifty-four miles to his home in Newport Beach, on the Balboa Peninsula right next to "the Wedge," one of his favorite surfing spots. The seventeen-room mansion was built in 1925 for razor heir King Gillette. The place was impressive, right on the bay, but there were a number of areas that Dick had started to fix up and never finished. I needed him to sign a two-page contract so we could include "Miserlou" on the first volume of our *History of Surf Music* series. I was only there a matter of minutes. Dick seemed preoccupied.

It took until 1986 before I was able to make a deal with him for a best of album and, at his insistence, a 1983 live album he had recorded and issued on his own label. Needless to say, sales of *King of the Surf Guitar: The Best of Dick Dale & the Del-Tones* trounced those of *The Tigers Loose.*

Karyn Rachtman was lowballing me on the fee for *Pulp Fiction*, pleading poverty, only offering $7,500, claiming that she had a lot of songs to license. It's not as if I felt like doing writer/director Quentin Tarantino a favor. I had met him only once, and he berated me because Rhino passed on putting out the soundtrack album to his first film, *Reservoir Dogs*. There was sound judgment behind that decision. I didn't think the movie would be seen by enough people to sell albums. I was right, as it only grossed two and a half million at the box office. The soundtrack sold well only after the success of *Pulp Fiction*. I did license "Little Green Bag" by the George Baker Selection to the movie.

Pulp Fiction's budget was $8 million. I could have turned Karyn down, but I liked her and thought she did a good job. I had also been friendly with her father when I was at UCLA and put on a concert with one of the acts he managed, Flash Cadillac & the Continental Kids. I made the deal. The prominent placement of "Miserlou" in *Pulp Fiction* is a good example of how a song in a hit movie can generate interest. It was a boon to Dick's career, and it sparked a financial windfall for both of us.

The soundtrack album sold over a million copies. In an interview in conjunction with the release, Tarantino arrogantly referred to burning the song's future appeal. He said, "'Miserlou' will be old news." I was offended. I licensed the song for big money to a few commercials. Sales of our *King of the Surf Guitar* album swelled to 275,000. Because of the popularity of surfing in Australia, I thought we could license the album there. We received this response from Warner Australia: "Is Dick Dale a comedian? No one around this office has heard of him!"

"Miserlou" also exemplifies how a quality piece of music can have an effect regardless of when it was originally recorded. The majority of people who took note of the song didn't know that the original record was released in 1962, and they didn't know who Dick Dale was. They were not relating to it as nostalgia or as an "oldie, but a goodie," but because it was a great record.

My friend Eddie Sotto, who worked at Walt Disney Imagineering, called me to get a phone number for Dick's manager. Eddie hired Dick to provide a new soundtrack for the Space Mountain ride at Disneyland. Dick played his trademark riffs over a newly recorded segment of the

Aquarium movement from Camille Saint-Saens' nineteenth century romantic composition *The Carnival of the Animals*. Dick's playing was so frantic, riders thought the ride's speed had increased, but it hadn't.

I got a call from Dick. He was going over his taxes and was surprised that on the 1099 tax form we had sent him, it indicated that he had made over $250,000 in the previous year. I felt gratified that Rhino had played a part in his resurgence. Only ten years earlier, his life was a mess. After defaulting on his mortgage, he was evicted from the dream home he never finished restoring. He barely survived a nasty divorce, and was reduced to living in his RV parked in his parents' driveway. Dick didn't express any appreciation. He called, he said, just to check that the amount was correct.

*   *   *

When Richard and I were producing comedy recordings in the early years of Rhino, we weren't consciously trying to make records like Stan Freberg—it was in our DNA. The antiauthority feelings and absurdist views we shared with Stan would make him our spiritual father. It came as a pleasant surprise when Gary Stiffelman called us to see if we would be interested in talking to his new client, Stan Freberg, about a possible project.

My appreciation for Stan's talent came at an early age, but at the time I didn't realize it was him. My favorite TV show when I was very young was *Time for Beany*, the adventures of Beany (a boy) and Cecil the Seasick Sea Serpent. Stan was one of the two main voice actors and puppeteers. In the 1950s Stan's comedic records—exceptionally well-produced mini-plays—scored more novelty hits than any other recording artist. Many were brilliant, like "St. George and the Dragonet," a parody of the *Dragnet* TV show which was number one for four weeks in October 1953. But Stan was eventually lured away by the creative challenges and big bucks of advertising, where the sense of humor he displayed had *Advertising Age* magazine credit him as being "the Father of the Funny Commercial."

Although Stan's singles had been collected onto LPs before, in 1961 he went into the studio for the first time to record an album. *Stan Freberg Presents the History of the United States* was so popular that it stayed on the charts for half the year. Recorded as musical theater, it spanned the time from Columbus' discovery of the New World through the Revolutionary War. Award-winning Broadway producer David Merrick (*Oliver!, Hello Dolly!*) loved it so much he had Stan write a subsequent volume, bringing the story up through World War I. The play never worked out and Stan was so disgusted with the experience he shelved the script for twenty years.

Rhino funded the recording of Stan's revised second volume and issued it in July 1996. A double album set—packaged with volume one—sold much better at 42,000 copies. The success made it possible for us to produce a proper box set of Stan's career, four CDs and a video tape that included his best commercials. (Stan won twenty-one Clio Awards for advertising.) Through Stan I met Ray Bradbury. It was a thrill for me as Bradbury had been one of my favorite authors. During Stan's busiest years he didn't have much time for acting, but in September 1966 he did appear on one of the best episodes of *The Monkees*, "Monkee vs. Machine."

One afternoon at our office, Richard was conversing with Stan and sensed that he was a conservative Republican. When he confronted him on it, Stan said, "What's wrong with being a Republican?" Richard said, "To us in the sixties, you were a hero of the antiestablishment: you were the first person we knew to take on modern consumerism, wanton consumption, and the shallowness of the media. You were like Lenny Bruce to us. To me, it would be like finding out Lenny Bruce was a Republican." Stan responded, without irony, "Lenny Bruce a Republican? That would be weird."

Richard and I never managed by instilling fear. We considered it counterproductive. As a result, just because we championed a project, it didn't mean that our freethinking staff was inclined to *"win one for the Gipper!"* and support it. This came to light on a project Martin Lewis brought to us in 1987. In order to show the governor of their state, Illinois, how much they wanted the new state prison to be built in their town, the civic leaders of Flora produced a song and video to promote their efforts. "Is We Is Or Is We Isn't (Gonna Get Ourselves a Prison)" by the Barbed Wire Choir featured creaky townspeople rapping sections of the song. It was like a real Village People come to life, including the police chief, the mayor, and the newspaper publisher. I thought the effort by these atypical rappers was funny and endearing, and it was getting enough national TV exposure to be worth a shot. Martin even arranged for Spencer Christian, the weatherman from *Good Morning America*, to intermittently report from Flora throughout the show. Our marketing, sales, and promotion people didn't know how to handle such an oddity, and weren't motivated to try. It was a low-money deal, and I wasn't expecting a big seller, but I was disappointed by our company's lack of effort. Flora didn't get their prison, nor did their Rhino release sell more than a minimal number of copies. But more to the point, it made me realize that if we didn't have the support of those department heads in the planning stage, a project might not be successful. And they weren't always right.

I read the screenplay for the movie *The Full Monty* and thought it was so good I would have even invested my own money in the production. The budget was only $3.5 million, and Twentieth Century Fox didn't need any contribution from me. But as a low-budget movie they did need our songs at an accommodating price. As a result, we were in first position to put out the soundtrack album. In June 1997, I set up a screening of a rough cut (not quite finished film) at Fox for our senior staff, marketing, and sales people. Other than me, the only person who wanted to put out the soundtrack was Julie D'Angelo, my former assistant who now headed up soundtracks for us. I was surprised that even Gary Stewart failed to see the potential of the film. I wasn't going to make the soundtrack deal if nobody else believed in it. The low-budget movie was a hit, grossing $45 million at the US box office and $200 million more outside of the country. RCA issued the soundtrack album in the States and sold close to half a million copies.

Ian Whitcomb was an anomaly among performers of the British Invasion. He had a top ten hit with "You Turn Me On" in the summer of 1965. He was a student of history, graduating with a degree from Trinity College in Dublin. As much as he was energized by 1950s rock 'n' roll, he was more taken with the music that was popular around the turn of the twentieth century, particularly with Ragtime. He was hired, briefly, as a consultant on the *Titanic* movie, but quickly became disenchanted when it was clear that the producers had no interest in recreating a musical soundtrack that accurately depicted what was played on the ship. When he told me this, I suggested to him that he should record such an album, and that we would put it out. The album was released midyear and was well in place when the long-delayed film debuted in December. When the movie hit big at the box office, people took notice of Ian's affectionate tribute, resulting in the biggest selling album—over 100,000 worldwide—in his career. *Titanic: Music As Heard on the Fateful Voyage* also won a Grammy Award for best packaging.

At the national WEA sales meetings in February 1999, we started our presentation with a short film that dubbed a Rhino sales pitch onto a 1967 film of Japanese superhero Ultraman. Richard was then introduced, but it wasn't he who came to the lectern, but—keeping in dub theme— a Japanese actor who mouthed Richard's words—out of synch—while Richard recited his speech hidden from view. The actor hammed it up, including one segment during which he drank water from a glass while Richard was still speaking.

Finally, we were given access to the Warner Brothers vaults, and at that meeting we previewed our first box sets, Deep Purple in March and Alice Cooper in April. Similar to Atlantic, we had to use a specific Warner Reprise Archives logo with diminished Rhino presence. Had the Warner execs not been so stuffy, we could have embarked on the Warner reissue program six years previously, with the Music Group benefitting from six years of additional profits. But events were only going to get stuffier.

CHAPTER 10

The Andy Warhols of the Music Industry

THE RHINO BROTHERS

When Richard and I attended art openings in our twenties and thirties, it wasn't that we were intrigued by the new crop of modern artists. We thought it would be a good place to meet girls, although that rarely paid off. Despite our motives, much of what we did could come under the category of conceptual art, in which the idea was more important than the execution or result. While Andy Warhol is more associated with pop art, his concepts were always much stronger than the artistry. He embraced a sense of humor and an absurdity in painting canvasses of cans of Campbell's Soup and garish images of Mao and Elvis Presley.

In a similar manner, our thought processes coalesced into recordings and other elements where the concept was stronger than the finished product. This was the result of active minds that weren't directed to broader or higher purposes. It also reflected our sense of humor, and channeled whatever antiauthority attitudes we had. Warhol is a reference, not an influence. Lurking in our subconscious minds was the gimmickry of low-budget horror filmmaker William Castle.

By our very natures, in the workplace Richard and I were fairly conventional, responsible guys. Although not outgoing, we were approachable and low-key, and tried to be helpful. We were not screamers, we didn't swear, we were not rude, and we weren't flamboyant or needing to bring attention to ourselves. Yet, there was that kernel of rebelliousness and a restlessness to push the limits, which found its way into our product.

That sense of mischievousness was a part of Richard's and my personalities, and we were able to express it at Rhino, whether or not it was perceived. In a sort-of tribute to the Warner Brothers, we referred to ourselves humorously as the Rhino Brothers. In designing the cover to one of our novelty compilations, Anne Brownfield came up with the concept of a circus to accommodate our many acts. Drawing upon the circus promoters Ringling Brothers, she coined the Rhino Brothers. I thought it was funny because Richard and I weren't brothers. Rock acts the Righteous Brothers and Walker Brothers weren't composed of brothers, either. I next used it for our publishing company name, Rhino Brothers Music, just like publishing giant Warner Brothers Music.

I find coming up with a novel idea or approach very gratifying. It shows my brain is working. Sometimes an idea falls short when realized, or gets changed by budget considerations or the involvement of others. Richard and I gave each other a reasonable amount of leeway to express ourselves creatively, even if our commercial expectations were low. Checkpoint Charlie is an apt example.

Howard Kaylan and Mark Volman were fans of Kraftwerk, a German all-synthesizer band that hit it big in 1975 on the strength of their *Autobahn* album and hit single. A few years later, the Casio Computer Company manufactured a cheap, toy-like synthesizer. Mark and Howard wanted to record an EP of Kraftwerk-like arrangements on their Casios. I oversaw the record, and had the cover written in German so it looked like it could have been an import. Mark and Howard called their "group" Checkpoint Charlie—after the name of the guarded crossing between East and West Berlin during the Cold War—and adopted pseudonyms of Salz and Pfeffer (German for salt and pepper). I resurrected an obscure concept, of mastering a record so that it played inside out. One put the needle on the inside where the label was, and the record played the music properly (not backwards) until the needle was on the outer groove. I thought if record fans didn't initially respond to the musical content, how could they not want to impress their guests with a record that played inside out? (The cover was clearly marked in English and German that it played that way.)

It got little media attention, and consequently sold less than 2,000. Later we found out there was a real German band named Checkpoint Charlie.

Sometimes the result is unexpected. A record we thought would sell little became a best seller for us. "Louie Louie" was one of the defining songs of the 1960s. The Kingsmen's cover of Richard Berry's original didn't become a national hit until late 1963, seven months after it was released. It was sloppily performed, sounding as though it had been recorded in a garage. Much of the vocals were unintelligible, to the point where the FBI made an investigation after the record became a hit because they heard that the lyrics were dirty. The song has endured because it captured the feeling of teenage abandon so well.

If an artist was fortunate enough to have had a run of hits, its record company would usually issue a "Greatest Hits" or "Best of" album which was a sure bet for impressive sales, without additional recording costs. But nobody had been crazy enough to put together an album composed of different versions of the same song. Who would want to hear one song, although differently arranged, numerous times? Richard got the idea from California radio stations KALX and KFJC, which played all the known versions, back-to-back, during "Louie Lou-a-thons." To make the album more contemporary, Richard and Bob Wayne produced an arrangement that copied the style of David Bowie's recent hit, "Let's Dance," as performed by Les Dantz and his Orchestra.

A nice inclusion was the version of "Louie Louie" by the Rice University Marching Owl Band. In the 1950s and 1960s, rock music was anathema to both college and professional sports. By the 1970s, attitudes had changed, and one would hear the novelty of a marching band playing a rock song during the half time of a football game. It was a good arrangement, and we kicked off the album with it. When I was able to license the recording to a couple of movies, including *Naked Gun*, it provided some bonus money for the school and for us.

Richard was in touch with Max Feirtag, the owner of 1950s R&B label Flip Records, who, as Limax Music, published the song along with his wife Lillian. Richard Berry's 1956 release of "Louie Louie" hadn't sold much, about 7,000 copies. Originally the B-side of his single, he felt the song wasn't worth much (and, three years later, was happy to sell the publishing and writer's share of that and the other songs he wrote for Flip to Feirtag for $750 because he needed money for his impending wedding and honeymoon). The "contract" was written on a napkin in a restaurant. Feirtag was fine with what Rhino wanted to do, as he stood to benefit from nine cover versions of the song. Because he was having difficulty with Richard Berry at the time, he refused Richard's request to license the original Flip Records version recorded by Berry. Feirtag failed to grasp the significance of the inclusion of the song's first recording.

Richard contacted Berry, and produced (also with Wayne) a version that matched the original so closely, he received a call from Feirtag's lawyer who thought we had bootlegged the original recording. When Richard told him that he had made a new recording of the song, the skeptical lawyer told him that they were going to "conduct laboratory tests" to determine if there was a difference. Richard's production was so faithful, we never received even one complaint that it wasn't the original version in the package.

As we were having a good year, the outrageousness of releasing one album of all the same songs appealed to our sense of fun more than the thought that we could possibly make money on the release. Richard was so sure it would be a sales flop, thinking it might only sell 3,000 records, he didn't even credit himself on the jacket. Because I thought he should, when I mastered the record I had the engineer inscribe into the inner groove "COMPILED BY RICHARD 'I WISH MY NAME WERE LOUIE' FOOS." We sold over 80,000.

Henny Youngman had a long career as one of America's best comedians. He was called "The King of the One-Liners," which meant that he favored short jokes. He even wrote his letters, vertically, with one-liners. His best-known one-liner is, "Take my wife—please!" A typical joke is this one, included on the album we released: "My wife said to me, 'For our anniversary I want to go somewhere I've never been before.' I said, 'Try the kitchen!'" We got in touch with Henny and licensed from him an album that was out of print.

In reimagining the album, Richard's inspiration was to take a 20 Greatest Hits-type of record and adapt it to Henny's accumulation of jokes, resulting in our title of *Henny Youngman's 128 Greatest Jokes*. (No, we didn't count how many jokes were actually on the album.) The design of our cover called to mind those albums that depicted gold records with titles of hits placed over them. On ours we had the opening joke phrase in place of the hit title. I expanded on the trick track process heard on Monty Python's *Matching Tie and Handkerchief*, wherein one side was mastered with two concentric grooves. When the listener plopped the needle onto the disc, he didn't know which of the two tracks he would hear. I elected to go for four. One complaint of comedy records is that after you've played them once, you'd heard all of the jokes. Side one contained four, three-minute sides. You put the needle at the beginning and it played to the end of the record. You could do that four times and not hear the same jokes. Although the album was among Rhino's steadiest sellers, the resulting innovative package didn't seem to ensure any additional sales. Henny questioned the gold records on the cover: "Why did you put doughnuts on the front?"

The Olympics, a light R&B vocal group from Los Angeles, were best described as a poor man's Coasters. Although their recordings were very credible, they weren't as sophisticated as their peers. They drew upon the same humor and references, as exemplified by "Western Movies," which was similar in subject to the Coasters' later-recorded "Along Came Jones." Their most remembered songs include "(Baby) Hully Gully," "Big Boy Pete," "Good Lovin'" (later a smash for the Young Rascals), and "Peanut Butter" (recorded originally by the Olympics under the name Marathons), which is familiar from its use in TV commercials. While the Olympics had only one national top twenty hit, they more than merited a best of, but that's not what motivated us to release an album.

We were bothered by the commercial trivialization of the Olympics sporting event, owing to the 1984 Olympic Games committee selling the name to all sorts of products with little regard to the relevance or nutritional benefits: the Snickers candy bar was the "Official Snack Food," Coca-Cola the "Official Soft Drink," Budweiser the "Official Beer," First Interstate Bank the "Official Bank."

We decided to comment on the absurdity by releasing *The Official Record Album of the Olympics*. We couldn't resist thumbing our noses at the organization as we developed a package that incorporated US flags, event tickets, and a special Rocky Rhino marathon runner bearing a lighted-torch logo. The actual theme music from the games was released by Columbia Records as *The Official Music of the XXIIIrd Olympiad, Los Angeles 1984*. Whew! We parodied the Olympic Games endorsements on our album jacket with group favorites: The Official Car of the Olympics: 1949 Convertible; The Official Drink of the Olympics: Ripple Wine; The Official Restaurant of the Olympics: Stan's Drive-In; The Official Dance of the Olympics: Hully Gully.

The Olympic Committee heard about the album and sent us a threatening demand letter, dated August 29, that we "cease and desist." We were amazed at the serious tone. Richard responded with a retort that explained that the band adopted its name in 1957 from LA's Olympic Boulevard, and suggested the committee "might also want to collect a royalty from the city of Los Angeles for using your name on their street signs." He pointed out that, unfortunately for us, "the average customer seems able to discern the difference as Columbia's LP has outsold ours, approximately 250,000 to 3,000." The Olympic Committee never responded.

Rhino's biggest seller in its early years was a concept of Richard's. He was bothered that many of the successful rock acts of the '70s had abandoned the irreverent and fun spirit inherent in rock, with Led Zeppelin being a prime example. In order to satirically expose the seriousness of their music, he thought of rendering their "Whole Lotta Love" performed on kazoos. I named the act the Temple City Kazoo Orchestra, and we recorded the song in a garage in Santa Monica. When it became the most popular cut on our *Rhino Royale* compilation album in 1978, we produced a few more songs in Michael Sembello's Encino garage with members of Stevie Wonder's band helping out. In 1983 Sembello scored a number one hit with "Maniac," a song from *Flashdance*.

We released a twelve-inch EP on multicolored *Disco Vinyl*, initially in a numbered limited edition. Unlike other studio recordings of fictional artists, we did not merely concoct a name, but created a persona and accompanying biography that explained the music. Richard's liner notes were inspired, claiming that the leader, David Humms, had transposed all nine of Beethoven's symphonies to be played on kazoo and revealing that the group had finished second in Temple City's annual Kiwanis Club talent contest, losing to a woman who played "Yankee Doodle" on her false teeth.

We received calls from radio stations requesting copies to play. We put together an ad hoc group and performed two songs on daytime TV's *The Mike Douglas Show*, the second one alongside Cheryl Tiegs, Lou "the Hulk" Ferrigno, Lee Grant, and comedian David Brenner. The TCKO, as we referred to them—our inside joke at the Electric Light Orchestra, whose name was abbreviated to ELO—played a UCLA parking lot concert and received a better response than local band X, who followed us.

The conceit of developing a humorous background for a made-up artist was first expressed on the Rhino label's fourth single, "Baseball Card Lover" by Rockin' Richie Ray. Richard had a knack for writing these "official bios," as evidenced here with an excerpt: "Rockin' Richie Ray was four years old when he first heard Gene Vincent singing 'Be-Bop-A-Lula.' He immediately discarded his corduroy playsuit for a leather jacket, and was soon expelled from Mother Goose Nursery School for organizing protection rackets on the milk and cookies run."

We tried to help where we could. I don't mean to say that we had been around Wild Man Fischer so much we could think like him, but we did have his patter down and could write songs like him. When we recorded *Wildmania*, he was having difficulty coming up with material, so Richard and I (as Kowalski-Schwartz) wrote six songs in his style. Fischer liked them, and he performed them on the album. Other times we stood in for him. When he failed to show up on a Saturday afternoon we were being interviewed on the phone by a radio station in Cleveland, Richard impersonated Wild Man. He stepped into those shoes a second time when, as Wild Man Jr., he effectively rendered "I'm the Creature from Outer Space" when Fischer failed to show for the recording session.

There were so many Elvis impersonators springing up following Elvis Presley's death in 1977, it got Richard to thinking: Elvis was such a worldwide star, there must be impersonators in many countries, and what would they sound like? That idea was the basis of our *The International Elvis Impersonators Convention* EP, which was released in 1979. Richard and I produced the various made-up acts in the studio. Richard wrote mini bios of the performers, with a large dose of humor, like this passage from the Japanese representative, Hound Dog Fujimoto: "Vastly popular from playing Elvis in over twenty-four Japanese movies, Hound Dog received his greatest acclaim in the classic Elvis versus Godzilla."

The cover of 1960's *Elvis' Gold Records—Volume 2* contained the phrase "50,000,000 Elvis Fans Can't Be Wrong." For our record, Richard adapted it to "20,000 Elvis Imitators Can't Be Wrong," and speculated that, at this rate, "by 1986 one in eleven employable males will make their living imitating the King of Rock 'n' Roll." In a case of life imitating art, an Elvis Presley Impersonators International Association Convention was held in 1990 at Chicago's Sheraton-O'Hare hotel, attracting 150 imper-sonators from around the world.

Faced with poor sales from our novelty records, Richard had largely bailed out of producing, but I was still coming up with ideas I wanted to try. While the world was inundated with Christmas rock songs, I had never heard one celebrating the joys of Hanukkah, so I wrote one for the 1981 holiday. The title "Hanukkah Rocks" was inspired by Ian Hunter's "Cleveland Rocks" (a song on his 1979 album *You're Never Alone with a Schizophrenic*). I rewrote Allan Sherman's "Twelve Gifts of Christmas" to the eight days of Hanukkah, and trivialized the chorus to "Hanukkah rocks all around my block"—instead of using "the world." I had Graham Daddy and Louis Naktin compose the music, and got a class of grade school students to sing the chorus, just like Roy Wood had on his mas-sive English hit "I Wish It Could Be Christmas Every Day." That, and the three other songs by Gefilte Joe and the Fish, were pressed onto blue vinyl in the shape of a six-pointed Jewish star that many were surprised actually played on their turntables. The sticker on the jacket invited the purchaser to "join the old wave . . . with the world's oldest and only known Jewish Senior Citizen rock band."

Will Ryan and Phil Baron, who recorded for the kids market as Willio & Phillio, were excellent at impersonating voices. I wondered what it would sound like if you had the Three Stooges sing a song by the Stooges, the rock band fronted by Iggy Pop. I copied the musical backing of the Stooges' "I Wanna Be Your Dog," had Will and Phil sing as Larry, Moe, and Curly, and released it as by the Seven Stooges.

In early 1981 Blondie had a hit with "Rapture," signaling the rush of white artists to record in this new style. Richard reasoned that if the Beatles were still together, they would have recorded a rap record as well, so we wrote "Beatle Rap" (as S. Fields and P. Lane). I produced the recording in the studio, impersonating two of the voices while Ryan did the other two. For the label of the single, we reproduced the yellow and orange swirl of Capitol's mid-1960s Beatles' 45s. It looked so good we used it for subsequent singles releases.

Sometimes we got lucky and licensed one of our original productions to a movie. I had heard that surfing was popular in Bombay, India, which spurred the idea that they must have their own version of surf music, and what would that be? I covered classic surf instrumental "Pipeline" using sitar and tabla, named the artist "The Bombay Beach Boys," and included it on one of our compilation albums. The second *Austin Powers* movie was going to play it in a scene, but the scene was cut, much to my disappointment. It was used in the movie *200 Cigarettes*, which paid us many times the $500 it cost to record. Similarly, *Sixteen Candles* used one of our Temple City Kazoo Orchestra recordings.

In the early 1980s, yearly wall calendars featuring large photos were being sold in bookstores. The more obvious titles displayed photos of rock groups or swimsuit models. I thought we could make our own calendars to give away as a means of branding. This way a buyer for a chain would be reminded of our company every time he looked at our calendar. Initially we used photos of music artists whose product we had released, but then changed to reprints of album covers from the previous year. Music fans loved them. One of the disappointments of Pete Townshend's life, or in February 1992 when he wrote me, was his absence on a Rhino calendar: "Harold, it's become my dream to feature, even in a very small way, in one of your calendars."

We included typical anniversary-type entries of rock star birthdays and significant events, like the Beatles' first appearance on *The Ed Sullivan Show*. I deviated from the standard expectations by adding less than landmark occurrences, such as on February 20: *1965: Keith Moon breaks his manager's dishwasher by using it to wash fruit.* I included trivial Rhino history, as on March 11: *1974: The Rhino Store creates a new way to get rid of non-selling records: it pays people 5 cents to take home Danny Bonaduce's album.* Some of the birthdates identified the band the performer was most associated with, such as *Steve Marriott (Small Faces)*. I threw in a few baseball players, similarly identified, such as on November 3: *1918: Bob Feller (Cleveland Indians)*. On days when there was no entry, I selected non-musicians whose work I appreciated, like Raymond Chandler and Mel Ramos. No one asked me about the baseball entries or the non-musicians. I also added half-tone messages, like *BUY A RHINO ALBUM TODAY*. The partially visible sales pitches were humorous stabs at subliminal advertising, inspired by Vance Packard's groundbreaking *The Hidden Persuaders*, which I read while at UCLA.

Comics, of course, are a staple of youth culture. Richard came up with the idea of having the cover of our 1982 product catalog look like a comic book. I thought it was a great idea, but the first one he oversaw while I was in France at MIDEM, had poor artwork. I took it over from then on, with superb covers illustrated mostly by Scott Shaw.

Our unconventional thinking also applied to our anniversaries. Most companies that have been in business a while, acknowledge familiar years like ten, twenty-five, and fifty. We commemorated our first ten years with a huge party on the Santa Monica Pier. I was fine with celebrating anniversaries, but the expense only made sense to me as a means to promote the company and the product; in other words, anniversaries were recognized primarily to increase revenue. We decided to do it differently, to do it the Rhino way, by selecting unusual year anniversaries that related to teenage/rock 'n' roll culture. Having a Rhino Bar Mitzvah at thirteen years was too close to our ten-year celebration. We next did a Sweet Sixteen, and five years after that a twenty-first anniversary. During these celebration years we held sales promotions and Richard and I traveled to five cities to do press and radio interviews. We produced special advertising supplements for *Billboard* magazine, deviating from the norm with a *National Enquirer* parody and a comic book.

As much as Richard and I loved novelty records, it was hard to continue producing them because they didn't sell. In the fall of 1993 he had an idea: he wanted to record "the 'In-A-Gadda-Da-Vida' version of 'Davy Crockett.'" Crockett, best known as one of the heroes of the Alamo, was the subject of a miniseries on Disney's ABC TV show in the 1950s. The impact created a cultural phenomenon. A second miniseries was produced, and even though kids had seen the programs for free on TV, they paid money at the movie theater to see two feature films edited from the footage. The phenomenon wasn't restricted to the United States. Phil Collins, growing up in London, was so enamored as a young child that when his income soared twenty-five years later as a member of Genesis, he started collecting Alamo artifacts, accumulating over a thousand objects. "The Ballad of Davy Crockett" became a top ten hit for three different artists in 1955. Additional verses were used in the program as story bridges. No one had released a version of the song with all twenty-nine verses.

"In-A-Gadda-Da-Vida" was a seventeen-minute song that made up one side of the Iron Butterfly's 1968 album of the same title. A three-minute edit was released as a single, but the popularity of the longer version sold so many copies that it was the biggest seller for Atlantic Records prior to the popularity of Led Zeppelin. What Richard suggested was to make a recording of "Davy Crockett" with all twenty-nine verses, a long song like "In-A-Gadda-Da-Vida."

Like Richard, I had been a big Davy Crockett fan as a kid, even owning a coonskin cap, just like Crockett's. I looked for a marketing hook to avoid producing another poor-selling novelty record. There were two proposed feature films garnering attention in the trades: a serious one on the Alamo, and a humorous one on Crockett written by the team responsible for the *Police Academy* series. I thought either one had a good shot to be produced. TV producer Alan Sacks recommended Riders in the Sky, and I worked with the Riders' Doug Green on the song selection. The album was recorded in Nashville over a three-day period in March 1994, and then sat on the shelf waiting for a movie to be realized. A year after I left Rhino, I asked David McLees, who succeeded Gary Stewart as head of A&R, to release it as a favor. The recording had already been paid for. I don't think he was that interested, but after a few months he reported that they couldn't find the tape. The comedy film never happened. It took until 2004 for *The Alamo*—which starred Dennis Quaid and Billy Bob Thornton—to hit the theaters. Riders in the Sky released the album themselves through their deal with Rounder Records. They thanked me as "That Guy at Rhino Who Got the Ball Rolling."

*   *   *

Hugh Brown shared our creativity and sense of humor, but he was an actual artist. His calling card described him as "Evil Genius." I met Hugh after a performance by the Dictators at the Keystone Berkeley in April 1977. He was a friendly guy and visited me at the Rhino store when he came to town later in the year. He brought a shirt he had made from a silkscreened pattern with repeated images of the notorious President of Uganda, Idi Amin. During subsequent visits to LA, he showed me other art pieces he had completed. The Keith Richards Blood Transfusion Kit, inspired by reports that the Rolling Stones' guitarist had his blood changed in Switzerland prior to the group's fall 1973 European tour, had medical tools set in a velvet-lined box. In the late 1880s, a convicted forger serving time in Sing Sing prison carved the Lord's Prayer on the head of a pin. Hugh was inspired to write the Lord's Prayer on an enlarged photo of circus performer Zip the Pinhead. His printed resume had a background of white raised lettering, a repeated pattern of "HIRE ME."

Hugh's first album cover credit was courtesy of the Clash, who used a work he created from altered Chinese propaganda imagery for their second LP, *Give 'Em Enough Rope*. Over the years I had him photograph and design a handful of albums for us, but what I wanted most was to hire him for Rhino. He kept putting me off, telling me that he liked the freedom he had freelancing. After giving up my quest, I was dismayed when he told me that he had accepted a job from IRS Records in 1989. In 1996 the label was about to fold when he accepted a job at Rhino as our creative director. He won three Grammy Awards (with shared credits) for *Titanic: Music As Heard on the Fateful Voyage* (1997), *Beg Scream and Shout!* (1998), and *Brain in a Box: The Science Fiction Collection* (2002). The last release depicted a brain floating in formaldehyde—as one might have seen in a horror movie—with three different lenticular (3-D) views of the brain on the sides of the box. Hugh created a number of inspired works after Richard and I left, including the top of an amplifier to house a heavy metal box, which featured a volume knob that rotated to eleven— instead of the standard ten—just like in the Spinal Tap movie.

CHAPTER 11

Fear and Loathing in Hollywood

The Artlessness of the Deal

The notorious author Hunter S. Thompson rarely traveled, but he had agreed to fly into Los Angeles to meet with us at Rhino Films to discuss a project or two. It wasn't much of a surprise that he was almost an hour late in meeting us in the lounge at the hotel where we had booked him a room. He was dressed exactly as a fan of his writing would expect: casual, wearing a Hawaiian shirt, holding a Bloody Mary cocktail. He was accompanied by his former girlfriend, Laila Nabulsi. He was in good spirits. The dinner party included Steve Nemeth, his sister (my wife) Stephanie, my partner in Rhino, Richard, and Laila. We sat at the large table in the dining room of the Westwood Marquis Hotel. Hunter placed an initial order from the waiter: "another Bloody Mary, three Heinekens, a triple Chivas—in a big, pretty glass with lots of ice—and a bottle of Schramsberg Blanc de Noirs Champagne."

Not too long after the waiter left, Hunter swept his right hand in a grand flourish, scooped up what looked like a blob of butter from the top of a ramekin and zeroed in on his nose. Sitting across from him as he pretended to snort cocaine, I thought, "Hunter is a funny guy." I soon realized that it wasn't a butter dish from the table that Hunter was holding, but a similar-sized container filled with cocaine. It was an audacious and possibly provocative gesture in a public place, but fortunately there had been no other diners seated nearby and no waiters hovering. Such flagrant behavior was not something I was comfortable with. Hoping that he would control his impulses made for a tense dinner. Hunter came across more like a character than a real person. After we finished our entrees, he requested one of every dessert for our table to sample. At the end of our dinner, he mumbled about needing to get in touch with Jack Nicholson in order to get some adrenalin to avoid having to call 911. I'd had enough of Hunter for the night. Steve went to Hunter's room and encountered actor Don Johnson coming out of the bathroom with a plate full of cocaine.

From whatever deranged behavior Hunter revealed in his autobio-graphical breakthrough *Fear and Loathing in Las Vegas*, to that depicted in subsequent writings and at times reported in the news, the surprise was that producing the *Fear and Loathing in Las Vegas* movie seemed to bring out the worst in peoples' behavior, with very little of the misbehaving being attributed to Hunter. It was as if the talent and the dealmakers were the victims in a small town where everybody goes crazy, like in *Invasion of the Body Snatchers*—except the bad behavior on display here, I suspect, was not a freak occurrence.

I was a fairly new subscriber to *Rolling Stone* when, in the fall of 1971, I was galvanized by "Fear and Loathing in Las Vegas," a two-part article written by Hunter S. Thompson. It was presented as factual—Thompson had tape-recorded part of the journey and taken copious notes—but the descriptions were so outrageous, especially the consumption of drugs, I had to presume that the truth was heavily fictionalized. Most of all, it was funny.

I read everything he wrote, mostly in the pages of *Rolling Stone*, and took interest in his campaign to run for sheriff in Aspen. I bought *Fear and Loathing in Las Vegas* when it was issued as a paperback and his other books as they were published. His first book, *Hell's Angels*, was difficult to find in those pre-Internet days, so I ended up reading it over a number of afternoons in the UCLA Research Library.

Early in 1971 Hunter was assigned to write an article for *Scanlan's Monthly* magazine about the mysterious death of Los Angeles newsman

Ruben Salazar, following a Vietnam War protest march that turned into a riot in East Los Angeles on August 29, 1970. Salazar was taking a break from covering the event, having a beer in the Silver Dollar Café, when a deputy sheriff fired a tear gas projectile into the bar. It struck Salazar and killed him. Because Salazar had been critical of the police's interactions with Mexican Americans in East Los Angeles, many thought the Los Angeles County Sheriff's Department had deliberately targeted him.

It was while working on his story that Hunter felt Oscar Acosta could be a good source for background information. Acosta was an activist Chicano lawyer who had been a friend of Hunter's for a few years by that point. Hunter wanted to get at the root of the problem in the community and see if Acosta was aware of any police conspiracy. The problem was that Acosta was always in the presence of bodyguards from the militant Brown Berets. He was defending a number of Mexican Americans who were charged with setting a series of fires at the downtown Biltmore Hotel during Governor Reagan's speech to four hundred Mexican American educators. Members of his retinue were suspicious of Hunter because he looked like a (non-Latino) member of the Establishment. In order to get Acosta to talk freely, to get him away from any surveillance or wiretaps, or worse yet, a bodyguard who might be a police informant, Hunter suggested during a meeting in the Polo Lounge at the Beverly Hills Hotel that the two of them drive to Las Vegas. Hunter could get their expenses covered by accepting an assignment from *Sports Illustrated* to cover the Mint 400 motorcycle race, starting March 21.

While holed up in a room at the Ramada Inn in Arcadia, California, across the street from the Santa Anita race track, Hunter found it emotionally grueling to write the Salazar article. After he was through with his day's work, he wrote about his trip with Oscar to Las Vegas for relief. The natural humor of this composition contrasted with the seriousness of the Salazar piece. When *Scanlan's* folded, "Strange Rumblings in Aztlan" found its way into *Rolling Stone*. Towards the end of April, Oscar and Hunter went back to Las Vegas to attend the National District Attorneys Association's Conference on Narcotics and Dangerous Drugs, primarily as a means to get more material. Hunter has referred to the resulting article as "a vile epitaph for the Drug Culture of the Sixties."

"Fear and Loathing in Las Vegas: A Savage Journey to the Heart of the American Dream" was published in two parts in *Rolling Stone* in November. Instead of using his real name, Hunter chose the pseudonym Raoul Duke. He did this because he didn't want the depravity he reported to affect his ability to get clearance from the White House to cover the 1972 presidential campaign. Similarly, he attempted to protect Acosta by referring to him as Dr. Gonzo, a Samoan rather than a Mexican American, because the description of his behavior and drug taking might have impaired his status with the State Bar of California. Acosta relished the notoriety that came with the popularity of the piece. Random House was ready to publish the book version when their lawyers requested that Acosta sign a libel release, which he would only agree to if he were properly identified. He was also sensitive about being referred to as a "300-pound Samoan attorney," rather than a 250-pound Chicano lawyer. It wasn't feasible for Hunter to make changes to the text, so the two of them were properly identified in a photo on the book's back cover, taken while they were in the lounge at Caesar's Palace. The hardcover was published in July 1972, with Hunter using his real name as the author. Inspired by the attention, Acosta wrote two books. He was a paid-up member of the California Bar when he disappeared under mysterious circumstances in Mazatlan, Mexico, in 1974, in what some have speculated was a drug-deal gone bad.

Through the years there have been many attempts to turn the book into a feature film. Max Palevsky made his fortune as a pioneer in computer technology. He stabilized an insolvent *Rolling Stone* magazine when he invested $200,000 in the company in early 1971 and became a director and board chairman. During this time he became friendly with Hunter. As a side-deal to a loan he made to Hunter, Palevsky optioned the rights to *Fear and Loathing* for Cinema X, the film production company he co-owned, with the contract written on a napkin in a bar. He slated Vernon Zimmerman to direct. Zimmerman's recent film, American International Pictures' *The Unholy Rollers*—which starred *Playboy*'s Playmate of the Year Claudia Jennings as a roller derby skater—had been released in November 1972. *Chicago Sun-Times* film critic Roger Ebert had a lot of nice things to say about the film, especially its "tough, sleazy vulgar vitality." Zimmerman, in turn, hired that film's writer, Howard B. Cohen, to pen the *Fear and Loathing* screenplay that was completed in March 1973. Cohen was one-quarter of the Conception Corporation, an excellent comedy ensemble similar to the Firesign Theatre.

Three guys calling themselves Shark Productions—Shark being the nickname of the white Cadillac convertible Raoul Duke drove in the book—optioned the property in 1975. John Jergens, heir to the hand lotion fortune, joined Shark with additional capital. Through the years many scripts were written, including one by Larry McMurtry for which he was paid $15,000. McMurtry is best known for his Pulitzer Prize-winning novel *Lonesome Dove*, and for cowriting the screenplay for the *Brokeback Mountain* movie. At one point Jack Nicholson was considered for the role of Raoul Duke, teamed with Marlon Brando as Dr. Gonzo.

A few years later as the popularity of *Saturday Night Live* (*SNL*) increased, it was Dan Aykroyd and John Belushi who were offered the roles. (Murphy Dunne, also from the Conception Corporation, backed up Aykroyd and Belushi as keyboardist in the Blues Brothers Band.) The movie wasn't made that time, either. Aykroyd and Belushi had Hunter come to New York to attend a taping of *SNL*. While there, he became enamored with Laila Nabulshi, who was an associate producer for the show. Laila had an exotic name and the alluring face of a woman of intrigue, but it was her sense of humor and mischievousness that drew them together. They became romantic. She moved in with Hunter in 1979 and helped him with his projects.

The book's two main characters, essentially, were the focus of 1980's *Where the Buffalo Roam*, which drew from Thompson's expanded writings. The movie, which starred Bill Murray of *SNL* as Thompson, was poorly received, critically and commercially. Hunter pocketed $100,000 from the production.

The following year Hunter and Laila went to London to attend a performance of *Fear and Loathing* in a small, theatrical setting, upstairs at the Latchmere Pub. That gave Laila the impetus to try to realize a feature film from the book. For a time Jergens provided the funds to pay writers to have more scripts written.

Laila succeeded Shark and formalized a new agreement with Hunter in 1987 in which she had seven years to make the film. She hadn't interested anybody when writer Bill Stadium introduced her to Steve Nemeth in 1992. As Richard and I were running our record company, we couldn't devote that much time to the film business, so Steve became our in-house producer. He thought this would be the perfect movie with which to launch Rhino Films. Laila sent Hunter a fax telling him that we were good guys and that we wanted to make the movie. We subsequently spoke to Hunter on the phone.

In June a number of our family members went to London for the confirmation ceremony in Westminster Abbey of Stephanie and Steve's Uncle Cyril's year term as Lord Mayor of Westminster. Laila put us in contact with Ralph Steadman, who had complemented Hunter's writing with his own outrageous illustrations. I first became aware of Steadman from his caricatures of the members of the Who on their "Happy Jack" single picture sleeve in 1967. Ralph took the train from Kent to meet Steve and me for afternoon tea at Fortnum & Mason.

In contrast to the perverse characters he realizes in his work, Ralph comes across avuncular, and with his bald head he reminded me of the actor Peter Boyle (who, incidentally, played Lazlo, a part similar to Dr. Gonzo, in *Where the Buffalo Roam*). Ralph was supportive, but despite our interest, didn't think the book would ever be made into a movie. He was still angry with *Rolling Stone* publisher Jann Wenner for never having returned his original artwork. Ralph's resign gave us more resolve to try to get the movie made. We didn't want to waste everybody's time (all over again). I reread the book on the flight back to Los Angeles.

Although we were charged with moving forward, Laila changed gears. Here, Steve and I were advancing toward the football to kick it like Charlie Brown in the *Peanuts* comic strip, and she, like Lucy, snatched it away. Our initial contracts had been generated, but before they were signed, Laila decided to try to make the film with Jake Scott, Ridley's son, who had directed a number of music videos and had a desire to direct feature films. Laila thought they could produce the film through Ridley's production company which had a deal with Paramount Pictures. The first step for them was to write a script together. I took note of the

"Peri Picks" column in an October 1992 issue of *Newsweek* that listed *Fear and Loathing* as one of five "hottest" books being read on college campuses that fall, remarkable for a twenty-year-old book.

By November, Hunter and I had established a rapport. As a consolation of sorts, Laila gave Hunter her approval for us to generate another project together, for cable TV. I had taken note of the miniseries format, specifically Sydney Pollack's *Fallen Angels*, John Landis' *Dream On*, and Robert Zemeckis' *Tales From the Crypt*. I wanted to do something similar with Hunter's edgy writings. Hunter and I engaged in a series of faxes that we sent to each other. I think I matched him pretty well. An early one from him used the letterhead from our nation's White House. I responded with one I had from a hotel in London, also called the White House.

I came up with a concept I thought would work. A Hunter-type freelance journalist lives in a remote cabin. Every show would start with him telling his recent adventure to his friend who would sketch as the story unfolded. This was similar to the way the Sherlock Holmes stories commenced, with Holmes recounting to his chronicler and friend Dr. Watson in the confines of their shared apartment. The artist was, of course, based on Steadman, with the expectation that he would provide the illustrations for the show. *The Wild Wild West,* a science fiction TV western from the late 1960s (made as a feature film starring Will Smith three decades later), was the first show that I remember that used illustrative art to define chapters—commercial breaks.

Then Came Bronson was a TV program that aired for one season, 1969-1970, starring Michael Parks as a disillusioned newspaper reporter who took off on his motorcycle every show for an adventure. In addition to appealing to the countercultural lifestyle, the show was unique as Bronson traveled to a different location every week and interacted with different characters. Similarly, the reporter in my idea would be assigned a different story every week and, like Thompson, would end up getting involved with the characters, participating in the event and changing the outcome. I thought I would be able to draw upon Hunter's collected works for the episodes. In reading and in some cases rereading his compendiums, there was very little to draw upon. Hunter was open to my concept, but he was pushing for his idea.

Hunter was passionate for "Off-Duty Cops." In one fax he wrote: "You will be at the mercy of a far more Sinister System, the Massive coast-to-coast Network of half-mad, brutal and frequently Psychotic Off-Duty Cops, WHO WILL DO ANYTHING FOR MONEY." His lead detective character, F. X. Leach, had a wife who "suffers from terminal Tourette's syndrome, and is also a Binge Drinker with a record of Public Violence." Hunter had no ideas for stories, only to say that they would be true. I personally wasn't interested in his concept, nor did I think it was a show that people would want to see, much less one that could be sold.

Prior to Hunter coming to Los Angeles to meet us, Laila got him to extend her start date on *Fear and Loathing* two additional years. The instructions Hunter gave us for the airline were: "Tell them I'm the Dalai Lama, traveling in disguise for spiritual reasons—and also that I need a wheel-chair, a large Lap Robe, and a Fat Young Boy for me to fondle and pray over during the flight to L.A., just kidding." Hunter was able to hitch a ride with actor and neighbor Don Johnson on Johnson's private jet.

When I saw Hunter in his room at the Westwood Marquis on December 1, the day after our dinner, it was apparent that he muttered, which meant that it was hard for me to hear everything he was saying even though we were the only ones in the room. It was a pleasant visit, getting comfortable with one another, but Hunter didn't offer much in the way of ideas. During that visit and at other times he asked, "Are we going to have fun?" I thought there was something childlike about that verbalized request. The sole reason *Fear and Loathing* was written was because Hunter had fun with the process. I was naïve; I didn't recognize the harbinger. I encouraged fun in the workplace as well as home, but for me there would be no fun because I was most responsible for the project. I tried to get him to visit Rhino, thinking he would be impressed with our organization and have more confidence in us. Even though the office was little more than a mile from the hotel, he didn't make it. He flew out the next day, with Johnson.

Unlike most record (or film) companies, we were very conservative with expenses. For his two-night stay, Hunter had spent almost $300 on room service (remember, it didn't include his first or last night's dinners) and another $120 in mini bar charges. Hunter wasn't totally insensitive to our economics. By getting a ride with Johnson, he saved us on the airfare from Aspen, so I didn't carp on the room charges. Before coming into town, I asked him what kind of car he wanted me to rent for him. He requested a Bugatti. I didn't know what that was, but I soon found out: an expensive French race car that was no longer in production. We rented him a Mercedes Benz. The day he checked out I got a call from Adele Baughn in our human resources department. It seemed that the previous night Hunter and Laila had consumed too much alcohol at a restaurant on La Cienega Boulevard to feel comfortable enough to drive back to the hotel in Westwood, so they took a cab. The next morning the car wasn't in the restaurant's parking lot. It seemed typical that Hunter lost a car. I don't know if it was ever located.

Towards the end of February 1994 Hunter came into town, this time staying at the Sunset Marquis. We had finalized an agreement to work together to develop the TV show. He requested the option money be delivered in cash in a paper bag. I brought the agreement and a check in a brown paper bag. In exchange, as a symbol to seal the deal, "like the Indians would," according to Hunter, he gave me a multifunction hand tool.

Laila's collaboration with Jake Scott hadn't advanced the project or even resulted in a screenplay she liked. She once again offered us the *Fear and Loathing* movie, and the TV show was put aside. We optioned the book in February 1995, with Laila getting Hunter to extend the start date through January 1997. Based on Steve's strong desire that *Fear and Loathing* should be Rhino Films' debut feature and his confidence that we could get a studio to fund the production, we paid Hunter $50,000 towards the purchase price. Using *Pulp Fiction*'s $8 million cost as a benchmark—because it also had an edgy tone—we thought we could produce our movie for $5 million. Within the next few weeks Steve had conversations with production executives at the studios. He thought that one would option the property from us and pay to have the script written. Only Fine Line made an offer, but the $15,000 option fee didn't come close to what we had advanced to Hunter, so we declined.

Johnny Depp and John Cusack were friendly with Hunter and had the inside track to play the lead role. We'd also heard from the agents representing Brad Pitt, Keanu Reeves, Sean Penn, Nicholas Cage, and Kevin Spacey, but they weren't aware of our low budget. Depp met Hunter through a mutual friend at the Woody Creek Tavern, Christmastime 1995. Cusack had codirected his brother Bill and Jeremy Piven in the New Crime Production of the book in late 1991 at the Gallery Theater in Chicago. Cusack and Depp were fine actors who we would have been happy with, but they weren't particularly hot at the time. I would have preferred Tim Hutton, who was one of Steve's best friends, because he looked like Hunter. After winning an Academy Award for best supporting actor in *Ordinary People*, he had squandered his appeal by making poor career choices. Depp lobbied harder for the role with Hunter and got the job. He agreed to work within our budget for a fee of $500,000, well below his usual quote. In hindsight, Cusack might have been the better choice. His career took off the following year with starring roles in *Grosse Pointe Blank* and *Con Air*, and he might have given a more appropriate acting interpretation. In addition, at six foot three inches, he was closer in height to Hunter, which meant he was more physically imposing (like Hunter) than the shorter Depp.

Finding a director who could convey the elements in the book and work within our proposed budget would prove to be a challenge. Jeff Stein wrote and directed the Who's 1979 documentary *The Kids are Alright*. He had directed the most consistently imaginative videos aired on MTV in its formative years. His direction for the Cars' "You Might Think" won the first MTV Video Music Award. Steve and I met with Jeff, but he was dealing with a personal issue at the time, and we didn't feel we had enough of a support system, like at a studio, to take a chance in giving him his first (nondocumentary) feature film opportunity.

Laila suggested Lee Tamahori and Alex Cox. Lee, a native of New Zealand, made an impressive feature film debut as a director with *Once Were Warriors*. Laila flew out to Aspen with Lee and his projected writer, Pat Kelly, to meet with Hunter at his house on February 23, 1996. Lee and Hunter bonded over firing guns in Hunter's backyard. I heard that his subsequent film *Mulholland Falls*, due to be released at the end of April, wasn't very good, and I developed reservations. I wasn't displeased when financial negotiations reached an impasse.

Initially I wasn't interested in Alex Cox, either. I liked two movies he had directed, *Repo Man* and *Sid and Nancy*, but then he hit a creative slide. Laila, Steve, and I met with Cox, but nothing he said impressed me. Steve met with Leon Ichaso, who was familiar with drug culture, having directed Wesley Snipes in *Sugar Hill* and Don Johnson in a number of *Miami Vice* episodes. So, not counting Jeff Stein, under consideration for director of a movie that takes place in Las Vegas, with characters in part searching for the American Dream, we had a Cuban, a Brit, and a New Zealander. The Brit was chosen.

Steve's oldest sister was married to Hy Zacks during this period. Zacks was an accountant and lawyer who wanted to help his brothers-in-law realize their ambitions to produce movies for the incipient Rhino Films imprint. He introduced Steve and me to one of his clients, Leslie Alexander, a very successful bond trader, originally from New Jersey and now living in Boca Raton, Florida. He reminded me of the character Dustin Hoffman played in the movie *Rain Man*: his anxiety manifested itself in a slight speech impediment and facial tics, and he was a wiz with numbers. He didn't seem to be particularly interested in the film industry. It was more a gambler's throw of the dice in a new area of business for him. Alexander was in the process of buying the Houston Rockets basketball team. He asked me if I wanted to invest, but I didn't have a spare million lying around. It would have been a good investment.

When somebody is offering you money to make a film, you tend not to ask many questions. Given that he was a client of our brother-in-law's, we didn't ask. In September 1995 we contracted with Alexander to cofund with us our first feature production, *Plump Fiction* (a parody of *Pulp Fiction*) and possibly other films. In August the following year our film was completed, but unsold, when we sent Alexander a proposal offering him to fund the entire $5 million budget of *Fear and Loathing*. Alexander agreed. We started spending money. When we were confident that Johnny Depp wanted to star, we increased our budget to $6 million and Alexander agreed to that. We continued spending. Alexander then changed the deal. He wanted us to kick in a million dollars. We didn't intend to do that, but since the clock was ticking, we reluctantly capitulated.

One issue in making a film is timing, a window where talent is available for the duration of the production. If there are too many delays, an actor might already have been committed to make a movie that would overlap on the now-delayed production, or an antsy actor might take another acting job rather than waiting for one that might disappear. During this time we were forwarding information on our proposed contracts and budgets to Alexander. On November 20 I faxed a draft of the revised deal points to Alexander and Zacks, and Zacks said he thought Alexander would agree to them.

Cox and his writing partner/girlfriend Tod Davies had finished the screenplay. Actually we found out later that Davies had written well over 90 percent. Steve thought Benicio Del Toro would make a good Dr. Gonzo because of his performance in *The Usual Suspects*. On the evening of November 21, there was a read-through of the screenplay in Rhino's main conference room. In a read-through, you're trying to get an idea of the rhythm of the dialogue, if any segments are too long, too boring, need clarification, etc.

It was a no smoking building, but Depp refused to comply. In the course of the evening he drank a six-pack of Rolling Rock Beer. I thought of sequestering the bottles to sell them on eBay, but it's not something I would have done. They went into the recycling bin. Not realizing that Depp was imitating Hunter's barely audible mumbling, which included displaying no emotion in his rendering, I was put off. Even worse was Del Toro's stumbling. How could anybody get an idea if the dialogue was working? Only later did Steve inform me that Del Toro—an overall exemplary actor—suffered from dyslexia. I did not find the read-through reassuring or beneficial.

In December Alexander wanted to change the deal again. By the end of the year we had no signed agreement with Alexander, he had given us no money, and we had spent $450,000 (in preparing the movie for a late January start date) when we hadn't intended to invest any of our own money at all. Actually the money was advanced from the record company, but Richard and I were on the hook for it. We tried into January to come to an agreement with Alexander, but we couldn't. Our late January start date would be a problem if we didn't have the financing in place. We were able to get Hunter to grant us an extension until March by advancing him $32,000.

On January 12, 1997, Cox and Davies visited Hunter at his home. Initially they were invited, and then discouraged from coming; they showed up anyway. It didn't work. Cox wasn't interested in joining Hunter in watching football on TV, and he spurned the sausage Hunter had specially cooked because he and Davies were vegetarians. More offensive to Hunter was Cox's desire to animate a scene in the movie, the so-called *wave speech*. He was referring to the metaphorical crest of the wave that represented the fullest impact of the optimistic values of the 1960s, before it dissipated. It was an important passage for Hunter, and he was offended that Cox wanted to cheapen it by making it a "cartoon."

Cox was on the outs with Hunter, but he claimed not to have sensed it. Soon thereafter, he attempted to get chummy with Johnny Depp and visited him at the club he co-owned, The Viper Room on the Sunset Strip. In support of Hunter's feelings, Depp in essence told Cox that he would not work with him. In early February Cox invited me to dinner with Davies at a restaurant in Santa Monica. I responded to his friendliness. He seemed to appreciate my musical ideas—or was he just being solicitous in hopes of keeping the job?

Steve made a deal with Patrick Wachsberger for his company, Summit Entertainment, to finance the film and represent the foreign sales. With Cox on shaky ground as director, Wachsberger engaged Jack Rapke at the Creative Artists Agency, who suggested Terry Gilliam. Wachsberger also thought he could get more money for the foreign rights with Terry as the director, which meant a budget closer to what Terry had been accustomed. We all liked the idea of Gilliam, primarily because he was so visually imaginative. At the end of the month it was clear we would need more time. Steve negotiated an extension on the start date through May for an additional $15,000.

As a rock movie in spirit, there would be enough music used in the film to make an enticing soundtrack album. Even though it was a Rhino Film, I thought it would be too risky for Rhino to expend the big advance for the soundtrack rights, but other labels were interested. Jolene Cherry, whom I met when she started out in the business as record producer Mike Chapman's assistant—later his girlfriend—alerted her boss, Doug Morris, the head of the Universal Music Group, about the film. He called me to inquire about the soundtrack rights. Richard and I had previously reported to Morris, but in a move that proved to be disastrous, he was fired from his position as US head of the Warner Music Group two years prior to this. He then was hired by Universal and built that company into the industry's leader as Warner's business declined. We had a good relationship with Morris, but I hadn't spoken to him since he left Warner. Morris wasn't a film buff and wasn't hip enough to have been familiar with *Fear and Loathing* when I let him know of our interest in 1992.

I told Morris I would consider a Universal label if he could interest the film company (they were owned by the same corporation) in distributing our movie. It wasn't an easy request. Morris called Casey Silver, the head of Universal Pictures, who was interested primarily because Terry's last film, *Twelve Monkeys*, had made money for Universal. I set a deal in motion with Silver for Universal to take over the financing, distribution, and ownership of the film in the United States, and in the foreign territories in which Summit hadn't already entered into contracts. Jolene thought the deal we were looking for was too rich for her division, so Morris had me set up meetings with Universal's DreamWorks and Geffen. Both were cold at the time and in need of a hit—neither had an album in the top fifty. Doug Mark, one of Steve's best friends from childhood and now a music attorney, negotiated a deal with Eddie Rosenblatt at Geffen for an advance against royalties of $1,250,000.

In mid-March we received notice that Les Alexander was suing us. He felt that he should have half of Rhino's profits, even though he reneged on his verbal agreement to finance the film. The law firm representing us in the litigation conducted a LexisNexis search on him. Most revealing was a lengthy article, "Greed Head," from February's *Houston Press*, the city's alternative newspaper. It was subtitled: "There's darkness at the edge of Clutch City, but one thing is clear, Les Alexander will get his. And maybe yours, too." The article is best summarized by this passage: "But since Alexander bought the NBA franchise in August 1993, his organization has left behind a lengthy trail of fired employees, stiffed vendors and angry sponsors. And their stories are remarkably consistent—a litany of broken agreements, unpaid bills and a mean-spirited cheapness that borders on pure greed." In essence, it seemed that Alexander used his deep pockets to bully people, and this seemed like what he was doing to us. Bob Bustman, the writer from the *Houston Press*, surmised that Alexander had difficulty relating to and empathizing with people. Alexander and his (then) wife were supporters of PETA, People for the Ethical Treatment of Animals. But it seemed that ethics, when it came to people, were of lesser consideration. He appeared to weigh transactions with a legal or liability perspective, rather than to consider the moral or humane impact. Given this insight, I wasn't going to let Alexander bully me, even if it cost me—and it did. If I gave into him, it would only perpetuate his bad behavior with others.

Alexander was shortsighted in attempting to sue us. His first and biggest mistake was initiating action prior to the movie coming out. He was banking on a big movie, with a settlement awarding him a portion of the profits. The movie tanked, so there were no profits. He should have waited until after the movie was released to see how it performed. Zacks told me that a primary reason why Alexander made the deal with Rhino Films was because of my integrity. I'm guessing that he forgot about that, and that he didn't realize how staunchly I would defend that integrity. I spoke to Zacks to appeal to Alexander, but he wasn't able to deter him. We spent money on mediation, but the mediator wasn't effective.

On March 25 we received a letter from Alex Cox's representative, stating, "fire Laila Nabulsi or Alex Cox will not direct the movie." For various reasons, that wasn't going to happen. Sensing that he was out anyway, it might have been a matter of saving face. Reluctantly, because of Directors Guild stipulations, we later settled with Cox. Two checks were sent to his company, Commies from Mars, for $62,500 (half from Rhino, half from Universal). Cox and Davies also made $46,800 for the screenplay that wasn't used. In addition, we had to settle with three people he had hired to work on the preproduction, and that cost us $5,000.

At this point we were in a precarious state. We didn't have signed agreements from the talent, we spent our own money without intending to, and we needed to get an extension from Hunter. We also got the feeling that if Hunter refused to extend, Laila could take the elements we had put together and go somewhere else, cutting us out of the action and the money we had spent. From here on out Laila claimed that she was acting in our interests, but we sensed that she was being duplicitous.

In order to protect our position, Steve threw down his trump card. If Hunter didn't extend and if everyone didn't formalize the deals their agents had verbally agreed to, Steve would commence a production by the contracted start-by date with the original low budget and with Alex Cox directing. If Depp bailed, we would get John Cusack (or another actor) to replace him. Depp's agent at International Creative Management, Tracey Jacobs, reacted most vehemently. Her profane-infused tirades would have made her a natural candidate to play the wife with Tourette's syndrome in Hunter's "Off-Duty Cops." She was a serial harasser. She would call Steve much earlier than normal business hours, at six or seven in the morning, awakening him with a typical opening like "You're no Scott Rudin and I'm a cunt." Johnny Depp called Steve at the office to inform him, "I'm in a tree outside your window, looking at you, jerking off." Steve was shocked. When he first met Johnny he thought he was a nice guy. He hung out at his house and drank draft beers with him. Steve managed a comeback: "I didn't know you found me that attractive."

It was all a bluff. Where would we have gotten the money? But the other side didn't know that. It worked. It got everybody focused, and Hunter granted us an extension—for more money, of course. As a consequence, Steve alienated Laila, Terry, and Johnny. He was excluded from having anything to do with the production, and he was the target of vitriolic verbal and written assaults.

In May, Terry and his writing partner Tony Grisoni got to work on the screenplay. With their initial draft and two subsequent drafts—that were then budgeted—they failed to comply with Universal's approved budget of $17,500,000. This caused more crucial delays, which contributed more stress.

On the morning of June 18, I met with Terry to give him my ideas on the music. One approach, which I don't believe anybody had done, was to use only songs that were played on the radio in the two-month span of the two trips. Four of the six songs mentioned in the book were from the period. The other was to draw from more obscure songs from that date and before. For example, I wanted to use "1970" by (Iggy and) the Stooges to establish the time. For a scene when we hear and then see the Shark as it comes into view, I wanted the audience to hear the banshee-styled wails of Robert Plant from Led Zeppelin's "Immigrant Song." Led Zeppelin had not granted a film license for one of their records since *Fast*

Times at Ridgemont High in 1982. I thought it would be a coup to get Led Zeppelin. The song was from the period and it would work with the scene. I thought we had a chance with the otherwise reluctant group because the request wasn't for "Whole Lotta Love" or their other more popular songs. In addition, a couple members had invested in the Monty Python film *The Holy Grail* and had made money, so they might have been positively disposed toward ex-Python Gilliam as director. He didn't seem receptive to any of my suggestions. For that scene he used a song from 1968, Big Brother and the Holding Company's "Combination of the Two."

Another idea I had was to have the Doors provide the score. In 1978, seven years after Jim Morrison died, the three surviving members reunited in the studio to create the musical backing for a number of poems Morrison had recorded in the year before his death. I found the result, released as *An American Prayer*, inspired. Because their sound naturally conveyed an ominous feeling, I thought their soundtrack would complement the story.

There was a party given by one of Hunter's friends at a home in the Hollywood Hills prior to production. Hunter welcomed my wife and me to sit with him on lounges in the patio. Singer Warren Zevon and actor Harry Dean Stanton hovered nearby. Hunter was gracious and mannered in a way that made him seem to us like a Southern gentleman. Stephanie continued to chat while I wandered off and broke the ice with Johnny Depp by asking him about his rock band days in Florida. He seemed shy, and his manner was low-key. We talked about amplifiers, and I asked him what his favorite group was. I was surprised and pleased when he mentioned the 1960s band the Zombies, as they were also among my favorites.

Benicio Del Toro asked me my vision for the movie. It was the only time anybody in the production asked me that question. I said hello to Jesse Dylan, who was directing rock videos and short films. Mostly I chatted with director Bob Rafelson, who had been Hunter's neighbor for thirty years.

On July 1 Steve received an insulting voice mail message from Terry, who expressed his anger that the production needed more money, and that some of his crew had threatened to quit: "What the fuck are you doing? . . . We're getting in deeper and deeper shit and you guys are playing your stupid games with money . . . stop pissing around . . . You'll want to talk to somebody to learn to make movies, and then you can talk to people {meaning him}. Until then, pay the money and then maybe one day you'll learn how to make movies!" Steve was shaken up. He played the message for a few people, including his girlfriend at the time, actress/writer Carrie Fisher. The following day she left a message on Steve's voice mail, deadpanning, "Where's my goddamn money?"

At this point, Terry still hadn't submitted a shooting script with an approved budget. By midmonth Universal had taken over the financing of the movie. As late as July 30, Universal's business affairs vice president Jeffrey Korchek wrote a letter to Terry's designated producer, Patrick Cassavetti, telling him that the proposed budget was "way in excess" at nearly $19 million. Finally, Terry came in with a script that was approved. When Steve questioned it, Terry said that they wrote that one only so they could get it approved, not that they thought it would work within the budget. Korchek was displeased when Gilliam later went over budget by more than $2 million, as that meant that Universal couldn't benefit from taking over Summit's foreign positions, and using the commission to reduce their cost.

The movie commenced production on July 26. On July 30 attorney Thomas F. Hunter wrote a four-and-a-half-page, single-spaced letter to Randy Paul, our production lawyer, on behalf of his clients regarding the "backend splits" (profit participation): ". . . you were about to show us your appreciation by trying to fuck us with some tortured, misdirected and ill-advised technical argument on behalf of your client." He threatened that Terry would buy the rights from Hunter, make the movie with Universal, and "fire Rhino." His postscript indicated that he had hired feared litigator Bert Fields to represent Terry on this issue. Although it was soon resolved, we still had to hire a litigating attorney to respond, which meant more money spent on lawyers.

In an attempt to patch things up, Steve splurged on three *Fear and Loathing* first edition books and sent one each to Johnny, Benicio, and Terry. I told him not to do it, that it wouldn't be appreciated, that it was a waste of his money. Depp sent his back, with a curt note that was unsigned. Steve didn't receive any response from Terry or Benicio. Later, in appreciation,

Terry sent a first edition book to Jeffrey Korchek, signed by him and Hunter. I wondered if it was the book that Steve had bought for him.

After the film had been in production for a couple of weeks, the head of music for Universal, Harry Garfield, had a conversation with Cassavetti regarding Terry's interest in hiring a music supervisor. He told him, "I know twice as much as those guys (the three Terry was considering), and Harold Bronson knows twice as much as me." Terry never got back to me on the tape of songs I left with him, nor did he respond to my two faxes. In one, I cautioned him against using the Rolling Stones' "Sympathy for the Devil." Hunter referred to it in the book because he played the *Beggars Banquet* album, from which it came, continuously while he wrote the piece. Allan Klein, the head of ABKCO, was notorious for charging exorbitant fees and for refusing to license the masters he owned for other companies' product, in this case the soundtrack album. I was relieved when I heard that it wasn't in the film, only to learn later that Terry paid $150,000 to use the Rolling Stones' "Jumpin' Jack Flash" over the end credits. The song didn't appear on the soundtrack album. No music supervisor was hired. Garfield saved the production money by providing those services. Terry overspent on the music, nearly $1.7 million. I thought I could come up with equally effective songs for about a third of the amount. I spoke to Casey Silver about it, but he seemed more deferential to giving Terry what he wanted than saving the over-budgeted production money.

In early August Steve ruffled more feathers when he innocently fielded a call from a reporter for the *Las Vegas Review-Journal* newspaper who wanted to confirm locations for the filming in Las Vegas. Terry's angry voice message over the published story closed with: "We offer you our condolences, and say, never come to the set. You will not be welcome. Don't even think about it, Steve. Now fuck off and keep your mouth shut. Goodbye." Cassavetti showed that he could rise above his "Money-money-money-money-we-need-more-money!" phone rants, with real flair in his writing. It's the only time I've seen "missive" and "bons mots" used in a letter. Steve responded, and Cassavetti countered with disdain: "I would appreciate not having to engage in further tedious correspondence on matters I would deem to be common sense." He closed with "Best Wishes."

Steve spoke to one of the lead actresses whom Gilliam directed in the movie *Brazil*. She told him that Terry needed an adversary in mounting his productions, which usually meant the studio, but in this case was us. Monty Python member Michael Palin affirmed, "He needs to feel that there's a battle he's engaging in." Fellow Python Terry Jones put it this way: "He has to have an enemy to get his juices going."

In anticipation of the movie coming out the following year, and with hopes that it would be a hit, I thought it would be opportune to publish a luxurious edition of the book. I talked to Hunter about it and he was game. It would sell for $100, and be limited to 1,000 or 1,500 copies. Hunter, and maybe Ralph, would sign them. The contents would include bonus material, including an original chapter involving coconuts broken open on the hood of a car that had been excised from the original.

In mid-October Hunter came to town to make a cameo appearance in the film. He called me to have lunch. Knowing his natural inclination to wake late in the day, I offered a later time. He insisted that he would be up, and that I should come to suite 59 at the Chateau Marmont at one o'clock. I came. I banged on the door. No response. I thought he might be in the restaurant or nearby. He wasn't. I called the room to no response. I came back to the room, and banged some more. After a while Hunter answered the door. It took him a while to fully wake. We didn't have lunch. Typically, there were filled room service trays scattered about. Some of the drinks hadn't been touched. There was food that had barely been eaten. It occurred to me that Hunter's excessive room service orders might be less about consumption than the psychological comfort derived from the clutter.

Hunter invited me to see his scene being filmed, but I told him that I was excluded from visiting the set. He was surprised and offered to rectify the situation, but I didn't feel I needed to be in a place where I wasn't wanted. We talked about his limited edition book and about the film. He wanted to have Keith Richards sing, "Home, Home on the Range" over the end credits. I thought it was a bad idea, and didn't fit the story. Interestingly enough, Neil Young performed the same song on the *Where the Buffalo Roam* soundtrack.

According to Hunter the original hard cover didn't sell that well, about 10,000 books. Random House printed many more, so he and Jann Wenner bought a large quantity of the excess copies and put them in storage, but neither could recall where. The fact that there could be pristine 1972 books hitting the collectors market concerned me a little. My proposed edition never happened, even though our basic deal was worked out. Those original hard covers never materialized if they, indeed, existed.

Laila was nice enough to invite me to the wrap party on October 22. It was an opportunity to check out the Planet Hollywood restaurant in Beverly Hills, but I barely knew anybody. The main stars, like Johnny Depp, didn't show, and I didn't know members of the production crew. On my way out I saw Terry. We had a nice, brief chat, and I felt good that our last encounter had been a positive one.

From the film's budget, Gilliam and Depp each made $500,000, Cassevetti $350,000, Nabulsi $250,000, and Del Toro $200,000. For the rights to the book and for consultation—although he didn't really do any—Hunter received $300,000. John Jergens, on behalf of Shark, received $175,000, which was the amount he said he and his partners had expended for optioning the book and hiring writers.

In February 1998 Steve received a letter from Laila who was upset that he was taking a credit as a producer. (Richard and I were the Executive Producers.) She felt that her many years trying to get the movie made justified her in having the only producer credit. Patrick Cassavetti also took a producer credit. For his early involvement John Jergens was given an associate producer credit. Those were the only feature film credits Laila and Jergens were to have.

Terry had another fight on his hands as the Writer's Guild of America wanted to deny him and Tony Grisoni credit for writing the screenplay. He appealed and they were given first position in a shared credit with Cox and Davies. I empathized with him and believed him when he said that he didn't use anything in the Cox/Davies script. As an adapted work, with both scripts drawing material from the book, I don't see how the WGA could make a determining evaluation.

The film was shown as a sneak preview at Universal City Walk's AMC Theaters. Steve and I weren't invited to attend. The evaluation cards the audience members filled out and the discussion with the focus group afterwards resulted in a poor response. It discouraged the executives from

Universal, specifically the marketing department. The film was not well received when it premiered on May 15, 1998, at the Cannes Film Festival, nor when it was released to general audiences in over a thousand theaters in the States a week later.

Many people like the film, but I didn't. I thought Terry missed the mark. First of all, the primary appeal of the book is that it's funny, which the movie mostly wasn't. Terry threw in a number of elements that weren't in the book and that didn't enhance the story, such as the casting of little people in various roles. Because the behavior of the two lead characters was so deviant, the movie needed to show more that they cared about each other and that they were supportive. The characters, primarily Johnny Depp's, should have drawn their interpretation from the depiction in the book. Rather than Depp—with Terry's guidance—conjuring up Raoul Duke from the pages of the book, he impersonated the Hunter of twenty-five years later. He spent weeks hanging out with Hunter at his home in Woody Creek to get the mannerisms down. The dedication was admirable, but I thought the affect was misguided, resulting in cartoonish, jerking movements and a low-key, unemotional speaking delivery. In real life Hunter muttered, but it wasn't part of Raoul Duke's character in the book.

I felt bad for Ralph Steadman, as his artwork was important to the book. I was disappointed that the non-Rhino producers relegated his illustrations to a sole image unimpressively displayed on the t-shirt of the hitchhiker in the movie. They marginally dispersed poorly reproduced images through the closing credits. If it were up to me, I would have used his illustrations over the opening credits, similar to that of the *Pink Panther* films. It would have been distinct and immediately link the film to the book.

Aside from all the craziness that emanated from Hunter S. Thompson, he did have an appreciation for the craft of writing and a respect for journalism. It was important for him to "get the story." The lengthy articles generated about the movie after it went into production focused on Johnny and Hunter. Not one writer asked to interview Steve or me, so nobody got the real story of how this movie got made over twenty-five years after the piece had been published. Had the movie been a hit or been the beneficiary of good reviews, there might have been more interest. The best-selling *Leonard Maltin's Movie Guide* rated it a "BOMB." Because the movie didn't do well, the timing wasn't right to pitch a Hunter S. Thompson inspired TV show, and we never revisited that idea.

Despite Terry Gilliam's boast that "the film is the bargain of the century," it only grossed $10.5 million in US theaters (with $4.6 million filtering back to Universal). Because of the depictions of the consumption of drugs, the movie was deprived of the revenue that would have been generated from a sale to network TV. It did prove to be a consistent seller in the home video market, but has still lost millions according to Universal Pictures' accounting department. I felt bad for Eddie Rosenblatt. He had made such a generous offer, but with sales of 125,000 copies, Geffen Records lost a lot of money on the soundtrack. Steve and I both felt the movie would have been better at our original low budget. Hunter made even more money when a reissued edition with the movie's key art on the cover sold well enough to top the best-selling paperback lists.

It took over two years to settle with Alexander. Our concessions were few, and he received no money. The impact on Rhino Films was severe. Even though our deal with Alexander to finance additional films was still in place, he failed to respond to any of the new properties we were contractually obligated to offer him. His suit cost us $200,000 in legal fees, an amount that otherwise would have funded our overhead and development for the next two years. We felt we had momentum, with three feature films released theatrically in 1998, only to be derailed by his action. Rather than his being in a position to help build our film company and participate financially if our films were successful, he essentially abandoned his position. In additional to the money expended, it wasted my time, but it wasn't merely time; it also took an emotional toll. One criticism of lawsuits is that the money spent on lawyers doesn't create anything, like a product (or in this case, a film) that can be sold. It's money being spent to extract (usually) money that already exists with another entity. His investment in *Plump Fiction* was paid back and, as of this writing, he has received royalties from the film for the past fourteen years. In recent years, *Forbes* magazine has ranked him among the four hundred richest people in the United States, with a net worth of over $1 billion.

Rhino received a producer's fee of $250,000, but after our expenses we were left with very little: $200,000 defending Alexander's suit; $32,000 for our portion of the Cox settlement; $5,000 more when we shut down that production; thousands more hiring additional lawyers to negotiate the Cox settlement and respond to the nasty letters we received from Thomas F. Hunter and Laila Nabulsi. From a nonmonetary standpoint we were equally unsatisfied: we were excluded from feeling like part of something, from the camaraderie of being part of a team, from making a contribution, and from seeing something we started through to completion.

Richard and I commiserated. As tarnished an image as the music business had, from what we witnessed the film industry was much worse. We were not used to this. We strived to run our record company with a high level of integrity. In 1996 the Clinton administration acknowledged us by having Secretary of Labor Robert Reich present us with a Corporate Citizen Award. It was the only one awarded to an entertainment company.

I enjoyed getting to know Hunter and Ralph, but dealing with Alexander's lawsuit and experiencing the anger and mean spirit unleashed at Steve resulted in the worst enduring experience of my life. People can express their positions with civility. Universal's Jeff Korchek was always civil and professional even when we disagreed. In Hollywood talent is indulged and so are their representatives. If Tracy Jacobs didn't represent an actor on the level of Johnny Depp, she wouldn't be able to get away with being a fire-breather. No one would want to deal with her. The same goes for the other agents who acted similarly. Terry Gilliam can be affable and charming. Given the commercial disasters he's been responsible for, one would think he would be more appreciative of his opportunities.

I liked Hunter, but he was well past his creative peak. I asked him questions about the story, for clarification, but he didn't contribute anything to the production while I was involved, nor do I think he did to Terry's. It seemed to me that Hunter didn't understand why, with all the drugs he had consumed and with his aberrant behavior, he hadn't died twenty years ago. It seemed like he was fumbling in his agenda on what he should be doing. He still wrote, but it wasn't inspired. I hadn't talked to him in years when I heard a voice mail from his assistant, about a year before he committed suicide in 2005, checking that my contact numbers were still the same. It was comforting to know that he thought enough of me to keep me in his phone book.

We heard that Terry Gilliam had a good rapport with his actors, particularly Johnny Depp, who agreed to star in his twist on Cervantes' seventeenth century novel *Don Quixote*. The film, budgeted at $32 million, started filming in October 2000, but then suffered irreversible setbacks of a flash flood and the actor playing Don Quixote being debilitated by a double-herniated disc. The production was terminated, with the insurance company eating the losses. Depp's connection with Hunter went further. Depp starred in 2011's *The Rum Diary*, based on a novel Hunter wrote in 1959 but had not published until 1998. The $45 million film only grossed $13 million in US theaters, resulting in tens of millions of dollars in losses.

While *Fear and Loathing in Las Vegas* was poorly received, it did win one accolade, The Governor's Motion Picture Award. As Executive Producers, Richard and I flew to Las Vegas on May 27, 1998, to accept a plaque from Nevada Governor Bob Miller at a large ceremony at the Las Vegas Hilton, solely because the production had spent so much money in the state. We wondered if he, or anyone else in the presentation, had even seen the film.

The First Teen Star
of Rock 'n' Roll

Frankie Lymon

And the Making of the "Why Do Fools Fall in Love" Movie

There were good reasons for making a movie about 1950s teen idol Frankie Lymon, but I never dreamed that a movie would actually be made. Frankie was an exceptional singer and personality whose records deserved to be heard. We now owned the master recordings, but as our *best of* album only sold 17,000, we would only see a notable increase in sales if a movie was produced.

Frankie Lymon was really the first teen rock 'n' roll star. He was only thirteen years old in early 1956 when his group, the Teenagers, catapulted to number six on the charts with "Why Do Fools Fall in Love." Teens responded strongly to them and bought their records because the singers were also teens. Other rock 'n' roll performers who scored their first hits around the same time were much older: Bill Haley, twenty-nine; Chuck Berry, twenty-eight; Fats Domino, twenty-seven; Carl Perkins, twenty-four; Little Richard, twenty-three; and Elvis Presley, twenty-one.

George Goldner, who was born Jacob Goldman, was an important record man in the early days of rock 'n' roll. He wasn't a lawyer or an accountant, but a garment dealer who had a passion for dancing and Latin music. He left his job to promote dances, and later formed a label,

Tico, to record Latin music. This led him to recording R&B and doo-wop vocal groups on subsequent labels. These groups described themselves as vocal harmony groups. Later, in the 1960s, the style acquired the descriptive name *doo-wop* because of the common repeated phrase that was first widely heard in the Turbans' hit "When You Dance."

Richard Barrett was a member of one of those groups, the Valentines. His first encounter with the record business was when he sold a song he had composed in the army to music publisher Morris Levy for $100. That song, "Creation of Love," later occupied the "B" side of Frankie Lymon's hit "Goody Goody," credited to "Levy." In addition to being a performer, Barrett worked as a musician and producer. He produced several of the Chantels' records, and played piano on their hit "Maybe." His solo single, "Some Other Guy," never made the pop charts, but was a favorite of Liverpool groups in the 1960s. The Beatles played it in the only known film of them performing at the Cavern Club.

In uptown Manhattan's Washington Heights, on the corner of 165th Street and Amsterdam Avenue, Frankie's group sang outside of Barrett's apartment and the market where Frankie had worked since he was ten. Barrett, having worked late-night sessions, used to be awakened by their singing, and he chased them away. One day he heard a song that made him want to talk to them.

Calling themselves the Premiers, the group was composed of three blacks, Frankie, Sherman Garnes, and Jimmy Merchant; and two Puerto Ricans, Joe Negroni and Herman Santiago. Frankie, a soprano, was thirteen. The others were a couple of years older. Negroni was the leader, Santiago sang most of the leads, and Garnes had an exceptional bass voice, especially for someone so young. Together they presented a strong vocal blend.

Barrett made a deal with Negroni: the group would stop singing outside of his window if he could arrange a recording session for them. He rehearsed with the Premiers in a music room at Stitt Junior High. He thought the combination of a Spanish-accented singer in a rock 'n' roll song could take advantage of the mambo craze. He set up an audition with Goldner. After hearing a number of songs, Goldner focused on "Why Do Birds Sing So Gay." On the night of the audition, Santiago's voice was hoarse from a cold. Merchant and Negroni couldn't sing the song because they didn't know the lyrics, and Garnes was the bass singer. Frankie piped up that he knew the words, so he sang it and impressed everybody.

Vocal groups liked to rehearse in hallways and vestibules to take advantage of the natural echo. Quite often the Premiers rehearsed in a doorway in Garnes' apartment building. A tenant, Richard White, got sick of hearing the group singing the same five songs over and over again, so he gave them poems and love letters written by his girlfriend Delores, suggesting they use them as lyrics for a song. During the audition, Goldner suggested a new title and lyric change to "Why Do Fools Fall in Love." It's difficult to know who contributed what: how much of the lyric came from Delores's poem, how much Goldner actually contributed to be credited as the cowriter along with Lymon and, initially, Santiago. Merchant, who came up with the "De doom-wop a doom-wop a doom-wop a doe-doe" intro, also claimed he contributed, but Goldner told him there wasn't room on the label for a fourth name.

It was not unusual for a record label head, or someone with influence, to end up with a writing credit without having made any contribution. Mostly, a young songwriter was all too willing to share credit if he could get a hit: disc jockey Alan Freed received credit—and remuneration—as a writer for playing Chuck Berry's "Maybellene," Dick Clark for giving exposure to an artist on his *American Bandstand* TV show, and Elvis Presley for agreeing to perform a song for one of his records.

The song was recorded at Bell Sound in Manhattan. Sax player Jimmy Wright was Goldner's music director. He suggested the group change its name to the Teenagers. Barrett's contribution was important, as the group was inexperienced in the studio. More specifically, he worked with Frankie's enunciation and phrasing. The song was a smash for the new Gee label. The composers were listed as *Lymon-Santiago-Goldner*. Soon thereafter, the credit was revised to just *Lymon-Goldner*. What could these unsophisticated teens know about royalties? They had no point of reference. The anticipated results of having a hit record were impressing your friends who heard it on the radio, playing more live dates with increasing audience reaction, and being able to charge more for public appearances.

The group followed with "I Want You to Be My Girl," which made it to number twelve. They were a sensation live. Frankie was a bundle of confidence, personality, and energy. Richard Barrett said of Frankie, "I never saw a kid with so much dynamite." The group's dancing was choreographed by Cholly Atkins, who later did the same for Motown's many acts. A highlight was Lymon and Santiago doing the splits in tandem. New York dates were followed by national tours, and appearances in two quick low-budget teen movies, *Rock, Rock, Rock* and *Mister Rock 'n' Roll*. The Teenagers were a phenomenon. In their first year the group had four Top 50 hits, which was all the more remarkable as Goldner's small, independent company was not well funded. The members wore a fashion-breaking sweater that had a large "T" on the front. Tommy Hilfiger later used a group photo to introduce the "Classics" chapter in his *All American* style book.

With his high tenor, Frankie was the Michael Jackson of his day. The impact that Frankie and the Teenagers had was comparable to that of the Jackson 5. They inspired such a fervent reaction from their young teen fans that many formed doo-wop groups of their own. Billy Vera holds the distinction of being the only artist with whom Rhino had a hit, "At This Moment," which made it to number one in January 1987. As a twelve-year-old R&B fan, he witnessed Frankie's performance at the Brooklyn Paramount: "Frankie was, bar none, the best kiddie performer and singer there ever was. I make that statement having also seen performances by Frankie's only real competition, Stevie Wonder and Michael Jackson, when they were kids. Great as they both were, and they both were amazing, neither could touch Frankie Lymon at that age." Veronica Bennett (later Ronnie Spector) heard the group's records when she was twelve years old and thought Frankie had the greatest voice she'd ever heard. Inspired by Frankie, Ronnie racked up a handful of hits as the lead singer of the Ronettes.

The group was even more successful in England where "Why Do Fools Fall in Love" hit number one in the summer of 1956. The next year they sold out the London Palladium twice and had three big hits: "Baby Baby," number four; "Goody Goody," number twenty-four; and "I'm Not a Juvenile Delinquent," number twelve. This last song, which was written by Bobby Spencer of the Cadillacs and then sold outright to Goldner, belied the group's nature. As effective as Frankie was in conveying the thrill and exuberance of being an innocent teen, by the time his first record was released, he had been introduced to the ways of the world: he had run errands for pimps, had sex with women twice his age, smoked pot, and drank alcohol. In London, fourteen-year-old Frankie took to smoking six-inch cigars.

In the 1950s version of rock stars destroying hotel rooms, the Teenagers were kicked out of the Park West Hotel for shattering beer bottles in their suite. They were asked to leave the hotel where they were booked in Manchester for unruly behavior. Back in the States, Frankie's drinking caused him to become unreliable and he missed more than a few dates. On those occasions the Teenagers used Jimmy Castor as a replacement. Castor scored a top ten hit in 1972 with "Troglodyte (Cave Man)."

For these young teens it was a matter of too much success too soon. The other members became jealous of Frankie because he got most of the attention. When they started out Frankie hadn't been the lead singer, and they were all equals. Because of the dissention, Morris Levy, who was managing the group, split them into two acts that he thought could both be successful, but neither was. While in London, Frankie alone recorded an album, *Frankie Lymon at the London Palladium*.

Frankie's voice began changing the following year, and more dramatically towards the end of 1959. It was still a good voice, now deeper and smoother, like that of a pop crooner's, but lacked the magic it had before. He had one more charting record, a cover of Thurston Harris' 1957 hit "Little Bitty Pretty One," but it only made it to number 58 in the summer of 1960.

He was introduced to heroin at a party in 1959 and became a junkie for most of the remainder of his life. He got into scraps. Once on tour with Chuck Berry and Bo Diddley, pint-sized Frankie jumped on a chair to punch a promoter in the face. He was convicted of stealing and for narcotics possession. In 1966, in order to avoid a heroin charge, he went into the army rather than serve time in jail. In December 1967 he received a dishonorable discharge from the army. On February 27, 1968, in his grandmother's apartment in New York, excited about a comeback recording session scheduled for the next day, he accidentally overdosed on heroin and died. He was twenty-five years old.

Within the following decade, George Goldner, Joe Negroni, and Sherman Garnes—who served time in prison—also died. George Goldner was a big gambler. He borrowed money from Levy to pay his debts, and Levy ended up owning Goldner's label when he couldn't pay him back. Goldner would start another company, he would have hits, and the pattern continued. As part of Roulette Records (of which Goldner was an original partner), Levy bought Tico, Gee, and Rama in March 1957. Later, he also acquired Goldner's subsequent labels, End and Gone. In 1964 he supplanted Goldner's name with his own on all of the songwriting credits. In 1984 Levy testified under oath about how he helped to write "Why Do Fools Fall in Love": "We really more or less wrote poems or put words together. You get a beat going, and you put the music and the words together. I think I would be misleading you if I said I wrote songs, per se, like Chopin." Morris Levy passed away in 1990. He had been convicted on two counts of conspiracy to commit extortion, but due to ill health never served a day in prison.

La Bamba, a feature film of 1950s rocker Richie Valens' life, was released in 1987 and became an unexpected box office success. The Hollywood studios reacted by developing similar biopics on Chuck Berry, Eddie Cochrane, and others, only to pull the plugs when a movie on Jerry Lee Lewis' life, *Great Balls of Fire!*, tanked. After Rhino bought the Roulette Records catalogue in 1989, it was always in the back of my mind to create feature films that could expose the music to a new audience and increase album sales. Roulette had neglected promoting its catalogue, diminishing the awareness of Lymon and the Teenagers to the extent that most people associated "Why Do Fools Fall in Love" with Diana Ross, who had a top ten cover in 1981.

I thought a movie could convey the appeal of the Teenagers' records and Frankie's immense charm and talent, as well as provide a glimpse into his tumultuous life. Many people had tried to make a movie about Frankie, including Martin Scorsese, but none had gotten past the script stage because of the problem posed by the final part of Frankie's life—a downward spiral that ended when he overdosed on heroin. The music he made with the Teenagers is so joyous, it contrasted sharply with the depressing last third of the scripts we had read.

Philadelphia-based writer Stephen Fried wrote an excellent article on Rhino that appeared in the April 1992 issue of *GQ*. When he came to interview Richard and me, he gave me a copy of the July 1989 issue of *Philadelphia* magazine that featured his lengthy piece on Frankie Lymon's three ex-wives battling it out for the windfall in songwriting royalties due from Diana Ross' hit. Drawing mostly upon transcripts from the court cases, Fried wrote a compelling account, peppered with colorful language and conflicting testimony.

It wasn't as if Morris Levy was easy to pry royalties out of. With his connections to the Genovese crime family, and his intimidating nature, artists and songwriters were fearful of suing for their money. The original twenty-eight-year term of the copyright was expiring, and Levy had to strategize in order to renew it. Because of Frankie's death, that right fell to his heir. Wife number three, Emira Eagle, initiated a lawsuit. In order to counter her claim, Morris Levy dredged up Elizabeth Waters (aka Mickey), who was serving time in prison for shoplifting. He offered to cover her legal expenses and pay her $15,000 if the court determined she was Frankie's rightful heir. In order to hedge his bet, Levy cut the same deal with ex-Platter's singer Zola Taylor, who the opposing lawyers referred to as his "bullpen wife."

Elizabeth Waters also had served time for prostitution and, like Frankie, had problems with drugs. She married Frankie in January 1964, but hadn't gotten a divorce from her first husband until the following year. In October 1965 Frankie married Zola Taylor. She was the only female vocalist in the Platters, who were extremely popular in the 1950s. In court, Zola couldn't furnish the divorce decree to her second marriage or the marriage license with Frankie, blaming their disappearance on when Frankie "trashed" her house. She said that she tried to get a duplicate of the license from the courthouse in Tijuana, but that it had burned down. Opposing lawyers submitted newspaper articles, one reporting that the marriage took place in Las Vegas and another quoting Zola claiming the marriage had been "a joke." This left Emira, a schoolteacher with no previous marriages. She met Frankie while he was in the army in Georgia and married him in June 1967.

By the time Fried's article appeared, the case still hadn't been settled. Subsequently, as the trial was in its final stages, Waters and Taylor, who hadn't spoken with each other for most of the trial, empathized with each other and decided to share their take if they won. A Pennsylvania judge ruled in Waters' favor, recognizing a common law marriage, but the New York Supreme Court prevailed in ruling Eagle the winner. The court cases involved five judges and nine lawyers.

I resolved the problem in dramatizing Frankie's sad story by making his former wives a prominent part of the movie by having each of them tell their own story of Frankie's life. I was thinking low budget, $1.5 million, something Rhino could handle (with partners). I envisioned a movie that would focus on the trial, with his ex-wives played by colorful character actresses. When Frankie's ex-wives would reminisce about him, I would cut to a performance by the group from one of their movie appearances. This way, viewers could see Frankie's real talent instead of an interpretation by an actor. I also thought of recreating scenes, without dialogue, similar to what is used to bolster documentaries.

I liked Fried, and I liked his writing. I offered him the opportunity to create the screenplay. As he'd never crafted one before, I told him I would work with him. He had optioned his book *Thing of Beauty: The Tragedy of Supermodel Gia* to Paramount Pictures. (In his book he coined the term *fashionista*, referring to a person devoted to the latest fashions.) *Gia*, an HBO movie, debuted on the cable channel in January 1998. It won an Emmy Award and two Golden Globe Awards, one for Angelina Jolie's performance in the title role. I thought that it would be an opportunity for him to learn how to write a screenplay in case he wanted to control that stage in the future for any of his stories that might interest Hollywood. I also thought we could get a screenplay written for far less than if we hired an experienced writer. Initially he was interested, but then opted out. He suggested I do what he did: get a copy of the court transcripts.

In 1996, when Steve Nemeth met with Warner Brothers movie executives Bruce Berman, Billy Gerber, and Gary Lemel, I was surprised to hear that they loved the concept. *Waiting to Exile*, which was released in December of the previous year, had been an unexpected hit and a big moneymaker for Twentieth Century Fox. It, uniquely, starred a black female cast: Whitney Houston, Lela Rochon, and Angela Bassett. Thinking *Waiting to Exile* had shown that there was an audience for such a cast, Warner was looking for a similar vehicle, and our movie fit the bill. Lemel, Warner's head of music, also saw this as an opportunity to establish his Warner Sunset imprint to produce music-based movies.

Tina Andrews loved Frankie's music so much that she wrote a script with hopes of selling it to Michael Jackson. Early in 1983, she got the idea when she saw Michael performing in his "Billie Jean" video on MTV. Making the connection between him and Frankie—their singing, their dancing—she was moved to write a script. She interviewed numerous people, including Zola Taylor, Richard Barrett, and Little Richard. When she submitted it to Jackson's representatives, she was devastated that they refused to look at it. Studios were impressed by her script, but thought the tone was too dark. She was influenced by *Lenny*, the film on comedian Lenny Bruce directed by Bob Fosse.

Tina contacted us after a friend read of our interest in producing the movie in *Variety* and notified her. Her script, like others we read, did not depict the trial. Of Lymon's three wives, Andrews only included Zola Taylor. She seemed like the perfect person to write our movie. Steve and I both thought she had a great attitude and we enjoyed working with her. I got her the transcripts from the trial. Consequently, much of the movie's dialogue, including some of the humor, was derived directly from those transcripts.

Gerber was a music guy and made many of the talent suggestions, including the director, Gregory Nava. Nava had impressed the Warner execs with *Selena*, starring Jennifer Lopez, which he wrote and directed. They gave him a production deal. They figured that as they were paying him anyway, they might as well absorb some of the costs with having him direct our feature. Gerber never sought my opinion, which I found surprising as the vision for the project originated with me. Especially in contrast with Terry Gilliam and Patrick Cassivetti on *Fear and Loathing in Las Vegas*, Nava and his producer, Paul Hall, were civil, personable, and even likeable. In addition, they were both Rhino fans. We could talk to them, but it didn't necessarily mean they valued our input.

In addition to Lela Rochon (Emira Eagle), who had costarred in *Waiting to Exhale*, Warner was considering the biggest black actresses of the day, including Diana Ross and Oprah Winfrey. I was excited when singers Toni Braxton and Queen Latifah were suggested for Zola Taylor's part. Nava put off Latifah with comments about her needing to lose weight for the role. Braxton initially committed, but then reconsidered. She felt the role would be too demanding for her acting debut. Eventually the starring cast was scaled down a notch or two, with ex-wives Zola Taylor and Mickey Waters played by Halle Berry—who hadn't yet become a star—and Vivica A. Fox, respectively. Larenz Tate portrayed Frankie.

I had some problems with the casting, and it was not because the actors didn't perform well. In films it's not uncommon to have a number of characters combined in order to make the story easier to follow. Even though George Goldner was important to the group and their records, he was incorporated into the Morris Levy character. Levy was physically imposing and intimidating. Paul Mazursky, who played him, is short. The opposite held true for the 1950s Little Richard character. Richard was short, that's why they called him *Little*, and Miguel A. Nunez, Jr. is tall.

In September 1965, a month before he married Zola, Frankie made his last TV appearance, on *Hollywood A Go-Go*. I suggested the scene to show how far he had fallen professionally. Lip-synching to "Why Do Fools Fall in Love," a song from when he was thirteen years old, he was grimacing as though he were in pain, and he was missing his two front teeth. In the movie, during this time period, Frankie was visiting Zola Taylor in Los Angeles. Andrews and Nava wanted a triumphant scene to represent Frankie's comeback, of him singing on the *Hullaballoo* TV show. I suggested it be changed to *Hollywood A Go-Go*, but it was filmed as *Hullaballoo*, even though Frankie never appeared on that show and it was taped in New York. In the movie the Kinks preceded Frankie, miming "All Day and All of the Night." The McCoys— and not the Kinks—performed their hit "Hang On Sloopy" on the *Hollywood A Go-Go* show on which Frankie appeared.

The location for Zola Taylor's house was the Case Study House #22 (aka Stahl House) in the Hollywood Hills. It was designed by Pierre Koenig and was the site for a famous photo taken by Julius Shulman. In actuality, she lived in a very nice Spanish house typical to Southern California. Nava liked the view from the backyard, and thought the modern house looked more photogenic. I would have gone for authenticity. Unlike in the movie, wife number three, Emira Eagle, initiated the lawsuit, not Mickey Waters.

Newly produced movies require a dynamic sound. Rather than use tapes recorded in the 1950s, which were lacking, film producers usually had new recordings made. For 1978's *The Buddy Holly Story*, Gary Busey, who starred as Buddy, sang on new recordings of Holly's songs. For *La Bamba*, Los Lobos recorded new versions of Richie Valens' originals. Unlike in those two films where the subject was dead—having died in the same plane crash—Jerry Lee Lewis was alive. He recorded new versions of his records for *Great Balls of Fire!* He was now in his fifties, however, and the difference could be heard.

The reason for the movie—to me—was to have the music of Frankie Lymon and the Teenagers heard, and I'm referring to the original recordings that people loved. I felt as though I were the caretaker of their music. Frankie's vocals were so unique I didn't think anybody could duplicate them. While he had a certain musical quality, it was his personality that made him effective. He was only thirteen years old; he had a narrow range and was not a technically good singer. In the early days of rock 'n' roll, all records were in monaural, which was a problem when using the original tapes. Yet, they were in good shape and had fidelity. Lemel could understand the dilemma, so we came up with the idea of enhancing the existing tapes by adding to them. He hired noted arranger Arif Mardin and had him duplicate some of the harmony vocals and instruments—like saxophones—that were already on the recordings and split these additional tracks into stereo. I conferred with Mardin, but he grasped what was needed and did a fine job. The music in the film was used during the group's live performances, so the addition of the crowd cheering added to the stereo effect.

I'm open to suggestions, and a good suggestion can come from anywhere. I was visiting my uncle in New Jersey when we pulled into the parking lot of a restaurant. He was familiar with the parking lot attendant, and he mentioned the movie I was producing. The attendant asked me if I knew "Out in the Cold Again." He thought it was a great record. It wasn't a hit, so I wasn't considering including it. When I came home, I listened to it again, and he was right. It was worthy of the soundtrack and I made it one of the group's six songs. I also included three of the Platters' hits: "The Great Pretender," "Smoke Gets in Your Eyes," and "Only You (And You Alone)."

The movie was shot in the Los Angeles area. Downtown substituted for Manhattan, with the Orpheum and other theaters for those in New York. Santa Paula, which is located in Ventura County, filled in for Augusta, Georgia. Moss was draped over the tree branches, and the paved street was covered with dirt to make it look like the South.

I didn't have much to do with the production, so I only attended a couple of the shoots. I recommended the actors playing the Kinks wear the red hunting jackets the group favored in that period, and supplied photos to the costume department to recreate the coats. Paul Hall promised me an outfit, but I never got it. I thought it would be fun to see the performances of Frankie and the Kinks at the *Hullaballoo* set, which was filmed at CBS Television City in the Fairfax district. The stage had been home to numerous TV shows and, for many years, *American Idol*. It was a return visit for me; Richard and I had performed in the Temple City Kazoo Orchestra on *The Mike Douglas Show* in 1979. I offered to choreograph the Kinks, but Nava declined. While there I chatted with Halle Berry. I was surprised that she didn't know much about Frankie, so I explained the impact that he and the Teenagers had. Paul Hall introduced Steve and me to the director John Singleton, who is best known for *Boyz n the Hood*. Later, John contacted us about making a miniseries for HBO about Stax Records, the seminal Memphis-based soul label of which Rhino controlled a majority of masters. Universal Publishing was less than workable, and the miniseries never got off the ground.

The other time I visited the set was for a courtroom scene. I helped negotiate Little Richard's deal, and I wanted to welcome him to his first day of shooting. Richard, Gary Stewart, Bob Emmer, and I met with Little Richard and his manager at the Hyatt on Sunset, where Little Richard lived in two adjoining rooms. He came downstairs in full makeup, talked with gospel references, and was as nice as can be. Although he agreed to record a Christmas album for us, the project never happened. Little Richard wasn't a natural actor, and Nava had difficulty directing him. In a moment of frustration, Richard exclaimed, "I'm playing myself!" It was hard to disagree with him. He energized every scene in which he appeared.

Rhino, as part of the Warner Music Group, reported to Bob Daly and Terry Semel, who were coheads of Warner Brothers Pictures. It was frustrating for Richard and me as they didn't understand the record business, and shouldn't have been given those responsibilities. I felt completely different about them after I attended a meeting to discuss a rough cut of the film. Also in attendance was noted editor Dede Allen. All three were in accord, and had astute comments. Nava had a good grasp on the artistry and symbolism of film, but he went a bit too far, incorporating elements that an audience wouldn't grasp. One scene featured a galloping white horse, which represented heroin—horse is slang for heroin—that they rightly had a problem with and thought should be deleted.

I chose the six songs performed by Frankie Lymon and the Teenagers that appeared in the film, for which the Rhino label received a licensing fee of $170,000, netting far less than half after paying artist royalties and our foreign partner. For our role in producing the movie, Rhino Films received a fee of $250,00, reduced to $191,250 after paying agents' and lawyers' commissions.

Shortly after filming was completed, I wrote a letter to Mark Reina, Warner Brothers' vice president of publicity, with some marketing ideas: producing a documentary film, commissioning a biography that would be published by a Warner Books company, packaging a tour with the surviving Teenagers as well as other artists featured in the movie like the Platters and Little Richard, and a promotion with the Rock and Roll Hall of Fame, to which the group was inducted in 1993.

In 1986 a group of doo-wop fans held a concert to raise money to pay for a proper gravestone for Frankie. Even though Frankie's brother Louis gave his support, there was a problem with the estate at the time, so the completed gravestone sat in a record store in New Jersey. I thought a renewed effort to install the gravestone would provide a unique news story that could draw attention to the movie. Reina never responded to my ideas.

I disagreed with the approach that Warner Brothers' marketing department took, which deemphasized the music. In a report from a test screening at Magic Johnson Theaters in Baldwin Hills, the consensus of the audience was that "the musical performances were the real stars of the movie." The colors of the poster were washed out, and the ensemble grouping looked like the attractive cast of a black soap opera. To coincide with the movie's August 1998 release, Oprah Winfrey based a show around it, but the theme was "Have you been a fool in love?" The cast were guests, but the discussion elicited confessions from audience members about their relationships rather than emphasizing Frankie as a character, the drama of the movie, or the music.

I had a problem with our Rhino Films credit as part of the credit block, which is the listing of those who are credited on the poster and in the initial printed ads. Our logo was included on the credit block for *Fear and Loathing in Las Vegas*, a Universal Film, but not on this Warner film. The presence of the Rhino logo is good branding as it increases awareness of the company that Warner now owned—and it didn't cost any extra money to do so. I spoke to Daly about it. He said that it was usually applied for production companies that contributed to the funding of a film, which we hadn't. I felt he could have easily had our logo included, and thought this was another call he got wrong.

Realizing the value of contemporary artists in marketing new releases, Sylvia Rhone, the president of Elektra, wanted to issue an album with artists and tracks her label could promote. She hired Missy Elliott to put it together for a release on the East/West label. As a music fan, I was offended that it was misrepresented to the public as the soundtrack, as most of the songs on their album weren't in the movie. Only Little Richard's "Keep a Knockin'" was in the film; songs by En Vogue and Missy Elliott ran over the end credits. There were no songs by Frankie Lymon and the Teenagers on the East/West album.

Even though our album was the genuine soundtrack, I was prevented from using that term, so I came up with *Original Versions from the Movie*. All of the fourteen songs were in the film, but I was disappointed that we couldn't include "Keep a Knockin'." Rhone was correct in speculating that her album would sell more than Rhino's, 127,000 to 41,000. Given that Elektra spent over $1 million to produce the album, it lost a significant amount of money. Ours made between $150,000 and $200,000 for the Rhino label. Our *Best of Frankie Lymon and the Teenagers* sold 9,000 in the five years we were working on the movie, and an additional 10,000 after the movie was released. Because stores ordered larger quantities of a new release rather than a catalogue title, we issued the *Very Best of Frankie Lymon and the Teenagers*, which sold 34,000. We were hoping for significantly more sales, but the movie wasn't a hit.

The big loser was Warner Brothers Pictures. The $12.4 million at the US box office distilled down to $5.2 million for Warner. They banked $7 million from pay TV and $1.7 million from home video sales. Usually there's additional money generated overseas, but when I finally talked to the person in the international department, I was rendered nearly speechless when she told me that the only country outside of North America where the film made it into theaters was Trinidad. Warner spent $34 million making the movie, and $17 million on marketing (mostly ads). The other main expense was the cost of the prints, which totaled $2 million. I estimate that Warner Brothers lost $40 million on the film.

Frankie Lymon and the Teenagers, the Platters, and Little Richard were all inducted into the Rock and Roll Hall of Fame. "Why Do Fools Fall in Love" was ranked #307 on *Rolling Stone*'s "500 Greatest Songs of All Time" (in a poll of 172 musicians, critics, and music industry executives in 2004). The Beach Boys, who had recorded the song on a 1964 album, performed it on their 2012 reunion tour. Emira Eagle Lymon made over a million dollars on the song.

CHAPTER 13

The Rhino Way
to Negotiate

This chapter is expanded from a lecture
I gave to Rhino employees.

The lawyer we used in the early days, who preferred to go by his last name, Ashley, was a smart guy who we would have been more inclined to continue with except for his habit of being very late in delivering agreements. He negotiated our contract for our second single, by Roky Erickson, with Erickson's manager who was also a lawyer. Even though the fee was reasonable at $200, it greatly cut into our profit as we only sold 2,000 records. Within a year or so I took over our negotiating and contract drafting, even though I had never been to law school or had any legal training. My negotiating skills surfaced when I was a preteen trading baseball cards in a time in which the cards weren't that valuable. I wasn't cutthroat, but learned that in some instances I could get two cards in return for one of mine. For the next ten years I negotiated most of our contracts.

The main points of a record contract are easy to grasp: royalties and advance. A royalty is how much is paid for every record sold. An advance is an amount that is paid up front in order to secure the deal and as a guard against getting stiffed by the *licensee* failing to pay royalties on records sold. A nonrecoupable advance meant that, in the event the record generated less in royalties than was paid in the advance, the licensor would not have to pay back the difference.

Record companies try to pay as little as possible. A common royalty in the 1960s, for even a successful group like the Monkees, was 5 percent. A decade later a good royalty was considered to be 10 percent. It was a percent calculated on the list price of the record. For example, if an album had a list price of $5.98 and an artist was to receive 10 percent, then that would calculate to 59.8¢ a record. Record companies further diminished that amount in their contracts. From the days when records were pressed on shellac, which was prone to break, contracts contained a breakage percentage of usually 10 percent. Breakage didn't occur when the medium changed to plastic (vinyl), so the companies kept the discount and merely called it a packaging deduction. Standard language was for the company to pay on 85 percent of the records sold. This was because, on occasion, as an inducement for a store to initially stock a record, or take a higher quantity than was desired, the label would give them one-in-ten, meaning that they would get one free for every nine they bought. (Because a store could return unsold product, certain heavily promoted albums in the 1980s were referred to as *shipping gold and returning platinum,* meaning that more copies were returned than sold.) This *free-goods* deduction was part of the calculation even if the label didn't give any away as a sales inducement. Using the above example, that would diminish the royalty further, to 46¢ per album.

In the early days of CDs, manufacturing was more expensive than vinyl albums so labels hiked their packaging deduction to 25 percent. Within a few years manufacturing costs were more in line with that of vinyl albums, but record companies still kept it at 25 percent. In the digital age, labels extracted more from the artist as a means of paying for their technological costs and for the legal fees expended in chasing illegal downloaders. Here's the breakdown from a typical download where the consumer pays 99¢ for the song on the iTunes store: 29¢ retained by Apple; 9¢ for the publisher; 46¢ for the label; 15¢ for the artist and producer. When labels license to a third party, like Rhino, the income is usually split 50 percent for the artist, 50 percent for the label. A label licensing to a company such as Apple for iTunes refuses to look at the income being subject to a similar split with the artist, but payable as an artist royalty, as though the label shipped physical product to Apple as it did to a store, generating much less income for the artist.

When I made our first license with a major label, with Warner Special Products (WSP) for a *Best of Allan Sherman*, we were given a standard agreement of a 10 percent royalty and an advance on sales of 5,000 copies. Unlike the major labels who had royalty deductions in all of their artist and producer agreements, WSP granted us no deductions as a licensee. As I soon found out, the agreement I signed with Warner Special Products, the licensor for all the Warner owned labels—Warner, Elektra, and Atlantic—was standard in the industry.

Among the initial best of albums I wanted to release was one that collected the recordings of the Standells, the 1960s rock group best known for "Dirty Water." The group had recorded for Tower Records, an imprint of Capitol Records. In February 1979, I wrote our request to Capitol's licensing person, Renny Martini, but he never responded. When I finally reached him on the phone, he replied that he couldn't license it to us. When I asked him why, he wouldn't give me any explanation. A couple of years later I found out the reason. Capitol didn't own the masters. Why couldn't he have just told me?

Richard and I wanted to reissue the recordings of Richie Valens and the Bobby Fuller Four, both produced by Bob Keane, but had difficulty tracking down the owner. I had been told to get in touch with PolyGram. Their response was, "We can't license this to you at this time." Because of Martini's subterfuge, this time I pushed for a reason. PolyGram's response was, "We don't know whether we own it or not." Paul Politi helped me get in touch with Bob, who was then selling home alarm systems. I made the deal with him, and it was a fruitful and long lasting relationship. The 1987 movie on Valens' life, *La Bamba*—for which Los Lobos did the music—pushed our best of album past 200,000.

Because the established labels had a difficulty in relating to rock 'n' roll in the fifties and sixties, most of the rock hits were on independent labels. These companies were often fly-by-night, or otherwise unsophisticated. What could we do if there was a track that we really wanted, but we couldn't determine the owner? Ken Sasano, a great guy, music fan, and product manager at Columbia Records, told me that when Columbia couldn't find the royalty recipient, it merely put the money into an escrow account in order to pay them when they were found. I learned later that Sasano probably meant that's what Columbia did on masters they owned. He didn't express that limitation to me, so I thought it was applicable for any record. As a result, we got into trouble.

In October 1982 we released a pumpkin-shaped, orange-colored record for Halloween that really played on turntables. It sold well enough to merit a follow-up the next year, a bat-shaped record. We felt it wouldn't be complete unless we included Bobby "Boris" Pickett's "Monster Mash."

Bobby had been an aspiring actor living in Hollywood who moonlighted with a vocal group called the Cordials. During their rendition of the Diamonds' "Little Darlin'," he hammed it up with an impersonation of horror movie star Boris Karloff. The crowd loved it, and eventually Bobby agreed to make a record with that voice. It was a take-off of Dee Dee Sharp's "Mashed Potato Time," and although expectations were low, "Monster Mash" provided the perfect musical accompaniment to the exploding monster craze sweeping the nation in the early 1960s. It topped the charts in 1962 and made the top ten again nine years later.

The record was originally on Garpax Records—see what I mean about small labels—but its most recent appearance was on Parrot, a PolyGram imprint. I requested to license the record from PolyGram, but the licensing person claimed they didn't own it. We tracked down Pickett and offered to license it from him, but he insisted PolyGram owned it. We called the label, told them what Pickett had told us, and they again claimed they didn't own it. Once again we checked with Pickett, who repeated his understanding. I figured we would use the track and put the royalties in an escrow account, as Sasano suggested.

On September 30, 1983, a day before the record was to be pressed, I was in New York having an initial meeting with PolyGram's head of licensing, Artie Fischer. When I told him what we were doing with "Monster Mash," he blew up and told me that PolyGram owned the song. I was nearly speechless and managed, "But you told us twice you didn't own it." Fischer said it didn't matter. When I offered to license it legitimately, he replied that it would take at least six weeks to get approval. I called Richard from his office and had him halt production.

We were down, but not out. Richard quickly rebounded, rounded up Bobby Pickett, and recorded a version that was virtually indistinguishable from the original. In order to afford the session, Richard agreed to write and produce a commercial for the Sears Halloween Shop, featuring Pickett. Despite the fact that Richard had never previously produced a commercial, it won second place in the national musical category of New York's Big Apple Radio Awards.

The aggravation we experienced, Richard's herculean effort, and the visually stunning bat-shaped record only mustered 5,000 copies sold. It was, unfortunately, not unusual for our inspired efforts to yield so little commercially. But there was a silver lining. Richard's version was so good, I licensed the song to a few TV shows, such as *The Simpsons*, and compilation albums, thus making more money than we anticipated on the song, and karmically depriving PolyGram of licensing fees that they otherwise might have received had they been reasonable.

In October 1967 I was watching *Upbeat*, a syndicated TV show taped in Cleveland. The Ohio Express performed "Beg Borrow and Steal," an infectious song with a chorded-rhythmic pattern similar to "Louie Louie" that I immediately liked. The group had a few subsequent hits, their most well-known being "Yummy Yummy Yummy." They and the 1910 Fruit Gum Company were in the vanguard of a two-year fad of lightweight rock referred to as "bubblegum." When I compiled two albums of the best from this genre, I experienced difficulty in licensing "Beg Borrow and Steal." The record had been a hit for the Cameo Parkway label, which Allen Klein's company bought out of bankruptcy. Even though he hadn't released any of the Cameo Parkway records in the over ten years since he bought the catalog, Klein wouldn't license us the track. As it turned out, the same record had been issued a year previously on Attack Records as performed by the Rare Breed. I licensed the record from the producer to complete my package, although I had to list the artist as the Rare Breed.

There weren't reissue labels like Rhino. What existed in the early eighties were hits packages that were advertised on TV by companies such as K-tel. The strategy was to spend a lot on advertising with the goal of selling hundreds of thousands of albums. In contrast, we were deemed small potatoes by the labels. Because Rhino's business was selling to retailers, in the early days we could only justify paying an advance based on 5,000 sales. The labels' contracts were geared towards the mail order companies and contained clauses that didn't apply to our business. The labels didn't want to alter their contracts for us, and we were denied deductions for items such as free goods, because they didn't apply to mail order companies.

We felt we were lucky just to have them return our calls. The major labels didn't appreciate that we were a new source of business for them. Capitol turned us down, then licensed us a few titles like *The Best of the Spencer Davis Group*, then cooled on us again. PolyGram Records initially wouldn't license to us at all. Sometimes CBS Records licensed to us, sometimes not. For the same bat-shaped record, Richard recorded an impressive, sound-a-like version of the theme song from *The Blob*, as by Little Stevie and the McQueens (actor Steve McQueen starred in the movie) because CBS wouldn't license us the original version. As a result, we felt we couldn't be aggressive in negotiating for a fairer contract.

In any negotiation one has to understand their position in relation to that of the other party. When we first approached other labels about licensing their masters, as the recordings were referred to, they weren't motivated. Never was I approached with the attitude of "Let's see how much business we can do together." It was more like they couldn't be bothered to deal with us. When it came to the other, more established record companies, regardless of how we were feeling, we had to make nice. We were dependent upon them to agree to license us their masters in much the same way the United States is reliant upon oil from the OPEC countries.

Never Before, an album of rarities by the 1960s group the Byrds, provides a good example. Bob Hyde was a record collector friend of Richard's who headed up Random House's record mail order division, Murray Hill Records. He was able to license the Byrds' masters from CBS Special Products. Because we helped him with the package, he agreed—as did CBS's head of marketing, Paul Smith—that we could issue the album to retail when mail order sales dried up. The album turned out exceptionally well, and sales were so good that Smith reneged, preferring to have CBS release it to retail. What could we do? We weren't going to complain because that would have affected our ability to license from CBS in the future. Smith threw us a bone by agreeing to license us most of the tracks we needed for a Roy Orbison hits package. CBS had recently obtained ownership of Orbison's masters from the country label Monument, which had filed for bankruptcy. Karma was in our favor as Orbison racked up sales of 475,000.

In our early days when we signed an artist like Barnes & Barnes, I provided a royalty of one dollar an album. As noted, the language in standard industry agreements often meant that the artist had no idea how much he was making on every record sold. I thought this would take some of the mystery out of the process by making it easy to understand and calculate. Using the Barnes & Barnes example, their 1980 album *Voobaha* sold 5,384, which meant that they would have received $5,384 in royalties.

Some artists had difficulty with that presentation. They preferred a percentage of list price as in most artist agreements. I thought a fair offer was the same rate that the major labels licensed to us, 10 percent of the list price with no deductions. This worked for a few deals, but then artists didn't think this sounded as much as their friends who were getting higher percentages from other labels. Of course, those percentages were with deductions. So, I increased percentages and incorporated a packaging deduction, but I avoided paying on less than 100 percent of records sold.

I.R.S. Records (which stood for International Record Syndicate, rather than Internal Revenue Service) started around the same time as Rhino. They were one of the labels that we were in envy of because they were interested in the same cutting edge artists as we were, but because A&M Records funded and distributed them, they were ahead of us in the game. The rapid success of the Police, whom owner Miles Copeland managed and who had signed to A&M, also gave them legitimacy as a label that could break new wave acts.

I was an early fan of Oingo Bongo, having seen them when they played during the summer of 1975 at the Daisy in Beverly Hills. Then named the Mystic Knights of the Oingo Boingo, they styled themselves after a 1930s jungle orchestra. A few years later, with a new lineup of superb musicians who played complex rock arrangements, the name-shortened Oingo Boingo were among my favorite local bands. I kept in touch with the group's lead singer and composer, Danny Elfman, and licensed "I'm Afraid," an early track of theirs, for our 1979 local bands compilation album, *L.A. In,* and even put their picture on the cover. Danny wanted to sign with Rhino, but I could only budget $500 for them to record an EP whereas I.R.S. offered them five times that amount, so they signed with I.R.S.

The Go-Go's were another band Richard and I wanted to sign, but who went with I.R.S. When English rock journalist John Ingham became their co-manager, he invited us to see them play in April 1980 at the Arena in Culver City. Early on their performances had been ragged, but at this point they had improved greatly. They were leaving the next day for a tour of England. By the time they had returned, Ingham was out, and so was our entre.

I also courted Stan Ridgway and his band Wall of Voodoo. In February 1980 we made an appointment for him to come in and discuss signing the band with Rhino. Days later he called to cancel because he said they had to prepare to play at a post-concert party for Pink Floyd, who were in town performing seven shows at the Sports Arena. I never heard from Stan again. I.R.S. signed Wall of Voodoo to record their first album. I.R.S.'s biggest success came with R.E.M., with whom they had one platinum and four gold records. But most of their artists didn't sell well, and they folded in 1996.

I'm not saying that Rhino could have done a better job marketing these acts than I.R.S., but we couldn't compete with them. This falls into being aware of what we could and couldn't do. We signed new artists with large local followings—like the Pop, and Nu Kats—to record EPs for us. As with these groups, and in other cases, we were thought of as a last resort label. That didn't mean that we squeezed them to make a bad deal. We wanted to be fair. It was just an awareness that we had leverage, and could use that position to negotiate for our benefit—unlike dealing with the majors where we had no leverage. For example, major labels sign artists to multi-album contracts. That's because if an artist becomes successful, the label will benefit from healthy sales on subsequent albums. We could have signed our new artists with options for future albums, but we didn't. I felt that we were offering so little in the way of an advance or recording budget—in order to lower our risk—I couldn't justify tying up the artist for the future. This backfired on us with one of our few successful new artists.

Danny Perloff, our college rep in the San Diego area, was enthused about a new country rock band named the Beat Farmers. We signed them and gave them a recording budget of $6,000. We broke the act and sold an impressive 50,000 albums. Before we could even mention having them record a follow-up for us, their manager signed them to Curb Records without even giving us a courtesy phone call. If Curb had been able to make the Beat Farmers into a hit act, we would have benefitted with more record sales from new fans wanting to hear their first album, but Curb's results were modest and we saw no upswing in sales.

We learned our lesson with our next signing, garage rock girl group the Pandoras. Even though we had options for more albums, after the release of their 1986 Bill Inglot-produced Rhino debut, *Stop Pretending*, they absconded to Elektra Records. I appealed to Peter Philbin, the label's West Coast head of A&R whom I had befriended when he was at Columbia, but he failed to be honorable. Rather than seek damages in an expensive lawsuit and risk Elektra snubbing our future licensing requests, we acquiesced. Karma railed against the Pandoras; Elektra never released their album.

Quite often when we had off-site company meetings, Richard brought in a motivational speaker. Once he even brought in a fake, standup comedian Robert Aguayo posing as a spiritualist. Richard took notice of Scott Alexander because his Rhino Press had published motivational books such as *Rhinoceros Success*. At a company meeting we had in Marina del Rey, Alexander told a story of a man who had a bird feeder in his backyard: a bird house with seed, mounted on top of a pole. A squirrel kept getting at the food. The man tried different things, including greasing the pole, but still the squirrel was successful. The point he was making was that the man might spend five to ten minutes a day thinking about how to protect his birdhouse, but the squirrel probably spent most of its waking hours thinking about how to get the food.

Richard and I, and many of our employees were similarly focused. This wasn't merely a business for us, but a passion. It was important to make the deal, to preserve the music, and to present it with quality so people could benefit from the power of the music. When I was negotiating with a lawyer, I was fortified by a need to make the deal happen. A lawyer would have been a dispassionate agent who was representing his client on the negotiation, as well as other clients with other deals with other companies. I was like the squirrel that was thinking long and hard about how to get the food. I definitely got a sense of this in some negotiations.

Albert Grossman, a high-powered manager who had previously guided Bob Dylan and Janis Joplin, started Bearsville Records in 1970. His label grew to signing over twenty artists, but only two were big sellers, Todd Rundgren and Foghat. The label had been distributed by Warner Brothers Records, but had ceased releasing new product by 1984. Grossman died two years later. As a Todd Rundgren fan, I had been having phone conversations with Bearsville for almost two years before I was able to make a deal to revive their catalogue.

We agreed on an advance of $300,000, which was by far the most we had ever paid anybody. Bearsville's accountant, Steve Constant, the person I negotiated the main points with, refused to accept the standard 10 percent royalty, claiming that his artists were at a higher rate. He wanted 14 percent, which was much higher than I wanted to pay. I wasn't privy to Bearsville's artist's contracts, their royalty rates, or how Bearsville intended to pay them. I had to accept Constant's position and work with it.

My goal was to find ways to bring the deal more in line with our comfort zone. While I had intended to pay a 10 percent royalty with no deductions, when he asked for 14 percent, I put in the agreement the deductions on packaging and free goods, which brought it down to a more manageable rate, although still more than 10 percent. I also put in a clause to represent the masters for licensing to third parties: to other labels for compilation albums and to producers of films, TV shows, and commercials. In our agreement, I made the income a fifty-fifty split. Because Constant was primarily concerned with the advance and royalty rate, he gave less thought to our other points. Not only did the licensing income provide another profit area for Rhino—at no additional advance—it also helped us recoup the advance sooner.

Constant was canny, but also disingenuous. Rather than paying artists the "high" royalty rates that he mentioned, Bearsville paid them much lower by splitting the income they received from Rhino. This was legitimate. Bearsville was no longer active as a label with a distribution deal with Warner Brothers. They licensed their masters to us. Most contracts of the time split licensing income fifty-fifty with the artist.

Bearsville also benefitted from outstanding recoupable advances. As an artist becomes successful, he's able to negotiate for a higher advance and recording budget on subsequent albums. When the artist loses popularity, quite often a label will end up unrecouped, meaning that the label advanced the artist more money than was paid back from royalties earned on more recent releases. This amount stays on the books and is slowly recouped—if at all—from catalogue sales and licensing. Foghat's best-selling albums were *Foghat Live* (1977), which sold 2.2 million, and *Fool for the City* (1975), which sold 1.3 million. Todd's best-selling album, *Something/Anything* (1972), sold 735,000. In the early 1980s, at the end of their term, Foghat was down to 37,000 and 15,000 on their last two albums, respectively, and Todd was averaging around 50,000.

Our first product was released in 1987. We did exceptionally well with Bearsville, and I renewed the deal for subsequent three-year periods at the same advance amount. Constant noticed the fifty-fifty split, and in renewing, renegotiated that down to where Rhino received 25 percent. Around the time I left the company, five of our Foghat albums had sold over 100,000 each. Todd Rundgren had four titles that averaged 150,000. I was disappointed that our *Best of Foghat*, which sold over 400,000, was still shy of gold record status. I would have liked to have given a gold record award to Foghat's lead singer, Dave Peverett, who died in 2000. He was a nice guy who helped us on some of our blues packages.

Oddly, this mission we were on, and with Rhino being a last-resort sort of label, I didn't feel intimidated when I negotiated contracts with some of the top lawyers in the business, for example for the Bearsville and unreleased Monkees contracts. If the owners felt they could get more money elsewhere, they wouldn't have been at Rhino. Part of the process of dealing with these experienced lawyers was their scrutiny of minor points that I thought was unnecessary, such as a clause that diminished the royalty rate

for product sold to the armed forces (a very small amount for us), a limit on
the time period a licensor could audit, and the jurisdiction in which a suit
could be filed, etc. Rather than representing their client's best interests—
and that includes being expedient rather than prolonging a negotiation to
add billable hours—some lawyers become combative, aggressively going
after points in order to satisfy a personal need to win.

I was under the impression that lawyers had to adhere to ethical standards in the same way that doctors take the Hippocratic Oath. There are
guidelines, but nothing as strong. Still, as a professional, one would expect
a lawyer to be ethical, but that isn't always the case. In 1977 Jeff Samuels,
the nicest guy in the record business, was signing acts for United Artists
Records. He liked a couple of songs I had written and allocated $500 for
me to go into the studio to record demos. Before I got the money, I had to
sign a one-page agreement prepared by UA's legal department. It had three
clauses, the third of which granted UA the right to publish my songs for
the rest of my career. For a measly $500—none of which was going into
my pocket—I thought this was outrageous. Jeff told me to cross it out.
He explained that it was included so UA could use it as leverage in case
they, or any other label, wanted to sign the act in the future. They could,
for example, give back the publishing in exchange for a lower royalty percentage or a longer-term contract. So, UA's lawyers knew they were being
unfair, and perhaps, unethical, but they did it anyway to take advantage
of naïve artists.

The best thing I can say about Michael Bishop is that he's a true rock
music fan, from when he was a teenager playing in bands on the Sunset
Strip in the sixties. On occasion he pitched me ideas for projects. He was
making a living as a composer for low-budget movies when he came up
with an idea while watching late night TV: a compilation album of original movie music as played by rock bands. I didn't think the idea would
sell, but one listing interested me. Sonic Youth had recorded the soundtrack to a 1987 film, *Made in U.S.A.* The movie fared poorly at the box
office, and the soundtrack had never been released to consumers.

I made a deal with the film's producer to issue the soundtrack and
with Bishop to mix the tapes for release on CD. Sonic Youth didn't like
the film and didn't want our soundtrack released. Their lawyer was, of

course, paid to represent their position. What was missing from this contentious exchange was a respect for the law and Sonic Youth honoring a contract that they had signed. Apparently this lawyer hadn't heard Abraham Lincoln's advice: "If you cannot be an honest lawyer, choose some other occupation." He said that if we released Bishop's mix, Sonic Youth would badmouth the album and tell their fans not to buy it.

In an attempt to ameliorate the situation, Gary Stewart stepped in and thought it would be best to have the band mix the album—at our expense. This made the soundtrack more costly and delayed its release, by which time Sonic Youth's popularity had slipped. I preferred Bishop's mixes. During this period Bishop, understandably, was very upset, and also in need of money. Having problems with his alcohol consumption, my assistant, Julie D'Angelo, and I had to endure numerous abusive phone calls from him. He suggested I buy him out of the project. Even though his mixes weren't used, I intended to honor our contract whereby he received a producer's royalty. We agreed on a buyout and were done with him. In his state, he didn't realize that his behavior had burned his bridges at Rhino on any future projects. A few years later he contacted me to be interviewed for a documentary he was producing, titled *Rage: 20 Years of Punk Rock West Coast Style.* I felt good that when I last saw him it was on a positive note.

One area we didn't do particularly well in was soundtracks. Even with the surprise success of *Valley Girl*, a soundtrack we put together and issued eleven years after the movie was released, which sold 230,000, we probably only approached breaking even. A relatively low budget film, *No Holds Barred*, was a breakout for wrestling star Hulk Hogan, grossing $16 million at the box office. Everybody had higher hopes for Hogan's next film, the bigger-budgeted *Suburban Commando*, including us, as we released the soundtrack album. It flopped, only managing $6 million in film rentals, which meant that too few people saw the film who wanted to buy our soundtrack. A song I wrote and produced was used as the second song over the end credits. A look at the accounting for our album showed a loss. But through the years the publishing income on the song brought the project close to breaking even. It's an example of an additional income source that helped to hedge the album's possible losses.

I was thinking long-term. I tried to make negotiations reasonable and congenial. I realized the importance of paying royalties fairly and regularly and being available for any questions an artist or licensor had. Because of my experience interviewing rock musicians in my twenties, I was comfortable interacting with them rather than being intimidated by being in the presence of a star. I made a deal with Howard Kaylan and Mark Volman for a five-song Turtles picture disc in 1978, our first year. We were still releasing product by them in my last year, 2001. I made a deal with producer Bob Keane in 1981 to release Richie Valens and Bobby Fuller Four masters. We were still doing business with him when I left.

The most important factor in preparing for a negotiation is evaluating what something is worth. Small deals were not as crucial. As we built our business and were perceived as being successful, people we negotiated with wanted more money. Selling businesses—or in this case music catalogues— relied on financial guys determining that the accounting made sense and was reliable, and then a standard factor was implemented. For example, if a catalogue—or business—averaged $500,000 in profits a year the previous three years, at a factor of six, the purchase price would be $3 million. If a factor of eight, it would be $4 million.

Richard, with input from our finance and sales departments, usually provided evaluations based on what albums we would release and what licensing income we could expect. He did an excellent job. Other labels didn't do this. They were so big that any purchased catalogue just got absorbed. They never evaluated whether a deal was good or not. Quite often the person who made the deal would be gone from the company and it wouldn't be of concern to his replacement. Because we were self-financed in the early days, it was important that we made good deals. If we even made one high-priced deal that bombed, we could very easily go out of business. I estimate that of all the deals we made and of all the albums we released, 75 percent were profitable, 15 percent broke even, and 10 percent resulted in a loss—and rarely a significant one.

We had made a licensing deal with Brunswick Records for masters by Jackie Wilson, the Chi-Lites, and Tyrone Davis. We were interested when the owner expressed a desire to sell the catalogue. Richard excelled at thinking outside of the box and put together a promising plan in order to finance the deal. A better-funded and larger company, like a major label, would want to own all of the rights and wouldn't even have considered the proposal that Richard conceived. Rhino's primary interest was to issue best of albums by the more prominent artists and to be able to use individual tracks on our compilation albums. He had deals in principle: with one company to take the foreign territories, one to take the synchronization rights (film/TV/commercials), and another to put out the albums that we felt wouldn't sell sufficiently for us to release. Ultimately the owner decided not to sell.

Mike Ross, the cofounder of Delicious Vinyl, came to see us about distributing his catalogue. Soon after it formed, the label scored three top ten hits in 1989: "Wild Thing" and "Funky Cold Medina" by Tone Loc, and "Bust a Move" by Young MC. Ross wanted cash to promote new artists. He would have sold his label, but wanted much more money than we felt it was worth. Richard came up with a novel, workable idea. We paid him much less than he wanted, $2 million, but made it a loan collateralized against the catalogue. This way we got the masters to sell and license, and Ross got money to reinvigorate the label. The loan would be paid back from his portion of the earnings from the joint venture. Of course if the loan wasn't repaid, we would end up with ownership of the masters.

Sometimes Richard would miss the boat. He had been negotiating with *Rolling Stone* magazine about issuing a box set to commemorate their twenty-fifth anniversary. It's a deal we should have made, but he was lax in returning publisher Jann Wenner's phone calls. Wenner became impatient and contracted with Time/Life for a seven-disc box set that proved successful in the marketplace.

One deal Richard made proved to be problematic. In contracts, sometimes a clause states the licensor will have approval of the product at various stages before it comes out. For example, they might have approval of the sound of the mastering, the album graphics, the booklet or liner notes, and sometimes the advertising elements. If I ever faced that clause I made sure I added the phrase, "not to be unreasonably withheld." Richard made a deal with Phil Spector's attorney, Martin Machat, to rerelease Spector's catalogue, including a box set. But he didn't add the "not to be unreasonably withheld" clause.

Phil Spector wasn't a singer or an instrumental artist, but a producer-songwriter who forged a unique style. The dense sound of his early 1960s recordings with the Ronettes, the Crystals, and other artists became known as the *Wall of Sound*. Although the contract was signed in January 1987, the deal stalled and we were only able to release one album that year, 1963's *A Christmas Gift for You*. Spector wouldn't approve anything else. Bill Inglot oversaw the mastering of the discs for the box set. Spector's long-time engineer, Eddie Levine, thought they sounded great. We had suggestions for the packaging, which Spector would approve, then quickly change his mind. He then wanted the box to look like a bible, complete with gothic lettering. The music he produced was so joyful, I thought that design would be a mistake.

Although Richard had made the deal, throughout all this time he had still not engaged Phil Spector. That was to change on Sunday night, December 13, when Richard met Art Fein at the Music Machine club in West LA to take in a performance by Bo Diddley. Art was a music writer from Chicago who moved to LA in the fall of 1972. He worked for a time at Capitol Records where he befriended John Lennon and Yoko Ono. Subsequently, he rolled his interest into side projects like music supervision, management (the Blasters), and promoting rockabilly at local clubs. Art hosted a music discussion show, *Li'l Art's Poker Party*—that had nothing to do with card games—on local access cable. Spector was a fan of the show, and in an odd twist on video dating, chose guests for Art to invite up to his house for social evenings.

When Art mentioned that Phil Spector might join them, Richard became anxious, not only because of the impasse in our deal, but because of Spector's reputation for bad behavior. Spector showed, and when Art introduced them, Richard felt Spector knew who he was, but then Spector said, "Richard, you're Art's butler, aren't you?" Richard thought it was easier to avoid a confrontation and agree. Richard recounted the evening, during which Spector behaved like "he was drunk on his ass." When Spector made a visit to the men's room, accompanied by Art, he snatched a lit cigarette from a seated patron and smoked it as though it were his own. Still, after the club closed, Richard joined him and Art in Spector's limousine: Art and the chauffeur in the front, Richard and Phil in the back.

Spector was acting completely insane, and was calling Ike Turner on the phone to invite him to join them. Spector mercilessly cut Turner up after he arrived with his son. Turner's response sounded like unintelligible grunts to Richard. Around 4 a.m. Art abruptly opened the front door, said, "Bye," and abandoned Richard. With Spector's bodyguard/chauffeur present, and the back door locked, Richard felt like he was a prisoner. Richard had heard about the parties Spector used to throw, when he made it difficult for guests to leave before he wanted them to—doors and gate locked, guard dogs patrolling the perimeter—which meant for extremely late nights. It was an inconvenience for guests to be in the presence of a legend, but most put up with it.

At 5:30 a.m. Spector, who had been irrational the whole time, changed gears. "In ten seconds he goes from falllng-down, slobering drunk," said Richard, "to the sharpest mind I've ever met in my life." He accused Richard of stealing from him. He rattled off specific language in the Rhino contract and gave his opinion why he didn't have to adhere to the clauses. Richard felt more uncomfortable. Finally, at 6 a.m. he saw an opening when they exited the vehicle to relieve themselves against the wall of the club, after which he scooted away.

Compounding the instability of the Spector deal was Martin Machat's poor health and subsequent death in April 1988. We had lost a voice who could reason with Spector. Martin's attorney son, Steven, attempted to fill that void, but it didn't work. We couldn't proceed because Spector wouldn't approve anything we did. Richard reasoned that because Spector didn't have much to do—he wasn't actively producing new artists—by prolonging the process, it filled his time.

Spector ultimately made a deal with Allen Klein for ABKCO to release the catalogue. Although we had a legally binding agreement, to have attempted to proceed would have meant being in a costly and time-consuming lawsuit, further engaging Spector's time and combative nature. Klein quickly reimbursed us for our expenses. But the disappointment among the fans of Spector's music at the company couldn't be reimbursed, nor the many man-hours expended on the project. When they made their deal, Klein and Spector joked that the two most hated men in the music business had joined forces.

The ABKCO box set came out in 1991 and unfortunately wasn't up to Rhino standards. Klein spent a lot of money on marketing, and ABKCO's distributor, PolyGram, shipped enough copies to earn a gold record. Rather than qualifying with sales of 500,000, as a box set with four CDs it needed only 125,000. Thousands of unsold boxes were returned by retailers. ABKCO warehoused them for many years hoping to sell them at their regular price, but further sales were a trickle. In the mid-2000s they were sold at cutout prices, at a discount of around 75 percent of list price to consumers. In November 2006 I ordered a couple from Amazon. com for thirteen dollars a box to give as holiday gifts. Art Fein bought his at Costco for around the same price.

We were passionate about our work and committed to putting out a superior product, and I was disappointed that it didn't seem to be much of a factor in making deals. The major labels didn't seem to care. Nor did Allen Klein, who never licensed to us, thinking that he would make more money if consumers only purchased ABKCO product. I thought artists would appreciate what we did, and they would be motivated to have great looking and sounding albums and the benefit of our effective marketing and sales departments. There was also our commitment to community service and giving back. I couldn't see how anybody could make a deal with another label. If our offer of an advance wasn't the highest, surely our reputation for paying royalties regularly would be a factor. If we put out the best product, showing the artist in the most favorable light, and if we were able to sell more product than any other company over the long run, then why wouldn't someone make a deal with Rhino? The reality was that it was down to what company paid the largest advance.

Sometimes deals weren't made due to other factors. In the early 1980s when I met with people at companies in London, their first response to a proposal was to come up with reasons why they couldn't make a deal. I couldn't understand this attitude. If a deal is made, everybody makes money, but if no deal is made, nobody does. After attending MIDEM in February 1982, I met with the BBC. I wanted access to the recordings they made with various artists that captured them live in the studio for broadcast on radio. They were flummoxed by my request. I had to get permission from the band members to even have them make me a cassette copy to listen to. It took three years until Rhino released *The Zombies Live on the BBC*. I was also interested in issuing similar albums by the Yardbirds and the Move, but the Zombies was the only one I was able to realize.

On May 3, 1985, I attended a party for Jerry Leiber and Mike Stoller at Le Dome restaurant in Hollywood. Jeff Beck was there with his model-looking girlfriend. I had been told that Jeff, who had been one of the rotating star guitarists in the Yardbirds, was keeping the project from going forward. I gingerly approached him, introduced myself, and expressed our enthusiasm for wanting to issue the BBC recordings. I had heard that Jeff was shy, but he barely looked at me, directing his gaze at the floor. His social discomfort made me feel uncomfortable, and I didn't probe him on how he felt about our request.

Pye Records had a rich catalogue from the 1960s, including the Kinks and the Searchers, which I wanted to license for the United States. After making two separate visits to London in 1987, I was frustrated that I couldn't close the deal with the current owners. It took Bob Emmer to finish it up for us. None of us had an ego of needing to be the proprietor of a deal. What was most important was that a deal was made. It was similar to when Richard constructed the offer for Delicious Vinyl and I completed the negotiations with their lawyer.

The Beatles' label, Apple Records, was one of my influences in starting Rhino. Apple's catalogue, primarily Badfinger, Mary Hopkin, and James Taylor (his first album), still hadn't been released on CD. In early 1990 I wrote a letter to Apple Records' head Neil Aspinall in which I offered $500,000 for the rights to the non-Beatles Apple masters for the United States. I thought it was a significant offer, but it didn't even merit a courtesy response.

I tried for years to license the Dave Clark Five and Slade catalogues for the United States, but I was unsuccessful. Both Dave and Colin Newman, the English accountant who represented Slade, held out for the exorbitant advances they wanted. They eventually got them from other companies who didn't fare well. By keeping their catalogues out of the marketplace for so long, they lost sales in the years CDs were initially available. Their inaction further devalued them, as the hits weren't being promoted to oldies radio or for use in film and TV.

Hits used in commercials can bring in lucrative amounts. Sometimes publishers weren't always reasonable. I tried to determine the music budget before I gave a quote on using one of our masters. The fair practice would be for the master rights holder and the publisher to be on equal footing, even though the publisher might receive more from performance play. If I didn't make a deal, I felt that it was money coming out of my pocket, regardless if I owned a percentage of Rhino or not. Employees at large publishing companies didn't feel that way. They wanted to keep their quotes high, but it didn't seem to bother them if they didn't make a deal. The two most difficult publishers that I dealt with, EMI and Warner/Chappell, were also the largest. They would want to maintain their quote, rather than considering the commercial's music budget or what would be fair for the record company to receive. This occurred a few times on hits by the Monkees when, in an effort to make the deal, I took less than the publisher.

The most egregious example affected Curtis Mayfield. Mayfield was a highly respected singer and songwriter who was a two-time inductee in the Rock and Roll Hall of Fame as a member of the Impressions and as a solo artist. In 1990, when lighting equipment fell on him during a performance, he was left paralyzed from the neck down. We had made a deal to reissue his solo recordings. In 1998 I was contacted by an advertising agency that wanted to use the introduction of Mayfield's hit "Superfly" in a commercial for the Visa credit card. The agency had only $150,000 for the music budget, which was on the low side for a national campaign, but the TV commercial was to be directed at a smaller, urban (black) audience. I was fine with making the deal for $75,000. Jack Rosner at Warner/Chappell wanted significantly more than that, claiming that the song was requested all the time. We checked with Curtis, who could have used the money as he had high expenses from being paralyzed. Assuming he would have received half—as the songwriter and recording artist—his share would have been $75,000. Even though Curtis expressed in a letter to Warner/Chappell that he wanted the deal to happen, Rosner refused to budge. I appealed to the company's chairman, Les Bider, a former accountant, but he was unmoved. In declining to accede to a sister company, Rosner and Bider even ignored Time Warner head Gerald Levin's pep talk encouraging synergy. I spoke to Rosner about it later. He clarified that while Warner/Chappell had received a few requests in the past, they had never actually licensed the song to a commercial. Rosner, perhaps feeling guilty, said that he probably should have agreed to the offer. This is the mentality I had to navigate.

Sometimes artists can seem to be unreasonable in turning down a deal. The Sweet were a 1970s English band best known for the hits "Ballroom Blitz," "Little Willy," and "Love Is Like Oxygen." We wanted to combine their hits which were on two different labels. Because the group had a bone to pick with Capitol Records, they withheld approval of our proposed album.

In the last few months I was at Rhino, Richard asked me if I could close a deal with the Doors for the use of "Break On Through" in a Cadillac Escalade commercial. Danny Sugerman managed the nonactive band's catalogue and merchandising. He was one of my oldest friends. I also had good relationships with the surviving members who had been involved with some of our early projects. Drummer John Densmore—lauded for *Riders On the Storm,* his book on the group—credits me with giving him his first writing assignment, the liner notes for a recording he did with guitarist Robby Krieger. We had recently made a deal with Danny to issue Doors concert recordings via mail order through our Handmade collectors division.

The use of the Doors song in the commercial was not something that would have benefitted Rhino. Tony Peppitone, the head of Warner Special Products, asked Richard to help as the income would be significant for the Warner Music Group, but he was having difficulty getting the group to approve. Organist Ray Manzarek was in favor. I felt Robbie would agree to it if I could persuade John. There is the issue of art being used for commerce. If songs are heartfelt expressions, using them in commercials can, in effect, debase them. I didn't feel that way. In addition, on rare occasions—more in England than in the United States—a song used in a commercial can sell significant records from the exposure.

Densmore's position was based on imagining what Jim Morrison's opinion would have been had he been living in 2001. In 1969 General Motors wanted to use the Doors' "Light My Fire" to advertise the Buick Opel. Manzarek, Krieger, and Densmore approved the hefty $80,000 fee—of which $60,000 was to go to the Doors. Morrison couldn't be contacted, but his lawyer approved the deal. When Morrison heard about the airing of the commercial, he became incensed, and the Doors never approved the use of their songs in another commercial. But who knows what Morrison would have thought in 2001? It was an extremely lucrative deal, especially for a song that was never a hit. "Break On Through" was the Doors' first single and only managed to chart at 126 on *Billboard*. The contract would have been for $8 million, from which the Doors—presumably—would have received $1 million apiece. I could not persuade Densmore. The producers replaced it with Led Zeppelin's "Rock and Roll," for less money. It was an extremely successful campaign and, uncommonly, General Motors used the song for three years.

Much to my disappointment, Frank Zappa had made a deal with Rykodisc for his masters. Rykodisc started out in 1983 as a well-intentioned CD-only high quality label of mostly folk and acoustic performers. Their artsy name was from the Japanese word that meant *sound from a flash of light*, which related to the laser beam in a CD player. They weren't doing that well when they shifted gears and tried to ape Rhino with rock reissues. After the success with Zappa's catalogue, they were emboldened to outbid Rhino on David Bowie's catalog. Bowie had been with RCA, but his recordings had reverted to him and his manager. I was able to get sales figures on his RCA CDs. This was prior to the more accessible sales information provided by SoundScan, which started in 1991. I was surprised to discover that Bowie's sales weren't that good. As the CD format had been in the marketplace for a number of years, I couldn't expect much of an upside—most music fans had already replaced their vinyl with CDs—and didn't think it was worth the $2 million they wanted. Unbeknownst to me—and my calculations—Bowie was planning a major greatest hits tour, which invigorated the catalog to Rykodisc's benefit. They also scooped us on Elvis Costello's masters.

Frank and Gail Zappa came to see us because they were not happy with Rykodisc. Richard was the point person. I wasn't involved. Frank knew he was dying, and wanted to make a deal with us for newer product as the older catalogue was with Rykodisc. We put out a few titles before Frank died in December 1993. Frank wanted Gail to sell the catalogue, preferably to Rhino, and not be involved in the business. She did otherwise, and was now in charge of Zappa Records. I was happy to not be involved, as Gail had a reputation for being difficult.

Gail wanted to sell Frank's masters for $20 million, which I thought was outrageous. Among all of Frank's albums that major labels had issued and promoted, Frank only had one that broke into *Billboard*'s top twenty. He didn't sell enough to merit $20 million. Richard thought we should offer $12 million, which seemed too much to me as well. He made his offer based in part on Gail's asking price, even though it was 40 percent less. Rykodisc was a natural suitor and they, obviously, had no idea of our offer. They came in at $22 million.

The result was that by trying to be Rhino, they made a horrendous deal that, in effect, bankrupted the company. They could no longer afford to operate, and the company was sold in 1998 to Island Records' founder Chris Blackwell. So, one bad deal ruined a good record company.

The Untold Story of 1979

"My Sharona" and The Knack

All years have big news stories, and 1979 was no exception: the nuclear accident at Three Mile Island, the Tehran hostage crisis, the Israel-Egypt peace treaty, gas rationing causing lines at the pump, and inflation. But the story of the biggest record of the year, "My Sharona" by the Knack, was left untold because the members of the band clammed up.

To a rock music fan starved for the type of music that dominated the charts in the 1960s—bands like the Beatles, the Who, and the Kinks—the Knack were saviors. When the Knack's first single debuted on the charts, there were no rock records in the top ten. "Hot Stuff" by Donna Summer, "We Are Family" by Sister Sledge, "Ring My Bell" by Anita Ward, "The Logical Song" by Supertramp, and "Chuck E.'s in Love" by Rickie Lee Jones were the top five songs.

Get the Knack was the best-selling album in America for five straight weeks. *Billboard* selected the Knack for "Top New Artist of the Year." Even though the members were music business veterans in their mid-twenties, with presumably more maturity and perspective than a band of impetuous teenagers, they still couldn't prevent success from slipping through their fingers.

The Knack's success would not have been possible were it not for lead singer Doug Fieger's infatuation with a girl whom he couldn't have:

one he was so obsessed with, one who frustrated him so much that he couldn't help but write songs about her, including a record that topped the American charts for six weeks.

In the late 1970s there was a proliferation of bands playing rock and a number of new clubs to cater to the increase. The main inspiration for these bands was the punk scene in England, primarily the Sex Pistols and the Clash. In Britain the music was an expression of frustration with social inequities; in America it was more of an artistic emulation. For the most part, the musicality of the American bands was lacking. They could barely play, they couldn't sing, and their songs lacked the comparative sophistication of the English bands.

Doug Fieger was floundering. In his mid-twenties, his dream of having hits as a member of a teenage rock band was years in the past. As a member of Sky he had recorded two poor-selling albums for RCA Records, produced by Jimmy Miller, who had guided the Rolling Stones and Spencer Davis Group. He moved to Los Angeles in 1970 as a member of Sky with dreams of becoming the bass player in the Doors (they didn't have one), and he was the only one who stayed when the band dissolved.

Doug grew up in Oak Park, a middle-class, mostly Jewish suburb of Detroit. His father was a labor lawyer and his mother a union organizer for the Michigan Federation of Teachers. He referred to his family as a violent one and consequently grew up "scared." As a kid he was interested in drama and played the lead in Peter Pan at the Detroit Institute of Arts. He involved the neighborhood kids in his productions. Once he enlisted his older brother, Geoff, in staging a convincing funeral for his sudden and unexpected death. Geoff, as funeral director, appointed the pallbearers and gave a eulogy. Doug was buried beneath a pile of leaves. Later on Doug studied acting with Lee Strasberg and Jeff Corey.

He met his girlfriend, Judy Halpert, in a ninth grade English class. Two years later at Oak Park High School they became "lunch buddies," and not long afterwards Judy moved into the permissive and progressive Fieger household. She joined Doug when he relocated to Los Angeles.

He was picking up a little money here and there as a bass player for hire. In 1974 he filled in for the bass player in the German progressive band Triumvirat. That same year he was paid to rehearse for three months with the Carpenters after Karen Carpenter broke up with her boyfriend, who had been the bassist. When Karen and her boyfriend reconciled, Doug was out. A few years later he played in local band the Sunset Bombers, but their record bombed. He also worked for a few months at the Licorice Pizza record store that was caddy corner from the Whisky a Go-Go on Sunset Boulevard.

He was disillusioned, but determined. No one was interested in his songs. A representative for the company that managed Jackson Browne seemed perplexed that Doug was writing about girls and dismissed his songs as "novelty music." In January 1978 Doug and his writing partner Berton Averre (pronounced like *of air*) enlisted drummer Bruce Gary to record a demo tape of three songs. They submitted it to various record companies, but didn't even get one to call them back.

Bruce met a manager from Elliot Roberts' company who managed high profile acts Neil Young and Joni Mitchell. Bruce told him about the prospective band, and he seemed interested in coming to see them play. Scott Bergstein, who worked for Casablanca Records, arranged for the group to use a soundstage Casablanca was renting in the Gower Gulch studio complex.

Bruce Gary was one of the first people Doug met when he moved to Los Angeles. With similar musical tastes, Bruce predicted that they would play in a band together some day. Bruce was struggling as well. When he was younger he was diagnosed with hyperactive disorder and ADD at a time where there was less understanding of its effect on learning. His parents had difficulty coping with their son and often directed their anger at him, to the point where he dropped out of high school to play drums professionally, originally touring with bluesman Albert Collins. Hustling for the next gig became part of his routine. His highest level of recognition was playing in a band with ex-Cream bassist Jack Bruce, ex-Rolling Stones' guitarist Mick Taylor, and noted jazz pianist Carla Bley, but according to Doug he never made much money.

Berton grew up in the San Fernando Valley and was bright and talented, but lacked drive and hadn't done much professionally. In the new band lineup, in order to be better able to sing the songs he and Berton had written, Doug wanted to play rhythm guitar. This meant they needed to find a bass player, and fast, as they had a showcase for a prospective manager little more than a week away.

Bruce knew Prescott Niles from the Los Angeles scene. The name sounded snooty, English, and upper class. He was born Prescott Niles Fine, but as a kid in New York he was simply Scott Fine. Prescott recorded an album in 1972 as a member of Hendrix clone Velvert Turner's band, and he was a good enough bass player to be asked to join various ensembles, though none had been successful. Handsome with curly hair, Prescott's look recalled that of 1970s glam rock star Marc Bolan.

Even though the four musicians didn't have much of a history together, they had a lot in common. They were twenty months apart in age—from Bruce, the oldest, to Berton, the youngest—and they were all, coincidentally, Jewish. It wasn't as if the members of the Knack were passed a secret formula for success. At this point, in their mid-twenties, being the next Beatles could hardly be an achievable fantasy.

Cream became the first rock "super group" when it formed in 1966. The idea was that each of the three musicians—Eric Clapton on guitar, Jack Bruce on bass, and Ginger Baker on drums—was the cream of the crop. In their own way, as it related to the burgeoning late 1970s Los Angeles rock scene, the Knack was similar.

Berton was a real gem. Although he had been in bands, he mostly practiced in the confines of his family's home, similar to Eric Clapton before he became known. Doug loved Bruce's drumming because "he could play crazy like the Who's Keith Moon, but with better technique." Bruce loved the British bands of the sixties, but was good enough to add complexity to the commercial song arrangements the Knack were seeking. Doug thought Prescott's bass playing was superior to his own.

Despite Cream's artistry and commercial success, the members were not friends. Tension was rampant, to the point where Ginger Baker described the second of the group's two years together as "agony." The Who and the Kinks, heroes to the Knack, didn't get along, either. The members of Knack were not friends, but were attracted to each other because of their musical gifts, as well as their shared passion for the music of the sixties. Doug was such a talent that the others put up with his "my-way-or-the-highway" attitude.

Doug explained his pushiness: "I wanted to be somebody and to have an identity. I didn't think I was good looking. I would look in the mirror and be repulsed because I thought I was hideous. I felt I had to push myself in order to make up for it. I also thought the business was brutal. It was like going to war. It took me a long time until I realized that my life wasn't my work."

During band rehearsals Bruce often played something other than the part he and Doug had worked out together. Doug would give Bruce a stare, Bruce would nervously snicker, and they would have to start the song again. At times Bruce would sulk or be sullen. Doug felt that he was the only one dealing with Bruce's attitude. He didn't get any support from Berton or Prescott, and this added to his frustration.

As a consequence of Doug's attitude, and in contrast to their music affinity, Berton didn't relish socializing with him. "One day he called me up to come over to his place to write," he said. "I needed a break from him. I told him I was going body surfing in Manhattan Beach. He said to pick him up; he wanted to go, too. I could have just got on the San Diego Freeway and driven straight to Manhattan Beach, but now I had to go into Hollywood to pick up Doug. He ended up on the beach covered in a towel so he wouldn't get sunburned, and he wouldn't go into the ocean because he was afraid that sharks might be lurking like in the *Jaws* movie."

Judy worked at Norm Tuch Hair Salon on West Third Street. She took breaks by walking in the area, which included looking at the trendy clothes selection in Denise's Place across the street. The store sold Chemin De Fer jeans, New Hero outfits, Comfort Shoes, and Korkeze. She became enamored with the savvy sales clerk, high school student Sharona Alperin, who worked part-time. Judy was so impressed, she told Doug about her.

Shortly after the band coalesced in May 1978, Doug was on his way to band practice when he stopped by Di Fabrizio Shoes to have Pasquale make him a pair of the type of boots the Beatles wore. Judy's salon was a few doors away, so Doug thought he would stop in and see her. She wasn't there, but he was directed up the street where he saw her talking to an attractive young girl who was minding her bosses' baby in a stroller. Judy introduced Doug to Sharona as "my husband." She made a strong impression on him. He invited her to the band's upcoming showcase.

For the rest of the day he thought about Sharona. Oak Park's population was predominantly Jewish. Doug only dated Jewish girls, and was primarily attracted to those who were Sabra, born in Israel, like Judy. Sharona's name was Israeli. Judy and Doug were both impressed at how self-assured she was, especially considering that she was only sixteen years old.

That evening, after rehearsal, when Doug returned home to the apartment he shared with Judy just down the street from the Whisky a Go-Go, he realized he had to make a move. It wasn't that he and Judy were arguing. It's just that, after ten years living together, they had grown apart. "Judy was like my mom," he said. "She took care of me. If it wasn't for her, I probably would have gone out without my shoes on, and I definitely wouldn't have eaten."

For the showcase the musicians invited their friends. Sharona came with some classmates who were very enthusiastic in response to the band's performance. The band played well, but no one from the management company showed up. It was a disappointment, but the musicians enjoyed playing with each other so much they decided to keep going as a band. It would be a way that Doug and Berton could get their songs heard, and they could pick up some money in the process. Doug convinced Berton to quit his job hanging drapes in order for them to be able to devote more time to the band.

The Knack's sound definitely harkened back to that of the rock bands of the '60s, but it was edgier, influenced by the recent punk movement. The lyrics were more contemporary. As Doug said at the time, "We're not living in the '60s, we're living in the '80s. Little 14-year-old girls do not want to hold your hand, they want to hold your kazoo. They don't want to fantasize about you as a dream lover, they want sweaty sex."

Doug thought the band should have a look like the early Beatles did in their collarless suits and in subsequent matching dress, but the band didn't have much money. Bruce's girlfriend, Ellen Brill, suggested a look where everybody wore black pants, white shirts, and black ties. The pants and shirts were common enough, and could be bought cheaply at thrift stores. She worked for a company that repurposed tuxedos, and was able to supply the band with black ties and vests made from remnants. This was very helpful to Berton, whose hapless manner of dress inspired the description "Hippy Huck Finn." These elements provided a unified identity for the band, but they weren't the first to make use of black ties. Some of the English punks sported the look, as well as the Los Angeles band the Heaters, whose members also wore vests.

When Donna Summer needed rehearsal space to mount her new stage show, Bergstein, who offered to be the group's manager, had to find another space for the Knack. They moved to a facility next to Bekins' storage building at Santa Monica Boulevard and Highland, run by three dope-smoking Rastafarians who kept telling the Knack that they played "too fast." Sharona and her friends often came by, fortifying the malnourished musicians with hamburgers from Carl's Jr.

At that time in the late 1970s in Los Angeles and other major cities, many bands were striving to be seen on the club circuit in order to have a chance at building a significant enough following to attract a major label contract. That put the club owners in an advantageous position. It was no longer common within the business to pay a new performer, even minimally, to provide the entertainment for alcohol-consuming customers. A new scheme was adopted by club owners: the owner gave the act tickets to disperse that would grant the holder free entrance into the club to see that band. The non-paying admissions added nothing to the pockets of the musicians onstage, but the two-drink minimum requirement for every member of the audience would do wonders for the club's revenue. In many cases the band got a share of paid admissions, but those tended to be minimal as a band was building a following. The motivation for a band such as the Knack was that it was a way to improve playing before live audiences, as well as a way to build a following that could help to launch a career. Given the club system, it took over six months before the Knack were paid anywhere close to what they should have made.

Danny Sugerman saw the band at their first club date on June 1, at the Whisky a Go-Go. "I never had so much fun at a show in my life," he said. "And it wasn't just me. Everyone in the place was on his feet, pressing toward the small stage. The band got four real encores. They were contagious and electrifying. No one in town had experienced this type of energy before."

Sharona had attended a yeshiva, a Jewish religious school, but for her senior year she transferred to the public school Fairfax High. Sharona's ethos was expressed in the title of the Kiss song she had written in marker on her bedroom wall: "I Wanna Rock 'n' Roll All Nite and Party Every Day." Sharona was very important in creating a following for the Knack by passing out these free admission tickets to her classmates, abetted by her best friends Nicole, Robin, and Leslye. She loved the music and the excitement of the Knack, and she liked Doug as a person.

The more time Doug spent with Sharona, the more he became captivated. She was dynamic and self-assured, but also cool, "like a female Keith Richards," as Doug put it. She also had a wild side. She did so much to promote the band that it would be easy to conclude that she was really into him. The main problem for Doug was that Sharona had a boyfriend, Marty Gurfinkel, which she reminded him about whenever he came on too strong. She later clarified that rather than being Doug's groupie, which would have been typical for the time, "He was my groupie."

Still, Doug tried to see Sharona as often as he could. They met for dinner at the Moustache Café across from the Improv comedy club on Melrose Avenue, or at Theodores next to the Starwood, or at Fuddruckers. At times they made out in the parking lot behind Pink's hot dog stand. She invited him to her house for a pool party, where she and her girlfriends performed a provocative run-through of the song "Time Warp" from *The Rocky Horror Show*.

The Knack closed their set with a driving cover of the Rolling Stones' rendition of "Not Fade Away." They wanted to come up with an original composition to replace it. Berton suggested the music to a song he built around a catchy riff inspired by Elvis Costello's "Pump It Up." They ran through it at rehearsal with Doug scat singing because there were no lyrics yet.

Back at the apartment, Doug got it in his head that Sharona might give him more time if he wrote a song about her. He was intrigued by the unique sound of her name. It soon became apparent that the end of Berton's riff fit Doug singing "My Sharona" perfectly. To Doug, the push-pull nature of Berton's rhythm represented the way Sharona seemed to entice him and then push him away. He had already written a song about his experience with her, "Frustrated." As Doug and Berton were working on the lyrics, Berton felt uncomfortable because Judy was in the next room and he thought she would take notice. Doug was so possessed that he pressed on and came up with the stutter on "my," similar to what Roger Daltrey sang on the Who's "My Generation."

The next day at rehearsal they ran through it even though the song hadn't been fully developed lyrically. After all, the sooner it was finished, the sooner the band could play it and the sooner it might win Sharona over. Bruce didn't like the song, thinking it was too simple. He refused to play it and Doug became incensed. This wasn't merely his drummer refusing to contribute to a new song for the band, this was Bruce sabotaging his gambit to win Sharona over. Doug, a man possessed, darted to the drum riser, raised his guitar over Bruce's head like an axe, and yelled, "I'm going to bash your head in if you don't start playing the drums, right now!" Bruce backed down. He eventually came up with a great drum part, atypically minimizing the use of cymbals in favor of rhythms inspired by surfer stomps and the Miracles' "Goin' to a Go Go."

Boyfriend or no, Doug couldn't possibly make a move while living with Judy, and the nitpicking between them increased. He expressed his frustration in writing "Let Me Out," in which he called on Sharona (not by name) to rescue him because "I'm just a prisoner of your love." Although Doug was an experienced, committed rock musician, he wasn't a typical philanderer. As he put it, "Even though I can be a serious, selfish bastard, and I was back then, I have very strong, middle-class morals. I could count on one hand the number of times I cheated on Judy. But I didn't feel comfortable doing it because it was against my personal moral code."

In August, a week before his twenty-sixth birthday, Doug moved out of his and Judy's apartment on San Vicente Boulevard and into Tim Prior's basement. Prior comanaged the Knack. He worked at Island Publishing, and Doug thought he would be good for the band because of his international connections and knowledge of music publishing.

Through a childhood friend, Doug was introduced to Scott Anderson. Anderson was an acolyte of music industry eccentric Kim Fowley, who was most familiar as the manager and producer of the all-girl band the Runaways, and was played by Michael Shannon in the 2010 movie about the band. Fowley described Anderson as "a rich kid from Pacific Palisades, an heir to Kaiser Aluminum." He appointed Anderson road manager of the band, but then had to fire him, which didn't leave Anderson with the best reputation. Having absorbed Fowley's confident spiel, he talked a good game.

Realizing that Scott Bergstein wasn't going to take the band where he thought it could go, Doug welcomed Anderson to the team in late July. He thought Bergstein could do the day-to-day coordination, Prior the foreign deals, and Anderson more of the strategic overview.

A week later, for his August 20 birthday, in order to cheer him up, Scott Bergstein and Tim Prior took Doug out to dinner at the Palm Restaurant. Afterwards, they went to the Starwood to see Nick Gilder, whose hit "Hot Child in the City" was making its way up the charts. While there, Doug became reacquainted with Abbe Beck. He first met Abbe on Halloween night in 1976, when he was playing bass for the Rats (later Sunset Bombers) at the Amber Glow biker bar on Tujunga Canyon Road. At the end of the evening at the Starwood, Abbe asked Doug if he would like to come home with her, and he happily did.

Abbe became his girlfriend, but he was still obsessed with and frustrated by Sharona and was still writing songs about her. His latest, "(She's So) Selfish," clearly identified her as "she's been working in the clothing trade." And Judy was still in the picture: he went over to her apartment to seek advice and solace over Sharona.

Sharona and her girlfriends took Doug out to celebrate his birthday at Knott's Berry Farm. All the while Sharona resisted capitulating, and this made Doug want her even more. "She made me feel like I was fourteen all over again," he said. "She was probably more mature than I was at the time. She had a positive attitude, always up and supportive. I never saw her depressed or sad."

A few nights after his birthday, on August 23, Sharona and her friends made the long drive to Monrovia to see the Knack play at the Woodsound cowboy bar. While watching the opening band, Bates Motel, Doug made out with Sharona. Marty was sitting on the other side of her, oblivious.

On September 30, the day of her seventeenth birthday, Sharona came to a rehearsal dressed in purple pants, a white shirt, and a purple beret. The Knack played "My Sharona" as part of their revised set. "The song was a metaphor for the sex I desperately wanted to have with Sharona,"

Doug said. "The song's arrangement had a climax and Berton's euphoric lead guitar solo." Sharona didn't realize until after she had departed that Doug was singing a song about *her.*

With Sharona still resisting Doug's overtures, he thought it would be less painful for him if he didn't see her, so he banned her from coming to the band's rehearsals. But he couldn't restrict her from coming to their club performances. When he saw her in the audience he talked about her on stage, of the hard time she was giving him, without mentioning her name. Of course he wrote about this, too. "Go Away, Stay Away" was a good song, but it wasn't recorded until the group's third album and was never finished.

In October there was a blowup between Anderson and Prior that resulted in Prior stepping down. "The Wooden Nickel in Lancaster was a long way from Hollywood," Berton explained, "but we owed it to ourselves to play as much as we could to build up the band's name." Unfortunately, the night erupted in two shouting matches. Although bands quite often play more than one set a night, the Knack had been contracted to only play one. "We didn't want to play two sets that night because it made our one performance special," said Berton. "After our set, Scott Anderson got into a shouting match with the owner of the club who wanted us to play a second set. On top of that, Scott got into a fight with Timmy Prior, who thought we should play the second set. It became so heated, Timmy ended up quitting right there. It was a crazy night. I don't think I'm ever going to forget the club owner screaming at Scott, 'Do you really think this band is worth $150?'"

Having three managers became unwieldy, but the Knack thought they needed all the help they could get. Anderson was the survivor. He expressed the division between manager and artist, according to Doug, with "The music and the band is your area. I won't stick my nose there. The business end is mine, and you don't stick your nose there."

The Knack were getting a lot of people out to see them live, but many times it was Sharona and her friends and their friends who benefitted from free tickets. Bruce Ravid, an A&R man for Capitol Records, was a fan and usually there. But what got the other record companies interested was when famous rockers joined the group on stage. First it was Ray

Manzarek of the Doors. Then Stephen Stills and Tom Petty and Bruce Springsteen. The Knack had worked up Eddie Money's hit "Two Tickets to Paradise" as part of their repertoire. On the November evening when Money came out of the audience at the Starwood to join them on stage, rather than performing an old rock 'n' roll song, they played Money's hit.

Flush with all the attention from the jamming superstars and from the thirteen record companies now interested in signing the band, Doug was very boastful in an interview he gave to Kristina McKenna that ran in December in the *Los Angeles Times*: "We're worth a lot of money and will be very big because the tunes are there and we play very well live. There's no filler in our set; they're all 'A'-side hits." He said that they wouldn't be happy with just one number one hit. He felt they would have at least ten. Even though his boasts were a front for his insecurities, his predictions did have merit.

Early in the new year, Doug and Sharona had sex for the first time. Steve Stills invited Doug to jam with him at the Record Plant where he was recording a new album. Sharona met Doug there, and afterwards they went back to Prior's basement. To Doug, Sharona's attitude was, "I'll do it with my body, but I'm not really doing it in my mind." The second time was when she joined him in San Francisco for a Knack show. He was still with Abbe, and Sharona was still with Marty.

The group calculated that, ideally, they wanted half a million dollars. They figured that would give them the money to record two albums, tour the world, and help with their living expenses during that time.

Warner Brothers was American's best label in the 1970s. Bob Krasnow, vice president of talent acquisition, wanted to sign the Knack. When president Mo Ostin came to see the band backstage after a performance at the Troubadour, he insulted them by asking how much they paid those shills to scream for the band. The insult was compounded when he made an offer that was less than the amount they felt they needed.

Freddy Hine from Polygram offered $4 million. He was such an over the top personality that they weren't sure if it was a serious offer or if it was made under the influence of cocaine.

Capitol Records seemed to be surviving on the sales of one major artist at a time. In the mid-sixties, it was the Beatles, whose product was initially rejected as being unsuitable for America. Then it was Grand Funk Railroad, and then the Steve Miller Band and Bob Seger.

The staff wasn't the hippest, either. Rather than music-obsessed record guys, upper management came across as beer-drinking, sports-watching, good ol' boys who, in-house, were referred to as the Coors Club. In meetings at the company, Doug was surprised at how often the executives wore football and baseball logoed clothes. Bruce Wendell, the head of promotion, came to work wearing a Philadelphia Phillies uniform because he was the team's batboy—a forty-year-old batboy—for two games when they came to town to play the Dodgers. But they were professional, and they were nice guys.

Rupert Perry, an Englishman who was head of A&R, felt that Capitol couldn't compete with the sales or finances of other labels, so he reasoned that they had to try harder. He encouraged Ravid to attend as many shows as he could. When Perry showed up, after the band's performances he would give Doug a quarter as a humorous installment payment indicating how much Capitol wanted to sign the group. But it was Ravid's attention that made the difference. As a reflection of what a big deal it was for Capitol, the group signed their contracts on the roof of the company's famous headquarters, the only time that's been done. When they got their check, Doug gave Perry back his quarters.

Doug and Berton were building a vast repertoire of songs and were pushing for their debut to be a double album. The execs informed them they would then have to charge more, and why make it more expensive for music buyers to take a chance on a new album? They said that sales of 50,000 would be good for a first album and would help to establish the group.

I was a friend of Mike Chapman, then the hottest producer in the world, having had hits with Blondie and Exile. I recommended that he see the band, thinking that he would want to sign them to his production company, but he never got around to it. Later, after they signed with Capitol, he read a news item in the *Los Angeles Times* that listed the producers the Knack were considering, and his name wasn't on it. His ego was slighted and that motivated him. Of course, his pop sensibilities made him an excellent choice to produce their debut album. The musicians were so good and so well-rehearsed that the album Chapman produced was completed in eleven days, recording from April 1 to 11 with two days of mixing.

The recording cost was only $18,000, remarkable in a time when the average major label album totaled $150,000. Many artists spent much more. The latest album by Fleetwood Mac, *Rumors*, cost $400,000, while Bruce Springsteen's *Darkness on the Edge of Town* cost $300,000.

While the group members were excited to be on Capitol Records, there were no rational expectations that the group would be selling like the Beatles, so the number of Beatles references on their record and elsewhere came from a sense of fun with these passionate record collectors rather than a notion that they were the second coming. Some references were coincidental. The album's title, *Get the Knack*, was thought to be similar to the Beatles' US debut *Meet the Beatles*, but "Get the Knack" had been a catch phrase used on the group's flyers a year before their album was even released.

They wanted their album cover to be the photo that was taken when they first got together. Randee St. Nicholas was an artist friend of Prescott who had never taken a professional photo before. She borrowed a camera and the Knack chipped in to buy one roll of film. In the photo Doug has a demonic expression because Bruce goosed him, and he in turn grabbed Bruce's crotch from behind, which resulted in Bruce having a much bigger smile than usual. At the time, only Doug liked the photo, but a year later they thought it best captured the band's personality.

Capitol's execs were perplexed as to why the group didn't want a color album jacket like all the company's other releases, but they agreed to the existing photo. The Beatles' first American album cover was also in black and white.

The back cover was in color, capturing the group playing in a TV studio in a nod to a scene in the *A Hard Day's Night* movie. The label on the record was the same style that was used by Capitol in the mid-sixties on Beatles records. The press kit featured question and answer sheets similar to those that were generated for teen magazines in the sixties. In this case, Doug fabricated the answers to make it more amusing to the reader. And, to top it off, Doug looked a lot like the Beatles' John Lennon.

Doug moved out of Tim Prior's basement and into the Via Valentino apartments on Highland Boulevard. "Sharona was a little drug addict," Doug said affectionately. "She would show up with bags of pills. I, of course, supported and encouraged it." Doug had her pose for the single's picture sleeve. She wore her usual getup of Levi's blue jeans and a white t-shirt that showed the outline of her nipples. Sharona held the Knack's first album cover, with her hand positioned to cradle Doug's photo.

After the band signed with Capitol, its ex-managers came with their hands held out. The band members acknowledged Scott Bergstein's contribution for providing the rehearsal space and stipends and for getting them gigs. According to Doug, Bergstein declined a royalty on record sales, which would have made him a lot more money than the $50,000 the band paid him. Tim Prior was another matter. Doug felt he had done little. Doug even had to pay him rent when he lived in his basement. Nonetheless, in order to avoid a lawsuit, the band paid him $50,000 as well.

Capitol was pleased with the new album, and in order to spread the buzz beyond the United States, they booked the Knack on a promotional tour of Europe beginning the third week of May 1979. The band members were excited. Berton had never been out of the country before. Prescott had lived in England from 1973 to 1975 and was returning in a hot new group with a new record about to come out.

In 1975 Prescott and a bandmate were driving home from a night at London's Speakeasy club. Their car was stopped by the police who were searching for bombs but found hash inside of a film canister. After spending the night in jail—with their Irish setter—they were allowed to leave after their lawyer failed to appear. Prescott thought he had a suspended sentence. When the Knack's UK trip was planned, he told his manager who assured him there would be no problem.

Prescott takes up the story: "We arrive in London. We get through customs. I can see the Rolls Royce limos parked, waiting for us. It's the biggest thrill of my life. I get a hand on my shoulder. 'Mr. Fine, come with us.' Apparently my situation had been worked out with immigration, but not with the police. The other guys were totally confused. I hadn't told them about my problem, and they didn't know my real last name was Fine."

Prescott spent the night in jail, at the Cannon Row Police Station in New Scotland Yard. He was freaking out, especially when a roadie speculated that the tour might have to be cancelled. "I rehearsed our set playing air bass," Prescott recalled, "moving up and back as though I were on stage. All the while I'm hearing the other inmates getting sick, groaning and screaming. The next day I went to a hearing and was fined 100 pounds. I got back to the hotel, quickly showered, shaved and dressed, and was ready for a day of interviews and photo sessions. I was relieved and very happy."

As the 1960s faded into the 1970s, rock's presence on the hit singles charts declined. In the early 1970s, soft rock (James Taylor, the Eagles) became popular. Later in the decade disco flourished. So when radio started to play the Knack it gave hope to rock fans everywhere. To provide some perspective, when "My Sharona" finally hit number one on August 25, 1979, it was the only rock record in the top five, the others being "Good Times" by Chic, "Main Event/Fight" by Barbra Streisand, "After the Love Has Gone" by Earth, Wind & Fire, and "Bad Girls" by Donna Summer.

I was hired by Capitol Records to interview Doug and Berton for a tape that was to be circulated to radio stations in the United States. It was July 19, and "My Sharona" was number 34 on the *Billboard* singles chart. Sitting in Studio C at Capitol, Doug and Berton were in good spirits, having just returned from a brief tour of Europe. It was an informative, fun interview, and the only extensive one they conducted at that time. I attempted to set the mood and acknowledge the band's Beatles parallels by injecting a few references for those listeners hip enough to get them. For example, in a press conference after the Beatles came to America the first time, they were asked, "How do you find America?" John Lennon replied, "Turn left at Greenland." I gave them the straight line of "How did you find England," so they could reply "Turn right at Greenland."

In two separate press releases Capitol Records made more overt Beatles comparisons, indicating that "My Sharona" was the fastest record to be certified gold in the history of the label since the Beatles' "I Want to Hold Your Hand" in 1964, and that *Get the Knack* was the fastest album to go gold—in thirteen days—since *Meet the Beatles* in 1964. The album eventually sold 2.9 million in the United States, but could have sold even more if the company hadn't had difficulty finding available pressing capacity. Because the record was selling so fast, in Capitol's pressing plants slower moving titles were displaced with the Knack's album to get more records pressed. But Capitol had contracted with Warner Brothers Records to manufacture their records as well, and they couldn't bump non-Capitol titles.

As much as the band, its label, and the fans were giddy with the Knack's success, the seeds of discontent had already been sown. Anderson wanted to create a mystique about the band, so he didn't want the members to do interviews, at least in the United States where they were more visible touring. He wanted to avoid Doug's tendency to arrogantly mouth off, as well as the issue of the members' ages, which, in their mid-twenties, made them much older than their teenage fans. This caused resentment among the press who had championed the band. In October, when *Rolling Stone* was compelled to run a feature article, the tagline noted ". . . this band shot to the top of the charts—without a word to the press."

The visual manifestation of this backlash was created by Berkeley-based artist Hugh Brown. He had designed the poster for a concert at UC Berkeley's Zellerbach Hall where the group opened for the Police in March 1979. He first heard about the Knack from a writer for *BAM* who was raving that the band were the second coming of the Beatles. Brown thought they were good, but not that good.

He originally designed the Nuke the Knack elements as a fun giveaway promotion for KSAN's Outcast Hour radio show, which featured punk acts. While its alliterative title was appealing, the recently signed SALT II treaty limiting nuclear weapons between the Soviet Union and the United States inspired the "Nuke" part. The kit consisted of a t-shirt, sticker, and button in a Nuke the Knack Sack. Kits were awarded to winners along with tickets to a punk show.

He brought a small quantity to the monthly Hollywood record collectors swap meet. I was keeping Toby Mamis company at his table when Brown came by, and I had Toby make some room for him to sell his items. It was Sunday, August 5, and the Knack had just heard that "My Sharona" had broken into the top ten. Doug was lugging a cardboard Buddy Holly in-store standup display when he came over to the table. He seemed amused, and approached Hugh with "Greetings from the entertainer to the artist." He bought a set for nine dollars, as did Bruce and Prescott.

Brown sold about two hundred of the kits. "I got mail from Knack fans asking why I hated them," he said. "They all had spelling errors and hand drawn happy faces. I sent back their letters, correcting the spelling and adding a frowning face." Only later, when Doug got wind that he was making "Honk if you slept with Sharona" bumper stickers, was Brown contacted by the Knack's lawyers to cease and desist. He complied.

Brown's biggest customers were the punks who resented the Knack's success. Local punk groups like X, the Weirdos, the Go-Go's, and the Germs now felt the major labels were only interested in the more commercial Knack-like ensembles, who were referred to as "skinny tie bands" after the Knack's dress.

Sniffing after Knack-like returns, in 1979 major labels signed and released albums by a number of Los Angeles-based melodic rock bands: the Pop (Arista), 20/20, the Beat (both CBS), the Shoes (Elektra), and the Scooters (EMI, in early 1980). None succeeded. Only the Shoes' *The Present Tense* album made it into the Top 100, crawling to number 50.

The week before "My Sharona" hit number one in the United States, the band was whisked away on a tour of the South Pacific: New Zealand, Australia, and Japan. Despite generally positive reviews of the album, there were some writers, like Kristine McKenna of the *Los Angeles Times*, who were offended by what they considered to be sexist lyrics.

The prevailing impression of accomplished musicians who have massively selling hit records is that they're cool. The members of the Knack may have been knowledgeable, passionate, and hip, but their star personas belied neurotic characters straight out of a Woody Allen movie.

In Woody Allen's movie *Take the Money and Run*, there's a scene where the young Woody, in anticipation of a bully ripping the eyeglasses from his face and stomping on them, preempts him by doing it himself. That desire to avoid confrontation is what Berton was like. He was smart, talented, and well-read, but lacked confidence and ambition. That's why he needed Doug and his drive to make it so much, and that's why he put up with Doug's slights.

Doug described himself as being "a rather nervous character." Although he could be charming, fun, and intelligent, often he communicated by giving orders or shrieking to his bandmates. While on tour, he would test the expediency of a hotel's room service by ordering a shrimp cocktail before leaving for the night's performance. After weeks on tour, at a prestigious concert in Seattle, his face broke out in giant welts and he barely finished the show before passing out and being rushed to a hospital. When it happened the next night in Portland, he learned that he was allergic to the iodine that had accumulated in his system from eating the shrimp.

The handsome Prescott, who always seemed to have a blond of the month on his arm (including actress Britt Ekland), seemed a bit odd. He was known to have hoarded food in his room. He carried his own tube of Hellmann's mayonnaise into restaurants and peppered waitresses with many questions about the menu selection.

Bruce had issues with food, too. On tour he took advantage of any spreads the band wasn't directly paying for, even to the extent of throwing up in the afternoon to make room for the hosted dinner that evening. If the band was paying, however, sometimes he ducked out early to avoid contributing to the check, even though he received a per diem for food while on tour.

On the band's first tour of Paris, they booked a table at the well-regarded La Coupole. Doug was particularly excited, as many famous people had patronized the brasserie in the past: Josephine Baker, Ernest Hemingway, Pablo Picasso, and F. Scott Fitzgerald, among others. When Bruce realized that he was paying for his meal, he declined the pleasure of more expensive items like grilled lobster and wine.

These were the band's best days. The Knack were appreciating their newfound success and there was less tension. They could enjoy each other's company and their shared experiences. Berton recounted an incident from their first Japanese tour: "We were fatigued and were consequently slap-happy when we arrived at a radio station to be interviewed. It was difficult to understand the Japanese-accented English, so we started free-associating. Doug said 'Elvis Presley,' then Prescott said 'Elvis Costello,' then I said 'Lou Costello.' At one point I said 'Frankie Frisch.' Prescott, who was drinking a Coke, almost spit it up. He looked like he had seen a ghost. He said if he hadn't been sipping his drink, he would have said Frankie Frisch, too. The coincidence of two of us saying the name of this baseball player from the 1930s St. Louis Cardinals Gashouse Gang, just because we remembered it from when we played the All Star Baseball board game at home as kids, has to go down as the strangest moment of my life."

Robert Hilburn, writing in the *Los Angeles Times*, thought the Knack's next single, "Good Girls Don't," was even better than "My Sharona." Written about Bobbi Ernstein, a girl from Doug's junior high school, the record debuted on *Billboard's* Hot 100 chart on September 1 at 82, while "My Sharona" still held the number one position. A demo of the song was on the tape that had been turned down by every label early the previous year. The record climbed to number 11, providing the group with their second hit.

Doug persuaded Sharona to meet him in Hawaii, where the band was playing the last show of the tour in early September. Marty told her not to go, that if she went, they would no longer be boyfriend and girlfriend. She went. Sharona and Doug became hot and heavy from then on.

It was remarkable what the Knack had accomplished after having been a unit for little more than a year. Rather than being elated, Doug had a different revelation: "Sitting on my kitchen counter with a number one single and a number one album, and realizing that it didn't fix the emptiness I felt was one of the lowest moments in my life. I dreamed it perfectly. I got everything I wanted: I was at the top of the charts and I had a freaky little Jewess who would do practically anything I wanted. Instead of feeling like a king, I felt like a peeled zero."

Doug gave Sharona a present of $10,000 and told her to spend it any way she wanted. He bought Judy a BMW and TV. He had taken recreational drugs since he was thirteen years old: pot, pills, and cocaine, mostly at the largesse of others. Now, record royalties flowing in, Doug had the money to buy as much as he wanted.

Doug and Sharona did the same things as other young couples: going to the movies, shopping, and listening to music. They also had dinner parties for their friends, but these were more like drug-taking parties. They vacationed at Big Sur resorts. When the Knack took an extended break the following year, Doug and Sharona spent two months in Paris, at the Hotel George V "at nearly $700 a day," according to Doug.

On October 13 the Knack played their most prestigious concert, headlining New York's Carnegie Hall, where the Beatles made their second US appearance in February 1964. The following month the group was paid $45,000 for two sold-out shows at the Arizona State Fair, the first big money they had received from a performance date.

When Doug was out on tour, he had Sharona drive around with a real estate agent looking at houses for them. "I would house-shop in the limo," Sharona said. "I would choose five houses and then show him. One of the agents said to me, 'I've never seen anyone show houses like you. You should be an agent.'" She found one that Doug liked, on Hedges Way in the Hollywood Hills. He bought it for $980,000, putting down $600,000 cash.

When Doug was recording with Sky at Olympic Studios in London, the Rolling Stones were recording *Sticky Fingers* in an adjacent room. He marveled at Mick Jagger's car parked on the sidewalk, a 1963 cream-colored Bentley Continental S3 with oxblood upholstery. He dreamed that when he'd made it, he would get a car just like that. In December, after he received his first big royalty check from Capitol, he and Sharona drove to the O'Gara Coach Company in Beverly Hills. To Doug's surprise, that car model had just been sold by baseball Hall of Famer Willie Mays. "The car of my dreams, literally, pulled up in front of me at the very moment I was finally able to buy it," he said.

At the end of the year the Knack's "My Sharona" was awarded *Billboard*'s #1 Single of the Year, based on sales and airplay. Overall, the Knack's unexpected sales boon was even more significant to Capitol's bottom line, as the Beatles' catalogue sales had slumped to an eight-year low.

In retrospect, the band suffered from a rash of poor management decisions that reeked of inexperience: declining all interviews from the domestic press, touring outside of the United States when the record was topping the charts, declining to appear at the *Grammy Awards* television show even though they were nominated in the Best New Artist category because they were on tour in Japan.

The band acknowledged that Anderson was good in the early days. But with the band becoming so successful so quickly, it was hard for him to adjust, and he didn't realize that he needed experienced help. Ten years previously, Led Zeppelin's manager Peter Grant kept that band from performing on TV as a means to encourage fans to go see them in concert. Anderson tried the same strategy ten years later, but in this case, it only alienated the industry.

Doug gave these examples: "Dick Clark's producer calls up and wants the Knack to appear on *The American Music Awards* TV show. Because 'My Sharona' was so big, we probably would have won an award. Not only did Scott decline, he also didn't permit them to use a thirty-second film clip of the band performing the song. He also turned down an appearance on *Saturday Night Live* because they wouldn't let us host. He alienated concert promoters, including Bill Graham. As a consequence, the only time we played San Francisco was before our first record was recorded."

Rupert Perry recoils when he thinks of having to go with Capitol's president Don Zimmermann to see Anderson at his office in a suite at the Chateau Marmont Hotel because Anderson said he was "too busy" to travel the two and a half miles to the Capitol building.

At the time Doug didn't see these decisions as missteps: "We had a number one single and a number one album. We were touring the world a year after we started. I had two girls out on tour with me and all the alcohol and drugs I could ever want. So what could possibly be wrong?"

In the music business, when an artist had a couple of hits and a big-selling album, the strategy was to release additional singles that could become hits and get airplay to sell more albums. For example, Michael Jackson's then-current album *Off the Wall* contained four top ten singles and so did Fleetwood Mac's *Rumors*. Capitol wanted to follow suit and release "(She's So) Selfish" as the third single, but Doug wanted to record a new album to make up for the double album the group was denied for their debut. Don Zimmermann said that it was too soon to record a second album, but Doug got his way.

Doug was thinking about the release frequency of groups in the mid-sixties like the Beatles, Rolling Stones, and Kinks, all of whom released at least two albums a year early in their careers. He didn't want to lose the songs he and Berton had written the previous year before the band moved on to a subsequent phase. The music on the Knack's first album was played so much on the radio that releasing a second album eight months later with essentially the same sound was a miscalculation.

Mike Chapman invited me to visit him while he was producing at Whitney Studios in Glendale, usually to hear a prime track as it was being finished or mixed. Mike's sessions were focused, productive, and usually fun. It was also a learning experience for me in how to produce records. I always called first because it was over twenty miles away and I wanted to make sure there were no problems before I left work. In mid-December I visited while the Knack were recording their second album.

When I arrived, Doug was in the studio with Sharona, singing, and I was told to wait. The other members were pacing in the lobby area. I felt a tension, and no one was talking. Even Bruce, whom I met a few times previously, was not his usual friendly self. It was atypical for a Chapman evening, and I didn't stay long. What I took note of was their shoes, a type I hadn't seen before. They were light, like a Capezio dance shoe. Instead of leather, the top was red canvas, while the bottom was molded plastic. I asked Prescott about them, and soon bought a pair of Crayons for my own.

I found out later that Doug's obsession with Sharona resulted in the rest of the band being excluded from the recording of their own album. For example, when Doug recorded his vocals, he only wanted Sharona in the studio with him. When he was finished, Sharona went into the waiting room to summon the others to have a listen. When Chapman, wanting to get away from the troubles facing him in town, elected to mix the album in London, he, Doug, and Sharona—not the other band members—flew to London on the Concorde supersonic jet. When Sharona joined the Knack on tour, she and Doug shared a limousine; the other three shared a second one. Another Beatles comparison comes to mind: the intrusion caused by John Lennon's obsession with Yoko Ono.

Get the Knack was such a success that the songs submitted for the second album weren't evaluated for quality as much as they should have been. Chapman and the band felt they could do no wrong. Chapman, who was antidrug when he moved to Los Angeles three years before, now had a drug habit, and was further distracted because his marriage was falling apart.

Doug had a dual relationship with Berton. He valued their songwriting collaboration but at other times he was dismissive. Once, when Berton asked if they could have a week off between tours, Doug grabbed his arm, quivering, and said, "Maybe you don't want to be in this band any longer." He praised Berton's guitar playing, saying he was "the most underrated guitarist in rock," but at other times told him he could be replaced. Even though Berton co-wrote many of the songs, including "My Sharona," quite often Doug talked about the songs as if he were the sole composer.

The title of the second album, . . . *but the little girls understand,* was a phrase taken from the Willie Dixon song "Back Door Man." The full phrase, "the men don't know, but the little girls understand," refers to a sexual awareness. The Knack's title implies that if the older rock critics don't understand the band, the group's teenage girl fans surely do. The front cover featured Sharona looking up at the very visibly phallic microphone stand, behind which Doug is presumably standing. Chapman, bloated with success and drugs, signed off on the credits as "Commander Chapman," and was depicted on the cover of *BAM* magazine dressed as General Patton. The liner notes he contributed included "The record is very dear to me and my bank manager." Everyone assumed the second album would also be a success, but compared with the first, it wasn't.

While the album included repertoire that was rejected for *Get the Knack,* there were still some good songs. The problem was that there wasn't a song strong enough to be a hit. "Baby Talks Dirty" was the first single, released in February 1980. The song, like many on the album, was inspired by Sharona, even though it featured Abbe on the picture sleeve. Built around a guitar riff, musically it was a poor imitation of "My Sharona," though Doug didn't see it that way. The other guys in the group were put off by the masochistic nature of the lyrics, but as Doug said, "The floor wasn't open for discussion. Sharona liked to be spanked and hurt. It wasn't my thing, but it was a very honest song."

Chapman had been the hottest producer in America, but he was at the end of his run. The Knack's second album sold a little more than 400,000 and was considered a disappointment. Although Chapman continued to have hits as a songwriter, as a record producer he had only one more big-selling album. Blondie's *Autoamerican*, released later that year, sold over a million copies in the United States.

The band's hubris in releasing a single with uninspired music and a theme too provocative for their teenage audience was a harbinger of their diminishing potency. Compounding the lesser sales, the band's poor management decisions frustrated the Capitol execs. The previous year had been a tough one for the record industry. Because of the decline in revenue, hundreds were laid off. The Knack's lackluster sales meant that Capitol now had to wrestle with its own financial reality. Still, among the newly recorded albums Capitol released in 1980, only Paul McCartney's *McCartney II* and Bob Seger's *Against the Wind* charted higher.

When the Knack should have been in the States promoting their new album, they were, once again, on a world tour. In February 1980, while the group was playing a number of dates in Japan, Prescott first felt that the bubble was about to burst. When the Beatles became successful, they were asked in a press conference, "What will you do when the bubble bursts?" In the '50s and '60s the career span of a teen-appealing recording artist was short. Three years was considered a long career, even for an artist as successful as the early Beatles. As the Knack's first record scaled the charts, with their similarities to the Beatles, this question was bantered about.

"It was winter and bitterly cold in Japan," Prescott recalled. "Our first time in Japan was a big success, but now we weren't drawing that well. Our promoter told us that for this time of year, when the kids were back in school and studying, we were doing okay, but none of us felt that. We were in Japan only five months previously, so why were we back so soon?" It was February 28, 1980. Instead of being seen by thirty-two million viewers on that evening's *Grammy Awards* TV show—where they were nominated in two categories—the Knack played before a few hundred in Sapporo.

"When we got back to the hotel, it started to snow hard," Prescott continued. "Jeff, our roadie, told me that we didn't win for Best New Artist. Rickie Lee Jones won. It was the most depressing day of my life. I had to get out of the hotel and take a walk. I hadn't prepared for the weather on this trip, so I had no winter clothes. I put on three Knack suit jackets and trash bags over my Beatle boots. I walked through a blizzard. My legs were freezing, but I didn't care. The new album wasn't selling that well, and we weren't on the *Grammy* TV show; things felt wrong. I thought of the great success and joy we shared in the beginning, and how that's gone. I thought that if I took a turn here or there, no one might ever find me."

Customarily the lead singer of a successful rock band took advantage of his appeal by having sex with any number of women while on tour. In this case, Doug chose to travel with his own harem of Abbe and Sharona. The girls liked each other, which made sexual threesomes usual.

The past two years of touring with too little time off, coupled with the excessive drugs and sex, took their toll. In early March, while the band was in London, Doug experienced a breakdown. Abbe found him passed out on the floor of their room at the Montcalm. She thought he was dead. "We had to leave early in the morning," Doug said, "so I didn't have time to see a doctor. I was wheeled onto the plane in a wheelchair. In Munich, I saw a doctor who shot me up with speed, or something similar. It was like, 'Yeah, I'm back and better than ever.'"

As Doug became more egomaniacal and boorish, and more affected by the drugs he could now afford, one wonders why his band put up with him. As he was the lead singer and main creative talent, what could they do? It was very similar to the Doors, who had to accommodate an erratic Jim Morrison. More to the point, after Morrison's death, the remaining three members—all talented musicians—recorded two albums together that were not considered successes (and in an effort to preserve the Morrison legend, have never been issued on CD).

After having released their second album too soon, the Knack took too much time before releasing their next album. Scott Anderson was pushing to have Bob Ezrin produce. Anderson had been a gofer for Ezrin prior to being hired away by Kim Fowley. An excellent producer, Ezrin had a good feel for working with rock bands and had produced albums for Alice Cooper, Kiss, and Pink Floyd. Upon further consideration, the group felt that Ezrin's strong musical personality would result in more of a Bob Ezrin styled album than one that captured the Knack.

Doug was adamant about not wanting to work with Bruce and wanted to fire him. It additionally bothered him that Bruce always said what a nice guy ex-Cream bass player Jack Bruce was, but complained about him. "Jack Bruce barely paid him," Doug said, "and playing with me he made a million dollars."

Anderson was strongly opposed to firing Bruce because he considered him vital to the group's sound. Doug now saw Anderson as unsupportive. He and the other band members were also angry that Anderson's ambitious plans in management resulted in offices and overhead of $30,000 a month that the band paid for, now with diminished record royalties. As a result, Anderson was encouraged to resign as the band's manager in December 1980.

On December 19 I ran into Doug and Abbe at the Roxy. We were there to see the Firesign Theatre, who had recently released their *Fighting Clowns* album on Rhino. I met them when I was a college rep for Columbia Records at UCLA. I had signed them to Rhino the previous year. Doug was a big fan of the surrealist comedy troupe. Todd Schneider and I sat with them during the show, and I took them all backstage afterwards to meet the Firesign members.

Bobby Colomby had been the drummer in Blood, Sweat & Tears, the first successful rock band to have featured a brass section. He was now in Capitol's A&R Department. He placated Doug by committing to work with Bruce on his playing so that the group's sound and chemistry would remain intact.

Jack Douglas, an excellent producer with credits including Aerosmith, the Guess Who, and Cheap Trick, was recommended by Capitol to helm the new album. Although the group's first two albums had been completed quickly, this one was protracted because Douglas had developed a severe drug problem. He had produced John Lennon's last album and was still reeling from the impact of Lennon's murder six months previously.

Although the album only took three and a half weeks to record that summer, it took two and a half months to mix. Douglas' time was also compromised because he had committed to produce an album with Graham Parker around the same time. "One night Jack said he was going to get a cup of coffee," Doug said, "and he walked out of the studio. I remembered that I wanted to ask him a question, so I walked out the door looking for him. Through a window I saw him shimmying down a drainpipe and running down the street. I found out he ran home so he

could get a couple of hours of sleep until his session with Graham Parker."
During the mixing sessions Douglas introduced Doug to heroin.

The album went way over budget, and Doug and Berton each had to
forfeit $50,000 of their publishing royalties in order to get the album fin-
ished. The band members made themselves available for interviews, but
it was a matter of too little too late, according to Berton: "The decision
to give interviews—or stop not giving interviews—was at the time before
the album's release. It was borne in on us that some—maybe a lot—of
the enmity of the press toward us was a result of our silence, which they
interpreted as not allowing them to do their jobs when we were a big story.
The tardy decision to let them in didn't work. The newspaper or magazine
invariably sent a lesser writer to conduct the interview. More often than
not the slant on the piece was biased, not to say jaundiced."

By the time *Round Trip* was released in mid-October 1981, it was
almost two years after . . . *but the little girls understand*. Again, there was no
hit single, and one was needed to reinterest the group's teenage fans, who
had largely moved on. The album sold 95,000 copies. The group played
its last show on New Year's Eve at Baby'O in Acapulco and broke up weeks
later, owing Capitol the last album on their contract.

Doug didn't take it too badly. He was free from having to play with
Bruce, and he still had Sharona. He bought her a wedding ring in New
York's diamond district. They became engaged, they fought, they broke
up, they got back together. "We were fighting all the time and it was no
fun," Doug said. "On more than one occasion, when we had one of our
breakups, I would show up at Sharona's house at 2 a.m. and bang on her
front door. Her parents didn't seem to mind because they thought of me
as a nice, Jewish boy and one who was successful."

A major issue was Doug's extreme, controlling nature. "On the inside,
I felt bombs going off," he said. "Because I couldn't control the inside,
I had to control the outside. We fought about that a lot. We were doing so
many drugs, I sometimes wonder why we didn't die. Sharona rarely drank
alcohol, but I drank constantly. And we didn't eat very well." Ultimately,
their relationship was so intense that in Doug's evaluation it "burned itself
out." They broke up in May 1982. "She never gave back the ring. She said
it was stolen by a friend of hers."

Doug submitted demos of new songs to Capital, but they weren't interested in signing him to a contract as a solo artist. Because of rare, extreme rains in Los Angeles, part of the hillside behind Doug's new house had slid into his living room. He spent lots of money trying to save it from the extreme damage, but he lost his entire investment. By the following year he was in a new house, and he was married, but not to Sharona.

In the fall of 1983 Doug returned home from a contentious cocaine-and-vodka fueled evening. He eased himself into a warm, comforting bath. He had lit candles around the room. He was ready to call it a night, to call it a life. He reached for the nearby razor blade, the one he always used to cut cocaine into thin lines, but this time he intended to slit his wrists. He was fatigued, and the over-used blade was now too dull. He only bruised himself. He heard a voice speak to him, but there was nobody else in the room. It said, "Doug, you're a very sick boy and you need help."

Doug emerged from the bath dripping water, put on the nearest clothes he could find—a pair of pants, his wife's sweatshirt, and his pink boots—and had his wife drive him to the hospital. It was the start to turning his life around. He joined Alcoholics Anonymous, and realized for the first time that what he had was a disease. He learned more about himself, and he finally had the support that he needed. He established friendships, ones not based on the mutual need to score drugs. Looking back, he speculated that had his Hollywood Hills home not turned into a financial disaster, he probably would have died, as he would have had more money to spend on drugs.

Through the years he was still involved with music: writing, performing, and producing new artists. He counseled other members of AA. He enrolled in a class at Santa Monica City College and got a car mechanic's license so he could rebuild cars and tend to his (non-vintage) Shelby Cobra race car. He renewed his interest in acting and appeared as one of Dan Conner's poker playing buddies in a handful of episodes of the TV show *Roseanne*. In 1994 "My Sharona" broke into the Hot 100 off of exposure in the movie *Reality Bites*. The Knack regrouped—without Bruce—and toured.

After a number of proposals from other suitors, Sharona finally married, divorced, married again, and had children. The experience she had with a real estate agent looking for a house for Doug to buy eventually pushed her into become a real estate agent herself in 1986. She excelled and had a number of celebrity clients, including Leonardo DiCaprio, and was able to make a good living. Her professional website is mysharona.com, on which she uses an audio clip of the hit. While at Sotheby's International Realty she was tops in sales for five straight years.

Danny Sugerman convinced Doug to reform the original band, intending to manage them. Danny set up a showcase at the Viper Room on April 7, 1997, and invited me to attend. The reconstituted band had only practiced a little, but the magic of those four guys playing that music was evident. I agreed to have them record a new album for Rhino.

The project soon ran into problems. Danny relapsed into taking drugs and ended up in rehab. Without Danny's stabilizing influence, Bruce expressed his feeling that he should be given a portion of the songwriting royalties for "My Sharona." As important as Bruce's drums were to the success of the record, he didn't contribute to the words or the melody, which normally forms the basis of writing a song. Reluctantly, Doug and Berton considered Bruce's request—a requirement for his continuing with the project—but Bruce wasn't satisfied and quit.

Although it wasn't what I signed off on—a reunion of the original members—Doug's willingness to work things out made it hard to relinquish the project. First of all, there was the material. Doug and Berton had a large number of songs written, and Doug was very open to the Rhino staff being involved in selecting which songs to record. It would be incorrect to dismiss Doug's songwriting as ineffective after having parted ways with his muse Sharona, as his writing was at its best. As a result, the material chosen was very good. One of the stronger songs, "Can I Borrow a Kiss," I had encouraged Doug to write after he told me of a chance encounter with a girl at a pop music festival.

In order to make up for Bruce's absence, I felt we needed a drummer with prominence to add interest and credibility to the project. Doug settled on Terry Bozio, a respected drummer who had played with Frank Zappa and Jeff Beck, as well as having been a member of the successful new wave band Missing Persons that featured his then-wife Dale on lead vocals. Richard Bosworth, who coproduced the album with the group, summed up the feelings of many fans. "As excellent a drummer as Terry was," he said, "I think it would have been a better album if Bruce had played. He had a better feel for the Knack."

The CD package was designed by Hugh Brown, the mastermind of Nuke the Knack, who was now Rhino's creative director. *Zoom* was released in July 1998, and the band hit the road for a tour of clubs. Attending a performance in August at the Galaxy Theatre in Santa Ana, I appreciated Doug's sartorial dedication to the1960s. He was wearing a blazer that was similar to the burgundy striped velvet jacket that George Harrison wore at the *Sgt. Pepper's* launch party in 1967.

Many of us who were fans of the British rock groups of the sixties also envied their classy and imaginative dress. The way the Beatles appeared on the back of their *Revolver* album was the standard to which all groups should have aspired. Rather than becoming slovenly, or given to relaxed hippie or grunge garb, Doug, even in his later years, was one of the few who kept that standard alive. As part of his wardrobe, he had jackets and shirts, many custom made, that would have fit comfortably for a stroll down King's Road or a rest at the Speakeasy in London's Swinging Sixties, as much as they were uniquely contemporary. He dressed like a Beatles fan-come-rock star.

Rhino spent a lot of money promoting the album, but radio programmers didn't care. Their decision was based more on the group having been out of the limelight, rather than one based on an evaluation of the music. With very little radio airplay, and with few of Bozio's fans curious enough to see the band live, the club tour didn't fare well. The last leg was cancelled when Bozio unexpectedly quit the band—even though Doug was paying him a guaranteed amount rather than a split of the take, whether or not the group drew well.

The album sold less than 10,000 copies, and Rhino lost a significant amount of money on it, but most of the loss was made up by the profits from *Proof: The Very Best of the Knack* with masters I licensed from Capitol Records. Despite its commercial failure, those of us at Rhino considered *Zoom* the best newly recorded album we ever released. Nearly twenty years after topping the charts, Doug had written his best songs and performed his best recording.

The Knack took another hiatus, and then regrouped—with a new drummer—for the occasional performance date or recording. In 2004 Doug learned he had cancer. Half of a lung was successfully removed. After a period, tumors were discovered in his brain, were removed, and then reappeared. He embarked on a healthy regimen of diet and swimming, while enduring radiation, surgery, and experimental trials. He had a positive attitude, and was able to play the occasional date with the Knack.

In 2000 I initiated production on a drama about the Monkees for VH1's new rock movies series. As it was among their better-rated movies, I pitched the executive in charge, Michael Larkin, a few other ideas. I was surprised that he wasn't interested in a movie about Sharona and the Knack. It was one of the few number one records with a girl's name in the title that related to a real romance. In addition to the relationship between Doug and Sharona, there was the story of the band and the Los Angeles music scene of the late '70s and early '80s.

Toward the end of 2008 I had lunch with Mark Helfrich. Professionally Mark was best known as director Brett Ratner's film editor. Ratner had directed the *Rush Hour* series and *X-Men*, among many other films. Mark wanted to direct, and got his chance with the comedy *Good Luck Chuck*. It was a relatively low-budgeted movie that did well at the box office. Mark was looking for another movie to direct. He asked me what ideas I had and I told him about this one.

The most compelling reason for dramatizing the life of a music performer is the music. I thought the Knack had quite a few songs that would work cinematically. With Doug's cancer, Sharona battling stage-four colon cancer, and Helfrich's interest in directing, I thought I would try to make their story my next movie.

Doug was very open in expressing himself. I had Jeff Ressner write the screenplay, as he was an ex-staff writer for *Rolling Stone* and *Time* magazine and had majored in screenwriting at Northwestern University. Hollywood movie executives have had difficulty understanding rock dramatizations. The movies tend not to be very good and lose money. Just as our script was close to being finished, a run of failed rock movies—starting with *Cadillac Records*, starring Beyonce, and ending with

The Runaways, starring Kristen Stewart and Dakota Fanning—indicated that it wouldn't be the best time to pitch such an idea.

Doug succumbed to cancer on Valentine's Day 2010. He was survived by his brother Geoffrey Fieger, an attorney based in Southfield, Michigan, best known for having represented Jack Kevorkian, and by his sister Beth Falkenstein, who had written for TV shows. In his last years he had been able to make annual visits to Paris, once taking his young nieces. He had good relationships, and remained in contact with those women whom he had been closest to as an adult, including Sharona. Abbe picked out the furniture for Doug's last house. His first (and third) ex-wife Mia Klein—a Fairfax High alumnus like Sharona, but a year younger—helped to care for Doug when he was most ill.

At this point, thirty years later, it's clear that "My Sharona" has transcended hit record status to join the ranks of rock's most enduring songs. Although its impact was initially felt among teens in the summer of 1979, it had the same effect fifteen years later when enough people bought the record after having heard it in *Reality Bites* to cause it to break into the Hot 100 singles chart for a second time. It placed at number 75 on *Billboard*'s Greatest Songs of All Time list, compiled in 2008. It inspired Michael Jackson to write "Beat It," the best song on his *Thriller* album, when producer Quincy Jones told him that "we need a black version of 'My Sharona.'"

Nirvana and Pearl Jam performed it in concert. Sex Pistols guitarist and cowriter Steve Jones played the song countless times but felt his punk image prevented him from telling people. "Weird Al" Yankovic launched his career when Capitol Records released his first record, a parody of the song as "My Bologna." The song has been sung in TV shows like *The Simpsons* and *Full House*. The music video game *Rock Band* included a cover version. President George W. Bush had it on his iPod playlist.

When Doug Fieger channeled his lust and frustration into a lyric to gain the attention of a sixteen-year-old girl, he never would have imagined that thirty years later three hefty truck drivers would be singing along to it in a British TV commercial—for Oatibix cereal—inspiring enough sales for the record to climb to 59 on the UK charts. Such is the unpredictability of rock. With "My Sharona," Doug Fieger and Berton Averre had written a classic.

CHAPTER 15

The Monkees in "The Movies"

Because of the Monkees' rapid popularity, there was talk early on of making a feature film, but there wasn't time to give it much attention. It was only natural for them to star in a motion picture. The Beatles, Herman's Hermits, and others had done it, and the Monkees were already contracted to the TV division of a major studio.

Director Bob Rafelson liked to expand and experiment in the medium in which he was working. While *The Monkees* TV show was certainly formulaic, the use of quick cutting and breaking the fourth wall (where the actors stop the drama and talk directly to the audience) were progressive by TV standards. During the second season Rafelson broke out of the routine format and presented episodes that were documentaries ("The Monkees On Tour," "The Monkees in Paris"), fantasy ("Fairy Tale"), and just plain strange ("Monkees Watch Their Feet"). Weirder still was "Mijacogeo (The Frodis Caper)," the last episode of the show, which Micky Dolenz wrote and directed. "Frodis" was the Monkees' slang for marijuana. Rather than expand a TV situation into a feature film, which was how it was usually done, Rafelson wanted the feature film to be markedly different, and so did the Monkees.

Davy, Micky, Mike, and Peter felt very strongly about wanting to influence the content of the movie. The group was riding high with their first four singles being big hits: two number ones, a number two, and a number three. And they had completed an extremely successful thirty-date summer tour. As a result, in November 1967 Rafelson invited the Monkees to join him, along with producer Bert Schneider, and Jack Nicholson, for a weekend at the Ojai Valley Inn. A lot of marijuana was smoked, and the participants made suggestions for what they wanted to see in a Monkees movie. At that point Nicholson was a TV actor with recurring appearances on *Dr. Kildare* and *The Andy Griffith Show*. Rafelson had met him at a film society screening and connected with his intelligence and humor. He liked the way Nicholson had structured his script for *The Trip*, an American International Pictures film about the new LSD culture. Primarily because Rafelson liked him, he hired him to take everybody's ideas from that meeting and write the script, with his input. Nicholson reported back to Rafelson: "These guys are mad, they think they're Marlon Brando!"

The film's original title, "Changes," reflected changes on many levels compared with the TV show. When it was determined that another film had claimed that name, the title was changed to *Head*. A slang usage of the term at the time referred to one who was a marijuana smoker, shortened from pothead. It also referred to the movie as taking place in somebody's head. Drugs influenced much more than the title of the movie. It was structured like an acid trip, and Rafelson and Nicholson wrote scenes for the script while tripping on LSD. An early form of solarization was developed to provide some color-changing psychedelic effects for some scenes.

Rather than a story, the film was composed of short episodes, many of them standard genres from the history of film: Western, World War II, musical, silent movie; dropped from the script was a lengthy scenario set in 1880s Japan with a samurai adversary named Godzilla. Rafelson wasn't sure he was going to be able to direct another feature, so he wanted to get an idea of what it would be like to sample various settings and styles. The boxing scenes were inspired by *Body and Soul* and the desert scenes by *Lawrence of Arabia*.

Unlike in the TV show, where the Monkees are charming and cute, in *Head* their characters are unlikeable. Some of the film reflected the Monkees' concerns: their manufactured image, smart Peter Tork's role being that of the dummy, and Mike disliking surprises. But most of it was bizarre; the scenes didn't add up. When I saw it for the first time in the mid-1970s, I thought even then that it was ahead of its time. The Monkees look great, the songs are good, and the mind is engaged trying to understand what it's all about. The film had high production values even though it only cost $790,000.

Rafelson was expressing himself as the director at the same time as he was trying to depart from convention and make a hip film to re-invigorate the Monkees. The film was so strange and the group so unlikeable, that members of the Monkees suggest that Rafelson, now tired of the TV show and wanting to direct features, intended to kill off the band. I disagree. Contributing to their suspicion is a scene where the Monkees leap from a large bridge into the ocean. But that scene was in the first draft of the script, submitted in December 1967, when the Monkees were at their most potent. Rafelson was not the only director of the TV show's episodes, and while it may have been clear to him that it was his last Monkees project, it's also clear that everyone involved desired to make a quality film. As an actor, Micky is particularly impressive, but he didn't get the recognition.

Had the film been released six months earlier when the Monkees last big hit, "Valleri," was still on the charts, there would have been more interest from Monkees fans. But by the time of the release of the movie in November, the Monkees had been out of the top ten for seven months. "Porpoise Song," the theme from *Head*, didn't even make the Top 50. With the TV series off the air, the group was cold, and marketing the film was a big problem.

Rafelson miscalculated big time in embracing Marshall McLuhan's philosophy on media and Andy Warhol's pop art imagery. He wanted his film to be appreciated by the hip cognoscenti. So, rather than market the film as a Monkees' feature, the dominant campaign was aimed at older moviegoers. It featured the head of avant-garde marketer and Warhol follower John Brockman in the poster, print ads, billboard ads, and TV commercial, sans Monkees. The film bombed at the box office. Years later, after Rafelson had established himself as a cutting edge director with *Five Easy Pieces* and producer with *Easy Rider*, people, like the Rolling Stones, had him set up screenings of *Head*. I've seen the film many times, and I still find it engrossing.

As part of Rhino's acquisition of the Monkees catalogue, I wanted to increase their exposure by producing a new feature film. On TV shows and in movies, actors usually play characters. Such was the case in *The Monkees*, except here, to some extent, they played themselves and used their real names. Because of that it was difficult for me to imagine a Monkees movie with other actors in the roles. The Monkees were in their early fifties, but so were the Marx Brothers when they were making movies.

The success of *The Addams Family* movie in 1991 ushered in a fad of reviving 1960s TV sitcoms as feature films: *The Adams Family Values* and *The Beverly Hillbillies* followed in 1993, *The Brady Bunch* in 1995. Those were very successful, but not all were. *McHale's Navy* bombed in 1997. It didn't take much imagination to see *The Monkees* on the list.

Early in 1994 we were alerted to an "open assignment" notice to talent agencies posted by Columbia Pictures looking for a writer for a Monkees movie. That's strange, I thought, as Columbia didn't own the rights to make a Monkees movie—we did. I called the executive who was mentioned, Lisa Henson (daughter of Jim Henson, creator of *The Muppets*). Barry Josephson called me back. He was stumbling on the phone, saying that it was the idea of the Brillstein-Grey Company and suggested I meet with their executive, Howard Rosenman. Brillstein-Grey managed mostly comedians and was involved in producing TV shows. They had an overhead deal with Columbia at the time. This meant that the studio was paying for overhead, and the only way Columbia could get that investment back was from fees paid to the producer if projects were realized.

Howard and a couple of his guys met with us. He said it was Josephson's idea to do the movie. He pitched a story of one-time Monkees' manager, used-car salesman Jon Lovitz, trying to get the group to reform twenty-five years later as a grunge group. It seemed that Rosenman was coming from a place of trying to capitalize on the TV movie fad rather than a love for or an understanding of the original TV show. The writers he invited to attend the meeting had never seen the show. Nonetheless, I was open, and tried to improve on their idea, but they lost interest.

In early 1995, Jeff Sherman wrote a script for the Monkees titled "The Foregone Conclusion." It had some nice elements and was a spy farce along the lines of *Austin Powers*, which came a couple of years later. Jeff was a staff producer and writer for the *Boy Meets World* TV show, and he also was writing with Micky Dolenz. I went on a few pitch meetings with Jeff, and a friendship developed, but no one was interested in his idea.

During the summer David Hoberman came to see me. I had met with him ten years before, pitching him movie ideas when he was an executive at Disney. He was a nice enough guy, if low on energy, but he had questionable taste. At the time he was excited about *Earnest Goes to Camp*. The low budget feature starred Jim Varney as Ernest P. Worrell, a character he had created who became popular from appearing in commercials, and it made a lot of money for Disney's Touchstone division. That film and its sequels represented lowbrow entertainment. They weren't well reviewed by film critics.

Like Rosenman, Hoberman was interested in making a feature of *The Monkees*, but seemed more of an opportunist than someone who expressed any ideas. I wasn't interested in merely making a movie for Rhino to pocket the licensing fees. The goal was to make a good movie, preferably one starring the original Monkees. Hoberman wanted a free option, which meant that he could tie up the rights to the film for a year without paying Rhino any money, even if he did nothing. We had a couple more meetings. I would have liked to make it work, but his interest waned. Subsequently, he was one of the producers who made a live-action movie of the cartoon *George of the Jungle*. The movie was not well reviewed, but it grossed over $100 million at the box office.

When Brandon Tartikoff was president of NBC Entertainment, he had Mike Nesmith produce a show titled *Television Parts* for the 1985 summer season. The show was based on Mike's groundbreaking 1981 video *Elephant Parts* that won the first Grammy Award in the Music Video category. *Television Parts* didn't fare well in the ratings, but Brandon and Mike established an enduring friendship. Brandon had NBC Productions provide financing for two of Mike's Pacific Arts feature films, *Tape Heads* and *Square Dance*. In June 1996, after initial discussions with Mike, Brandon met with me to express his idea for a Monkees movie. He suggested setting it in the town where the *Weekly World News* was published and incorporating the strange events they reported in their pages. The supermarket tabloid was similar to *The National Enquirer* (and printed on their former presses when the *Enquirer* went to color), but was more implausible, with stories about space aliens and Elvis sightings.

Mike was friendly with Bob Katz, who became interested in the project. Bob rented a hangar at the Santa Monica Airport to house his motorcycle collection across from the one that Mike used as his office. Katz was partnered with Moctesuma Esparza in a production company. I had met with them previously when they were interested in teaming with us to produce the *Fear & Loathing in Las Vegas* movie. Even though I didn't like Brandon's idea, I valued what Mike had put together, so I was supportive. Katz was going to put up the money to develop the movie, which meant having a script written.

The other Monkees were all too willing to star in another feature film. Negotiations were proceeding, with each member of the Monkees to be paid $250,000 to act, which meant a million dollars for the group of four. All of a sudden Davy decided he wanted a million dollars, just for himself. It was an unreasonable demand, especially because it was difficult to determine if the Monkees could attract enough ticket buyers to justify the budget of such a film. Davy couldn't be dissuaded. The project fell apart, and his action attracted the others' disdain.

*   *   *

In the fall of 1998 I got a call from Vin Di Bona Productions, who were interested in producing a Monkees biopic for TV. They told me that VH1 was starting a new division to produce low budget TV movies of rock music stories. Vin Di Bono was best known for producing *America's Funniest Home Videos*. I couldn't see what they could bring to the production. From the meeting I had at their office with a handful of their executives, I didn't get a sense that they were either passionate or knowledgeable about the Monkees. They were only offering a fee to Rhino of $75,000.

I wanted to get more of an understanding of what VH1 wanted to do, so I set up a meeting with Mike Larkin, the vice president of VH1's Motion Pictures division. I thought that if Rhino Films was the producer, the picture would be better and the record company would make more money. In addition to telling the Monkees story, I wanted it to be more authentic than similar docudramas. Larkin had no allegiance with

Di Bona and was fine with having Rhino Films produce, but wanted to have us work with another company that was experienced in producing movies made for TV. He recommended his previous employer, Howard Braunstein of Jaffe-Braunstein Productions. Their business was making TV movies, mostly in Canada to take advantage of the tax breaks the Canadian government gave for not only location filming but also for the use of above-the-line Canadian talent, which could include producers, writers, actors, or the director.

Larkin liked the script that Ron McGee had written for VH1's *Meat Loaf: To Hell and Back* and recommended him to write the Monkees. I worked with Ron on the story. When the script was written, I forwarded a copy to each of the Monkees, Bob Rafelson, ex-manager Ward Sylvester, Don Kirshner, and Monkees experts Andrew Sandoval, Bill Inglot, and Eric Lefcowitz. Nobody pointed out any inaccuracies, and Peter and Micky gave me their approval.

In February 2000 I received a letter from Mike's attorney, objecting to his off-screen life being depicted in the movie. It wasn't clear to me if Mike read the script or had any specific objection. The letter said, in part, "it will be viewed as an infringement of Mr. Nesmith's rights and will be vigorously defended by him." Just because an attorney is paid to write a letter and make a claim on behalf of a client doesn't make it a valid one. In this case, given that we were making a facts-based movie, I thought Mike and his attorney were off base. I felt personally hurt by the two letters his attorney sent me.

I thought I had a good relationship with Mike, going back twenty-nine years. While most of our interaction was business, some of it was social, and I thought we enjoyed each other's company. I had worked with him on enough projects for Mike to know that I had artistic integrity as well as a commercial sense. I was always sensitive to his and the other members' wishes. That he didn't pick up the phone and call me to express himself, and instead had a lawyer send me letters, was a big disappointment and changed the way I felt about him.

Braunstein was great to work with and allowed me the freedom to forge the creative elements while he dealt with the physical production, the financing aspects, and suggestions from VH1. For me, I like actors to look like their subjects. For example, around the time we were casting our movie, *The Beach Boys: An American Family* miniseries aired on TV. The actor who played Beach Boy Brian Wilson did a fine job, but I kept thinking he didn't look like Brian, which pulled me out of the movie as a viewer. In *Little Richard*, a TV movie that aired around the same time, the actor who played Richard was good, but he was about a foot taller than the real Richard.

With the Monkees being so recognizable from the TV show, it was important to me to get actors who looked like them. I chose three of the actors in Los Angeles. Peter Tork said of L. B. Fisher, the actor who played him, "He looks more like me than me." George Stanchev was another find. He showed up to the initial casting interview wearing a longhaired wig, and made an immediate impression. He was also short. He got as close to projecting Davy's charm as I believe anybody could. Only after the filming was completed did Davy suggest using his nephew. "He looks just like me," he said. Micky Dolenz was a hard one to cast because his features are so flat. Davy used to call him "Skillet Face." It was a tough role for Aaron Lohr, who hadn't much experience, but he pulled it off. Jeff Geddis, who was cast in Canada, looked remarkably like Mike Nesmith. He assumed the role so well that at times when I watched the finished movie, I forgot I was watching an actor. They were all young actors with great attitudes and looked more like their subjects than any ensemble cast.

Colin Ferguson, who is best known for his later role of Sheriff Jack Carter in the *Eureka* TV series, played a composite of the Monkees' producers Bob Rafelson and Bert Schneider, and he looked like them. Early on I told Rafelson about the project and asked him if he wanted to be the director. He was ten years past his last significant feature, *Black Widow*, and had recently finished an HBO film, *Poodle Springs*, from Raymond Chandler's incomplete novel. Rafelson thought about it, but decided that he didn't want to revisit that period of his life. Later, expressing privacy issues, he asked me to not have his character named in the movie. I minded, but not too much, as it was a composite character and I didn't think he was that well known.

The main casting problem I had was with VH1's selection of Wallace Langham to play Don Kirshner, the Monkees' music supervisor. I was familiar with Langham, who is best known for having portrayed a writer on *The Larry Sanders Show*. But Langham was skinny. Kirshner was plump, Jewish, and spoke with a New York accent. Because of all the unknown actors, VH1 wanted someone who was more familiar to the kids and had us pay him a lot of money, $70,000, for a week of work.

I chose all the music for the film and negotiated all the licensing deals. "All of Your Toys" was an unreleased song that Bill Inglot found in the tape vaults. It was recorded during the *Headquarters* sessions. The song wasn't released at the time because Screen Gems publishing, which was owned by Columbia Pictures, didn't publish the song and didn't want to give away the income to another company. It sounded to me like it would have been a hit had it been released back then. Because it was largely unfamiliar to Monkees fans, I wanted to give them a treat, and featured it in the movie.

Howard Braunstein's priority was to get the picture finished so it could be delivered to the network in order to meet the scheduled airdate. For him it was a matter of expediency and completion, not artistry or quality. He had produced a lot of TV movies, but none were memorable. My point is that, whether you have a small amount of money or a huge amount, a good movie can be made.

I would have preferred to film in Los Angeles, where the story was set. The funding came from VH1 ($1.9 million), World International Network ($800,000), and the Canadian government ($500,000). Because of the tax subsidy, it was filmed in Toronto, where there are no palm trees. It was shot in four weeks, March to April.

For a low-budget movie, the location manager did an excellent job. A recently cancelled Canadian soap opera, *Riverdale*, provided many sets in one location. Lake Ontario stood in for the Santa Monica beach scene at the end of the movie. Of course there were no waves. Viewers failed to see the snow on the ground in the distance at the scene that took place at a farm in Beeton.

I had the Monkees beach house interior recreated. After filming wrapped, I thought it would be cool to have the set reconstituted in our lobby. I was told the trucking fee would be so costly that it would have been cheaper to construct the set from scratch in Los Angeles. For the scene where Jimi Hendrix opens for the Monkees, I had wardrobe copy the "eye jacket" that Hendrix wore on tour in 1967.

Copps Coliseum, with an ice floor set for hockey, stood in for the concert hall for the Monkees' live scene. Stanchev told me he experienced what it was like to be a Monkee on stage. Even though he and the others were miming to the Monkees' thirty-year-old live recordings, the teenage extras in the audience were genuinely caught up in the experience and responded like real, emotional fans.

Davy called me and suggested that he play the role of his dad. It was such a good idea, how could I have not thought of it? Davy would fly in on a Tuesday, act his part on Wednesday, and fly out on Thursday. We offered what we thought was fair, $35,000 for the one day of work. I thought he was going to do it, but then he decided that he wanted double what we offered. We couldn't justify that in a $3 million budget. Much to my disappointment, he passed. From what he was making as a solo act, he would have to have worked a few weeks to earn $35,000. He would have benefitted himself financially, made the movie better, and ingratiated himself to Rhino. It's another example of Davy making a poor business decision. The actor who was cast in Canada was bald. Davy's father had hair. Why wasn't an actor used who had hair? Would it have cost more money?

I suggested having Micky Dolenz direct. He had experience directing for TV and theater in England and had an excellent comedic sense. Because he hadn't directed a TV movie before, Larkin rejected him. Neill Fearnley was chosen because he was competent and he was Canadian. It frustrated me that he wasn't better. I viewed the scenes that were shot— the "dailies"—a day after. I could weigh in on what takes I preferred but I couldn't suggest what should have been done. In one scene the Monkees flee from chasing fans into a hotel and pass a waiter balancing a bottle of champagne on a tray. There was an opportunity for comedy in having the bottle fall, but it was missed. The actor who played John Lennon in a party scene looked way too old and had the wrong mustache for the "Sgt. Pepper" period. The reason the Monkees wore the same hairstyles was because Fearnley said that in using the same location for different periods, it would take too long to change the wigs. I wish he was more sensitive to Micky's hair, as his style was totally different during the TV show's second season. The fans were obviously critical of that, and didn't know the reason why.

Daydream Believers: The Monkees' Story ran a number of times in July 2000 on VH1. It was a success across the board. It was among the highest viewed in VH1's movie series. Larkin called the movie "terrific" and thought Fearnley did "an amazing job." Micky told me, "I was pleasantly surprised. It was honest, loving, accurate, and sensitive. It was great. It captured the spirit very well. I'm glad you did it." Peter and Davy gave me compliments as well, as did Ward Sylvester, although he thought we were too easy on Don Kirshner. I never heard from Mike.

The only disappointment came from CD sales. As an entertaining movie with great music throughout, I thought it would be reasonable to expect 10 percent of the viewers to purchase a "Greatest Hits" or other Monkees' album. In the initial period in which it was shown, we sold 20,000 more albums than usual, which we calculated was about one album sold for every one hundred viewers.

*   *   *

When Simon Fuller was in town to set up *American Idol,* he scheduled an initial meeting at Rhino to discuss producing a "New Monkees" TV show. I couldn't see much point in it. Nor did I see it with the *New Monkees* TV show, that ran in syndication in 1987 and performed so poorly that not all the completed episodes were shown. There were some good elements to that show, but it seemed more like Schneider and Rafelson taking the money and running. To me, the Monkees were the Monkees, those four guys and no one else. If you want to do something similar—don't forget, the Beatles were similar—call it something else. I suggested this to Fuller, but he wanted to take advantage of the Monkees' exceptional repertoire by having the actors record new versions of the old hits.

Simon Cowell, soon to be the star judge of *American Idol,* attended the second meeting with the intention of having the new group's recordings released on his custom label through RCA Records. I like learning about new areas that I have an interest in. This was an opportunity to learn about producing a weekly network TV series. Fuller suggested that the two of us produce the show together. Similar to the *Why Do Fools Fall in Love* and the *Daydream Believers* movies, Rhino Films would coproduce the TV show, and the Rhino label would derive a licensing fee for use of the Monkees' property.

Because of the immediate success of *American Idol*, the executives at Fox TV were interested in any of Fuller's projects, and that included the "New Monkees." But Fuller thought he should establish relationships at the other TV studios. NBC, with languishing ratings, was interested. The proposed series was championed by Ted Harbert, a big Beatles fan. Fuller's time was spread too thinly. He wasn't in LA enough to physically meet with NBC. He designated Alan Barnette, who had worked as a producer on the *S Club 7* pop group's TV show. Barnette and I got along really well, but Fuller's absence worked against the project. Ex-*Simpsons* writers and producers Josh Weinstein and Bill Oakley wrote a pilot episode that NBC liked. Most of the casting was in place, with Jay Baruchel slated to be the drummer.

On February 13, 2003, there was a big meeting at NBC in Burbank. Alan and I and the writers met with the NBC executives before they were to meet the cast. We were ushered into an office where Jeff Zucker, president of NBC Entertainment, was excitedly watching the debut of *Are You Hot? The Search for American's Sexiest People*. Although it was an afternoon meeting, Zucker was viewing an East Coast feed of the show as it aired on ABC. With his bald head, Zucker struck me as a cross between Homer Simpson and comedian Don Rickles. On the TV, Lorenzo Lamas, one of the experts on the show's panel, was aiming his laser pointer at a contestant's breasts while verbalizing his assessment. Zucker was exclaiming, "This is a train wreck!" I took his excitement to mean that he thought the public would respond to this show and make it a hit. If this was his sensibility, I thought I would have difficulty relating to him. The show was cancelled five weeks later.

Zucker liked our cast and the script and said he was "green lighting" the production of the pilot episode. The production of a pilot, or sample show, doesn't guarantee that the network will like the show and add it to their schedule, but it's a necessary step to see what the show's all about before more are ordered and money is spent. Before our pilot could advance, because of NBC's poor ratings, executives were fired, including Hartley. At the same time, another pilot script Oakley and Weinstein had written was picked up, and NBC thought they would be unavailable for the "New Monkees." I was given both reasons as to why Zucker reneged on "green lighting" our pilot. Oakley's and Weinstein's other show, *The Mullets*, was the lowest rated show of the season. When we later approached Fox TV about the "New Monkees," their interest had cooled.

From Junkmen to Heroes

The Story of Rhino Home Video

In the early 1900s, when Eastern European Jews immigrated to New York City they found that there were a great many businesses they were excluded from entering. As a consequence, many of them became fish men, peddlers, and junkmen, pushing their carts through the Lower East Side.

For our part, Richard and I were junkmen. Our store and stock of records were worlds away from that of a Tower Records. Our record label offices were in an un-air-conditioned, windowless loft, with asbestos taunting us from the unfinished ceiling. In our early years we didn't have the respect or even the attention of the industry because we didn't make hit records. Warner Brothers president Mo Ostin called us "the bottom feeders of the music industry." Our albums cobbled together old castoffs that the major labels wouldn't sully their hands with. This stigma was even truer with Rhino Home Video.

With his long blond hair, beard, and pale skin, Martin Marguiles—who went by the name Johnny Legend—could pass for Yosemite Sam's svelte brother. At the store we had sold large quantities of notorious ex-professional wrestler Fred Blassie's seven-inch EP featuring "Pencil Neck Geek." Martin had cowritten and coproduced the song based around Blassie's catchphrase. In 1978 we took the four tracks and enlarged the record into a Rhino twelve-inch EP, pressed on "Blood Red Vinyl." We became friendly with Martin, Richard much more than I.

Martin and his wife, Linda Lautrec, cowrote and codirected an hour parody of the 1981 feature film *My Dinner with Andre*, shot on video at Sambo's Restaurant in downtown Los Angeles. Whereas *Andre* presented an intellectual conversation about the theatre and the philosophy of life, *My Breakfast with Blassie* depicted comedian Andy Kaufman and Freddie Blassie improvising a dialogue about mundane things, like discovering that they both were germaphobic to the extent that they carried Handi Wipes. As an example of reality programming, it was twenty years ahead of its time. It was amusing, but Martin had difficulty in getting anybody to buy it. He suggested Richard take it—for no advance—and use it to establish Rhino Home Video.

I remember seeing Andy Kaufman when he'd breeze into the Rhino store and head straight for the bargain bins. I didn't find out until much later, that from the way he was dressed, he must have been on a break from his job as a dishwasher at the Nosh in Beverly Hills. Andy wasn't doing it for the money—he was already an established comedian—but for the experience/research.

Some record companies had Christmas parties. Having survived four years as a label, we decided to celebrate by throwing a Hanukkah party in December 1981 at the club At My Place in Santa Monica. It was a good event. We had a couple of bands play, a mock rabbi/comedian who emceed, and we gave away promotional yarmulkes. We served potato latkes and egg cream sodas. Andy was invited, but showed up after it was over. We were cleaning up when he arrived, and he proceeded to wrestle a woman, which was one of his bits at the time. It was a hard-fought contest that Andy barely won. There was more tension than I would have liked, and I felt uncomfortable with the late-night match.

To coincide with the release of our video, we held a premier party at the Nuart Theater in West LA on March 20, 1984. Kaufman attended, as well as Marilu Henner from *Taxi*. Richard borrowed eight toasters, and we served cheap waffles in the lobby in keeping with the breakfast motif. I was surprised at how ravenously they were consumed—none more so than by writer Richard Meltzer, who downed eight—and we had to make another run to the market for more. Because of the demand, the toasters kept overloading the electrical outlets, shutting off the power.

We gave complimentary seats to about 80 individuals, and the remaining 335 seats were sold. I was surprised that the theater sold out. There wasn't even a seat for me. I had seen the movie, so I didn't mind. I stayed in the lobby, and was surprised at the many laughs coming from the theater. It was another example of comedies being most effective when watched by many people.

Martin's attractive sister, Lynne, met Andy on the set and became his girlfriend. Two months after our screening, Andy passed away from cancer. R.E.M. referred to the movie in their 1993 tribute song to Andy, "Man on the Moon." Richard liked the reaction we received from *Blassie*, and with Martin's enthusiasm, developed the division. I liked the idea of Rhino Home Video, but I wasn't interested in their direction. I told Richard that he could do what he wanted, as long as it didn't lose money, but that's not what happened.

From the video compilations Martin produced for Rhino, his interests were those of a teenage boy hung up on wrestling. Scraping together movie trailers of obscure films and public domain footage, Martin compiled a number of videos with titles inspired by the world of wrestling, including the annual event *WrestleMania*. A sampling included: *Battle of the Bombs*, featuring the best scenes from the world's worst movies; *Sleezemania*, trailers from such films as *Jailbait* and *The Flesh Merchant*; and *Dopemania*, a potpourri of antidrug public service films from decades past. Other releases were titled *Weird Cartoons* and *Rhino's Guide to Safe Sex*. Martin's packaging was very creative, but the videos sold minimally.

In the early days of home video, it was so novel to watch a movie at home on one's own machine that mediocre titles sold much better than they should have because the movie studios were reluctant to enter this field. This encouraged companies to release marginal videos to get into the marketplace because it seemed as though everything was selling. By the time we entered the arena, the bloom was off the rose.

Our most notorious release was *Orgy of the Dead*, a little-seen movie written by the world's worst director, Ed Wood. Wood's reputation was solidified in Harry Medved's 1978 book *The Fifty Worst Films of All Time*.

The total from the three thousand ballots submitted by knowledgeable film fans resulted in *Plan 9 From Outer Space*—which Wood wrote and directed—topping the list. It required considerable detective work from Martin to track down *Orgy*'s producer, Stephen Apostolof. Contrary to public opinion, Apostolof considered Ed "a great filmmaker and a great man." Unlike some of Ed's more interesting bad movies, this one is little more than strippers dressed as ghouls disrobing in a graveyard set. Wood adapted it from his, ahem, novel. In 1994 sales of our Wood titles increased further after the release of the feature film *Ed Wood*, starring Johnny Depp as Ed and directed by Tim Burton.

Randy Friedman approached Richard about heading up our video division. Randy was in charge of I.R.S. Video, which meant he was the record company's sole employee dealing with home video. He told us that his bosses, Miles Copeland and Derek Power, had wanted to enlarge I.R.S. Video and spin it off as a public company. The people they were proceeding with turned out to be scam artists. As a result, to avoid any legal problems, they thought the best move was to close I.R.S. Video. Randy came over in early 1985, bringing I.R.S. Video's *The Police Around the World* concert program for Rhino to rerelease.

Randy Friedman was a friendly, good-hearted soul who had the misfortune of looking like one of the klutzy characters drawn by *Mad* magazine cartoonist Don Martin. Chuck Taylor's description of a typical Martin character could have described Randy: ". . . big-nosed schmoes with sleepy eyes, puffs of wiry hair . . ." He had an unbelievable number of contacts and had that salesman's gift of being undaunted in making cold calls. Capitol only sold to record stores. Randy expanded our distribution to video stores and, on occasion, nontraditional outlets like 7-11. He brought over other I.R.S. product of new wave bands, like *The Cutting Edge* and *New Wave Theater*.

Randy was impressed with the videos Martin put together, in part because they cost so little money. He liked the cachet they gave Rhino Video and felt he got more attention because of it. Ultimately, despite his intentions and efforts, he was fired after two years because the division was operating at a loss. Still, Richard thought enough of him to bankroll his next start-up company. With his future at Rhino in doubt, Randy recommended

Arny Schorr, who had experience in sales in both records and video, as his replacement. A music fan who displayed framed handbills from 1960s Fillmore concerts in his office, Arny had the sheen of a salesman and was always in motion.

In the midst of all this lowbrow programming were significance releases. Richard agreed to provide seed money for a documentary that explored the causes of the United States' 1989 invasion of Panama in exchange for the home video rights. *The Panama Deception* won an Academy Award for best documentary for 1992. The director, Barbara Trent, came by and Richard and I got to hold her Oscar. Sales were minimal. The Mamas and Papas' *Straight Shooters* won an American Video Conference Award for Best Documentary. We released a series of Emmy winning TV dramas from TV's early years, including *Requiem for a Heavyweight*.

The incipient home video business was a great idea, if of questionable legal status. Videotape of a large format had been used professionally for decades, but an effective, smaller format threaded into a cassette that people could watch on machines at home was a revelation. Tapes were at first sold to consumers on two formats, Betamax and VHS (for Video Home System). In the early days of home video there were gray areas. When Warner Brothers Pictures produced a movie like *Casablanca* (in 1942), they paid for it, owned it, and took the position that they could do anything they wanted with it. When the Turtles appeared on *The Ed Sullivan Show* to promote their new single "Happy Together" in hopes of creating sales, they would have signed off on a standard agreement giving the show full rights to their appearance. But the expectation at the time was that the show would air once on the CBS network—and maybe a second time as a rerun if they were lucky.

Ten years later the producer could take the unfair position that their rights were unrestricted, and they could issue the appearance on home video. Or they could take the fair position that they needed to get the rights from the participants, which meant tracking down each member of the band and negotiating with them or offering a flat fee. If it was rejected by even one unreasonable member, the performance could not be used. The group had agreed to perform on the show, but not to have their performance sold—with others—in a product that didn't yet exist.

We faced many of these issues when we made a deal with ABC to release videos of the mid-1960s TV show *Shindig!* The show was a must-watch for pop music fans and featured the top acts of the day from the Beatles and Rolling Stones on down. Unlike on most TV shows of the time, the majority of the performances were live. ABC insisted we pay everyone who appeared on camera. For example, we may have only been interested in a performance by the Kinks, but if dancers were in the shot, or members of a backup band, we had to track them down and pay them as well. Initially we felt *Shindig!* was perfect for us. It was quality programming, had never been out on home video, and it fit with our resurrection of great music from rock's past. It was more time-consuming and expensive than we anticipated. When the videos hit the stores in 1992, there were far fewer people who treasured the show in the way that we had, and we lost money on the deal.

It was tough going for Arny. It took him a while to understand Richard's vision. He added more music titles and expanded his staff, but getting quality programming was always a problem. The movie studios released their own movies and TV shows. The record companies released programs by those artists who were signed to their respective labels. Where could he go? We didn't want to go low-rent as Atlantic Records' A* Vision had, by inking a deal to release video produced by *Penthouse* magazine.

In addition, because Video's profitability was always in question, Arny felt he couldn't risk paying high advances or production expenses. It was difficult for him to get footing. It depressed him to sit in on department finance meetings and to keep reporting that his area was still in the red. As a consequence, by 1993 Rhino Home Video had diminished from a staff of seven to two: Arny and a designer. Arny was dispirited, but he loved Rhino and was determined to build a viable home video division for the company.

As the home video industry matured, it was better able to accommodate home video releases, but not fully, as was the case with a prospective Monkees compilation. After we made a deal for the Monkees catalogue, a potential big seller would be a greatest hits collection of the group's music segments from the TV show. To use a clip from a show we would not only have to pay the Monkees, but the director and writers of the episode—even if they had no contribution to the musical segment. Because of the union stipulations, the expense made the project unviable. From our experience, the publishers also were unreasonable. If one were to take a TV show, *The Monkees* or otherwise, and evaluate the cost of the production, the contribution of the actors, director, and writer, and compared it to the time during which a song was played, there's no way the publishers could justify their high rates.

I came up with the idea for *The Monkees* box to look like an old TV set. The fall 1995 release included twenty-one VHS tapes—fifty-eight episodes and the *33 1/3 Revolutions Per Monkee* TV special—and an impressive forty-eight-page booklet. The list price was $400, which was the most expensive box set for a video release. We manufactured three thousand, and were surprised that they sold out in ninety days. The subsequent demand was so strong that we decided to do another run. But it took a long time to manufacture because of the custom elements, primarily the box and booklet. A year later, we sold another 1,500, but when we wanted more, we found that Warner—without asking us—had destroyed the inventory on those custom elements. *The Monkees* box and the individual releases of the TV shows contributed greatly to making Rhino Video profitable.

Our success with *The Monkees* box got me thinking about a bigger and more profitable TV show release, *Batman*. Also popular in the mid-1960s, *Batman* ran for 120 episodes, none of which were ever on home video. Early in the series a script was written for the cast to star in a quickly made TV movie. It wasn't as good as the episodes, but it was the only product with that cast to have been released on home video.

Graphic novelist Frank Miller revived Batman with a darker tone. His take was so popular that it spawned a series of Batman movies commencing with *Batman Returns*, directed by Tim Burton in 1992. I had heard that Warner Brothers didn't want the TV shows out on video because they thought the campy tone would impair their new franchise, forgetting, of course, that there was one campy video in the marketplace. Because 1997's *Batman & Robin* had underperformed both critically and at the box office, there was a lull at Warner in plotting a successor. I thought it would be a good time to try to make it happen. Even though Rhino was part of the Warner Music Group, I thought that we were still perceived as being independent—as compared to being a competitor. As an *independent* company, I thought I could broker a deal between Fox and Warner, and cut each in on the profits. Time Warner owned DC, which published Batman comics. I projected a minimal profit of $3 million. If I cut DC and Fox in for 25 percent each, Rhino would make $1.5 million. It may not have been much for such large companies, but it would have been for us. I called the woman who headed DC and told her what I wanted to do. She put the kibosh on it.

Mike Nesmith invited me to a thirtieth anniversary reunion of those who had been involved in the production of *The Monkees* TV show in mid-September 1996 at the restaurant DC3 in Santa Monica. Other than the four Monkees, I knew few people and felt like an outsider. Mike introduced me to a table of guests sitting near the entrance. I exchanged a few lines with comedian Gary Shandling, but spent much more time talking to writer/director David Mirkin. The result was a deal he fostered for us to release the early 1990s sitcom *Get a Life*, starring Chris Elliott. Mirkin cocreated the show, served as its executive producer, primary director, and sometimes writer. The first two volumes did well enough so that we released a second set. As Shandling's *Larry Sanders Show* is among my all-time favorite TV shows, I made an offer of $250,000 to executive producer Brad Grey (of Brillstein-Grey Entertainment) for the home video rights. I never received even the courtesy of a reply to my letter, nor a return to my follow-up phone calls.

Another noteworthy project that never materialized was the original edit of the movie *This Is Spinal Tap*. The film only runs eighty-two minutes, but director Rob Reiner's original cut was four and a half hours. Because there were so many ardent fans of the film, I thought we could do well with a limited-edition release. Originally produced by Embassy Pictures, the film—and other assets—was sold to a succession of companies, with Paris-based StudioCanal ending up with the rights. With all the changes in ownership, the long edit couldn't be located. Some scenes—including ones with Billy Crystal—were included as a bonus on later home video releases.

Even though Gerald Levin, head of all of Time Warner, was a proponent of synergy, it didn't mean that his words alone carried enough weight.

When Arny met with two department heads at Warner Home Video who had blocked Rhino's request to license specific TV shows, their response was, "Why should we license to you when we can put it out ourselves?" Well, they weren't going to put out what we requested. Major studios, like Warner Brothers, were focused on the big-selling titles of their hit movies. Many of their old movies and TV shows weren't released because they would sell too few units to be worthwhile. We were experts in this area, and I had old TV shows like *Have Gun Will Travel* and *77 Sunset Strip* on my list. Licensing those dormant titles to us would have resulted in four profit centers: a licensing fee for the program, profit on the manufacturing of the video tape or DVD, profit from distribution, and profit from their ownership of Rhino—all from programs that were sitting on the shelf.

Their next argument was that any new SKU (stock-keeping unit) would compete with one of theirs. Essentially, they would feel competition for the home video release of *Lethal Weapon 4* from *Have Gun Will Travel*. Richard called Warren Lieberfarb, president of Warner Home Video, who hung up on him. I appealed to Bob Daly, but he was of no help.

We received our first gold video award for sales of 25,000 of *Rainbow Bridge*. I saw a long cut of the film in a screening room at Warner Brothers Studios in the 1970s. The film seemed interminable: a group of spaced-out hippies at a meditation center in Maui, with a short concert appearance by Jimi Hendrix midway through the film. Hendrix and his band played well, but the sound and visuals were substandard throughout the film. Arny was so happy that he had a best-selling title, he wanted to celebrate by giving me (and a few others) award plaques. Even here, I couldn't resist a (minor) joke. Sometimes when a record company orders plaques to present to artists, the person ordering them is so clueless that they make up presentation plates to a dead person, as *PRESENTED TO JOHN LENNON*. Rather than have a brass plate with my name, I told Arny to make mine *PRESENTED TO JIMI HENDRIX*.

Sometimes sales fail to meet expectations, which we experienced with *Shindig!* Other times you get lucky, as was the case in 1996 when Arny made a deal with Comedy Central to release their programs on home video. Our initial titles didn't sell well: *The Daily Show*, Bill Maher's *Politically Incorrect,* and *Dr. Katz, Professional Therapist* were among the cable channel's higher rated shows. The following year *South Park* became an unexpected hit. Primarily because of the videos we sold in 1998, Rhino Home Video experienced a surge in profits. It carried over into the next year with twelve *South Park* videos in the catalogue. We made so much money for Comedy Central, it would have been natural for them to renew the deal. Warner Home Video, seeing the large numbers we posted, elbowed us out. As Comedy Central was co-owned by Time Warner, we had no clout. There was no respect or consideration for Rhino as a company or for what we had accomplished.

Howard Kaylan turned me onto *Mystery Science Theater 3000* (aka MST3K), a TV show that aired on Comedy Central. It was based around Joel Robinson, who was trapped in space on the *Satellite of Love* (from the Lou Reed song) with four robots. As part of an experiment by an evil scientist to find out which bad movie would be most effective at making people crazy—to use as a weapon to take over the world—Joel was forced to watch bad movies. Viewers could see him silhouetted, seated as in a theater at the bottom of the screen with the robots, during which they made humorous comments, elevating otherwise unwatchable movies into novel entertainment. I loved it.

The concept of adding to, or changing the content of existing films was introduced to me in the early 1960s. Jay Ward, the mastermind behind the *Rocky and Bullwinkle* cartoon show, produced a season of *Fractured Flickers* in which segments from silent films were rewritten and dialogue dubbed in by actors. Comedian Soupy Sales, similarly, narrated silent film segments as part of his show. Woody Allen advanced the concept in his 1966 film *What's Up, Tiger Lily?*, in which he combined the footage from two Japanese spy thrillers and wrote a new story with entirely new dialogue dubbed in English. In the late 1970s the LA Connection made wise cracks to appropriate vintage films while sitting in the front row of a theater to the entertainment of paid ticket holders.

Richard and I dug the concept, and for a couple of years we were looking to follow in the footsteps of Woody Allen with a Mexican film that pitted colorful wrestlers against familiar horror villains. We screened a number of these hard-to-see films, like *Santo vs. Las Mujeres Vampiro*, but couldn't find one that had the right balance between action and dialogue. Unable to resist the concept, in 1986 we took one of these movies, 1964's *The Wrestling Women vs. the Aztec Mummy*, added rock music, and changed the title to *The Rock 'n' Roll Wrestling Women vs. the Aztec Mummy*.

Starting in 1992, I called MST3K creator Joel Hodgson, who also portrayed Robinson, numerous times trying to make a deal for home video. Either he was extremely untogether, so focused on the show that he couldn't fixate on my offer, or daunted by the unfamiliar business aspect of home video. It took me three years to close the deal with executive producer Jim Mallon. Hodgson had been replaced by head writer Mike Nelson, and the show's popularity had slipped. Still, titles like *The Brain That Wouldn't Die* proved to be steady sellers. Shortly before I left Rhino, I called Mallon to tell him I was leaving. He revealed that they had received nearly $1 million in royalties at that point.

Arny did an exceptional job of picking up good music titles by artists such as Neil Young, Paul Simon, Cheap Trick, and Pat Benatar, as well as the Who's film *Quadrophenia*, and worthy TV shows such as *The Lone Ranger*, *The Real McCoys*, and *Flip* (Flip Wilson). His taste was inconsistent, and he released duff titles such as the TV show *Pink Lady and Jeff*.

Sony Wonder had the rights to the 1970s TV shows *The Transformers* and *G.I. Joe*—both originally Hasbro toys—but didn't want to put them out on video, so Arny made a deal for an advance against royalties of $50,000 each. *G.I. Joe* sold well, but *The Transformers* sold much better than anybody anticipated, to the point where it earned a rare platinum award (sales of 50,000) for Rhino. Hollywood took notice; the feature film rights were optioned in 2003. Unlike the low budget of the original TV show, DreamWorks and Paramount spent $150 million making the film that was released four years later. It grossed over $700 million worldwide at the box office. It probably would not have happened had Rhino not primed the franchise.

As a result of the strength of the catalogue, Rhino Video accumulated $10 million in sales in 2001, with a good profit. For the next year Arny projected a healthy increase to $13 million and a profit of $3 million. By the end of 2002, the momentum of the division had raked in a profit of $8 million on sales of $22 million. It was a remarkable achievement, even more so in light of how Arny built the business back up from its lean years. It's an example of how, no matter how bad things get, you don't quit—you battle back. Richard and I worked well with Arny and appreciated how he was able to forge a successful division competing with companies with much deeper pockets and with access to better programming. But not everybody shared our opinion.

Arny met with Scott Pascucci, who succeeded Richard and me. Pascucci's son was into extreme sports, and Pascucci wanted to make a deal with ESPN for their X Games video programming. Arny told him he didn't think it would fit with Rhino. Ultimately, it wasn't something Arny had to bother with, because he left the company at the end of the year, unappreciated, having been denied a salary increase, and having been told by new WEA head Jim Caparro that he would have to prove himself in the next year to get a raise.

Let's look at the numbers again. Arny had exceeded his projections and brought in $8 million in profits. Arny could have asked for an extra hundred thousand or two, and been perfectly reasonable. But he asked for a lot less; he merely wanted to be brought up to par with what the other senior vice presidents at Rhino were paid. Arny's salary had lagged because of his division's struggle for profitability. He left at the end of the year, after sixteen years at Rhino Home Video, for a better deal at another company. Pascucci's X Games deal turned out to be a big money loser. Without Foos, Bronson, and Schorr, Rhino Home Video declined as a business, and ceased to exist by 2005.

The Rock Star and the Godfather

Tommy James and Morris Levy

Isn't it terrible when the only pictures you can find of the executives at your record company are their mug shots?

—Tommy James

The first time I saw Tommy James perform live, in June 1976, it was a revelation. Five years after his last Top 40 hit—"Draggin' the Line"—he and his five-piece band delivered a tremendous set of hits performed with verve and faithfulness. Tommy's voice was strong and his band's four-part harmonies were superb. The set was remarkable for another reason: there were only thirty people in the audience at West Hollywood's Troubadour nightclub. It made no difference to Tommy, as he delivered the kind of performance one would have expected had there been thousands of fans cheering him on. Towards the end of the set, while the band was vamping during "Mony Mony," he leaped off the stage and jogged around the club, shaking the hand of everyone in attendance. The way he expressed his appreciation made a big impression on me.

When Tommy James and the Shondells were getting airplay with their hits in the 1960s, I liked enough of them to buy their best of album when it was released. While their previous albums had worthwhile tracks, they were typical of the time, composed of mostly filler material. In my freshman year at UCLA, I carpooled with a couple of high school friends to a campus parking lot. One had bought an eight-track tape of Tommy's *Crimson and Clover* album, which was a marvel. The long version of the title track—the single of which hit number one—was one of the better psychedelic records of the time. Atypically for a band known for Top 40 hits, most of the songs on the album were good and were recorded with uncommon clarity and dynamics. I bought the album and the group's follow up, *Cellophane Symphony*, which included some perfectly acceptable arrangements featuring electronic instrumentation by way of a Moog synthesizer. The album was recorded at Broadway Sound, a studio co-owned by recently retired Yankees pitching great Whitey Ford, who had purchased the Moog from the Monkees' Micky Dolenz.

In October 1964 the Shondells, Tommy Jackson's band (he was known by his real surname at the time), recorded a song that Tommy had heard a rival band perform, titled "Hanky Panky." The term isn't used much these days, but was a playful expression for improper sexual behavior. Nobody knew much about the song, including the full set of lyrics. The song originated as a B-side to the Raindrops' "That Boy John," released in late 1963. The Raindrops were actually Jeff Barry and Ellie Greenwich, who were beginning to distinguish themselves as hit songwriters with "Be My Baby," "Da Doo Ron Ron," "Leader of the Pack," and "Do Wah Diddy Diddy" among their credits. Barry called "Hanky Panky" "a terrible song." The idea was to have an inferior B-side so a DJ wouldn't be tempted to play the wrong song—the one not being promoted—on the radio.

A local DJ at WNIL recorded the Shondells in the radio station studio and released a single on the Snap Records label. It received some impressive airplay in Michigan, Indiana, and Illinois, but by the time Tommy graduated from high school in June 1965, the record was no longer being played. Nearly a year later, a Pittsburgh dance promoter popularized the record in his area, resulting in tens of thousands of bootleg 45s being sold. Tommy needed a deal, and fast, to counter the bootlegged sales. His promoter/manager had him sign with Roulette Records. Because the original master tape couldn't be located, Roulette made a tape from one of the bootlegged records. It climbed to number one in July, almost two years after it was recorded. It's probably the only big hit to have been taken directly off of another record.

With the original Shondells dispersed, Tommy hired a Pittsburgh club band and the ensemble was now billed as Tommy James and the Shondells. The Beatles inspired the new era of rock 'n' roll, but not everybody who joined a band felt comfortable with the cultural path the Beatles blazed. Tommy and his bandmates were initially slow to embrace the changes, as their first tour program indicates: "They all have fairly short hair . . . not crew cut but short, and they are very definitely against the scruffy look as exemplified by some of the British acts."

A remarkable run of hits followed. From the time Roulette released "Hanky Panky" in June 1966 through the end of the 1960s, the group had more top ten hits than any other American rock group. The appeal of the original records was reconfirmed in the 1980s when three covers hit the top ten: Tiffany's "I Think We're Alone Now" and Billy Idol's "Mony Mony" were back to back number ones in November 1987, while Joan Jett & the Blackhearts' "Crimson & Clover" made it to number seven in 1982.

I saw Tommy play next in August 1988 when he shared a bill with the Rascals at the Universal Amphitheatre. Backstage after the show, I introduced myself and had a brief exchange with him. I told him that we were negotiating to buy the Roulette catalogue. He confirmed for me Roulette's reputation for not paying royalties. I told him that if we made the purchase, he would get royalties from us. He was cordial, but I don't think he gave it much consideration.

The owner of Roulette Records, Morris (Moishe) Levy, was a Damon Runyon character: tall, stocky, and gruff, with a manner acquired on the streets. He had a tough childhood, with his father and an older brother dying when he was very young. He learned the value of music publishing when he was in his twenties as the co-owner of the Birdland jazz club in Manhattan. He cobbled together a catalogue of masters from labels he was a partner in, invariably buying out his associates when they needed funds to cover gambling debts. Levy had a reputation among executives in the business that his word was his bond, while at the same time having the notoriety among his recording artists and songwriters of failing to account properly for royalty payments. When Levy's artists asked for their money, he would often reply with, "Royalty? You want royalty, go to England!" That he was physically intimidating and linked to the Genovese crime family meant that there were few who challenged him. A joke circulated for many years that scientists were looking for the quietest place on earth in which to conduct experiments and they had finally found it: Roulette's royalty accounting department.

He was aggressive in his business dealings. He managed DJ Alan Freed and attempted to trademark the term "rock and roll." On songs he published, he sometimes added his name as a songwriter, even though he had nothing to do with the creation. Morris came up with a smart way to distribute payola. He paid DJs for introducing acts at record hops and live dates. He understood the value of charity and raised millions of dollars for the T. J. Martel Foundation and United Jewish Appeal, of which he was that organization's Man of the Year in 1973.

Morris always denied that he was in business with the mob, claiming that these were old friends from early in his life. He would point to a framed photo of himself and Cardinal Spellman hanging on the wall in his office. His standard line was, "That don't make me Catholic." His activities caught up with him, and a Federal jury convicted him of extortion in 1988. Federal authorities described him as "the Godfather of the American music business." Although he had sold his publishing business, there were few companies interested in his masters because executives feared a rash of lawsuits would face the new owner from emboldened artists who no longer had to deal with Morris for the royalties they were owed.

He wanted $5 million for the rights to his masters, but there were no takers. Richard quarterbacked the evaluation process, making a chart on notebook paper: A&R provided him with a list of titles that we could release, and sales and marketing gave him an estimate of the sales we could expect. He had a separate category of titles we didn't think we could sell enough copies of to justify releasing ourselves, those we could license to another company. My main contribution to the process was surveying a number of music supervisors and film and TV licensing people who reported difficulties in dealing with Roulette since they frequently failed to returned calls. So, I knew there would be a big upside in media licensing. Because the purchase price was so hefty, beyond what Rhino could afford, we approached our distributor, Capitol, who contacted their international company, EMI Music, about partnering with us on the deal.

After Bob Emmer joined the company in October 1987 and got up to speed, he proved to be a big asset. In addition to anchoring our new business affairs department—and relieving me of drafting and reviewing most of the contracts—he was also adept in making deals. He wasn't so good at administration and at times lapsed into "speaking jazz," as Richard referred to Bob's concocted excuses when he failed to accomplish a task or forgot a previous discussion, because he improvised, like a jazz musician. Bob was sociable in a way Richard and I weren't, so in May 1989 we sent him to New York to meet with the EMI team and see Morris.

The negotiations did not go smoothly. Morris wandered around his apartment with his bathrobe hanging open, revealing his underwear. He had a problem with his sciatic nerve, and he had to lie on his back to relieve the pain. The first meeting did not go well, and he dismissed Bob and the EMI team. Walking through Central Park afterwards, Bob felt bad, called Morris, and persuaded him to meet the following day, which he would agree to only if Bob did all the talking among the buyers. This arrangement in place, anytime anybody from the EMI team had a question, they had to ask Bob to ask Morris, even though he was sitting mere feet away on his sofa.

Morris agreed to proceed, but gave the team 72 hours to go through the 101-page agreement. They met in a law office day and night, as it was the weekend. The office wasn't air-conditioned, so after the paralegals left, the team stripped down to their underwear to withstand the heat. Morris was surprised at the scene when he delivered a Sunday night dinner of Chinese take-out. He admonished them because he knew that the offices of the law firm two floors up were air-conditioned on the weekend. The deal was agreed to, subject to Morris meeting Richard.

Richard flew in and he and Bob drove to Ghent to visit Morris at his farm. Bob noticed that the framed family photos on the wall had heads cut out in the pictures. He asked Morris about them, and Morris responded, "I love my children; I hate my fuckin' ex-wives." Richard was struck by how frail Morris seemed, especially after dinner, when the fatigued Morris continued discussing the contract in his bedroom: Morris in bed, Bob and Richard sitting on it.

The purchase price was a bit under $5 million. Rhino put up a little more than half for the North American rights (excluding the jazz titles). EMI got the rights for the rest of the world (including the jazz). To guard against claims of unpaid royalties, Morris agreed to a "basket" of $350,000 for a period of a year. This meant that we could withhold that sum of money from the purchase price, subject to any claims. The only one we received was from New Orleans funk band the Meters, and that was worked out for a relatively small amount. Mitch Ryder, along with his group the Detroit Wheels, had hits with "Devil with a Blue Dress On" and "Sock It to Me, Baby!" The group had recorded on the DynaVoice label that Morris had acquired, but there didn't appear to be a contract anybody could locate. Ryder's lawyer, Neville Johnson, contacted us. Even though he was a friend of mine, I thought he was being overly aggressive in squeezing us for a higher royalty than his client would otherwise have received. After we came to an agreement, I couldn't fault Neville, and didn't let it impair our relationship.

Morris died of liver cancer in May 1990, without having served his time in jail. Morris was right when he told us that we would do well. Owing primarily to the robust sales of Tommy James and the Shondells (three titles sold well over 100,000) and KC and the Sunshine Band (whose *best of* sold over 500,000), we made back our money in less than three years.

Permit me to digress. Despite Rhino's reputation, KC—real name Harry Wayne Casey—didn't trust us enough to even let us borrow his master tapes, which were better than what we had received from Roulette. The band's records were well-produced, and Bill Inglot wanted to use KC's tapes to get the best sound for our reissues. KC put him off for months. Finally, Brian Schuman sent freelancer Bob Fisher to Miami. He spent hours outside of KC's house—actually his mother's house, as KC had run into problems with the IRS. He knocked on the door all day, but KC didn't answer because he was asleep until 6 p.m. KC whined about how Henry Stone (owner of KC's original label, TK Records) and

Morris Levy had ripped him off. Somehow Bob was able to finesse borrowing the tapes to do the work at nearby Criteria Studios. Bob reported back that KC's tapes were stored under his bed, in clothes closets, and in nooks and crannies throughout the house. He had no gold records on the wall. The only signs of success were photos of him with celebrities like Bob Hope and Dinah Shore.

The visibility of our KC and the Sunshine Band releases helped to revive interest in him. Early in our relationship, he was always calling us to accelerate his royalty payments. It seemed like he always needed money. In a few years, renewed interest in him had grown to where he was considering which offer to accept to play on New Year's Eve for a fee of $1 million dollars. He no longer called our royalty department.

When I heard about HBO scheduling a new series about the Mafia in January 1999, my thought was, hasn't this been done to death? In addition, the novelty of a crime boss like Tony Soprano seeing a psychiatrist (Dr. Melfi) paralleled the roles of Robert De Niro and Billy Crystal in the movie *Analyze This,* which was released in the middle of *The Sopranos* first season. *Analyze This* was a hit movie, grossing over $100 million, so how many people would care about *The Sopranos*? When the show's viewership doubled in its second season, I thought it would be opportune to pitch a movie based on the relationship between Tommy and Morris. My working title was "The Rock Star and the Godfather." There was even a character in *The Sopranos* based on Morris. Hesh Rabkin was Jewish, tall, and physically imposing, had made his fortune in the record business in the fifties and sixties, and owned a horse farm in upstate New York.

In the fable of the Scorpion and the Frog, a scorpion asks a frog to carry him across a river on his back. The frog is reluctant, because he says the scorpion will sting him. The scorpion counters that he wouldn't do that, because then they would both drown. The frog agrees. Half way through the water, much to the frog's surprise, the scorpion stings him. As they are both sinking, the frog asks the scorpion why. His reply is "It's my nature." Despite a person's intentions, sometimes they're unable to go against their basic nature, even if it negatively affects their life. From hearing Tommy tell his story, there was real affection between the two, a genuine father and son relationship, but Morris still couldn't help himself from ripping Tommy off. It was his nature.

The success of *The Sopranos* showed that people weren't tired of Mafia-themed dramas, and I was interested in fleshing out this relationship. Tommy's story presented a unique twist—one that was true—with great music for the soundtrack. I ran the idea by Ron McGee, who wrote the script for *Daydream Believers*, the Monkees movie. He was interested, and so was Tommy. What follows are excerpts from two lengthy phone conversations the three of us had in 2000—one in September and one in November—to determine the elements of the story. Where clarification is needed, my additions are in italics.

HAROLD: In the early days, did you get a sense that Morris had mob ties?

TOMMY: It was in May 1966, at the signing of my record deal. Morris' goons came in and one of them said, "Morris, we've got to talk to you right away." Morris went from being this charming guy to a serious one. I overheard them telling Morris that they just beat some guy to death in New Jersey.

HAROLD: Were there other things you saw that were mob-like?

TOMMY: There were meetings in Morris office with these guys every few weeks. I knew these were serious people because Morris introduced them to me as "Mr. . . ." These were scary people; they all looked the same and talked the same. Vincent "the Chin" Gigante [*who became head of the Genovese family in 1981*] was a regular. Morris seemed to be in charge of the meetings.

HAROLD: What was Morris' reason for not paying you your royalties?

TOMMY: His position was that I was always in the red because my studio bills were so high. [Laughs] The occasional statements I received always showed that I owed him money. Here we were selling millions of records, and I never seemed to recoup my recording expenses. The money I earned as a songwriter was also put towards recouping those costs, so it made no sense. After the three-year deal I signed was up, we probably sold 30 million records, and he's saying we haven't sold enough to recover our recording costs.

[*Tommy's figure was indeed his estimate, as he never received a full account of what he had sold. In the 1960s an artist's collected sales were calculated in this way: one record sold for every single, and five records sold for every album, as a single consisted of two songs and an album usually had between ten and twelve. In Tommy's example, his 30 million in sales might have been from four million albums and ten million singles. This method was abandoned in the 1970s when albums were acknowledged for regularly selling in large amounts.*]

TOMMY: Morris would ride that pony as long as he could. Other times he told me he couldn't pay me because he wasn't paid on time from his independent distributors. By 1968 I realized this was really a scam.

Morris got me out of the draft. It was in late 1968 or early 1969 when I was called to the draft board. Previously I had a deferment because I was married, but they needed more soldiers to report to Vietnam, so they changed my status from 3A to 1A. I thought the change might have been initiated by the Nixon administration because I had backed Hubert Humphrey and played at a number of rallies to support him in his campaign for president in 1968. Humphrey was paranoid around young people because they had given him a hard time over the protest against the Vietnam War. We were the first group of longhaired freaks who were friendly. Back at the hotel room, after the rallies, he wanted to know our opinions on things, of what the young people wanted. If he won the election, he promised me a position heading a national youth commission. I had him write the liner notes to our *Crimson and Clover* album. We remained friends until his death.

I don't know how this would play to the Vietnam veterans, if we put this in the movie. I freaked out. I hired psychiatrists and other doctors to write me letters. It just so happened that Morris was on the board of directors of Chemical Bank. One of his best friends, who was also on this board, happened to be the head of the Selective Service in New York. As fate would have it, this guy put in the fix. I took my physical at the draft board on Whitehall Street. At the end of the day, they said I had night color blindness, and I was given a 4F. And I know it was because of what Morris did.

HAROLD: How did Morris intimidate you?

TOMMY: You've got to understand that Morris intimidated people. He looked like Al Capone, or a character right out of a movie. He talked with a gruff Bronx accent. But he never threatened me. One time he came up to my apartment. My wife, my secretary, Morris, and I were all talking. He said, "Come here, kid," and he took me out on my terrace. He grabs a hold of the front of my shirt, and he says, "I'm gonna tell you something." He goes into a tirade about how there was a dispute at Birdland, the jazz club he owned, and a mob guy killed his brother instead of him. He gets more agitated when he tells me that he killed the guy who killed his brother. Then he gets very physical: "I took out a knife and I stuck it like this!" With his finger he jabs me in the stomach! "And I stuck it like this, and his intestines were hanging out." He said he was going to throw him off a building—like this one—but didn't. While he's telling me this, I'm freaking out. I'm wondering, why is he telling me this? This was Morris' way of letting me know that behind everything we're talking about, he can be a threat. This was his way of letting me know he was nobody to be messed with.

HAROLD: During this period, was there anybody you could go to?

TOMMY: I felt very alone, and ill-equipped to take him on. I once sent a couple of lawyers up to see him, and they ended up in business with him. I didn't feel there was anybody I could even go to for advice. I didn't want to do anything that would destroy my career. I didn't want to interrupt the flow of records. I wasn't sure what to do.

HAROLD: So, if you sued him and he put an injunction on you, or suspended your contract, or a similar action, it would stop the momentum you had.

TOMMY: Exactly. And it probably would have. A few years later, that's what I had to do to get out of my Roulette contract, and that's the effect it had. The bad feelings had been building. It came to a head in 1969 when my contract was up, and I was going to leave. That year was huge for me because we became an album act. We weren't being paid. It wasn't like I wasn't getting any money at all—just not close to what Morris owed me. When I told him I needed money, when he felt like it, he would give me a check here or there for $10,000 or $25,000. I was put into the position of having to beg for my money. I was frustrated and humiliated in having to do it, to beg like a bum, rather than being paid properly as a normal person.

HAROLD: But you re-signed.

TOMMY: Suddenly, Morris was my best buddy. We went to the World Series together [*the New York Mets beat the Baltimore Orioles in five games in 1969*]. [*Jazz musician*] Lionel Hampton went with us. I spent weekends at his farm. Sometimes I took my wife. Morris and I hung out together. We'd drink all weekend and have fun. Celebrities and other interesting people came up. One of the first times I visited, he had Dr. Joyce Brothers and her husband. He didn't hang out with wise guys, except, like on Tuesdays. He had the most amazing gun collection I've ever seen in my life, rows of high-powered rifles and Remingtons. I saw a happy family man. His farm was his oasis in the desert; he wasn't like he was in New York.

Morris had an amazing operation, a multimillion dollar dairy farm. Everything the guy touched seemed to turn to gold. He said to me, "Why don't you get a place close by. Let me look into it." He bought me an 1100-acre farm in upstate New York. He made the initial payment—and took it out of my royalties—and I made the mortgage payments.

Morris liked to get out and work. He put on overalls and shoveled manure and baled hay, like one of the farm hands. He loved it. He loved being with his son Adam. The three of us went target shooting, or hung out with the cows. The evening ritual would be a huge dinner around a gigantic table. Afterwards, we sat in front of the fire in the large fireplace, drank brandy from snifters, and talked until three in the morning. Once we talked about sci-fi movies from the fifties. I probably knew him as well as anybody. He would tell me how old he felt. He told me his life story, how to get back at a teacher who humiliated him in class; he lifted her wig and poured ink on her head. He was expelled from that. He kept bringing it up, saying, "If my teacher could see me today."

I got buzzed enough one night and asked him why he got involved with gangsters. I told him, "You've got a mind like a computer. You could have been one of the biggest businessmen around." He blew my comment off. The only thing he would say was, "I am what I am."

Morris talked me into staying by offering me a real big payout: a large advance, with guaranteed regular payments every year over and above any royalties that were due, a tailor made agreement with additional perks, including me becoming Roulette's in-house A&R man. At that time I was producing myself. He said, "Why don't you produce other acts for Roulette? You can help me run the label." It was Morris's way of showing that he respected my talent. He was impressed that I was writing and producing my own records.

After the first year, he stopped making payments. I sent my accountant over to talk to him, and he came back shaking. When I confronted Morris, his attitude was, "What are you going to do about it?" Morris never threatened me outright. He had no problem threatening the accounting people I sent up there to get my money.

HAROLD: What impresses me is that, not only were you successful as an artist, but also when you started to produce. [*Tommy cowrote and coproduced "Tighter and Tighter" by Alive N Kicking, which became a top ten hit for Roulette in July 1970. In the previous summer, a Texas group called the Clique had a hit with "Sugar On Sunday," a song Tommy wrote for the Crimson & Clover album but didn't release as a single.*] How could Morris have killed the bird that laid the golden eggs? How could he have not taken care of you?

TOMMY: He was the most penny-wise, pound-foolish person I ever knew. He could be sitting there with $75 million, and he would still cut your heart out for $5,000. He owned an unbelievable catalogue of songs and the masters to go with them. He could have made a deal with a major label distributor from which he would have made even more money. But then he wouldn't have been able to screw somebody out of 20 percent. It was interesting how emotionally disturbed the guy was. He was paranoid. He would not let anybody else run his publishing company. He liked playing the role of the gangster, but because of that, people wouldn't have anything to do with him. If he played it straight, he could have been even more successful. In one respect, he was one of the most reckless people I've ever met, and at the same time, one of the most anal. I was angry because I knew I was getting ripped off. At the same time, I knew that the money I was making—from touring, from radio play, and from commercials—was because Morris was spending money promoting my records. If it wasn't for Morris Levy, there wouldn't be a Tommy James.

One consequence of Morris's nonpayment of royalties was that Tommy lost the crack songwriting/production team of Bo Gentry and Ritchie Cordell, who provided the string of hits following "Hanky Panky," which included "I Think We're Alone Now" and "Mirage," and fostered Tommy's first credit as a hit songwriter with "Mony Mony"—inspired by the flashing neon sign on the building of the Mutual of New York insurance company. Despite their success, and the profits it brought to Roulette, Morris couldn't help stiffing them either, and they departed. They continued to have hits, most notably with "Indian Giver" by the 1910 Fruit Gum Company, which climbed to number five in the spring of 1969. By necessity, Tommy rose to the occasion as both a songwriter and producer, and commenced his most fruitful period.

HAROLD: One thing we need to go into here is your consumption of drugs. In your book you refer to it as a way you dealt with stage fright.

[*Tommy forwarded us a few early chapters of the book he was to publish in 2010 as Me the Mob and the Music.*] Was your frustration with Morris also a factor?

TOMMY: Popping pills was a way to stay up for twenty hours straight when I was working on an album. Beginning in 1967, everybody I worked with in the studio—musicians, producer, engineer—seemed to be popping pills. Someone gave me a Dexedrine, and I kept taking them. We had the studio booked every Tuesday and Wednesday. After a Saturday night gig, I would pop pills to stay up to write songs for the following week's session. I was writing with a sense of desperation because we needed songs to record the following week.

Although I became a born-again Christian in 1967, I was still popping pills, so I was not walking the walk for a long time. But it had a profound effect on my music. A number of the songs I wrote were religiously oriented, like "Crystal Blue Persuasion," which came right out of the Book of Revelation in the Bible. "Sweet Cherry Wine" is about my conversion experience. "Ball of Fire" was also taken from the Bible. I find it interesting how the good Lord would choose to bless me through a guy like Morris Levy.

Morris had been on me to stop taking the pills for a long time. He was very upset with the death of Frankie Lymon. He came to see me at the studio that night [*February 28, 1968*] to tell me that Frankie had died. He said, "Frankie was a kid who had it all, and fucked it up, and that's what's going to happen to you if you don't stop this shit."

I took pills for such a long duration that it finally caught up with me in 1970, at a gig in Birmingham, Alabama. I fainted on stage and had to be taken to the hospital. I had lost weight. I had been up for a couple of days. Some reporters got the story wrong and said that I had died. When I called the Roulette office the next day, they were surprised because they had heard I had died. The doctor told me that I had to stop taking pills, and that I had to take six months off. I never stuck a needle in my arm or took acid. I was scared of that stuff. You can kill yourself just as well with booze and pills. During this period I got a divorce from my second wife. During my recovery, I would go up to the office once a week. Morris always wanted to know how I was. He would tell me to stay out of the studio, to do what the doctor told me.

A consequence was that I lost my band. I didn't intend to break them up, but that's what happened because they weren't working. [*The Shondells were an important component of Tommy's success. Bassist Mike Vale cowrote a handful of their hits; drummer Pete Lucia cowrote "Crimson & Clover." With some personnel changes—Shondells' guitarist Ed Gray and keyboardist Ron Rosman left—the group became Hog Heaven and recorded an album for Roulette, but it didn't sell.*]

HAROLD: Rock stars are usually depicted as being cool, but you're more like a rock 'n' roll Woody Allen.

TOMMY: That's right. Every time we tried to be cool, something would happen. I've got my act on stage down pretty good, but inside, I'm anal-retentive. I'm a perfectionist, and it kills me when I can't be perfect, which is all the time. So I live my life in this terror, especially when I'm on stage. I'm shy, by nature, so I picked the wrong business to be shy in. Doing TV shows has always scared the piss out of me.

RON: When did it fall apart between you and Morris?

TOMMY: It came to a head in about 1972. In 1971 the Gambinos were taking over New York, and people were getting killed. Morris was aligned with the Genovese family. He and Nate McCalla left the country for a year. They went to Spain. Two of his partners were killed: Tommy Eboli—who also went by the name Tommy Ryan—and Morris Gurlak.

[*Eboli was murdered on the night of July 16, 1972, blocks away from where Tommy was performing at the Paramount Theater in Brooklyn. Nate McCalla, at over six feet tall and 250 pounds, was a physically imposing black man from Harlem who, according to Tommy, had been a highly deco- rated paratrooper in the Korean War. He was Morris' enforcer and bodyguard, and accompanied Tommy at Morris' request. Morris loved him and gave him*] *his own label, Calla Records, on which J. J. Jackson had a hit with "But It's Alright." McCalla was found murdered, shot in the back of his head, in Ft. Lauderdale in 1980. Neither crime was solved.]*

TOMMY: I was left holding the bag at Roulette. I was still trying to make music amidst all this craziness. At some point I was summoned to my attorney's office. He reasoned that if people were looking for Morris and he wasn't around, they might come after me, as I was the only thing that was making money for Morris. He said that I should make myself scarce, too. The first thing I did was to go up to my farm and stay there. Then my lawyer put together an album for me to record in Nashville, with [*musicians*] Pete Drake, and D. J. Fontana and Scotty Moore, who had recorded with Elvis. I spent four months in Nashville making a country-influenced album. I handed it to Joel Kolsky, a New York street guy who was one of Roulette's radio promotion guys, and was now running the label with his brother. He looked at me like I was from Neptune: "What is it, you're wearing cowboy boots now?" Roulette was no longer a friendly place. I finally made up my mind that I was through with Roulette.

When Morris came back in 1972, we had a real blowout. I had reached a point where I didn't care: put me in cement boots if you like, but let me out of here! I went up to the office and said to Morris that it was over. It became a real screaming match. I had never heard Morris yell so loud at me. He said, "You ain't fuckin' going nowhere." He was not going to give in, so I had to sabotage my career. I played crazy. I was sick all the time. I couldn't go into the studio. I could never quite get anything done. Morris was still releasing records he had in the vault. All charted, but none were big hits. When he ran out of masters in 1974 he finally let me go, but I had to leave my publishing with him, for any songs I had written, or would write through 1979.

RON: After the blow out, did you still see Morris?

TOMMY: No matter how much we yelled and screamed at each other, two days later we were friends again. I went up to the office three years later, and he offered me a deal for my own label.

*   *   *

Tommy was, and would be, great to work with. When we finished our second phone meeting he said, "I want you to know that I'm very honored that you would think my touchy story would be interesting enough to make into a movie." I thought we had something. Even though the Monkees and Meatloaf movies (both of which Ron wrote) had been among VH1's highest rated, Mike Larkin, the executive in charge of that division, wasn't interested. We submitted the proposal to Showtime because I had heard that Jerry Offsay, the president of programming, liked rock 'n' roll. He had green lit the Jimi Hendrix movie that Showtime ran in 2000. Ron and I pitched it to one or two more producers, but no one was interested.

In October 2001, as I was about to leave the label, Tommy called me to express his appreciation: "You're one of the hippest people in the music business. You've led the way with reissues. You're a stand-up guy." A little over two years later, I received a call from him. He was concerned because his royalty payments from Rhino had dropped precipitously. I think he was fearful of his experience with Roulette being repeated. Although I could only presume, I assured him that Rhino was probably paying him properly. There were different people at the head of the company now. His music was no longer a priority.

The Rhino Label Part Four

The Long Goodbye

Wishing You Joy and Peace
At Christmas and
Throughout the New Year

Roger Ames, Warner Music Group

It was a nondescript Christmas card featuring an illustration of a tree ornament on the front. It certainly wasn't worth keeping for its visual appeal, but I kept mine. It was in the early days of January 2001, and knowing Ames, I thought his wish for a joyful year would ring hollow.

Ames was the fifth head of the Warner Music Group (WMG) in six years. Rhino's joint-venture deal with Atlantic Records was made with Bob Morgado, when he was head of the WMG. He had been New York Governor Hugh Carey's chief of staff. After he divested Warner of Atari, its troubled video game company, Warner CEO Steve Ross put Morgado in charge of the Music Group. His specialty was mergers and acquisitions, and his strengths were politics and organization. He wasn't a music guy. When we first met with him in 1991, his excitement wasn't about Rhino, but the deal he made to issue a series of CDs in conjunction with the 1992 Barcelona Olympics. He wasn't evaluating the project based on the music. He played some tracks for Richard and me. I thought it was a bad idea. It lost a lot of money.

Because Morgado didn't inherently understand the business, Warner Brothers Records head Mo Ostin had no respect for him, and caused consternation by refusing to report to him. Morgado thought he had a solution and created Warner Music U.S., selecting Doug Morris to preside.

We had reported to him when he was president of Atlantic Records, and we liked Doug. Unlike our experience at Capitol, where label head Joe Smith failed to notice that we had our best sales month when we met with him, Doug knew our numbers. Unlike a lot of company heads, he was good at recognizing executive talent, and giving them the freedom to be successful. He was warm, he smiled a lot; you could talk to him. We liked Doug's CFO Mel Lewinter even more. He smoked a pipe and would have been perfect casting as the "understanding uncle" character. Doug was a music guy, having produced and written songs for Laurie Records in the 1960s. As much as that suited us—and he aided in freeing up some Elektra projects for us—he was totally out of his depth when we brought up nonmusic ventures such as merchandising, feature films (*Fear and Loathing in Las Vegas*), animation (the Monkees), and theme restaurants (Club Rhino). Morris lasted about a year in his new position before Danny Goldberg orchestrated a power play in June 1995 that got a group of them fired, at the direction of Time Warner's chairman Gerald Levin. We were sorry to see Doug and Mel leave. That, coupled with alienating Ostin and other music executives, resulted in Morgado getting fired.

Because of our success, I was surprised Doug didn't call us in for a meeting to see if he could lure us away after he became head of Universal Music. Instead, with Bruce Resnikoff at the helm, he decided to bolster Universal's own reissue program. I liked Bruce. He started out selling bootlegged t-shirts in parking lots outside of concert venues, then got a law degree, and found himself in charge of licensing at Universal. He did a great job, and I thought about hiring him when we weren't sure if we would be able to retain Bob Emmer as our head of business affairs.

Doug got it in his head to call their new reissue label Hip-O, with the logo of a hippopotamus, in the same ballpark as our name and logo— although ours was a *hipper* looking one than theirs. If you were going to start a reissue label, you would call it something like Vault or Archive or Legacy, not name it after an animal, unless you were trying to evoke Rhino. Remember, we named our label after our retail store. When we protested to Bruce, he said that he was unable to dissuade Doug. Richard made his appeal to Mel Lewinter, who joined Doug at Universal, but Doug wouldn't budge. Assuming Bruce and Mel expressed our objection to Doug, I thought he was shortsighted in jeopardizing a good relationship over the name of a supplemental label.

After Doug left, we were told to meet with Michael Fuchs, who now assumed those duties. Because Fuchs had done such a good job building HBO, and because he wanted a new challenge, Levin gave him the Music Group to head as well, rather than risk losing him to another company. Richard and I were skeptical because he wasn't a music guy. When we met with him in mid-July in his bungalow at the Beverly Hills Hotel, he seemed more interested in rattling off his accomplishments than asking us about our business, or our assessment of the WMG. He went into the next room to show us his recent award as an inductee in *Broadcasting & Cable Magazine*'s Hall of Fame.

Fuchs was smart, a quick study, and he zeroed in on what Rhino was all about. This came to a head on October 27 during a presentation in the Warner Brothers Records conference room when Fuchs had an argument with Warner president Russ Thyret over Russ' refusal to grant Rhino access to the part of the catalogue he wasn't exploiting. He told Russ that no one bought a record because it was on Warner Brothers, but people bought Rhino records because the name had meaning. (*Brandweek* magazine concurred: "Not since Motown has a music label forged a meaningful brand identity.")

I was embarrassed to have witnessed the heated exchange. Considering that Fuchs was responsible for Thyret's promotion, one would think there would have been more cooperation in the room. At the end of the meeting, even though I felt emotionally drained, I felt good that Fuchs had gone to bat for us. His style rubbed people the wrong way. Three weeks later, he was gone.

Bob Daly and Terry Semel had been successful running Warner Brothers Pictures for a long time. In negotiating to renew their deal with Levin, they wanted to add the Music Group to their responsibilities so they could justify getting paid more in the way of salaries and bonuses. They also made a case for the Music Group reporting to them as a means to end the executive turmoil. It made sense to Levin. They took over from Fuchs in November.

Semel and Daly were well regarded within the film community, but they weren't music guys: they didn't understand the music business, nor were they fans. Levin didn't understand the music business, and neither did Richard Parsons, to whom the Music Group chairman later reported. Parsons was the president of Time Warner and his background was in banking. These guys may have been savvy enough to deal with (stock) investors and to understand balance sheets and profit/loss statements, but they had no inherent feel for music or the music business, so how could they make smart decisions about running the division?

It took a long time for Semel and Daly to get up to speed, and for us to get access to the Warner masters that we had been denied. They reasoned that the only way we should be given access to those masters was if we were fully owned by the WMG. It wasn't a path we would have pursued, but we were driven by the prospect of being able to properly reissue the Warner and Elektra masters. It took two and a half years after Semel's and Daly's appointment to effect that change.

In March 1999 Richard, Bob, and I joined other Warner executives at the vice president level and above for a presentation by the corporate execs in the Steven Ross Theater on the Warner Brothers lot. We sat in the second row, and before the meeting started, we introduced ourselves to Ted Turner. He responded with "I guess I am a Rhino," referring to his name being on our Turner Classic Movies soundtrack releases.

I bought into Gerald Levin's vision of the benefits of Warner's pending merger with AOL. In his talk, he encouraged synergy between the various companies, but I disagreed with his bottom-up strategy. He suggested that by talking about it, executives would apply it on their own. From the difficulty we experienced in trying to forge synergistic projects within Warner, we saw no motivation. I felt that it should be top-down. If executives failed to take advantage of mutual opportunities, then there would be repercussions.

Afterwards, I was surprised that Levin wasn't mobbed by glad-handers. I said to Richard and Bob, "Let's meet him." Either they were too shy, or they weren't interested. I introduced myself, and he welcomed me to walk with him to the lunch reception in a tented area nearby. I gave him my opinion on synergy, but didn't press the point. Mostly in the few minutes I had with him, I gave him a quick overview on what Rhino was and what we were trying to do.

Ramon Lopez was head of WEA International. The division wasn't doing well, and he was encouraged to step down. His handpicked successor was Roger Ames, who had been the president of the PolyGram Music Group and the owner of the (revived) London Records label. In one of my infrequent walks around our neighborhood with Zach Horowitz, president of the Universal Music Group, I asked him about Ames. He didn't have good things to say and speculated that his London label had lost $8 million in the United States the previous year. He said Ames had difficulty making decisions and was a loner and a poor communicator.

From our management training with Stan Slap, we understood the value of a good manager and the qualities a good manager needs. When one is managing other employees or division heads, one must be accessible, have good people skills, and be a good motivator. Among the most important qualities an executive should have is the ability to evaluate candidates to hire. From my perspective, I think the senior Warner executives missed the mark.

In order to get Ames to be part of the Warner Music Group, Semel and Daly had to buy his London label and bring it to the Music Group. Ames couldn't very well be at Warner if his own label was distributed by Universal (which had purchased PolyGram the previous year). Semel and Daly didn't have the confidence or knowledge to have looked upon the hiring of Ames as too costly and to have considered somebody else. In order to affect his coming to Warner, in January 2000 the Warner Music Group paid $210 million for London with, I'm presuming, a majority of that money going to Ames. Given that the worldwide profits for the label were $1.5 million in 1998 and $10.5 million in 1999, it seemed like a horrendous deal. The purchase price couldn't be justified by the profitability or the assets; $201 million was valued as "good will."

Prior to all this, in April 1999, Ames was invited to attend the Warner Music Group meeting in Hong Kong. I introduced myself to him at the opening cocktail party. Rather than being warm, or even civil, he replied in gibberish that made me think of Noel Redding's sped-up voice on "EXP," the first track on the Jimi Hendrix Experience's *Axis: Bold as Love* album. Peter Pasternak, our head of international, was right there with me, and couldn't believe his odd response. How respectful of Semel and Daly could I be when they were so shortsighted as to hire a jerk like Ames? The next day for dinner at the Repulse Bay Hotel, we were seated at the same table, although not next to each other. I overheard Ames talking about fly-fishing, so I attempted to engage him by asking him if he had read *Double Whammy*, Carl Hiassen's book that featured the sport. He responded that he had, and that he liked Hiassen's writing, but I was unable to interest him further.

At Warner Brothers Pictures all was not well. Semel's and Daly's contracts were not renewed. During their four years as coheads of the Warner Music Group, profits had declined almost 25 percent. As a result, in August 1999 Semel and Daly chose Ames to succeed them as the Chairman/Chief Operating Officer of the Warner Music Group. Time Warner President Richard Parsons gave it his rubber stamp. Ames had been president of Warner Music International for a mere four months.

The ink on the press release was barely dry when Ames presided over the Warner Music International meetings in Dublin. Peter Pasternak and David McLees, a rising young star at the label, represented Rhino. David had started out as an unpaid intern and rose to the number two position in the A&R department. He was little prepared for Ames, who greeted his presentation by feigning boredom: he put his head in his hands as his head dropped to the table. When David finished, Ames raised himself up to announce, "Let's get one thing straight. We don't give a fuck about Rhino!" David and Peter were shocked. Was Ames acting out for effect, attempting to ingratiate himself to his beleaguered European cronies? Or was he really expressing how he felt about Rhino and hinting at his game plan? Read on.

My interactions with Ames were minimal, mostly in the context of budget meetings. His style was to put everyone on the defensive. At the meetings, he smoked cigarettes—he was the only one to do so—in non-smoking buildings. He didn't have the courtesy to ask for the permission of those in attendance. His overall manner was to intimidate, and the result was that others tried to say as little as possible.

When we negotiated our joint-venture agreement with the Warner Music Group, I had language inserted that stipulated that we could run our company in the same manner as we had previously. For the past few years, we had done so, with minimal interference by the Warner Music Group, or Atlantic Records.

The first breach came when Dave Mount, who succeeded Henry Droz as head of WEA, said that our sales staff could no longer be Rhino employees and instead had to work for the newly formed WEA Strategic Catalogue Marketing Group. He placated us by promising us that not only would our former sales people still be selling Rhino, but so would WEA salesmen. It sounded good, and though we were skeptical, we had to comply. Even though Rhino's sales continued to be strong, we felt the change adversely affected us. As Rhino employees, our sales people were responsive to our direction. As WEA employees, they took their orders from someone else.

Richard had an idea to sell albums from our catalogue that were so limited in potential sales, we couldn't justify releasing them on Rhino through our regular distribution. He created an imprint, Handmade, and had interested Amazon.com in taking the line to sell exclusively. The idea was that these unique albums sold by Amazon would draw additional customers to the website. The plan was for Amazon to bring in thirty titles and guarantee that they would buy at least four thousand of each. We proceeded in conceiving the series and designating the titles. Then Amazon decided that they didn't want to make the deal. Richard tried to interest other companies, but none wanted the line. He decided we should do it ourselves, selling it through our own mail order division, Rhino Direct. From a financial consideration, I was skeptical after the guaranteed sales from Amazon fell through. On the other hand, I was all for making music available to those who wanted to hear these specialized titles.

In the January 2000 meeting at Warner Brothers in Burbank, Ames wanted to know about this new imprint, Handmade. I took it upon myself to explain/defend our reasons for the label. The example I gave was our recently released Stooges *Fun House* box set. In most recordings, the instrumental backing track is recorded first, with vocals added later to the best—of many—takes. Here, Iggy sang with the band on nine run-throughs of the album. The performances were of a high level, and the sonic quality was dynamic. We were selling them in an edition limited to three thousand box sets at $100 each, which meant that we made a profit of over $200,000 if the box sold out, which it soon did. Maybe this was chump change to Ames. He wasn't impressed, and he said he didn't know who Iggy and the Stooges were.

In October we joined other executives in a budget meeting for the upcoming year at Warner's New York offices in the Time Life building. Originally Ames had scheduled the meeting on Tuesday the tenth, giving no consideration to Jews who would have had to travel on the previous day, which was Yom Kippur. By 2000, many of the Jews who had the top positions when we joined the WMG in 1992—Atlantic (Doug Morris), Warner Bros. (Mo Ostin), Elektra (Bob Krasnow), WEA (Henry Droz), Warner Special Products (Micky Kapp), WMG General Counsel (Fred Wistow)—had been replaced by gentiles (Val Azzoli, Russ Thyret, Sylvia Rhone, Dave Mount, Tony Pepitone, and Dave Johnson, respectively).

Ames was, again, smoking in a nonsmoking conference room, and didn't ask the rest of us—all nonsmoking—if we would mind. Sitting next to him, I scooted my chair away when he lit up, and then scooted back. He didn't react to the hint. Then he lit into us, Rhino and Warner Special Products, on our number of employees: "What do they do all day?" As Roger had never been to Rhino, I invited him to tour our offices so he could see for himself what everybody did. He replied in the negative, saying, "I don't want to see everybody standing around."

As it was clear, and despite our high profitability and standing in the music business community, Ames had no respect for Rhino. I don't know if he was jealous because Rhino was more profitable than London had been, or if his idea of a successful reissue label was one that racked up big sales from TV-advertised collections as was the case in Britain where he lived. In America, TV advertising was much more expensive, which made these projects risky compared to Rhino's more assured business model.

In November Richard came into my office and asked if we should negotiate an extension of our employment agreements, which were due to expire at the end of the following year. I said that we should see how we liked working under Ames. I had concerns, and I didn't want to be saddled with an extension if we disliked working for him. Plus, we had a year to find out.

Richard expressed his trepidation over the AOL-Time Warner merger, with their strategy to cut costs using *purchase price allocation* (sometimes called purchase price accounting), or PPA. The salaries of terminated employees who had time on their contracts would ordinarily be an expense that would lower the earnings of the company. In a merger year, it's considered an acquisition cost and not one affecting the company's profitability or earnings per share of stock. It baffled me that the US government had a law that encouraged a company to fire its employees. Let me provide an example. If I were terminated with ten months left on my contract, the expense wouldn't lower the company's earnings—even insignificantly—by that amount. The company would not benefit from my services if I were no longer working, even though it was required to pay me.

Sometimes in corporate America decisions are made not for the long-term health of the company, but to address short-term goals like improving stock price. Time Warner was no exception. Price cutting—firing employees—to improve profitability could be effective, but at the expense of future profitability and growth.

In 2001, on the morning of January 23, I was in good spirits. At the beginning of the year my family and I had an enjoyable vacation on a Disney Cruise. The previous week I attended festivities leading up to the marriage of my good friend, long-time bachelor Paul Almond. The previous night Stephanie's cousin Maurice Summerfield was in town and hosted a lively dinner attended by Jon Kellerman and Andy Summers. And that day was my daughter's sixth birthday.

Richard came into my office. He looked ill. He reluctantly told me that I was to be terminated early under the PPA provision. Richard had expressed to Dave Mount that he was uncomfortable telling me, that he thought Dave should do it, but Dave insisted that Richard give me the bad news. He drafted a letter as though Richard had written it and faxed it to him. Richard showed me. I was shocked. I hadn't thought much about it. If anything, I thought I would have left at the end of the year when my contract specified.

When we made our joint venture with Atlantic, in the agreement there was a provision that we would meet on occasion for board meetings, which specified Richard and me, and the two head guys at Atlantic, Doug Morris and Mel Lewinter. We hadn't had a board meeting since they left Atlantic in 1995. Late in 1999, we were directed to report to Dave Mount. The only meetings I attended with Mount were in the context of being in a larger group. Richard and I, as the coheads of Rhino, had no reporting meeting with him, and I hadn't had a one-on-one meeting, either.

Two days after Richard showed me Mount's fax, I gave a lunchtime lecture at UCLA's Anderson School of Management for those in the MBA program. At a point during my talk on being an entrepreneur and distilling the Rhino story, I had to fight to contain the emotion I felt because of my situation.

Over the subsequent days my discussion with Richard was how I should respond to this directive. Should I appeal to Ames, to Mount? He didn't think it was a good idea. I wanted to stay as long as I could, in part to finish up the deals I was working on and to organize my files, and as a personal obligation to come as close as I could to fulfilling my contract. There were larger issues. Although I was no longer an owner, I cared about the company. It seemed like I was the only one who considered that, if I left sooner, there would be a negative effect on the morale of the company. I was a constant in the employees' professional lives. I was there from the beginning.

Stan Slap encouraged us to manage by walking around so we could interact with all of our employees. It was a manner developed by David Packard, cofounder of Hewlett-Packard. The intent was to avoid an ivory tower affect, whereby senior executives of a company isolate themselves from most of their employees, feeling more comfortable with executives on their own level. I saw this in Hong Kong, where Semel and Daly only sat with other senior executives during meals, rather than with others, as Richard and I would have done.

On February 1, we had a company retreat at the Ojai Valley Inn that included the employees of Warner Special Products, as the two divisions were slated to merge. During the presentations I gave a short speech. It was tough maintaining my composure.

How would the drop in morale affect the company's profitability? The longer I stayed, the more stable the company would be as other employees lost their jobs under Mount and Ames' direction. The more profitable the company, the larger my bonus would be when it was paid the following year. In addition, Richard had planned to take a month-long vacation in July (on a yacht cruising the Amalfi Coast). If I were gone, there would be no leadership in place. Nobody was considering that, either.

Richard thought, presciently as it turned out, that there were so many people being released, if I wanted to stay longer, I should do nothing—just be low-key—and that I would be lost in the volume of WMG employees being processed. And that's what I did. When I got the form contract from the WMG legal department —which didn't even apply to my position as cohead of Rhino—I did nothing.

Because of the way it was handled, and because of my decision to prolong my departure, I experienced the worst year of my life. My visibility and participation at Rhino was unchanged, and very few employees knew of my future. I withdrew from any WMG meetings, but I was like a stowaway, but on my own ship, anxious about being discovered. Richard was right, I had been forgotten about by WMG's lawyers. This subterfuge, as well as the prospect of leaving the company I had started with Richard, resulted in a low-grade depression that stayed with me most of the year.

I made time to organize, which few of us like to do. I went through my files, which consisted mostly of older contracts I had negotiated. For the benefit of the subsequent regime, I removed the extraneous material and forwarded the files to the legal department. My secretary departed at the beginning of the year, so I did the same for her files. I held a "garage sale," which meant that I was freely giving to those employees who wanted them the excess items from my storage cabinet that were mostly samples of Monkees licensed items. I sidestepped a couple of employees who asked me if this meant I was leaving the company.

In a few cases I sold masters back to the artists for low but reasonable fees. It was highly unlikely that Rhino was going to issue the four albums by Barnes & Barnes on CD, so I sold them back the two albums they didn't own. In this way they could either make a licensing deal with another company or issue them themselves.

I knew the EP we released on Bebe Buell was special to her, and Rhino was never going to issue it on CD. As she didn't appear to have disposable money, I gave her back the masters for no compensation. I should have done it more, but I didn't have the focus to track down those artists from the early Rhino days with whom I was no longer in contact.

The attitude of major labels is that they never sell their masters. The main reason is that they're too caught up in trying to make a profit to put time into evaluating older product that would be less profitable. What never gets discussed is the cost of storage through the years. An album that the label will never again derive any income from might take up several feet of storage space because of the two-inch multitrack tapes from the recording sessions. What would be the cost of storing three feet of tape for thirty years, times a thousand albums? Labels don't do that type of analysis.

One of the few bright spots was Rhino's release schedule for the year, which may have been our best ever. It was a tribute to the company that, twenty-four years in, we had not run out of ideas and were still capable of putting out great product. Titles that got me excited included box sets on the Monkees, the Yardbirds, Buffalo Springfield, Dead Can Dance, Richard Pryor, urban folk music, and 1960s British psychedelia with *Nuggets II*; an expanded Love's *Forever Changes* and a best of Alice Cooper; *Bride of Firesign*, a new album by Firesign Theatre; more *Mystery Science Theater* and *Get a Life* DVDs, and the Rutles on DVD. The Yardbirds' *Ultimate!* was particularly gratifying. It was as though I had come full circle, from a passionate UCLA sophomore who had proposed a Yardbirds compilation to CBS Records thirty-one years previously, to holding in my hand the superb career-overview bearing my company's logo.

As the year progressed, Richard let me know that he wanted to form a new company. He did not suggest we start one together, nor did he lessen the blow of excluding me. He could have put it into a context like, "I thought of asking you but then thought I'd rather do it on my own." I asked him then, as well as a few months later, why he wanted to form a new label. My point was that it was highly unlikely he was going to approach what we had accomplished at Rhino, especially in this economic climate—and without me! He nervously chuckled and said, "When I figure out why, I'll let you know." He never did. Part of his motivation was that Bob Emmer and Garson wanted him to start a new company so they could be equity participants (owners) this time.

Why not choose another business? I was focused on producing for film and TV. I think Richard was fearful of what he would be doing after Rhino. Now that he didn't have to worry about making a living, I would have expected him to reimmerse himself in the social work he was so passionate about when I first met him. What it came down to was that Richard still liked the business, and felt challenged to help build another company. He had discussions with Ames about having a custom label at the WMG, but it appeared that he was being placated.

Richard's vacation ran into turbulent waters because of Ames. He had it booked, after which Ames scheduled a WMG meeting. Richard's travel agent was able to reschedule, but forfeited a number of days that he had already paid for. Then Ames cancelled the meeting. When Richard was away, I was in place. Members of INXS came by the office to meet our staff, and to have a photo taken for the trades to announce the release of their new Rhino anthology *Shine Like It Does*. Since Richard wasn't in the office, I was asked to pose with the band. I borrowed an employee's eyeglasses to wear as my inside joke at a disguise, since a couple of members of the band also wore glasses.

Richard, Bob, and I had a good relationship with Fred Wistow, the Warner Music Group's general counsel. He was smart, had a dry sense of humor, and was a true eccentric: after retiring from Warner, he spent a month in a monastery. The search for a senior executive with a marketing background to head Rhino was proving difficult. Wistow's replacement, Dave Johnson, had worked with Scott Pascucci at Sony and recommended him for the job. With some desperation, Mount responded to Johnson's suggestion and hired him.

Pascucci had been senior VP of business affairs at Sony Music. Based on the West Coast, Pascucci lived in Malibu and loved the California lifestyle, but accepted a position at Arista in New York. He soon realized his mistake and saw the Rhino job as a means of getting back to Malibu. It wasn't that he was a fan of the label. In fact, he seemed to know little about us.

Amiable and, despite his paunch, good-looking enough to pass as a Baldwin brother, Pascucci wasn't close to being a Richard or a Harold.

Richard met Scott for breakfast in late August. He said that Pascucci had complimentary things to say about Rhino, not based on his knowledge or awareness, but from what he had been told when he asked his previous staff members. Pascucci responded to Richard's inquiry by revealing that, in the hiring process, he hadn't been informed of any mandate, or any problems or issues at Rhino.

The following week Richard met with Mount, and one topic that came up was where Pascucci's office would be. Mount suggested my office, that unbeknownst to him, I was still using. Richard didn't respond. The next day he told me of their discussion, and that he thought it would be disingenuous to not be honest with Mount. He called him and told him that "my deal" still hadn't been worked out. Mount was surprised. I was able to work out a timetable, with Mount's approval, to leave on October 12. I still had not communicated with Mount directly.

Pascucci's contract stipulated a salary much higher than either of ours. On his first day in the office, I welcomed him. I told him to let me know if he had any questions, and I asked him out for lunch. We never had lunch, nor did he ask me any question about Rhino's business.

My October 2 e-mail to Rhino's staff:

I want to let each of you know that I will be leaving Rhino as of October 15th. Although my contract is through the end of this year, I am required to leave earlier so that AOL Warner may benefit from the provisions of the merger, which allows it to write off part of my salary.

I think what we've created through the years has been truly remarkable. I only wish the best for all of you, and hope that you're given an opportunity to help Rhino to accomplish even more in the future. I will be readily available to you through October 12th, at which point I relinquish my duties as Managing Director.

My October 12 e-mail to Rhino's staff:

On the occasion of my last "official" day at Rhino, I want to summarize what I find are the most gratifying accomplishments of the company I cofounded with Richard nearly 24 years ago.

(1) We created jobs for 167 people, at our peak. For Richard and myself, we didn't take over a Company, or inherit a company from relatives, but Rhino was created from literally nothing. I'm most gratified in knowing that 167 people not only earned a living by working at Rhino, but because of the product we produced and the environment we created, most of those people actually looked forward to coming to work every day.

(2) We changed the industry as we dedicated ourselves to quality. The primary success of Rhino is derived from the following reason. The music that we grew up with was important to us, and Rhino reissues should show our appreciation to the artists and music fans by giving back to them a quality product. Not only did this provide the backbone of Rhino's success, but as the company sold more and more albums, the other labels established their own mini versions of Rhino, emphasizing quality much more than they had previously. Although there was more competition for us, our success was the catalyst that changed the industry, benefiting music fans everywhere.

(3) Community Service
I'm happy that our company has introduced the concept of community service to many Rhinos, and has provided a program to encourage employees to participate.

(4) Our imagination has not limited us to being only a record company. The prevailing attitude in our business is that record companies are only record companies. If they did anything other than music, it was releasing a minimal number of videos generated by their artists. With Rhino, we've been able to do much more. Rhino Video's scope is much broader than that of any other label. With Kid Rhino, we've succeeded in the children's market. Rhino Films has produced three feature films and two TV movies. We've produced a handful of documentaries and PBS live concerts. Rhino has even published 14 books. And our packaging is the most imaginative in the business. I find it all remarkable.

The outpouring of appreciation from employees was touching. But I also received phone calls from managers, like Eric Gardner, and artists, like Tommy James and Dave Clark.

Richard's lawyer, Alan Lenard, advised him that he would have more appeal if he were still gainfully employed, which is one reason why he stayed beyond the term of his contract when Pascucci asked him to. As a consequence, we didn't leave around the same time—me in October, him two months later. We started it together; if he didn't want to stay on by accepting Pascucci's new offer, then I felt we should have gone out together. It would have reflected the good partnership we had, and what we had accomplished. To use a familiar phrase from a TV show then airing, I felt as though multiple fingers were pointing at me, accusing, "You are the weakest link!"

Richard felt the Warner Music Group was playing games with him in his quest for his own label deal. "They are incredibly incompetent, or stupid, or a little of both," he said. When Dave Johnson refused to return the calls from Lenard, Richard set his sights elsewhere. He later admitted that we should have left together. He departed the company in March 2002, shortly after we—he invited me to join him—accepted a label of the year award from NARM at their yearly convention, in San Francisco. Paul Vidich told me that, over the previous ten years, the Warner Music Group's purchase of Rhino was the best deal the division made.

Even without me, I couldn't understand why Richard was having such difficulty getting a distribution deal, as he was the president of a very successful label. Nobody in the industry, let alone Atlantic Records or the Warner Music Group, ever did an evaluation of what Richard and I did, or an assessment of our strengths and weaknesses. If Richard and I, along with a number of Rhino's senior executives who were available, aligned ourselves in a new company, it would have made for a more attractive package. It took Richard until the end of the year to make a distribution deal, with Sony.

With so many problematical areas, Ames could have offered to extend our contracts and focus his energies on the areas most in need. Sales in the music industry peaked in 1999. They declined less than 2 percent in 2000, but over 4 percent in 2001. In contrast to the industry trend, not only did Rhino's sales increase in 2001, but profits were up significantly. In relation to our expenses, Rhino was the most profitable of all the Warner labels.

When we departed, there was no farewell party held for us. It's not as if I had a need to attend such a party, but it would have been nice to have gone out with a celebration of the company Richard and I had created. When Semel and Daly left, Warner had a big party for them. When Bob Emmer left, we threw one for him, as we did for many of our valued employees. Maybe Pascucci felt that he couldn't justify the expense from Rhino's $32 million in profits for 2001.

My biggest mistake was being so caught up in my situation—and as it related to the company—that I gave scant attention to the large number of options I had of AOL Time Warner stock. My logic was that I didn't need the money presently, and if I exercised my options—and sold the stock—I would be subject to income tax. As it was such a large company, I reasoned that, even with the price of the stock sliding precipitously, it would go back up. If I had responded to my early departure with an attitude of "I want nothing more to do with this corporation," I would have sold all my stock. With the price declining continuously, to a low close to 10 percent of what it had once been worth, I was never able to exercise my options, leaving millions on the table. Richard and Bob were astute enough to have exercised a portion of theirs. Years ago I would have beaten myself up over such negligence. In my maturity, I had the perspective that, given my lifestyle, it was money that I didn't need.

For the first time, Richard and I weren't paid our bonuses—for Rhino's performance in 2001—in a timely manner. Ames held up the payments until May 2002. We did receive a modest amount of interest added, but we felt disappointment for our now former employees, for whom we allocated over 20 percent of our share.

I haven't seen Ames since that time, and I am no longer on his Christmas card list. If I saw him in a small, social setting, I would ask him why he got rid of us. The obvious answer is that he wanted his own guy in there, one beholden to him, rather than two independent-thinking, self-made men. Within the year or so after we left, Emmer ran into him and asked him. Ames said he felt that, as we no longer owned part of the company, we wouldn't be motivated to make it more profitable.

This, like many of Ames' assumptions, was off the mark. The last three years we were at the company were the most profitable, and that's after the Warner Music Group took full ownership. Whether I owned 50 percent of the company, or 25 percent, or no percent at all, I always made decisions as if I were an owner. For Richard and me, our salaries were modest, as were our expenses. We were most interested in doing what was best for our company rather than our personal enrichment. A few months later, Emmer was chatting with Bob Daly who admitted that hiring Ames had been a mistake.

In the immediate years after leaving Rhino, it was clear to me that it was no longer Rhino, or the Rhino that Richard and I had created and developed. Sure, most of the employees were the same, and the product was up to our standards, but the other elements were lacking, the ones that came from our character and personalities: sense of humor, passion, humanity, integrity, vision, and so much more. In those years I read a biography on MGM studio boss Louis B. Mayer, and saw the documentary on how the Warner Brothers forged their film company. It made me realize, in a way I never had before, how companies are more than names or logos. The company name can remain, but the essence of the company can change. This was never truer than with MGM, which was formed from three companies—Metro, Goldwyn, and Louis B. Mayer. There were good reasons why an out of touch Mayer should not have continued to head the company, but MGM was never the same after he left, and declined.

Unlike MGM and Warner when they were sold, we were having our best years. To use a lofty example, would someone buy Apple and then get rid of Steve Jobs or buy Oracle and get rid of Larry Ellison? How about Amazon without Jeff Bezos? In addition, it seemed that our successors didn't value the history of the label that embodied the histories of all the other labels or attempt to understand the roots of our success. If you don't value history, you can't repeat it.

Richard was asked to come up with a way to combine Rhino with Warner Special Products. His plan was so well thought-out that it was adopted. Richard and I handed over the company, and no major problems or discrepancies were experienced. The company continued to do well, owing to some degree, to the deals we had put in place. Not long after Richard left, the company name was changed from Rhino Entertainment to Warner Strategic Marketing, and there was no further effort to brand the Rhino name. All mention of Richard and me, including our bios, disappeared from the Rhino website.

The Outro

Monty Python's fourth movie, *The Meaning of Life*, starts with a short film, *The Crimson Permanent Assurance*, in which the elderly employees of a long-standing accounting firm recently bought by a new American company rebel and take it over—as creaky, swashbuckling pirates. Similarly, I thought of taking back the Rhino offices after the company moved to Burbank in December 2002. The move was at the request of WEA head Dave Mount, whose desire was that all of the record companies be housed together in the same building complex near WEA. The Warner-Chappell publishing company in the sister building to Rhino's had the fortitude and profits to resist the uprooting. After spending hundreds of thousands of dollars on the move into a new building with much more space at a higher rent per square foot, Mount was canned, and his replacement relocated WEA to Manhattan, rendering Rhino's expensive operation unnecessary. Not foreseeing the contraction in the business—with the writing already on the wall—Rhino took much more space than was needed, paying for empty offices.

I wasn't being totally serious, but here's what I suggested to Richard. As we could still use the Rhino name for our film company, we rent our now-vacated former offices, with Richard, Gary Stewart, me, and other recently departed Rhinos back behind their desks as though they never left. The marble Rhino logo sign out front was still in place. It was an audacious idea, more funny than practical. But it would have been a futile attempt at recapturing something that was now gone. By following our bliss, Richard and I had created a company greater than anything we could have imagined, but now we, too, had left the building.

Index

About the Author

Harold Bronson co-founded the Rhino Records label, and co-ran the company with Richard Foos for twenty-four years. Rhino has been considered the best reissue label in the world, and for a number of years was awarded label of the year—among all the labels in the music industry—by the record retailers organization NARM. During the Clinton administration the company received a special corporate citizenship award from the Dept. of Labor as a reflection of how well they treated their employees.

He oversaw the Rhino Books division as well as Rhino Films, executive producing the feature films *Fear and Loathing in Las Vegas* and *Why Do Fools Fall In Love*, among others.

In his twenties, Bronson wrote about pop music for the *Los Angeles Times, L.A. Free Press, Rolling Stone*, and various music magazines. His last book is *Hey, Hey, We're the Monkees*.